Compensation for Criminal Injuries

Compensation for Criminal Injuries

David R Miers LLM, D Jur

Senior Lecturer in Law
Cardiff Law School

Butterworths
London, Dublin, Edinburgh
1990

United Kingdom	Butterworth & Co (Publishers) Ltd, 88 Kingsway, LONDON WC2B 6AB and 4 Hill Street, EDINBURGH EH2 3JZ
Australia	Butterworths Pty Ltd, SYDNEY, MELBOURNE, BRISBANE, ADELAIDE, PERTH, CANBERRA and HOBART
Canada	Butterworths Canada Ltd, TORONTO and VANCOUVER
Ireland	Butterworth (Ireland) Ltd, DUBLIN
Malaysia	Malayan Law Journal Sdn Bhd, KUALA LUMPUR
New Zealand	Butterworths of New Zealand Ltd, WELLINGTON and AUCKLAND
Puerto Rico	Equity de Puerto Rico, Inc, HATO REY
Singapore	Malayan Law Journal Pte Ltd, SINGAPORE
USA	Butterworth Legal Publishers, AUSTIN, Texas; BOSTON, Massachusetts; CLEARWATER, Florida (D & S Publishers); ORFORD, New Hampshire (Equity Publishing); ST PAUL, Minnesota; and SEATTLE, Washington

A CIP Catalogue record for this book is available from the British Library.

ISBN 0 406 12324 1

Printed by Biddles Ltd, Guildford and King's Lynn

For John and Anne

Preface

This book describes the interpretation, implementation and impact of the law governing state-funded and offender-funded compensation for victims of personal crime in England and Wales. Chapters 1-7 deal with the interpretation that the courts and the Criminal Injuries Compensation Board (CICB) have, over the past 25 years, given to the terms of the Criminal Injuries Compensation Scheme, and describes the changes that have been made to it as a result of the revisions which took effect from 1 February 1990. These revisions substitute for the commencement of the statutory Scheme established in the Criminal Justice Act 1988, itself regarded by the Board as the most significant advance since the Scheme was originally established in 1964. Chapters 8-11 deal with the provisions in ss 35-38 of the Powers of Criminal Courts Act 1973 governing the making of compensation orders upon conviction. Here too, there are important changes effected by the Criminal Justice Act 1988, supplemented by new Home Office guidelines. Both sets of provisions have generated a substantial jurisprudence, and if further justification were needed for a detailed treatment of these important remedies for victims of personal crime, it lies in the increasing numbers who, encouraged by the government, are likely to seek compensation under their terms.

The text explains and evaluates the procedural and substantive aspects of these two remedies, and is directed principally at those who work with them or wish to make use of them. However, the establishment and implementation of state-funded and offender-funded compensation for victims of personal crime raises a number of broader issues which are also addressed, in particular in chapter 12. Where appropriate, the scope of these remedies is compared with the approach taken by the law of tort to such injuries, which raises the more general question trenchantly analysed by Atiyah, whether the unique provision for victims of personal crime contained in the Scheme is justifiable. In the case of compensation orders, there is discussion of their place within the sentencing options of a criminal court. I argue that despite the superficial attraction of requiring offenders to compensate their victims, there are serious theoretical and practical difficulties which have not been fully thought through. Substantial parts of the text here are relevant also to the making of compensation orders for loss of and damage to property. Particular attention is paid to recent research on the effectiveness of these arrangements in achieving the compensation of victims of violent crime in England and Wales. The text does not directly deal with the law of Scotland, but the Scheme applies there (as do slightly different provisions concerning compensation orders), and where there are differences in the manner of its implementation occasioned by differences in Scots law, these are remarked upon.

I should like to thank my colleagues at Cardiff Law School who read chapters in draft, especially Peter Alldridge, Vivienne Harpwood and Stephen White. I should also like to thank Tim Newburn of the Home Office Research and Planning Unit for many helpful discussions. I owe a particular debt of gratitude to Sir Michael Ogden QC, the immediate past Chairman of the Criminal Injuries Compensation Board, who read and commented upon all the chapters describing the Scheme. The Board's secretariat also responded quickly and positively to inquiries I made of them. None has any responsibility for any errors or for the opinions that are expressed in the text.

David Miers
Cardiff
July 1990

Contents

Table of Statutes

References in this Table to *Statutes* are to Halsbury's Statutes of England (Fourth Edition) showing the volume and page at which the annotated text of the Act may be found. Page references printed in **bold** type indicate where an Act is set out in part or in full.

Table of Cases

H

J

K

L

M

Chapter One

Establishing the Criminal Injuries Compensation Scheme

A. INTRODUCTION

The Criminal Injuries Compensation Scheme (the Scheme), by which the state makes unique financial provision for the victims of crimes against the person, was established in 1964 by written parliamentary answer.[1] This Scheme was only the second to be set up in a common law jurisdiction, but heralded the establishment within the following decade of many similar arrangements in the United States, Canada and Australia. The unison in which these were introduced is the more striking when compared with the negligible interest in the crime victim's emotional, financial and social needs which had existed prior to the enactment of the first comprehensive scheme in New Zealand earlier in 1964.[2]

Against the background of the rhetoric of the victims' movement of the late 1960s and early 1970s,[3] recurring efforts were made by their promoters to justify the introduction of criminal injury compensation schemes funded by general revenue. Apart from the constant repetition of the apparent injustice implicit in the discrepant treatment by 'the system' of

1 697 HC Official Report (5th series) cols 89-94 (24 June 1964), coming into force on 1 August 1964. For the background see D Miers *Responses to Victimisation* (1978, Professional Books) and 'Victim compensation as a labelling process' (1980) 5 Victimology 3-16, C Harlow and R Rawlings *Law and Administration* (1984, Weidenfeld and Nicolson) pp 388-393, and P Duff 'Criminal injuries and "violent" crime' [1987] Crim LR 219-230.

2 B Cameron 'Compensation for victims of crime: the New Zealand experiment' (1963) J Public Law 367-375. The *Index to Legal Periodicals* now contains many references under the title, 'Crime, victims of', a heading not to be found before 1964.

3 On the victims' movement, see R Mawby and M Gill *Crime Victims* (1987, Tavistock) chs 3 and 4, M Maguire and J Pointing *Victims of Crime: A New Deal?* (1988, Open University Press), P Rock *A View from the Shadows* (1986, OUP), and Miers (1980).

victims and offenders, reliance was placed on the commonly observable fact that, for most victims of violent crime, the civil remedy that is in theory available to them is in reality hollow, given that most offenders go unapprehended or, if apprehended, typically have insufficient means to make compensation. Clearly the victim is at a disadvantage in these respects, but so too is the victim of property offences or of offences of dishonesty committed by a commercial enterprise that goes bankrupt. The difficulty with the argument that the state should stand behind the offender is that it argues too much; when the Scheme was introduced in 1964 the government was at pains to deny that any equivalent 'liability' existed for victims of property offences.

The further suggestion, that a compensation scheme is justifiable on the ground that the welfare state has as yet done nothing for the victim of crime 'as such' can be resisted on the ground that it has as yet done nothing for the victims of cancer or multiple sclerosis 'as such'; but as Atiyah has commented, both points of view miss the target.[4] No welfare state disburses money to the disadvantaged 'as such'; what it does is to attempt to alleviate the *consequences* of such misfortunes — loss of earnings and earning capacity, the costs of coping with permanent or temporary disability:

'What has to be justified is giving compensation to this particular type of case rather than in others, in giving more than is given by welfare state benefits, in giving where the welfare state gives none, and in giving by methods wholly rejected by the welfare state.'[5]

Four general justifications appear in the literature.[6] Some emphasise a doctrinal analogy with common law concepts

---

4 P Cane *Atiyah's Accidents, Compensation and the Law* (1987, 4th edn, Weidenfeld and Nicolson) p 295. The influence of Atiyah's criticisms is reflected in the 1978 House of Lords' debate on victims of crime where Lord Wells-Prestel, replying for the government, remarked that, looked at rationally, the distress suffered by victims of crime 'is very little different from the shock and suffering caused by being casualties on the roads, by industrial accidents and the tragic births of children with severe physical and mental handicaps . . . We have to ask ourselves whether we can say that victims of crime are intrinsically different from other disabled people in the community', 395 HL Official Report (5th series) op cit, col 306.

5 P Atiyah *Accidents, Compensation and the Law* (1970, 1st edn, Weidenfeld and Nicolson) p 324 (the quotation does not appear in the latest edition).

6 S Schafer *Compensation and Restitution to Victims of Crime* (1970, Patterson Smith) pp 117-135, P Burns *Criminal Injuries Compensation* (1980, Butterworths Canada) pp 97-144, R Elias *Victims of the System* (1983, Transaction Books) pp 19-48, L Lamborn 'The propriety of governmental compensation

and remedies, while others look to notions of social justice or to the optimality of spreading losses, but each is, for various reasons and to varying degrees, unconvincing.

(1) General justifications for state compensation of victims of crime

The first justification is based upon the notion of an attenuated contract between the state and the citizen. In consideration for his acceptance of laws regulating the private use of force in the pursuit of grievances and of the state's effective monopoly over the prosecution, trial and disposal of offenders, the state promises to compensate the citizen in the event of a breach of contract, that is, his sustaining a criminal injury. The contract is attenuated because the standard prerequisites of a contractual relationship are patently absent; but granting their absence, it is a weak argument, both in law and in reality. No common law system entails a proposition to the effect that its enforcement agencies promise to protect all people at all times. Apart from the fact that this would entail an absolute liability rarely to be found outside legislation controlling nuclear installations and the like, it contradicts the well-established discretion which those agencies enjoy concerning such matters as the allocation of manpower and resources, and the apprehension and prosecution of suspects. Moreover, the argument would presumably extend to theft and criminal damage, a liability which, as has been noted, the Home Office denied when the ex gratia scheme was introduced in 1964.[7] A second objection can be more shortly stated: in real terms the citizen gains far more than he loses as a result of the state's intervention in the policing and prosecution of offences.[8]

Also unconvincing is the analogy to the law of negligence. Here the state is regarded as a tortfeasor because of its failure

of victims of crime' (1973) 41 George Washington LR 446-470, S Teson 'Forgotten victims: the Missouri solution' (1981) 50 U Missouri and Kansas City L R 533-562, R Scott 'Compensation for victims of violent crimes: an analysis' (1966) 8 William and Mary LR 277-293, JUSTICE *Compensation for Victims of Crimes of Violence* (1962) and various symposia: 'Victims of criminal violence — a round table' (1959) 8 J Public L 191-253, 'Compensation to victims of crimes of personal violence' (1965) 50 Minn LR 211-310, 'Governmental compensation for victims of violence' (1970) 43 S Cal LR 1-121.
7 Infra, pp 9–10.
8 A Ashworth 'Punishment and compensation: victims, offenders and the state' (1986) 6 Oxford J Legal Studies 86-122, 102-104.

to prevent criminal activity. This argument is predicated on the legal possibility of a duty of care inhering in the state, a proposition that faces formidable problems even given the possibility of liability under the Crown Proceedings Act 1947. One obvious point is that the police are not officers of the Crown. Were a duty to be thought to inhere in a government department, for example, concerning the supervision of a borstal institution,[9] there remain complex issues of fact and law which would need to be resolved before liability could be fixed. These would centre on whether, for example, an assault on an elderly person in an enclosed area on a council estate was indicative of a failure to take care (assuming a duty in these circumstances at all) because (a) more police officers should have been assigned to a high crime rate district, or (b) the local authority had made inadequate provision for lighting the pathways and vestibules or had allowed the estate to become run down and further vandalised, or (c) because the architect's designs, as approved by the relevant planning authorities, can now be shown to facilitate rather than to deter crime, and whether the victim's injury, though foreseeable, was in part caused by his own physical condition or lack of care. Even if the victim's injury were foreseeable, this would not, as Lord Keith emphasised in *Hill v Chief Constable for West Yorkshire*,[10] be a sufficient test of liability; some further ingredient would be needed to establish that proximity of relationship between the plaintiff/victim and the defendant/police which the law would recognise as creating a duty of care. As this case clearly illustrates, such a duty does not exist between the police and members of the public at large; moreover, the House of Lords held, even if there were such a relationship, the police ought, for reasons of public policy, to be immune from actions for negligence in the performance of their routine policing function.

In *Hill v Chief Constable for West Yorkshire*, the plaintiff was the mother of a girl killed in 1980 by one Peter Sutcliffe, who was popularly known as the Yorkshire Ripper. Some time after Sutcliffe had been convicted of a number of serious offences, including murder, it transpired that the police had, early in their investigations into the first of his many offences, interviewed him on a number of occasions, but had eliminated him from their inquiries. The plaintiff argued that the duty of the police

9 *Home Office v Dorset Yacht Co Ltd* [1970] AC 1004, [1970] 2 All ER 294, HL.

10 [1989] AC 53, [1988] 2 All ER 238, HL.

was to exercise reasonable skill and care to apprehend suspects which in this case they had failed to do. Her allegations were based inter alia on the failure of the police to collate all the evidence against Sutcliffe, to make sufficient use of photo-fit pictures, to re-evaluate earlier suspects, and on their undue reliance upon hoax information and their uncritical acceptance of a single alibi provided by his wife. The issue was 'whether the individual members of a police force, in the course of carrying out their functions of controlling and keeping down the incidence of crime, owe a duty of care to individual members of the public who may suffer injury to person or property through the activities of criminals, such as to result in liability in damages, on the ground of negligence, to anyone who suffers such injury by reason of breach of that duty.'[11] Her claim had been struck out at a preliminary hearing on the ground that the police owed her daughter no duty of care; her appeal to the Court of Appeal was dismissed.

While acknowledging the general duty of the police to enforce the law (and the absence of any general exemption from the common law in their favour), the House of Lords declined to accept the further proposition that a failure to enforce the law in a given case would give rise to a cause of action, even though it was possible for the police to have acted otherwise, and a risk of injury to the victim was foreseeable. Relying on Lord Wilberforce's two-stage test of liability in *Anns v Merton London Borough Council*,[12] Lord Keith, who gave the principal speech, held that, unlike the facts in *Home Office v Dorset Yacht Co Ltd*,[13] there was no special relationship between the police and 'one of a vast number of the female general public who might be at risk' from Sutcliffe's activities.[14] If, as that case decided:

'there is no general duty of care owed to individual members of the public by the responsible authorities to prevent the escape of a known criminal or to recapture him, there cannot reasonably be imposed on any police force a duty of care similarly owed to identify and apprehend an unknown one. Miss Hill cannot for this purpose be regarded as a person at special risk simply because she was young and female. Where the class of potential victims of a particular habitual criminal is a large one the precise size of it cannot in principle

11 Ibid, p 59.
12 [1978] AC 728, [1977] 2 All ER 492, HL.
13 Op cit.
14 [1989] AC 53 at 62. See further his Lordship's speech in *Murphy v Brentwood District Council* [1990] 2 All ER 908 at 915.

affect the issue. All householders are potential victims of an habitual burglar, and all females those of an habitual rapist.'[15]

Hill v Chief Constable for West Yorkshire confirms that the argument that the state should compensate victims where it has failed to comply with its duty to protect them from harm is untenable because its major premiss is unsupportable as a matter of law or is contrary to public policy. The Court of Appeal's decision in this case also contains an interesting reversal of the argument under review: were it not for the existence of the Scheme, then it might be argued that a duty should exist:

'Historically, English law has left the consequences of the tortious acts of criminals to be borne by the members of the public who suffered them. What we are concerned with in this case is whether it is just and reasonable (or, if it be preferred, whether as a matter of policy) that a cause of action should lie against the police in the alleged circumstances of the present case . . . If the state made no provision at all for criminal injuries that might be a reason for imposing a legal duty of care upon the police in the conduct of their investigations, though for the reasons which I have indicated, I think that would produce unfair results between the victims of crime . . . [The Scheme has made] quite wide provision for compensation for such persons as are likely to suffer financial loss as a result of a crime of violence. It would not be desirable that inequalities should be produced by providing additional remedies for negligence. Either such remedies will merely duplicate the scheme, or they will give rise to inequalities which may be offensive to the families of other victims of crimes of violence in cases where no negligence by the police was involved.' [That is, inequalities between victims of crime and victims of other actionable injuries.][16]

More persuasive is the argument based on social welfare. This suggests that as the state is prepared to allocate funds from general taxation towards the relief of financial hardship occasioned by chronic unemployment, physical or mental disability or illness, so it should intervene where such consequences are occasioned by criminal violence. So far as the Scheme in Great Britain is

15 Id. Cf Lord Foot's assertion that it was right to compensate victims of crime because 'society has let the injured person down and has failed to give him the protection to which he is entitled', 446 HL Official Report (5th series) col 290 (14 December 1983), which simply begs the question confronted in *Hill v Chief Constable for West Yorkshire*, namely, to what sort of protection *is* the victim entitled?

16 [1988] QB 60 at 73 per Fox LJ.

concerned, however, this argument cannot readily be relied upon. A system of social welfare is characterised by the payment of benefits designed to alleviate poverty or serious hardship, these payments typically being conditional upon proof of need. While there is a financial threshold in the Scheme, its express purpose is not to filter out the unneedy, but to enable transfers of expenditure to other parts of the Scheme and to reduce administrative costs. Apart from this, and a further financial limit on the total payable for loss of earnings, the Scheme provides, to all intents and purposes, the compensation that would be payable in a civil action against the offender. Thus the Scheme goes well beyond the occasions for, and the amount of, the financial help that is available through the various Department of Social Security (DSS) payments. Once a government envisages compensating for such losses as pain and suffering and loss of amenities, the expenses incurred by a victim employing domestic help or private nursing care, or not taking into account moneys received from other non-taxpayer sources, it has moved beyond benefiting a person in need and as such its decision cannot be based on welfare philosophy alone.

Some supporters of compensation schemes seek justification in the argument that is is economically more sensible to distribute losses occasioned by criminal activity at large, rather than let them fall on the individual concerned. This argument has traditionally been based on an analogy with no-fault automobile accident schemes.[17] These are justified in part on the reasoning that as most accidents on the roads are referable to risks inherent in the activity, those who benefit from it should bear its concomitant costs. Likewise, as criminal behaviour is, by many, seen as being endemic in our social-structural and economic arrangements, so those who ultimately benefit from those arrangements — taxpayers — should also bear the costs.

This can be a persuasive argument, but again the realities of existing schemes go beyond the support it can offer. Schemes which recognise pecuniary loss as the only compensable head of damage may be criticised on the ground that they are unnecessary as separate institutions. As they are in effect performing a social welfare function, it would arguably be more efficient to disburse compensation via the existing social welfare agencies. On the other hand, in the case of schemes which additionally recognise some elements of general damage as being compensable, the distribution of loss argument is difficult to

17 See the discussion in Cane (1987) pp 560–570.

sustain since pain and suffering and so on are referable to other notions of social equity, in particular to restitution and the notion of full compensation implicit in personal injury actions. Moreover, where, as in Britain, the victim of crime is afforded from the taxpayer compensation assessed on principles and to a level inapplicable to the victims of other risks which might also be considered endemic to our economic arrangements — industrial injuries are an obvious case — the argument will not support what is claimed for it. It is implicit in the loss distribution argument that we regard *the loss sustained,* and not *the manner of its occurrence,* as the relevant ground on which to compensate. So long as we continue to have a separate criminal injuries scheme that gives victims of crime greater compensation than is available to other accident victims, or gives it in circumstances where it is denied to others, there will be difficulty in justifying it on this argument.

What is fundamentally unconvincing about these four attempted justifications is, therefore, that two of them are based on propositions that are either untenable as a matter of law or require acceptance of a fiction, and the other two, while they could support a scheme confined to those in need, cannot support the kind of scheme, based essentially on the principle of *restitutio in integrum,* that was introduced in Britain in 1964.[18]

(2)   Justifying the Criminal Injuries Compensation Scheme in Britain

The Scheme was based on recommendations which took shape in the deliberations of two Home Office Working Parties,

---

18 Similar problems have attended the justification of the *European Convention on the Compensation of Victims of Violent Crimes* (1983) European Treaty Series No 116 which the United Kingdom ratified on 11 January 1990; House of Commons, Home Affairs Committee *Compensating Victims Quickly: the Administration of the Criminal Injuries Compensation Board* (1989–90, HC 92) para 46. See D Miers 'The provision of compensation for victims of violent crime in continental Europe' (1985) 10 Victimology 662-671, K Horton 'Criminal injuries compensation in West Germany' (1980) 180 New LJ 468, A Tsitsoura 'The role of the victim in the framework of crime policy — international aspects' (1983) 8 Victimology 47-53 and 'Criminal justice responses to victimisation' (1985) 10 Victimology 574-584, M Boland and D Martin 'Victim compensation schemes and practices: a comparative approach' (1985) 10 Victimology 672-678, and M Joutsen *The Role of the Victim of Crime in European Criminal Justice Systems* (1987, Helsinki Institute for Crime Prevention and Control) ch 9.

reporting in 1961[19] and 1963.[20] The former addressed two options, one based on the industrial injury scheme, the other, which was ultimately accepted, on common law damages, but neither really came to terms with what was being contemplated by the introduction of the Scheme, namely the creation of a system of state funded compensation for the victims of intentional torts to the person. But in accepting the desirability of making provision for the victims of crimes of personal violence, the Home Office nevertheless made it quite clear that there was no question of the government acknowledging a right to compensation. Such a contention was both fallacious and dangerous:

> 'Fallacious because we do not believe that the state has an absolute duty to protect every citizen all the time against other citizens: there is a distinction between compensation for the consequences of civil riot, which the forces of law and order may be expected to prevent, and compensation for injury by individual acts of personal violence, which can never be entirely prevented. Dangerous, because acceptance of public liability for offences against the person could be the basis for a demand for acceptance of liability for all offences against property.'[1]

This rejection of liability was consistently undermined by those government spokesmen advocating the Scheme, who repeatedly referred to the desirability of the state accepting a 'responsibility' for the victims of violent crime. Elsewhere, the Home Office urged that compensation was justifiable on 'practical' grounds. Since these grounds were not regarded as being a sufficiently sound base on which to enact legislation, one may speculate about what precisely they did comprise, apart from well-meaning expressions of sympathy. On the other hand, if the practical grounds upon which enforceable rights were not to be based were nonetheless regarded as sufficient to warrant the expenditure

---

19 Home Office *Compensation for Victims of Crimes of Violence* (1961, Cmnd 1406).
20 Home Office *Compensation for Victims of Crime of Violence* (1963, Cmnd 2323).
1 Home Office (1961) para 17. The matter was more shortly, though equally forcefully, put in the 1964 Report which contained the details of the Scheme introduced later that year: 'The government do not accept that the state is liable for injuries caused to people by the acts of others,' Home Office (1964) para 8. Twenty years later the 1986 Working Party established to pave the way for the introduction of a statutory scheme reiterated the point: 'the state is not liable for injuries caused by the acts of others . . .', Home Office *Criminal Injuries Compensation: A Statutory Scheme* (1986) para 4.2.

of public money, the argument that their rejection as legal rights would cut the ground from any analogous treatment of victims of property crime looks weak, since the critical question appears to be not whether such victims have a right to be compensated, but, more pragmatically, whether the exchequer can afford to compensate them.

Forced to the point, the government could find 'no constitutional or social principle on which State compensation could be justified'.[2] Likewise, a number of those supporting the introduction of the Scheme frankly relinquished the search for an acceptable justification, and relied instead on the 'commonsense' of compensation for victims of crime. Cross, for example, commented:

> 'I am content to do without theoretical justifications . . . After all, these are questions of public welfare and they should be determined by public opinion. Human needs account for most of the welfare state, and its evolution has nothing to do with tortuous reasoning . . .'[3]

As we shall see, the state compensation of victims of crime in Great Britain is not the same thing at all as an issue of public welfare: the Scheme continues to provide assistance to victims of crime which goes substantially beyond what is provided for victims of other misfortunes.

The failure to identify sound reasons for its introduction led directly to many of the problems that the Scheme encountered in its early years, and indeed which continue to beset its implementation. Nor have more recent of the Scheme's supporters shown any greater sophistication. The Royal Commission on Civil Liability and Compensation for Personal Injury devoted a short chapter to the Scheme, concluding lamely that it was right that victims of crimes of violence should receive appropriate compensation,[4] but why appropriate compensation should be

---

2 Home Office (1961) para 18. Harlow and Rawlings, pp 388-393.
3 R Cross 'Compensating victims of violence' (1963) 49 The Listener 816 (16 May 1963). See also D Chappell 'Compensating Australian victims of violent crimes' (1967) 41 Aust LJ 3-11, and Lord Elwyn-Jones in debate, who remarked that the introduction of the CICB 'reflected the public sense of responsibility for and sympathy with the innocent victims of crime, and it was inspired by the feeling that it was right that there should be reasonable provision for victims of crime, as indeed for victims of accident and disease. It was an appropriate part of the provisions of the welfare state', 446 HL Official Report (5th series) op cit, col 287.
4 (1978, Cmnd 7054) ch 29.

substantially equated with common law damages was never discussed.[5] Likewise, the Working Party that reported in 1986,[6] whose recommendations formed the basis for the statutory Scheme, has continued this largely unreflective tradition: criminal injury compensation is justified because it gives effect to 'the strong public sympathy for those innocent victims of crime, who are unlikely to obtain redress against the offender'.[7] Having accepted the desirability of such financial provision, the common law model was, without more ado, to continue to be the persuasive analogy.[8] We consider some detailed implications of this analogy in later chapters.

This chapter turns now to consider the Scheme's legal status, the funding and staffing of the Criminal Injuries Compensation Board (the Board), and the controls that exist over the details of the Scheme and over the Board's interpretation of them.

B. THE LEGAL STATUS OF THE SCHEME

After 24 years as a non-statutory arrangement, the Criminal Justice Act 1988 placed the Criminal Injuries Compensation Scheme on a statutory basis. However, for reasons which will be discussed later, no commencement order had been made by the time of writing, and it is highly unlikely that one will be made for some years yet. The current version is the revision contained in a written parliamentary answer given by the Home Secretary on 8 December 1989.[9]

By para 1 of the 1990 revision, the Compensation Scheme will be administered, as it has been since its inception, by the Criminal Injuries Compensation Board, which is assisted by appropriate staff. So far as its status is concerned, the *locus classicus* is the judgment of Diplock LJ in *R v Criminal Injuries Compensation Board, ex p Lain*:

> 'The Criminal Injuries Compensation Board is not constituted by statute or statutory instrument but by act of the Crown, that is the executive government, alone. It administers on behalf of the executive government moneys granted by Parliament to Crown for distribution by way of compensation to persons who have suffered personal injury

5 Cane (1987) pp 296-297.
6 Home Office (1986) para 4.2.
7 Id.
8 Id, para 12.4.
9 163 HC Official Report (6th series) cols 411-417 (8 December 1989).

directly attributable to criminal offences, the prevention of crime, or the apprehension of offenders. So far there is nothing novel about this. If the matter rested there no persons would have any right to obtain any payment out of those moneys which would be enforceable in courts of law by action or controllable by prerogative writ.

But the matter does not rest there. The executive government announced in Parliament and published to intending applicants a document called "The Scheme." It took the form of a statement expressed in the future tense of how the distribution of compensation to applicants would be carried out. It stated that the Board would entertain applications for payment of compensation where specified conditions were fulfilled, and laid down the procedure for the determination by the Board of such applications. The procedure at any rate bears all the characteristics of a judicial or quasi-judicial procedure; and the Board when determining applications in accordance with that procedure is clearly performing de facto quasi-judicial functions, that is, acting as an inferior tribunal. Its authority to do so is not derived from any agreement between Crown and applicants but from instructions by the executive government, that is by prerogative act of the Crown. The appointment of the board and the conferring on it of jurisdiction to entertain and determine applications, and of authority to make payments in accordance with such determinations, are acts of government, done without statutory authority but nonetheless lawful for that.'[10]

Two reasons were commonly advanced at the time for the creation of this 'constitutional anomaly'.[11] The first was that to place the Scheme on a statutory basis would be to create rights in law which the government had consistently denied during the period of consultation prior to its introduction; the second was that in any event the Scheme was intended to be an experiment. It may be argued that the Scheme had, some years before it achieved statutory status, long since moved from the experimental stage; writing in 1980 the Board observed: 'we think that it can be said with confidence that the Scheme is now part of the nation's legal and social system.'[12] Even allowing for the fact that this is a partial judgment, few would question the significance of the Scheme for the many thousands — 415,926 — of victims of crimes against the person who have been compensated under

---

10 Per Diplock LJ in *R v Criminal Injuries Compensation Board, ex p Lain* [1967] 2 QB 864 at 883.

11 As both Lord Elwyn-Jones and Lord Bridge referred to the Scheme in debate, 446 HL Official Report, op cit, cols 288 and 297.

12 CICB 16th Report (1980, Cmnd 8081) para 1. In the same vein, see the remarks made about the Scheme during the Second Reading of the Criminal Justice Bill 1986, 106 HC Official Report (6th series) col 471 (27 November 1986).

its terms since its inception on 1 August 1964.[13] The demand that the Scheme be placed on a statutory basis was prompted by a number of factors: a desire to see victims 'properly' treated (that is, by law) and to hold the government to its promise to introduce legislation; a feeling that there was insufficient parliamentary scrutiny of expenditure by a branch of government in 1988–89 of just over £69m in compensation and costing some £3.5m in administration; and the continuing unease that, while it had never happened, it remained theoretically possible for the Crown to deny the payment of an award notwithstanding an applicant's eligibility within the Scheme.

(1) The legal status of the Board's decisions

A decision of the Criminal Injuries Compensation Board made under its non-statutory authority cannot, as Diplock LJ said in *Ex p Lain*, 'give the applicant any right to sue either the Board or the Crown for that sum.'[14] Nevertheless, the Board's decisions are not without legal effect; they make lawful a payment from the government that would otherwise be unlawful. So far as the applicant is concerned, though in theory the Secretary of State can disallow or reduce payment even where he falls within the terms of the Scheme, in practice the Board has no such discretion: 'the Board has always regarded itself as obliged to award compensation to anyone who satisfied the conditions for payment of compensation.'[15] The denial of the right to sue for payment was therefore of little moment; on the contrary, government spokesmen have been at pains to confirm the proposition that applicants who fell within the terms of the Scheme indeed have a 'right' to compensation.[16]

Even if this 'right' were one exercisable only as a matter of practice, that did not resolve the question considered in *R v Criminal Injuries Compensation Board, ex p Tong*,[17] namely, *when* did the applicant become entitled to payment. The victim, a rent collector, had been injured in a robbery. He was made an interim award, and some time later a final assessment was made by a single Member of the Board. However, before he was

---

13 CICB 25th Report (1989, Cm 900) App A.
14 Op cit, p 888.
15 Home Office (1986) para 2.2.
16 Baroness Trumpington 446 HL Official Report, op cit, col 304.
17 [1975] 3 All ER 678, [1976] 1 WLR 47, DC; revsd [1977] 1 All ER 171, [1976] 1 WLR 1237, CA.

notified of this award, he died from other causes. The Scheme then provided, as it does now,[18] that an award of compensation is personal to the applicant and does not survive for the benefit of his estate. After a special hearing, the Board decided that if the victim died before he had accepted the award offered, the offer lapsed. While the dependants specified in the Scheme were free to apply for compensation, they would only be eligible for an award based on a fatal accidents action, thus excluding any compensation for general damage. The Scheme also provided, as it does now,[19] that where the victim dies otherwise than in consequence of the injury, the Board may make an award to a dependant in respect of any reduction in earnings sustained by the victim between the injury and the date of death, and any expenses and liabilities incurred by him as a result of the injury. This did not, however, apply in *Ex p Tong*, as the victim's loss of earnings had been wholly met by his employer; the Board's final assessment was for general damages, which would not survive for the benefit of the widow, nor be available under the Fatal Accidents Act 1976.

The Divisional Court refused the application for certiorari, holding that the cut-off point was not when the offer was accepted, but when payment had been made: 'if no payment has been made, then there is no entitlement.'[20] The Court of Appeal, allowing certiorari, found this to be unacceptable. In its view, compensation was vested in the applicant as soon as the award was decided upon by the Board, irrespective of whether he had been notified of it. The court was especially concerned that the Board's view would mean that an applicant's entitlement could well depend on the speed with which offers of compensation were dispatched. If, in *Ex p Tong*, notification of the award had been sent the day after it was made (25 February 1971), the applicant would, since he died on 6 March 1971, have become 'entitled' to it, and hence his widow likewise. Lord Denning MR thus preferred the common law analogy, that once the verdict is given, the entitlement to compensation inheres in the applicant.[1] The Board experienced difficulties with this decision, and held some awards as provisional pending the outcome of the Home Office review then being conducted.[2] In the event,

18 Para 15; infra, pp 152–153.
19 Para 16; infra, p 153.
20 [1975] 3 All ER 678 at 681.
 1 [1977] 1 All ER 171 at 174.
 2 Home Office *Review of the Criminal Injuries Compensation Scheme: Report of an Interdepartmental Working Party* (1978).

the Working Party agreed with the Board's view that 'an applicant will have no title to an award offered until the Board have received notification in writing that he accepts it',[3] and the Scheme was duly amended in the 1979 revision following the Working Party's Report.

The Working Party that reported in 1986 recommended that 'entitlement to an award made by a single member should vest in an applicant 28 days after receipt by the Board of the applicant's written acceptance or on payment of the award, whichever is the earlier. Entitlement to an award made at a hearing should vest on payment of the award.'[4] The purpose of these in-built delays was to allow the Board to take account of new or changed circumstances, and, if it accepted that a mistake had been made, to alter the award. This would operate to the applicant's benefit, who, under the statutory Scheme, would otherwise have to obtain a court order in cases of error. Although the 1990 revision does give effect to many of the Working Party's recommendations that were included in the legislation, this is not one of them, and by para 22 of the Scheme, entitlement is stated in the same terms as those used in the 1979 revision.

(2) Amending the non-statutory Scheme

One consequence of the Scheme's mode of creation is that it has been readily susceptible to amendment, as indeed was intended. Apart from changes in the financial minimum, the major changes to the Scheme (all effected in the same manner) took place in 1969, 1979, and in 1990 in lieu of the commencement of the statutory Scheme. The most important of the 1969 changes, which were based on the first few years' experience of the Board and may thus legitimately be said to be the results of experimentation, reformulated the definition of offences that attracted compensation and extended the scope of the provision entitling the Board to reject undeserving applicants.[5] The 1979-80 changes were more extensive, implementing recommendations made by the Interdepartmental Review of the Scheme which was set up in 1974 and which reported in 1978.[6] The most significant of these changes were the introduction of powers to compensate the victims of domestic violence and to re-open cases where there

---

3 Para 22, and Home Office (1978) para 21.7.
4 Home Office (1986) para 22.18.
5 784 HC Official Report (5th series) cols 99-104 (21 May 1969).
6 Home Office (1978) op cit.

had been a marked deterioration in the victim's medical condition following the making of an award, the introduction of time limits for the submission of applications and of requests for hearings, and an increase in the Board's powers to administer awards where that would be in the victim's interest.[7]

A further review was initiated in 1984 following the announcement in December 1983 that the government intended to place the Scheme on a statutory basis (as the earlier review had recommended).[8] The Working Party reported in 1986;[9] its particular recommendations are dealt with in their appropriate places in the following chapters. Until this announcement the Home Office had resisted a number of attempts to introduce legislation, although it had endorsed the recommendations of both the 1978 review and the Pearson Report as to the desirability of this course.[10] The reason given was that the government wished to acquire sufficient experience of the Scheme's implementation following the 1979-80 changes so as to minimise the risk of early amendment;[11] accordingly it opposed Bills introduced by Lord Longford in 1979 and by David Alton MP in 1982.[12] A further explanation of the government's earlier unwillingness to act may have been the inertial effect of relative success: there is little point in encouraging political controversy (although legislation for victim compensation is bound to attract wide support, many will think it does not go far enough[13]) when existing arrangements are progressing with only minor hiccoughs.

The promised statutory Scheme was enacted in ss 108-117 of and Schedules 6 and 7 to the Criminal Justice Act 1988. The delay in making a commencement order to bring the Scheme into force was initially attributed to the Board's (and the Home Office's) desire to ensure that the regulations made under Schedule

---

7 CICB (1980) para 4.
8 Lord Elton 451 HL Official Report (5th series) col 1127 (10 May 1984).
9 Home Office (1986), op cit.
10 *Royal Commission on Civil Liability and Personal Injury*, op cit, para 1591.
11 The Home Secretary 971 HC Official Report (5th series) cols 17-25 (23 July 1979), and Lord Belstead 401 HL Official Report (5th series) col 1876 (3 July 1979). Also (1979) 130 New LJ 746.
12 401 HL Official Report (5th series) cols 228-43, 254-84 and 1877-98 (3 and 24 July 1979), 402 HL Official Report (5th series) cols 341-46 (30 October 1979), 26 HC Official Report (6th series) cols 903-06 (30 June 1982), 27 HC Official Report (6th series) col 618 (9 July 1982), and 28 HC Official Report (6th series) cols 280-81 (22 July 1982).
13 See, eg, the Opposition's complaint that the provisions in the Criminal Justice Bill 1986 were 'mean and niggardly', 113 HC Official Report (6th series) cols 1009-1112 (31 March 1987).

7 were right, but it became clear during 1989 that the Board was in serious difficulties with the backlog of applications that had been building up over the years, and was now unwilling to devote resources to preparing for the implementation of the statutory Scheme. In its inquiry held in December 1989, the Home Affairs Select Committee agreed that the preparation of the Criminal Justice Act 1988 had given the Board 'a wrong signal about priorities',[14] and acknowledged the desirability, indicated by the Home Secretary earlier that month, 'of the urgent need to tackle the backlog and improve the Board's service to present and future claimants.'[15] It was agreed that this would be more readily accomplished if the Board did not have to implement the statutory Scheme itself; however, because it contains features designed to improve the Board's productivity, these were included, along with a number of substantive changes, in the revision announced in December 1989 and which came into effect on 1 February 1990.

(3) The terms of the Scheme

The Scheme contains a mixture of prescriptive and descriptive propositions; it informs the reader both of what the Board's discretion is, and how it typically exercises it. The Board has, throughout its life, annexed to its Reports a short guide — 'The Statement' — to its interpretation of some of the Scheme's provisions. It should be emphasised that this is written for guidance only: 'each application will be decided on its merits and [that] what is said in this statement does not limit the discretion of an individual Board member or Board members at a hearing.'[16] In the chapters that follow, unless otherwise stated, references to 'the Statement' are references to the Statement appearing in the Board's 25th Report and references to 'the Scheme' are references to the 1990 revision. The text of the 1990 revision is reproduced in Appendix 1.

---

14 House of Commons (1989–90) para 16. For a discussion of the reasons for the backlog problem, infra, pp 307–309.
15 163 HC Official Report, op cit, col 410.
16 CICB (1989) App D. The emphasis on discretion was included following *R v Criminal Injuries Compensation Board, ex p RJC* [1978] Crim LR 220 in which the Divisional Court held unlawful a statement by the Board that purported to divest itself of its discretion in a given class of cases.

C. THE BOARD'S FUNDING AND ESTABLISHMENT

(1) Funding

By para 2 of the Scheme, the Board is provided with money through a Grant-in-Aid; the net expenditure falling on the Votes of the Home Office and the Scottish Home and Health Department. In addition to its grant in 1989-90 of £77,469,000,[17] the Board had a small income of £72,994 from operating receipts, being principally moneys recovered by victims from their offenders. From this fund is paid the awards made to successful applicants, which consume most of it, the wages and salaries of the Board Members and its staff and the Board's various operating costs. Details appear in each year's Report. By para 3 the Board is required to prepare and to submit a statement of accounts for each financial year to the Secretary of State which is examined by the Comptroller and Auditor General. These accounts, together with a report on the operation of the Scheme are required to be laid before Parliament annually.

The level of funding, which has increased every year since the Scheme was set up, has in recent years become a matter of public concern to the government. In 1983, when the bereavement award (£3,500) became available under the Scheme following its introduction in s 3 of the Administration of Justice Act 1982, the government sought to cover the cost (estimated at some £600,000 in the first year[18]) of making this payment in (virtually[19]) every case arising from an unlawful killing by increasing in November 1983 the minimum loss figure from £250 to £400, an increase that both followed quite closely upon the step from £150 to £250 (in April 1981), and was significantly above the rate of inflation. However, somewhat more drastic measures were mooted in 1986. Although the exact number cannot be known, it was clearly within the government's thinking that the enactment of legislation would increase the number of successful applications and hence the cost of the Scheme. To counter this, it was proposed to increase the threshold to £1,000, thus eliminating perhaps 50% of applicants, with an estimated saving

---

17 CICB (1989) p 23. The budget for 1990–91 is £115m.
18 House of Commons, Home Affairs Committee, *Compensation and Support for Victims of Crime* (1984-85, HC 43) para 32.
19 As under the Fatal Accidents Act 1976, cohabitees cannot receive the bereavement award, infra, p 176.

of £16m.[20] This proposal was greeted with derision by a number of interested groups; and the Chairman of the Board expressed considerable reservations about it.[1]

A primary reason why the Scheme will continue to be expensive is that compensation is awarded on the basis of common law damages. This means that with some qualifications (in particular concerning loss of earnings and, in the past, the deduction of state-funded collateral benefits), victims stand to receive that award which they could expect to receive in an action against their offenders. Where the injuries are severe, involving paraplegia, blindness or other disablement, the general damages award in particular will be substantial. The Scheme is unusual in this respect. Almost all other criminal injury compensation schemes impose not only a minimum, but a *maximum* amount that will be compensated, usually simply expressed as a fixed or proportional figure. This raises the question, why *should* criminal injury victims receive compensation according to the common law model?[2] The Board's Reports have not been sufficiently detailed to allow the reader to estimate what savings would be made if there were a limit of, say, £25,000 on any general damage award. Nor is there any evidence that alternatives such as this have been considered. If there must be a gross limit on expenditure under the Scheme, the issue is whether some whose injuries are sufficiently serious will continue to receive 'full' damages based on the common law model (notwithstanding the many objections that have been made to the continuation of that model), or whether a significantly greater number will receive some compensation, of whom a proportion will continue to receive, within the limit, what they would have received under the old model. Apart from such other considerations as encouraging positive attitudes towards the criminal justice system through the general availability of (limited) compensation for criminal injuries, as a matter of social policy it seems preferable that more injured victims should receive some compensation, than that most should not and that the minority who are very seriously injured receive full compensation. This does not

20 Times, 21 May 1986, Guardian, 27 May 1986.
1 M Ogden 'The work of the Criminal Injuries Compensation Board' (1984–85) 52 Medico-Legal J 227-241.
2 Infra, pp 157-161. The Northern Ireland scheme is similar in this respect to the CICB, D Greer *Compensation for Criminal Injuries to Persons in Northern Ireland* (1990, 2nd ed, SLS Legal Publications, Belfast), and D Greer, 'The Criminal Injuries (Compensation) (NI) Order 1988' (1988) 39 Northern Ireland Legal Q 372-379.

however represent the government's current thinking. It now takes the view that the Scheme should concentrate on injuries that 'substantially affect people's well being.'[3] So do serious industrial injuries, but this has not led to the provision there of benefits on the common law model.

(2)   Establishment

Paragraph 1 establishes a Criminal Injuries Compensation Board to which appointments shall be made by the Secretary of State and, in Scotland, by the Lord Advocate. No member of the Board may hold office for more than five years, beyond the retiring age of 72 or after ceasing to be qualified for appointment, but in each case the Secretary of State may renew or extend the appointment. In the case of the five year limitation, the Secretary of State exercises his discretion to renew as he considers appropriate; in the other two instances, if he considers it to be in the interests of the Scheme. Conversely, the Secretary of State may discontinue the appointment on the ground of incapacity or misbehaviour.

Board members must be practising barristers, advocates or solicitors. The majority of appointments have always been drawn from the first two categories; of the 40 members listed in 1989, 35 were Queen's Counsel. In its evidence both to the original working party in 1961 and to that which reported in 1986, JUSTICE proposed that the Board should include 'doctors, court officials, academic lawyers, accountants and insurance assessors'.[4] At its inception, the argument that an experimental scheme required legal expertise for its implementation prevailed; to that has been added the argument that the Board now has over 20 years' experience to draw upon, so that 'their appointment would have no advantage over the present arrangements for obtaining expert medical and other professional advice, as and when required, by means of written reports or the attendance of expert witnesses.'[5] No changes were made in the 1990 revision.

3 106 HC Official Report (6th series) col 471 (27 November 1986). See further the Home Secretary, 163 HC Official Report, op cit, col 410.

4 Suggestions that some lay members, and some with medical qualifications be appointed, have similarly been resisted by the government in the past, 775 HC Official Report (5th series) cols 556-57 (oral answers, 12 December 1968), and an amendment to the Criminal Justice Bill 1986 to permit such appointments was also unsuccessful, HC Official Report (6th series) Standing Committee F col 750 (24 February 1987).

5 Home Office (1986) para 1.3.

From the members of the Board, one is appointed its Chairman. The first was Sir Walker Carter QC, and the current Chairman, who assumed office in April 1989, is Lord Carlisle of Bucklow QC. Between 1976 and 1989 the Chairman was Sir Michael Ogden QC. During his tenure the Scheme was subject to the substantial reviews reporting in 1978 and 1986.[6] His influence on the development of the Scheme was substantial but not always uncontroversial, in particular concerning the desirability that the Scheme should compensate only the 'innocent' victim.[7] As we shall see, the terms designed to give effect to this objective have not been easy either to formulate or to implement.

The Board is supported by clerical and administrative staff, though not sufficient in its judgment to process and finalise applications as quickly as it would wish. This has been a matter of concern to the Board for some time, and in its 1985 Report used the opportunity afforded by the Home Affairs Committee's sympathetic treatment of the issue[8] to underline the growing discrepancy between the increases in its workload and in its staffing allocation:

'In the past ten years the number of applications received by the Board has increased by 145% without any corresponding increase in staff. The Board's complement was 162 until 1983 when it was increased to 183. In the past two years alone there was been an increase of 18.5% in the number of applications but the complement still stands at 183 and the Board's staff are now experiencing serious difficulty in dealing with the volume of work.'[9]

The Committee accepted the Chairman's evidence and recommended that there should be a gradual increase in the Board's establishment. In 1986 the Home Office allocated a further 13 staff to the Board, and later that year announced that an additional £114m would be available over the fiscal years to 1989-90 to assist in reducing the backlog of applications.[10] A

6 CICB (1989) paras 27.1-27.2.
7 Miers (1978) and (1980).
8 House of Commons (1984-85) paras 30 and 49.
9 CICB 21st Report (1985, Cmnd 9399) para 1. See further 47 HC Official Report (6th series) col 425 (3 November 1983). Greater increases in private over public sector salaries have also inhibited recruitment, especially in London, CICB 24th Report (1988, Cm 536) paras 5.4 and 11.3.
10 445 HL Official Report (5th series) cols 1278-80 (8 December 1983), 473 HL Official Report (5th series) cols 78-80 (8 April 1986), 481 HL Official Report col 1249 (6 November 1986), and HC Official Report, Standing Committee F col 981 (10 March 1987).

major component of this assistance was the establishment in 1987 of a second Board office, in Glasgow. It was expected that by the summer of 1988 this office would have reached its full complement of 109 trained staff and would have made substantial inroads into the backlog,[11] but the reality confounded these expectations. By December 1989 the backlog had increased to 92,000 applications, equivalent to 600 man years of work,[12] while the proportion of applicants having to wait more than 12 months for their applications to be resolved was 73.1%; only four years earlier this figure was 30.4%, and in 1974 it was 4%.[13] In its 1990 Report, the Home Affairs Committee recommended an increase of 60 in the Board's 333 staffing establishment, being the Chairman's revised estimate of what the Board needed to 'reduce the workload to what we consider to be a reasonable proportion and a reasonable time'.[14] However, the Committee also endorsed the Home Office's view that the solution to the Board's problems did not lie 'in having resources thrown at them',[15] and as we shall see in the following chapter, made a number of recommendations to remedy what it perceived to be some inefficiencies in its procedures.

D. ACCOUNTABILITY

(1) Parliamentary

Paragraph 3 of the Scheme provides that the Board's decisions will not be subject to ministerial review. Accountability was thought to be sufficiently met by keeping the general working of the Scheme under governmental review, and by the imposition on the Board of a requirement to submit annual Reports to the Home Secretary and the Secretary of State for Scotland. These Reports are open to parliamentary scrutiny, but this has been relatively rare, and with the exception of the Lords' debate in

---

11 CICB (1988) para 52.3. See further, ibid, paras 5.4 and 52.1-52.2.
12 House of Commons (1989-90) para 22.
13 Ibid, para 5.
14 Ibid, para 19.
15 House of Commons (1989-90) para 15, Home Office *Compensation and Support for Victims of Crime* (1985, Cmnd 9457) para 14.

December 1983,[16] not especially informed. Indeed, formal debate has largely centred on whether the government should introduce legislation; the Board's annual Reports typically prompting only Parliamentary Questions about delay in resolving cases, or the minimum threshold. It was, as Lord Allen put it in the 1983 debate, extraordinary that a body 'involving as it does substantial expenditure, the employment of substantial numbers of staff and its own legal code',[17] should be subject to such minimal parliamentary supervision. This lacuna was one of the prime factors that prompted the increasingly powerful lobby for legislation. Neither is the Board subject to supervision by the Council of Tribunals, which omission the 1986 Working Party recommended should be rectified.[18] As the Board is not a Crown body, it does not fall within the jurisdiction of the Parliamentary Commissioner for Administration, but as he is an ex officio member of the Council, he may direct to it complaints to him of maladministration.

The Home Affairs Committee noted the government's intentions that its executive functions should wherever possible be carried out by agencies, and recommended a study of the feasibility of giving the CICB agency status. The effect would be to give the CICB a measure of independence in achieving the productivity targets that its Framework Document would contain; for the Committee, this holds out the hope that greater management flexibility will, provided the CICB receives adequate resources, assist in the short term in the speedy reduction of the backlog, and in the longer term, in a more efficient use of its resources.[19]

Turning from specific questions about the Board's activities, there have been three reviews of the 'general working' of the scheme, two of which have been published. 'Beyond determining the terms of the scheme', however, neither Secretary of State has sought 'to influence the Board in the exercise of their discretion.'[20] While this may have been the practice, it is an open question whether the Secretary of State can, nevertheless, alter a decision

---

16 446 HL Official Report, op cit, cols 283-309. Earlier debates are 245 HL Official Report (5th series) cols 245-319 (5 December 1962), 395 HL Official Report (5th series) cols 255-307 (18 July 1978), and 401 HL Official Report, op cit.
17 446 HL Official Report, op cit, col 286. This view was shared by the government, ibid, col 303.
18 Home Office (1986) para 3.5.
19 House of Commons (1989-90) paras 41-43.
20 20 HC Official Report (6th series) col 298 (23 March 1982).

of which he doesn't approve. The non-statutory Scheme is amenable to change at the stroke of a pen,[1] and it has been the case that where the Board has reached decisions unattractive to the government (and perhaps to the Board too), amendments have been made so as to prevent a repetition of the decision should similar facts arise. This practice is, of course, perfectly proper; but it is theoretically open to the Secretary of State to reduce or disallow the compensation proposed to be paid, at least before the applicant has become 'entitled' to the award by an acceptance in writing of the Board's offer. Thereafter, the applicant can obtain judicial review if the Board refused to make payment, but prior to that entitlement and 'egged on perhaps by officials in the Treasury anxious to exercise a tighter and more direct control over the administration of the Scheme',[2] the Secretary of State can it seems veto payment. This decision can be reviewed neither by the courts nor, since he does not require its approval for such action, by Parliament. Such uncontrollable executive action Lord Bridge considered constitutionally undesirable, and it was one of the reasons why he saw the urgent need for legislation.[3] As the statutory Scheme remains unimplemented, such action continues to be a possibility.

(2) Judicial

(a) APPEALS AGAINST BOARD DECISIONS

The Scheme explicitly excludes the possibility of an appeal on the merits of a decision of the Board.[4] However, as indicated in the earlier quotation from Diplock LJ's judgment in *Ex p Lain*,[5] it was shortly established that its decisions are subject to judicial review. The Board had argued in that case that as the Scheme was no more than an administrative arrangement, *certiorari* could not go since the Board had no legal authority and could not determine questions affecting the rights of subjects.

---

1 Lord Allen, 446 HL Official Report, op cit, col 285. Or as the Minister of State put it, if less graphically, then more bluntly: 'in theory, a Secretary of State could wake up one morning and say, "that's enough of criminal injuries compensation", and that would be that.' HC Official Report (6th series) Standing Committee F col 738 (24 February 1987).
2 Lord Bridge, 446 HL Official Report, op cit, col 299.
3 Id.
4 Para 3 of the Scheme.
5 [1967] 2 QB 864, [1967] 2 All ER 770. Also Harlow and Rawlings (1984) pp 393-395.

Rejecting this, a strong Divisional Court (Lord Parker CJ, Diplock LJ and Ashworth J)[6]:

> 'saw no reason in principle why the fact that no authority from Parliament is required by the executive government to entitle it to decide what shall be the form of the administrative process under which compensation for crimes of violence is paid, should exempt the Board from the supervisory control by the High Court over that part of its functions which are judicial in character.'[7]

This example of judicial ingenuity, 'exercised in response to a sound judicial instinct, appreciating, as the court did, that decisions of a body such as the compensation board are essentially decisions of a kind which ought to be subject to review by the courts',[8] was thought remarkable at the time and remained thereafter a matter of curiosity:

> 'As a matter of strict jurisprudence, I have never been able to understand how a payment described in the Scheme as being *ex gratia* can become enforceable as of right, pursuant to an order of the court, nor how a board interpreting a scheme which consists of a series of administrative instructions can make an error of law, since the instructions do not form any part of the law of the land.'[9]

While there may be some trace of irony in Lord Bridge's retrospection, his Lordship also raised the more serious question, what response would the courts make if the Secretary of State sought review to quash a decision in favour of an applicant? If the Board were in error, then it must be in the public interest that the Secretary of State should be able to apply for review, though such an application does not appear ever to have been made. The Working Party thought it both inappropriate and unnecessary to include such a power in the statutory Scheme, the Attorney-General always being able to bring proceedings to prevent the Board from exceeding its powers.[10]

Though the Working Party did not consider that any injustice had been done in consequence of the lack of a formal appellate procedure, the exclusion from the non-statutory Scheme of a formal avenue of appeal has for some time been a matter of

---

6 The quality of the court was so described by Lord Bridge, 446 HL Official Report, op cit, col 299.
7 Lord Bridge, ibid, col 298.
8 Id.
9 Id.
10 Home Office (1986) paras 3.11-3.12.

adverse comment.[11] Many of those who submitted evidence to the Working Party favoured the provision of a statutory right of appeal, though opinions differed as to what the grounds should be.[12] In the event, the Working Party recommended only that there should be provision for appeal by way of case stated. It was considered unnecessary to permit appeals on questions of fact or on the amount of compensation, given the two-tier structure of the Board and the essentially discretionary nature of the assessment of general damage. The position now remains as it has always been, with an 'appeal' in the form of a hearing conducted by the Board itself, and the availability of judicial review.

(b)   INTERPRETING THE SCHEME

When interpreting the Scheme the courts have repeatedly said that it should not be approached as though it were a statute, but that 'members of the Board ought to be free to deal with [these] eventualities when they arise in a flexible manner having regard to the whole object of the Scheme'.[13] Likewise, the courts have taken the view that they should interpret the Scheme so as to give effect to its underlying policy, adopting the interpretation of a reasonable and literate man.[14] Whether, in practice, the courts always reached interpretations of the Scheme's provisions that were consonant with their policy is open to question: in *Ex p Tong*[15] the award did survive for the benefit of the victim's estate, which was clearly out of line with the Scheme's intentions, and in *R v Criminal Injuries Compensation Board, ex p Schofield* the Court of Appeal permitted a bystander to recover compensation when she was injured by either a robber or the person trying to apprehend him, when she herself was making no effort to engage in any act of law enforcement, again,

---

11 401 HL Official Report, op cit, col 235, 446 HL Official Report, op cit, cols 838–40, and 26 HC Official Report, op cit, col 903. See also, Home Office (1986) para 3.10. Of the 455,183 applications the Board has received since 1964, very few have resulted in applications for judicial review. CICB (1987) para 52.

12 Home Office (1986) para 3.7.

13 Per Wien J, *R v Criminal Injuries Compensation Board, ex p Tong* [1975] 3 All ER 678 at 680.

14 Lawton LJ, *R v Criminal Injuries Compensation Board, ex p Webb* [1987] QB 74 at 78, CA. See also Bridge J, *R v Criminal Injuries Compensation Board, ex p Schofield* [1971] 2 All ER 1011 at 1015.

15 Op cit.

an interpretation inconsistent with the Scheme's intentions.[16] Besides these, no other reported cases suggest that, had the Scheme been statutory, the courts would have reached interpretations other than those which they did in practice. If and when the statutory Scheme comes into force, it is unlikely that the Board will approach its interpretation in any manner different to that it currently employs.[17]

16 Infra, pp 139–140.
17 CICB (1987) para 57.

Chapter Two

The Board's Procedures

A. THE VOLUME OF WORK

In its 15th Report, the Board commented:

'The predominant factors in the volume of our work must relate to the number of crimes of violence, awareness of the Scheme and the decision of a victim to apply for compensation'[1]

and in the following year the Board added to this list the various extensions to the scope of the Scheme made in 1969 and 1979.[2] The impact of these revisions upon its volume of work, and more particularly upon the annual number of new applications is complex, and we should hesitate before ascribing to these changes responsibility for fluctuations in that number.[3] This is so firstly because, as a matter of definition, the Board's volume of work cannot be equated simply with the annual totals of new applications: volume of work involves a qualitative as well as a quantitative dimension, as the Board's observations on the difficulties that attend the consideration, for example, of late applications indicate.[4] Secondly, it is in practice very difficult to identify either the relationship between different subsets of figures that may be attributable to these revisions, or

1 CICB 15th Report (1979, Cmnd 7752) para 3.
2 CICB 16th Report (1980, Cmnd 8081) para 4.
3 See, eg, the Board's comment that it would be unwise to conclude that the decrease in the number of new applications during 1977-78 was attributable to an increase in the financial minimum from £50 to £150 in 1977, CICB 14th Report (1978, Cmnd 7396) para 2. See further CICB 23rd Report (1987, Cm 265) para 2, and 24th Report (1988, Cm 536) para 2.2 where the Board observed that 'it is very questionable whether it can safely be assumed that the steady upward trend [in applications] will ever be more than marginally affected by modest increases in the lower limit.'
4 CICB 17th Report (1981, Cmnd 8401) paras 38-39, 18th Report (1982, Cmnd 8752) paras 12-16, and 22nd Report (1986, Cm 42) para 7.

the impact that they may have had on the total of new applications. The issue is made more difficult because these revisions have both widened and narrowed the scope of the Scheme. For example, in 1979-80, the Scheme was widened to include victims of intra-family violence and to empower the Board to re-open cases where there had been a serious deterioration in the applicant's medical condition.[5] To March 1985, 877, and to March 1989, 1,306 applications respectively are specifically attributable to these extensions. On the other hand, another change in 1979-80 narrowed the ground on which compensation would be available to those accidentally injured while engaged in law enforcement.[6] The effect appears to have reduced the number of awards to policemen injured on duty from 3,065 in 1979-80 to 1,017 in 1983-84.[7] While we might expect that policemen would have continued to apply on the basis of the unrevised Scheme even after the introduction of this change, we might also suppose that within a short time, following the publication in the Board's Reports of guidelines indicating how the amended paragraph was to be interpreted, there would have been a reduction in the number of applications concerning such injuries, sufficient perhaps to offset the new applications prompted by the changes elsewhere.[8] It is not possible to tell since the Board's Reports do not break claims down according to the ground upon which compensation is sought; at all events the global figure of new applications since those various changes in 1979-80 has continued to rise every year.

(1) The number of crimes of violence

In 1988-89 there were 36,285 new applications in England and Wales to the CICB.[9] This represents 16.7% of the 216,100 notifiable offences of violence against the person, sexual offences and robbery recorded by the police in 1988.[10] This represents a reversal

---

5 On domestic violence infra, pp 153-156, and on re-opening cases infra, pp 61-62.
6 Infra, pp 141-143.
7 CICB (1979) para 41 and 20th Report (1984, Cmnd 9399) para 44.
8 Since the restriction applies to injuries which are sustained 'accidentally', it is unlikely that applications arising in such circumstances would or could be submerged in the much greater number of those arising from the commission of a crime of violence.
9 CICB (1988) para 2.1.
10 Home Office *Criminal Statistics England and Wales 1988* (1989, Cm 847) Table 2.1.

in the proportion of new applications to notifiable offences which has been increasing slowly over the past decade. However, if the figure for this group of notifiable offences in 1989 is, as the Home Office predicted in December 1989,[11] in the region of 220,000, the proportion of new applications in England and Wales that the Board has predicted that it will receive in 1989-90 (53,000, of which around 20% arise in Scotland) will resume the trend.

APPLICATIONS (fiscal year: England and Wales)		NOTIFIABLE OFFENCES (calendar year, 000s; violence against the person, sexual offences and robbery)		PRO-PORTION %
1979-80	18,948	1979	129.3	14.6
1980-81	20,613	1980	133.3	15.4
1981-82	22,099	1981	139.9	15.7
1982-83	24,635	1982	151.2	16.2
1983-84	26,828	1983	153.8	17.4
1984-85	29,050	1984	159.3	18.2
1985-86	33,420	1985	170.7	19.5
1986-87	35,967	1986	178.2	20.1
1987-88	35,940	1987	198.8	18.0
1988-89	36,285	1988	216.1	16.7

As the Board has observed, care must be exercised when drawing inferences from these figures;[12] in particular, they say nothing about the size of the eligible population within the terms of the Scheme and thus offer no basis for determining its success or otherwise in reaching that population. Neither, as the Home Office emphasised in its evidence to the Home Affairs Committee, is there a stable relationship between the number of crimes of violence and of applications for compensation;[13] rather, the determination of the parameters of any relationship is a matter both of complexity and of some uncertainty, as the following paragraphs will attempt to show.

In 1983 (this year has been chosen because it is possible to make some comparisons with British Crime Survey (BCS)

11 House of Commons, Home Affairs Committee *Compensating Victims Quickly: the Administration of the Criminal Injuries Compensation Board* (1989-90, HC 92) Minutes of Evidence, p 23.
12 CICB (1978) paras 1-2.
13 House of Commons (1989-90) para 23.

estimates relating to that year) there were, in round figures, 154,000 offences of personal violence (wounding, robbery and sexual offences) recorded by the police in England and Wales, and as the table above shows, the Board received in 1983–84 26,828 applications. There is no direct chronological correspondence between these figures, but they may be used, for want of better data, as the base from which some observations about the potential size of the eligible population for the purposes of the Scheme may be made. Two issues arise: firstly, how many more incidents than the 154,000 might have given rise to compensable injuries had they been reported, and secondly, given that the number of applications received by the Board was 17.4% of those offences that were recorded, how many more of them might have sustained a successful application? BCS estimates can help to elucidate these issues, but while the quantity of offences is clearly an important factor in determining the likely rate of applications for compensation, and by extension, the likely administrative and compensation costs, numbers alone will be poor aids to prediction. What is critical is the *severity* of the injuries sustained, since applications to the Board will not be met unless the injuries and consequential losses sustained exceed the minimum threshold, currently £750.

The BCS estimated that in 1983 there were between four (616,000) and five (770,000) times the recorded figure for 'crimes of violence', and its best estimate for wounding, robbery and sexual offences in that year was 635,000.[14] However, it also observed that the dark figure 'does not indicate that there is four to five times as much crime of the *same severity* as is now recorded in *Criminal Statistics*';[15] thus this figure should be refined according to some criteria of severity. One criterion used by the BCS was whether the victim required medical help. On this basis, the BCS concluded that 'most assaults and crimes of violence did not result in any serious physical injury; in only 12% of cases did the victim need any sort of professional medical attention, and in less than 1% of cases the victim was admitted to hospital.'[16] This suggests that arising from the best estimate of crimes of violence, some 82,550 victims required medical or hospital attention, a figure which is comfortably within the

14 M Hough and P Mayhew *Taking Account of Crime* (1985, Home Office Research Study 85) p 10. See further in P Mayhew et al *The 1988 British Crime Survey* (1989, Home Office Research Study 111) ch 2.
15 M Hough and P Mayhew *The British Crime Survey* (1983, Home Office Research Study 76) p 13.
16 Hough and Mayhew (1985) p 9.

154,000 such offences recorded in 1983, most of which would almost certainly have been reported to the police, but many more than the 26,828 applications received by the Board. Before we consider how many of that estimate might have given rise to compensable injuries, some other complicating factors should be mentioned.

Since one precondition to the obtaining of compensation is that the incident be reported to the police, the very fact that an injury does result from a dark figure crime will almost always be fatal to an application in respect of it.[17] In this formal sense the number of recorded offences does indeed represent the outer limit of the potentially eligible population, but not, of course, the outer limit of those injuries that are sufficiently severe to warrant compensation. Secondly, the BCS classification 'crime of violence' is not coterminous either with notifiable offences for the purposes of *Criminal Statistics*; and neither of these is coterminous with what constitutes a criminal injury for the purposes of the Scheme. To predict how many of all the offences which can constitute criminal injuries for the purposes of the Scheme could give rise to compensable injuries, it would be necessary to know their proportion of the total of applications. As the Board's Reports give no guidance on this issue, it is a matter of conjecture how many of the BCS' estimate for medically attended victims of 'crimes of violence' did apply, and how many victims of other offences made applications. Thus as it is not possible to say how many more victims of 'crimes of violence' may be eligible, neither is it possible to say how many more victims of, for example, offences under s 34 of the Offences against the Person Act 1861,[18] fall within the eligible population.

Returning to the BCS estimate of severity, we noted that some 82,550 victims of wounding, robbery or sexual offences would have required medical or hospital attention in 1983. What remains a matter of speculation is how many of these incidents might have given rise to injuries sufficiently severe to meet the Scheme's lower limit. Twenty-five years ago, McClintock's study, *Crimes of Violence* indicated that a large proportion of victims suffered no serious injury; 75% were back at work within a week, about 12% were off work for ten days and less than 2% suffered permanent

---

17 Infra, pp 73–74.
18 Trespassing on a railway line in circumstances likely to cause injury to the person; this has been the basis of a number of applications from train drivers who have suffered nervous shock upon seeing the consequences of 'railway suicides'. Infra, pp 114–116.

disability.[19] A similar picture emerges from the compensation survey conducted by the Centre for Socio-Legal Studies.[20] From 35,085 individuals who were collected from the screening survey, 3,630 reported some incapacity lasting two or more weeks arising from injury or illness in the previous 12 months, while a supplementary question screening for accident cases in the four years preceding that 12 months yielded a further 1,406 cases. These 5,036 cases constituted the compensation survey, from which only 21 were victims of crimes resulting in personal injury.[1] These were, by definition, injuries which had resulted in two weeks' or more interruption in normal activities, and of these, only seven made successful claims to the Board. Not too much, perhaps, should be made of this last figure; the 21 cases displayed a variety of factors which would in any event have created problems in the application, such as intra-family violence, or a failure to report the incident. What is significant is the very low incidence of criminal injuries apparently severe enough to come within the Scheme. The Survey team also remarked on the methodological problems:

'The size of the sample is a reflection of the relatively rare occurrence of serious criminal injury in the general population, combined with the difficulty, without a specially designed survey instrument, of screening out of the general population victims of personal attack.'[2]

The Compensation Survey underlines two points that have been stressed by the BCS: firstly, the relative infrequency of crimes against the person,[3] and secondly the relatively non-serious consequences of personal victimisation.[4] Two other surveys, however, point to a greater degree of harm, and suggest that the population of eligible victims (that is, who could expect an award) is certainly larger than the number who actually apply.

Shapland's study of 218 victims of criminal violence in the Midlands showed that 45 of the 54 who applied to the Board received either full or reduced awards; the number applying was

19 D McClintock *Crimes of Violence* (1963, Macmillan) p 54.

20 D Harris et al *Compensation and Support for Illness and Injury* (1984, Oxford UP).

1 Ibid, pp 30-36 and ch 6.

2 Ibid, p 203.

3 Hough and Mayhew (1983) p 15.

4 P Mayhew *The Effects of Crime: Victims, the Public and Fear* (1984, Council of Europe, European Committee on Crime Problems) p 4.

nearly 25% of the sample.[5] Leaving aside the presence of factors obscuring any unambiguous inferences about those who could have applied, or about those who did apply but were rejected, Shapland's sample, though based on offences that typify the vast majority of crimes which come before the Board, was drawn from a narrower range than that which comprises notifiable offences for the purposes of the *Criminal Statistics*. Accordingly, the percentage of those making an application may be considered to be a low estimate of those who might, given the full range of criminal injuries recognised by the Scheme, be eligible applicants. The second, more recent study, is Maguire and Corbett's account of their interviews with victims previously sampled by the BCS.[6] Over a third of their sample who had suffered personal victimisation reported themselves as being 'very much affected' by the offence.

On the basis of these two studies, the eligible population of those victims who have suffered injury as a result of a crime of personal violence in England and Wales would be between 25% and 35% of the total of such reported crime, in 1983 between 38,500 and 46,200 individuals. As noted above, there were 26,828 applications received by the Board during 1983-84. A number of these would of course be unsuccessful, being below the minimum limit or otherwise precluded by the terms of the Scheme. It is not possible to make a direct correlation between the number of applications the Board receives in any year and the number of those which are successful, as the Board's Reports do not distinguish, in the tables showing how live applications have in any one year been resolved, the year in which the application was made. However, as the cumulative total to 1989 of all applications received throughout Great Britain, 498,568, shows a success rate of 65% (323,528 applicants have received either full or reduced awards), 17,438 of the 1983-84 applicants could have been made awards. Using this percentage, it may therefore be suggested that from the estimated eligible population in 1983, between 25,025 and 30,030 victims of crime would have been compensable under the Scheme if all those who might have been had applied. These estimates must of course remain tentative so long as there is so little reliable data on the relationship between

5 J Shapland et al *Victims in the Criminal Justice System* (1985, Gower) ch 7 and p 150.
6 M Maguire and C Corbett *The Effects of Crime and the Work of Victims Support Schemes* (1987, Gower), ch 3. See further T Newburn *The Settlement of Claims at the Criminal Injuries Compensation Board* (1989, Home Office Research Study 112) pp 12-13.

the number of recorded offences, the measurable impact of the offence, and the relative proportions of the various criminal injuries that comprise the global figure of applications to the Board.

The problem of identifying with any tolerable degree of accuracy the size of the eligible population or the likely increase in the number of applications from year to year was well illustrated by the evidence presented by the CICB and the Home Office to the Home Affairs Committee. Whereas the number of applications in England, Wales and Scotland had in the years 1987-88 and 1988-89 increased by only 1.8% and 0.8% respectively, from 42,301 in 1986-87 to 43,054 in 1987-88, and to 43,385 in 1988-89, the Board estimated in December 1989 that at the rate of applications then being received, the total for 1989-90 would be in the region of 53,000, an increase over the previous year of 22%.[7] Viewed against the annual increase in recorded crimes of violence, this figure is not exceptional, representing about 24% of an estimated total of 220,000 notifiable offences for 1989,[8] but viewed against the need to plan the allocation of resources to the Board, such unpredictable increases have arguably contributed to the present substantial backlog.

Forecasting the annual increase in crimes of violence against the person and the proportion of that figure who might be expected to apply to the Board has assumed increasing budgetary importance, but it has never been an exact science. In 1980 the Board was advised by the Home Office that following the 'regular and significant increases' in applications in the 1970s, there would thereafter be a 'small but steady annual increase'.[9] This is indeed broadly how it fell out, though there was an increase of 13.8% in applications in 1985-86 over the previous year and a decrease in 1987-88 over 1986-87. In response to questions from the Committee, the Home Office admitted that it was using 'a less sophisticated method than one might try to achieve' to make its demand projections, and also indicated that obtaining a more sensitive instrument had not been a high priority given that under current funding arrangements, all items on its research agenda compete with one another.[10] Acknowledging the importance of cost effective research, the Committee recommended that the

---

7 House of Commons (1989-90) Minutes of Evidence, Q 148.
8 This estimate is based on the evidence given by the Home Office to the Home Affairs Committee, ibid, p 23.
9 CICB (1980) paras 6-7. A complete set of figures showing rates of application is contained in House of Commons (1989-90) ibid, p 21.
10 House of Commons (1989-90) para 24.

Home Office should 'establish precisely what research would be necessary to estimate more accurately the future level of demand upon the CICB'.[11]

(2)   Claims consciousness

What is clear is that, with the exception of 1987-88 which showed a 0.1% decrease by comparison with 1986-87, the number of applications received each year has consistently exceeded the Board's annual predictions, and has also exceeded the annual percentage increases in the number of notifiable offences. Thus there may be some support for the view expressed by the Board in 1977 that the growth in the number of new applications is indicative of a greater willingness on the part of victims to seek compensation,[12] though exactly what constitute the determinants of such willingness is a complex and largely untested issue. Equally unclear is the extent to which this 'steady upward trend' reflects the uncovering of the dark figure of eligible victims on the one hand, or an absolute increase in that population on the other.[13]

'No doubt pure ignorance accounts in many cases for failure even to consider making a claim'.[14] It is trite to observe that knowledge of the existence of the Scheme is a precondition to making an application, but despite the Board's constant efforts to publicise its terms, there has for some time been an apparently widespread ignorance about it. In the early 1980s Shapland found that while 39% of her sample knew of the existence of the CICB, 51% knew of no method by which they could be compensated,[15] a level of ignorance underlined in Newburn's survey of the use of compensation orders, in which he tested awareness of compensation possibilities.[16] The issue of publicity is of importance both to victims and to the Board. For the Board, decisions as to when, how and to whom to target information quite clearly have implications for the efficacy of its publicity

11 Id.
12 CICB 13th Report (1977, Cmnd 8401) para 1.
13 CICB (1988) para 2.2.
14 P Cane, *Atiyah's Accidents, Compensation and the Law* (1987, 4th edn, Weidenfeld and Nicolson) pp 201-202.
15 J Shapland et al p 124.
16 T Newburn, *The Use and Enforcement of Compensation Orders in Magistrates' Courts* (1988, Home Office Research Study 102) pp 36-37.

effort, and for the allocation of its financial and staffing resources should that effort produce an increase in applications.

An idea of the effort that the Board has made can be gained from looking at the way in which it has publicised changes to the Scheme. In a Parliamentary Reply in 1981, the Home Secretary said:

> 'As a matter of routine, police officers normally supply information about the Scheme to persons who have suffered physical injury as a result of violent crime. Publicity material has also been issued to hospitals, victim support schemes, Women's Royal Voluntary Service branches, citizens' advice bureaux, magistrates' courts [and] local offices of the DHSS.'[17]

Some 250,000 leaflets describing the 1979-80 changes were distributed to these bodies and to public libraries; and as the Board noted in its 13th Report, changes to the financial minimum have routinely been notified by the Home Office to Chief Constables, Chief Probation Officers and Clerks to the Justices.[18] In addition, the Board responds quickly to inquiries from the public,[19] and from the media;[20] in the latter case, subject to the constraint of confidentiality.[1] Against this background, the Board has cautiously suggested that increases in the number of new applications, and increases made within one month of the incident are attributable to these efforts; in its 20th Report it noted that it had received several hundred applications as the result of a television programme about its work.[2]

Given these efforts, whose broad outlines are periodically reiterated in its Reports,[3] it is not surprising perhaps that the Board has been sensitive to criticism that the low level of take-up, and the apparent persistent public ignorance of the Scheme, are attributable to a failure on its part to publicise its terms. In its 12th Report, the Board announced that it intended to discontinue its practice of presenting the number of new

---

17 15 HC Official Report (6th series) col 185 (17 December 1981). Also CICB (1980) para 12, (1983) para 12 and (1987) para 1.3.

18 CICB (1977) paras 4-5.

19 CICB (1978) para 3 and (1981) paras 16-18.

20 Even though the media have, in the Board's view, occasionally misrepresented its decisions, CICB (1979) para 10, and (1986) para 50.

 1 Para 27 of the Scheme. CICB (1981) para 18, (1983 Cmnd 9093) para 12, and (1986) para 50.

 2 CICB (1984) para 12. Also CICB (1977) paras 1 and 32, (1979) para 36, (1981) para 47, and (1986) para 50.

 3 CICB (1988) para 1.3. Also CICB (1984) para 12, and (1985) para 13.

applications each year as a proportion of crimes known to the police (at that time, 19%), the reason being that these figures 'have been consistently misunderstood and an inaccurate impression has been created about the effectiveness of the Board's efforts to bring the attention of those eligible for compensation to the existence of the Scheme.'[4] While we may have sympathy with the Board's wish not to be misrepresented, the decision to discontinue recording information of this kind is also regrettable; despite the fact that the Scheme has been in existence for over 25 years, there is still very little reliable evidence about the number of victims who may be eligible under its terms, and yet who remain ignorant of them.

Shapland's research suggests that quality of information is the most significant factor predicting whether victims will seek compensation.[5] Since the source of information will almost always be the police, their contribution is crucial. Despite the formal position recounted by the Home Secretary in the quotation above, Shapland found that police advice was variable in quality (uncertain, out of date) and that CICB leaflets were not always available in police stations. In 1988 the Home Office published a circular encouraging the police to give advice and assistance to victims about the possibility of compensation (including compensation orders), and giving information about the Board,[6] advice that is repeated in abbreviated form in the *Victim's Charter* published by the Home Office in February 1990.[7] In response to the marked increase during the late 1980s in the number of applications arising from child abuse, the Board took the initiative itself and sent a new circular on this matter in 1988-89 to local authorities and other interested organisations.[8] It remains to be seen whether these various moves will result in the kind of change in institutional routines within the police that will enhance victims' awareness of the Scheme, and in an increase in applications to the Board, given of course that the Board will be able to cope with any increase. Evidence on these questions may be available in time if the Home Office acts on the Home Affairs Committee's recommendations firstly that it

4 CICB 12th Report (1976, Cmnd 6656) para 1, and (1983) para 12.
5 Shapland et al pp 124-5.
6 HO Circular No 20/1988, 'Victims of Crime'. See further Home Office *Compensation and Support for Victims of Crime* (1985, Cmnd 9457) para 12, and J Shapland and D Cohen 'Facilities for victims: the role of the police and the courts' [1987] Crim LR 28-38.
7 167 HC Official Report (6th series) cols 906-907 (22 February 1990).
8 CICB 25th Report (1989, Cm 900) paras 1.7, 21.4-21.5.

should 'fund a marketing study to discover how the work of the CICB may be brought to the attention of all qualifying victims,' and secondly that it should conduct 'a special campaign to make sure that every local authority is aware of the rights of child victims to receive compensation'.[9]

These initiatives generally confirm the Board's long held view that unfocused publicity by itself is unlikely to be efficacious in the long term.[10] It remains convinced that consciously mounted publicity efforts should be directed to victims through the police, and more recently through victim support schemes, whose increasing reach are in part responsible for what the Board perceives to be a greater claims consciousness among victims of crime.[11] There is also the consideration that a better informed applicant can submit a more complete application, thus anticipating matters which the Board would otherwise have to follow up itself.[12] In addition, where the Board can itself identify those who have suffered criminal injuries, it will send application forms directly to them or endeavour to contact them via the police or local victim support groups, as it did following the killings in Hungerford in 1987 and the plane crash at Lockerbie in 1988, once it had been established that the explosion in the aircraft had been caused by a criminal act.[13] The Board's objections to unfocused publicity are that it is costly, given that the incidence of victimisation among the general population sufficiently severe to be compensable under the Scheme is very low, and that it is dysfunctional, creating misconceptions and false expectations in some members of the public.[14]

(3) The decision to apply

As might be expected, the primary reason why victims choose not to make an application is because they regard their injuries

---

9 House of Commons (1989-90) paras 44 and 45.
10 House of Commons, Home Affairs Committee *Compensation and Support for Victims of Crime* (1984-85, HC 23) para 44.
11 CICB (1988) para 1.4. Victim support schemes are important 'not merely because of the aid and comfort they can bring to victims, but because their assistance to victims so far as compensation from the Board is concerned tends to result in earlier application with sufficient information to enable cases to be processed more quickly', CICB (1979) para 9.
12 CICB (1989) para 1.7.
13 CICB (1988) para 8.1 and (1989) para 7.1.
14 The fact that awards under the Scheme are ex gratia has encouraged the view among some applicants that the Board is free to compensate those for whom it feels sympathy, but who do not fall within the terms of the Scheme, CICB (1979) para 15.

as being too trivial. This was the main reason (38% of respondents) given by Shapland's sample when asked why they had not applied to the Board.[15] In a healthy and robust person a sprained wrist sustained, for example, while attempting to prevent the offender from snatching a camera or handbag may indeed raise no issue about the 'triviality' of the injury (although this need say nothing of the victim's sense of anger or loss), but in marginal cases the exact components of this judgment become critical. Since we can hardly expect victims untutored in CICB Reports to be able to determine whether their injuries are ones for which, by para 5, 'the total amount of compensation payable after deduction of social security benefits, but before any other deductions under the Scheme, would be not less than the minimum amount of compensation', the judgments of others, such as the police, victim support groups or the victims' friends, family and workmates are likely to be influential;[16] but as with so many aspects of the CICB, there is little hard evidence on this matter.

One factor which clearly emerged from Shapland's research as being significant is the possibility of the victim being able to quantify the loss or injury. The reasons given by the applicants in her sample were dominated by the wish to recover for lost earnings, medical and dental expenses, lost or ruined clothing and for property loss or damage (in particular, to spectacles).[17] It is perhaps not surprising that victims are more likely to make an application where their injuries can be translated into real and tangible losses, but this possibility does not assist victims whose special damages are not significant by comparison with the effects of the injury to their health.[18]

Yet there has continued to be a significant proportion of victims who, though fully aware of the Scheme, and whose injuries would surely have warranted an award, have not made an application.[19] The Board made a special effort, for example, to inform all those who had been injured by a terrorist bomb explosion at the Old Bailey in March 1973 of the existence of the Scheme, and sent each one of them an application. Of 223 victims, it was estimated that 186 were eligible for compensation (the others suffering only minor injuries), but only 103 (55%) made an application. As to the possible reasons for the shortfall, the Board commented that

15 Shapland et al (1985) pp 122-123.
16 B Ruback et al 'Social influence and crime-victim decision making' (1984) 40 J Social Issues 51-76.
17 Shapland et al (1985) p 121.
18 CICB (1980) para 12.
19 CICB (1979) para 4.

this was probably attributable to the victims' 'desire to forget their painful experience as quickly as possible', which factor was 'of paramount importance to them.'[20] As noted above, the Board made a special effort to contact the victims and relatives of the indiscriminate shooting and killing in Hungerford in August 1987. The Board's 1989 Report recounts the number of applications received and settled, but does not indicate the proportion of potentially eligible applicants which that number represents.[1]

The shortfall between eligibility and take-up is an experience that is by no means unique to the CICB; it is a perennial feature of schemes in other common law jurisdictions, and is a common phenomenon in other areas of public benefit allocation. There are a number of factors that may explain this discrepancy: divergent perceptions of loss, of need and of the utility of the benefit to meet those losses or needs; differences in beliefs and feelings about the application procedure, including in the case of the Scheme, an unwillingness on the part of victims of crime 'to have their conduct, character and way of life investigated';[2] inability to cope with official forms and enquiries; and a desire simply to forget a distressing experience. These are no doubt all factors which singly or in combination may discourage victims from applying; their precise role remains, however, a matter of speculation.

B. APPLYING FOR COMPENSATION

(1) Verifying the application

Applicants are required to complete a form detailing various aspects of the incident and of the injury to which it gave rise (a copy is reproduced as Appendix II). By para 22 this has to be submitted 'as soon as possible after the event' and at any rate within three years of its occurrence. Shapland's account of the application form's requirements is succinct:

'This asks for details of the offence, whether and how the circumstances were reported to the police; the extent of the injury

---

20 CICB 10th Report (1974, Cmnd 5791) paras 1 and 10. Also (1976) para 1, (1979) paras 3-4, (1980) para 12, and (1988) para 1.2.
1 CICB (1989) para 7.3.
2 CICB (1974) para 1.

and the treatment received; earnings lost and out-of-pocket expenses incurred; social security, pensions, gratuities, compensation and insurance payments received; and particulars of any previous applications. The applicant also signs a certificate authorising the Board to obtain any details they may require from medical practitioners, the police, the social security or other public benefit authorities, the applicant's employer and government-sponsored training or rehabilitation units.'[3]

When received, a case file is opened and held centrally until all reports required by the Board — typically from the police and from medical authorities — are received. It is then taken over by one of the case-working officers (CWOs) who scrutinises the file to see whether the application is prima facie within the Scheme and whether there is sufficient information to make the initial decision. Until the 1990 revisions, the CWO would, if satisfied on these matters, pass batches of files on to Board members in rotation, but under the revised Scheme, CWOs will themselves be authorised to make initial decisions. If not satisfied that the file is ready, it is the CWO's responsibility to obtain the missing information.[4]

The CWO will routinely check the details given by the applicant with the police, hospital or medical authorities named in the application, and with any other relevant person or agency. The police may additionally be asked:

'whether, in their view, the injuries were due to a crime of violence, arrest of an offender or prevention of an offence . . . whether the injuries resulted to any extent from the applicant's own conduct; whether there were any material facts about the applicant's conduct, including his conduct before and after the incident and his background; whether the applicant has previous convictions; and the result of any prosecution.'[5]

This process of verification can take some time. Where discrepancies appear or sufficient information has not been given or is unavailable (for example as to the victim's medical condition or prognosis), the Board will seek further information from the victim, or await the outcome of treatment. Of potential

3 Shapland et al (1985) p 152.
4 For a description of these procedures see D Williams *Criminal Injuries Compensation* (1986, Waterlow) ch 3 and Home Office (1986) para 22.1. Reproduced in Appendix III is the Guide to the Scheme that the Board sends to each applicant.
5 Shapland et al (1985) p 152.

significance to many applications will be the outcome of criminal proceedings. Where these are pending, it is the Board's practice to defer determination of the application. Such factors of course conduce to delay in the resolution of applications, a matter which has been for some while the object of criticism.[6] In its inquiry into the Board's procedures the Home Affairs Committee was critical of the outdated record keeping practices employed by the Board, whose London office was 'a world of filing cabinets and heaps of paper, not of VDUs and instant data retrieval.'[7] The implications for processing applications and monitoring progress upon them are serious; the Board has depended, essentially, on bringing forward dates which, given its chronic understaffing, are not met. We consider further in chapter 12 the Committee's response, but in fairness it should be observed that however effective its own monitoring systems, the Board will inevitably be dependent on the efficiency of those upon whom it relies for answers to its questions.

Occasionally, applications are revealed as being fraudulent. In some instances the applicant may simply invent an injury for the purpose of applying for compensation,[8] more common are cases in which injuries are presented as being inflicted during an assault that were in fact sustained when the applicant fell over while drunk or were self-inflicted.[9] It has been the Board's practice to ask the police to investigate, and where possible, to prosecute such cases. Such prosecutions rely for the most part on offences under the Theft Act 1968,[10] but the 1986 Working Party considered these inadequate and recommended the creation of a specific statutory offence, akin to those common in social security legislation, of knowingly or recklessly, and without reasonable excuse, making a statement to the Board which is false in a material particular.[11] The recommendation has not been acted upon, perhaps because, as the Board's Reports indicate, the number of such cases is very small by comparison with the total number of applications received.[12] Neither has the Board any power to re-open a case following the making of an award

6 Eg 474 HL Official Report (5th series) col 702 (7 May 1986).
7 House of Commons (1989-90) para 26.
8 CICB (1989) para 13.2.
9 M Ogden 'The work of the Criminal Injuries Compensation Board' (1984–85) 52 Medico-Legal J 227-241. See also CICB (1987) para 56, (1989) para 13.3 and Williams (1986) para 7.31.
10 CICB (1988) para 51.1
11 Home Office (1986) para 22.4.
12 CICB (1984) paras 56-58, (1985) paras 49-51, and (1986) paras 44-46.

should it subsequently learn that it was fraudulently obtained; in such a case it would almost certainly seek to prosecute the applicant. However, where an applicant, having made one genuine claim in 1984 in respect of which the Board made an interim award, subsequently made a number of fraudulent claims, the Board, exercising its discretion under para 6(c),[13] refused to make any further award for the genuine application, as would otherwise have been standard practice.

Of those applications that are genuine, a small number have each year been abandoned; 2,859 out of 38,830 resolved in 1988-89.[14] The Reports do not indicate the reasons why such applications are not pursued; it may be that these are simply not known to the Board.

(2)   The initial decision

Once the CWO has decided that the file can go forward, each application was, prior to the 1990 revision, considered by a single member on the basis only of the documentary evidence submitted by the applicant and generated in response to the Board's inquiries. The single member could make either a full or a reduced award, reject the application altogether, or where he considered that he could not make a just and proper decision himself, refer it to a hearing by three members. Where the application was rejected or resulted in a reduced award, the reasons would be given to the applicant; in any other case the notification of award has normally included a breakdown of the assessment, unless the Board considered that to be inappropriate.[15] What have constituted the criteria of propriety for the exercise of this discretion are not publicised in the Reports. The Scheme has, since its inception, provided that an applicant may, if dissatisfied with this initial determination, ask for a hearing before three different Board members.

The 1986 Working Party felt that there was 'no justifiable reason for proposing any radical change in the two-tier structure of single member decisions and hearings which has operated well for over 20 years,'[16] but it did suggest two amendments to

---

13 CICB (1988) para 52.3. On para 6(c), see infra, pp 75–79.
14 CICB (1989) App A.
15 The Working Party was keen that the Board should routinely explain to applicants the basis of its determination in each case, Home Office (1986) para 22.15.
16 Home Office (1986) para 22.2.

the Scheme. One of these is intended to channel aspects of the initial decision away from the single members to the Board's administrative staff, the second to eliminate from the hearing procedure cases which disclose no substantive ground for reconsideration. Both of these are given effect in the 1990 Scheme, which otherwise continues the earlier procedures. The changes to the hearing procedure are considered in section (3) following.

Regarding the initial decision upon the application, the Working Party was concerned that Board members' talents were often being expensively employed on matters that its administrative staff were, by virtue of their experience with the Scheme, wholly competent to decide.[17] The same point was made in evidence to the Home Affairs Committee, where it was observed that in other contexts, notably the determination of insurance claims, it is unnecessary to have qualified lawyers involved at all stages or in all cases.[18] On the other hand, both bodies recognised the value of the single member procedure for encouraging confidence in the Board's decisions and, though this is difficult to verify, for discouraging any higher level of hearing requests.[19] Nevertheless, there was general agreement that it would be desirable for the Board to be empowered to delegate some decisions to its staff, not only to improve productivity, but also to enhance their job satisfaction.

Accordingly, para 22 of the revised Scheme provides that the 'initial decision on an application will be taken by a single member of the Board, or by any member of the Board's staff to whom the Board has given authority to determine applications on the Board's behalf.' The Working Party identified applications based on traffic accidents or which have led to a very trivial injury as the kind of matter which could be dealt with by Board staff,[20] but the evidence given by the Home Office suggested that the threshold below which they would be authorised to take decisions on eligibility and quantum might be as high as £2,000 or even £5,000.[1] In the event, the Board has adopted the more cautious approach favoured by its Chairman. Initial decisions may be taken only by the Board's advocates (who are all qualified

---

17 Ibid, para 22.4.
18 House of Commons (1989-90) para 33.
19 Ibid, para 9 and Home Office (1986) para 22.6. See also the Board's own evaluation of the single member procedure, (1989) para 14.3.
20 Home Office (1986) para 22.6.
 1 House of Commons (1989-90) para 10.

lawyers) and only in respect of the questions whether the applicant has complied with the requirements of para 6(a) and whether the injury is a criminal injury within para 4.

Besides the undesirability of delegating to staff issues that they would find difficult to determine, there were other considerations that the Home Affairs Committee thought encouraged caution. Without a commensurate increase in staff, delegation of substantive issues would of course exacerbate the backlog problem, but it was also thought that the administrative model might not be as well received, and that there would therefore be an increase in applications for judicial review.[2] If this is to be avoided, the Board will clearly have to be very careful in the manner in which it implements the power provided by para 22. One measure of quasi-judicial control lies in the possibility of the 'designated member of the Board's staff' exercising the option which has always existed for the benefit of the single member, of referring an application to a hearing 'where he considers that he cannot make a just and proper decision himself.'

Most applications to date have resulted in a full award, and most single member decisions (to whatever effect) have been accepted. Of the 35,971 applications resolved in 1988-89 (after abandoned claims), 32,482 were single member decisions accepted by the applicant.[3] Whatever the outcome of the application, the applicant was, until the 1990 revision, absolutely entitled to a hearing. The vast majority of hearings have taken place at the instigation of dissatisfied applicants: 6,037 in 1988-89 and 4,583 in the previous year.[4] During the 1980s there was a considerable increase in hearings. In 1985-86 there were 10% more hearing requests than in 1984-85,[5] while between 1982-83 and 1983-84 there was an increase of 43.5%.[6] The reasons for these increases, which were out of line with the earlier pattern, are not always clear, though the increase of 32% over 1987-88 may be explicable simply by the fact in 1988-89 the Board determined more applications than in any other previous year.[7] While, by contrast, single member referrals have been relatively infrequent — in 1983-84 (the last year for which figures are given) there were 220

2 Ibid, para 11.
3 CICB (1989) App A.
4 CICB (1988) para 11.1.
5 CICB (1986) para 11.
6 CICB (1984) para 51.
7 CICB (1989) para 10.2.

hearings instigated in this way — it may be that their frequency will increase as Board staff find that they cannot make just and proper decisions by themselves. We consider further in chapter 12 the implications of hearing requests for an evaluation of the Board's work; the next section concentrates on the procedures that the Scheme lays down.

(3) Hearings

(a) THE GROUNDS FOR A HEARING

By para 22, an application for a hearing has to be made in writing 'within three months of notification of the initial decision', although the Chairman, whose decision on the matter is final, can waive this limit where an extension is requested within the three month period, or where it is otherwise 'in the interests of justice to do so.' This application must set out the reasons why the hearing is sought, and include any additional evidence that the applicant wishes to draw to the Board's attention and which may assist it to decide whether a hearing should be granted. Hearings have always been, and will continue to be, oral only, but some important changes were introduced in the 1990 revised Scheme which for the first time imposes restrictions on the applicant's right to a hearing.

During the 1980s the Board became increasingly concerned about the demands placed upon its resources by the fact that the Scheme gave all applicants the unqualified right to a hearing before three members of the Board, excluding the member who made the initial decision. In response to the Board's evidence, the 1986 Working Party recommended the second set of controls mentioned earlier. In formulating these, its principal concern was to balance the desirability of reducing the Board's workload by eliminating some hearing requests with that of retaining for the applicant a right to have the initial decision upon his application reviewed in any case where there are possible grounds upon which the Board could reach a different decision. Once it became clear that the legislation was unlikely to be brought into force, the Board sought to have these controls introduced into the existing Scheme, as

'a way of sifting out obviously unmeritorious as well as frivolous hearing applications so that the time can be more profitably spent on those cases which plainly require the Board's attention. By the same token we consider that the Scheme ought to provide for certain cases to be reconsidered on paper rather than invariably by oral hearing.'[8]

Paragraphs 23 and 24 of the 1990 revision give effect to these objectives in two ways.

As an initial step, para 23 seeks to eliminate from the hearing procedures applications that simply raise questions about the accuracy of the primary facts. Where the reasons given in support of an application for a hearing suggest that 'the initial decision was based on information obtained by or submitted to the Board which was incomplete or erroneous,' the application will be remitted for reconsideration by the single member who made the initial decision or, where this is not practicable or the initial decision was made by a member of the Board's staff, by any other Board member. This paper reconsideration does not however preclude the possibility of a subsequent hearing, which is expressly preserved by para 23.

The changes introduced by para 24 are substantively more important. They are designed to prevent applications going to a hearing unless they satisfy the criteria set out in that paragraph. These provide that an applicant will be entitled to an oral hearing only if:

'(a) no award was made on the ground that any award would be less than the sum specified in para 5 of the Scheme and it appears that applying the principles set out in para 26 below, the Board might make an award; or
(b) an award was made and it appears that, applying the principles set out in para 26 below, the Board might make a larger award; or
(c) no award or a reduced award was made and there is a dispute as to the material facts or conclusions upon which the initial or reconsidered decision was based or it appears that the decision may have been wrong in law or principle.'

Paragraph 26 provides that at a hearing:

'the amount of compensation assessed by a single member of the Board or a designated member of the Board's staff will not be altered except upon the same principles as the Court of Appeal in England

---

8 Ibid, para 1.8.

or the Court of Session in Scotland would alter an assessment of damages by a trial judge.'

The first two grounds are quite specific: para 24(a) is concerned only with the minimum loss provision, and para 24(b) only with cases in which the applicant is seeking an increase in the award. Paragraph 24(c) is considerably wider in scope: it contemplates all those cases in which the Board has discretion to withhold or reduce compensation. Hearing requests invoking para 24(c) will typically involve applications rejected because the injury did not constitute a criminal injury as defined by the Scheme or because it was made out of time, or applications that resulted in an award being withheld or reduced in value because the applicant had failed to notify the police of the incident, had not co-operated with them, had provoked the incident in which he was injured, or had a series of convictions for offences of dishonesty.

Accordingly, neither an applicant whose application was initially rejected by a Board member or by a designated member of staff or was rejected by a Board member upon a reconsideration under para 23 because his injuries were valued at less than the sum specified in para 5 — £750 — (para 24(a)) nor one who seeks to challenge the award made (para 24(b)), will be entitled to a hearing unless the initial decision was wrong in principle or the amount awarded was so very small as to make it (in the judgment of the Court of Appeal) an entirely erroneous estimate of the damage to which the applicant is entitled.[9]

Given that it applies to cases in which there is a dispute as to the material facts or the inferences drawn from them, or it appears that the initial or reconsidered decision may have been wrong in law or principle, para 24(c) would be of much wider scope were it not for a further qualification in para 24. This provides for the review by not less than two Board members (not including one who made the initial decision), should it appear that the application is likely to fail the criteria in paras 24(a)-(c). Should they then consider that:

'if any facts or conclusions which are disputed were resolved in the applicant's favour it would have made no difference to the initial or reconsidered decision, or that for any other reason an oral hearing would serve no useful purpose, the application for a hearing will be refused.'

---

9 Adapted from Greer LJ in *Flint v Lovell* [1935] 1 KB 354 at 360. See generally H McGregor *McGregor on Damages* (1988 Sweet & Maxwell) paras 1833-1744.

This qualification applies to all three of the criteria specified in para 24(a)-(c), and contains two conditions upon which a hearing may be refused.

Suppose, first, an application based on the facts recounted in para 18.1 of the Board's 25th Report. Here a policeman sustained 'numerous slight bruises and abrasions in addition to a bite on the upper arm' while struggling with a suspect who was resisting arrest. His application for compensation was refused on the ground that his injuries did not exceed the minimum loss provision. An application for a hearing would surely be refused on the basis of para 24(a), and it would also be refused following the two member review even were they to give the applicant the benefit of a doubt, for example, as to whether the bite would take four rather than two weeks to heal. Similarly, where there is a dispute about the facts upon which the award for general damages was based, then on the assumption that there would have been no alteration to the assessment had the Court of Appeal been considering the facts as found by the Board, the application would fail under para 24(b), and would also fail under this additional qualification where, even giving the applicant the benefit of a doubt for example as to his medical prognosis, there would have been no other outcome but that reached at the initial decision or reconsideration. Finally, suppose that the applicant had been assaulted as he stepped off a British cross-Channel ferry at Calais, and that he had a conviction a few years earlier for armed robbery. The Board could dismiss the application on the ground that, the injury being sustained in France, it had no jurisdiction. But it would also almost certainly refuse a hearing on the basis of the qualification as it applies to para 24(c) because, even allowing him the benefit of any evidence that the assault actually took place on the ferry, the Board would very rarely indeed compensate applicants having convictions for serious offences, and thus the conclusion reached at the initial or reconsidered decision would have been no different.

It is also possible for the two member review to refuse a hearing in any one of these three instances if for 'any other reason' they consider that a hearing 'would serve no useful purpose.' This is intended to allow the Board to refuse hearing requests on the ground that they are vexatious, frivolous or otherwise unmeritorious, as for example if the Board were to receive an application in which it is alleged that the applicant's injuries have been caused by the use of invisible rays projected by ill-disposed beings from foreign planets.[10] While this second condition gives the Board a wide power to refuse a hearing application, such refusal will be unlawful if it is 'so outrageous in its defiance of accepted logic or of accepted moral standards that no sensible person who had applied his mind to the question to be decided could have arrived at it.'[11]

While, as the Home Affairs Committee observed, these new provisions hold out the possibility of a significant increase in applications for judicial review,[12] the Board has sought to preserve the judicial model in the hearing procedures. This can be seen in the requirements firstly that reconsiderations under para 23 must be conducted by a Board member where the initial decision was taken by a designated member of staff, secondly that in paras 24(a)-(c) an oral hearing will, subject to the further qualification in para 24, be granted where a court would interfere with a trial judge's decision or where there is a dispute about the facts or it appears that the Board erred in law, and third in the need for two members to decide upon hearing requests that are subject to review.

However, that review is itself expressed to be discretionary, and thus raises the question, how hearing applications are to be dealt with. Under the provisions in para 5(4) of Sch 7 to the Criminal Justice Act 1988, the Board is empowered to refuse an application for a hearing if it is 'of the opinion that there is sufficient reason to do so', and, if requested, is required to issue the applicant with a certificate to that effect. The Act further entitles the applicant to apply to the High Court for an order of *mandamus* requiring the Board to reconsider the application. On the assumption that a decision by the Board's staff not to refer for review an application for an oral hearing that in their opinion is likely to fail the criteria in paras 24(a)-(c) would itself be open to judicial review, it may be expected that hearing applications which do not clearly meet the criteria will routinely be reviewed by two Board members.

To summarise: the procedures established by paras 23, 24 and 26 provide:

(a) where the application for an oral hearing suggests that the initial decision was based on erroneous or incomplete information, it will be remitted for reconsideration, without

---

10 See 489 HL Official Report (5th series) col 749 (23 November 1987).
11 Lord Diplock, *Council of Civil Service Unions v Minister for the Civil Service* [1985] AC 374 at 410, HL.
12 House of Commons (1989-90) para 12.

prejudice to the applicant's right, if dissatisfied with the ensuing decision, to apply for an oral hearing (para 23);

(b) where the application for an oral hearing appears likely to fail the criteria in paras 24(a)-(c) it will be reviewed by two Board members: should they decide that, even giving the applicant the benefit of any factual or inferential doubts the initial or reconsidered decision would have been no different or for any other reason an oral hearing would serve no useful purpose, the application will be rejected. That decision is final, though open to judicial review.

The reviewing procedure is expected to filter out between 5–10% of applications for an oral hearing; in a further attempt to reduce the Board's workload, the Working Party also considered whether it was necessary that three Board members should be allocated to every hearing (making four members who have given consideration to the application):

'That such expertise and care are *available* to deal with claims on the Scheme is to its credit and is a feature whose termination we would recommend only with reluctance. The application of such resources to *every* case in which an applicant chooses to call upon them, however, strikes us as a luxurious arrangement which must necessarily come under question in the light of the great increases in the volume of applications which have occurred and may yet occur. We are not aware of any corresponding field of public administration in which as a routine and at the sole behest of the applicant, it is found necessary to apply such a concentration of legal expertise.'[13]

On the basis that hearings are wholly different from the initial decision, and not merely lateral appeals, the Working Party concluded that, unless there were exceptional circumstances in which it might be advantageous to have more than one member taking part, hearings could routinely and appropriately be conducted by one Board member only.[14] In the event, the Scheme has been amended so that at least two members shall participate in hearings, and in the new review procedure. There is no change to the established position that the members participating in a hearing requested by an applicant should not include the member making the initial or reconsidered decision, but para 22 does now permit a hearing requested by a single member to include that member.

13 Home Office (1986) para 23.1.
14 Ibid, para 23.2.

One matter that has not been significantly changed concerns the position of an applicant whose application has already been referred by a single member or a designated member of staff to a hearing and who, dissatisfied with the outcome, would now himself like to request a hearing. There was and is, with one exception, no provision for such a case. The statutory Scheme makes provision for partial hearings, which allow an application to be referred for a hearing on a specified point, thus leaving open the possibility of a hearing requested by the applicant on an issue excluded from the referral. This procedure, which goes some way towards meeting the criticism of the pre-1990 Scheme that in cases of single member referrals the applicant was precluded from exercising his entitlement to a hearing, was not introduced in the 1990 revision. It might be argued that hearings referred from a designated member of staff to a panel of at least two Board members reproduces the judicial model of the normal hearing procedure, but in neither this case nor the case where the single member has referred the application to a hearing, does the applicant have the possibility either of a paper reconsideration or an oral hearing. The one exception, where the Board adjourns the hearing, is discussed in the following section.

(b) THE CONDUCT OF THE HEARING

Cases set down for hearing, whether as the result of referral or at the applicant's request, have been shared between eight teams of members who sit at various centres in England, Scotland and Wales (a ninth was added in 1987). In 1988-89 they sat on 491 days, resolving 3,153 cases.[15] Despite an increase in productivity over the past few years, the substantial increase in the number of hearings has placed a very considerable burden upon Board members, a burden which is exacerbated by requests that are abandoned or by applicants (or their representatives) who are not fully prepared for the hearing.[16] In its 1987 Report, for example, the Board commented:

15 CICB (1989) para 10.3. On hearing days Board members also carry out inspections of an applicant's injuries as a means of verifying and judging their extent, prior to a decision being made on his application; id, para 10.5.
16 CICB (1984) para 53. For earlier discussions of the hearings procedures see CICB (1977) paras 37-39, (1980) paras 33-35, (1981) paras 50-51, (1982) paras 62-67, and (1983) para 40. The increase in manpower brought about by the establishment of the Glasgow office will itself result in further demands for hearings as there will be more single member decisions made, CICB (1988) para 11.2.

'The number of cases prepared for hearings was substantially higher than the number actually resolved. There are still far too many applicants who simply fail to attend, or who give insufficient notice of their unpreparedness thus creating last-minute gaps in the Board's hearing lists. Other cases may have to be adjourned for further medical evidence or for the purposes of resolving some dispute as to the applicant's financial loss. A common example is the case in which the applicant's solicitors have failed to supply the Board before the hearing with a properly quantified and substantiated documentary account of their client's loss of earnings.'[17]

Permitting itself the observation that such poor preparation would, in litigation, be reflected in the order for costs, the Board indicated that it had taken further administrative steps 'to ensure that applicants fully appreciate their responsibilities in this regard.'[18] These steps essentially involved amendments to the forms for and advice concerning the hearing that the Board sent to applicants, but a more effective solution was sought in the 1990 revision. It has always been open to an applicant who has requested a hearing to withdraw, with the Board's consent, before it has begun, but there has been no sanction against those who simply failed to show up. Paragraph 25 now provides that the Board may dismiss an application if the applicant fails to attend the hearing and has offered no reasonable excuse. The Chairman may relist the hearing upon a request in writing, but his discretion is final.

Paragraph 25 permits the Board to adjourn a hearing once commenced 'for a reason'. This may be of its own motion, perhaps because the evidence it requires to make a decision is not available, or at the request of the applicant. Where the applicant is refused such a request, judicial review will not lie if the basis upon which the applicant makes the request could not in any way affect the members' decision.[19] As a further concession to the

---

17 CICB (1987) para 12.
18 Id. In 1988-89 443 applicants failed to attend the hearing for which their application had been listed (this is slightly higher than in the previous four years); House of Commons (1989-90) Minutes of Evidence Q 258. This is about 10% of the total of hearing requests. Applications are listed for each day's hearings, and the applicant is given an hour from the time scheduled to make an appearance. Thereafter his application is treated as abandoned, subject to the Chairman's discretion to relist it.
19 *R v Criminal Injuries Compensation Board, ex p Gould* (1989) CICB para 26.4.

desire to reduce the workload of Board members, an application considered at an adjourned hearing may be remitted for determination by a single member in the absence of the applicant if the only issue remaining is the assessment of compensation. However, in such a case, the applicant has a right to apply for a further hearing if he is not satisfied with the final assessment. This hearing application is subject to the provisions in paras 22-24.

A hearing should not be regarded as an appeal in the sense that that term is normally understood. So much is clear from the fact that a single member or designated member of staff can refer an application to a hearing without first deciding any issues of law or fact. Where the hearing is at his request, the applicant is reminded that the Board 'looks at the application afresh and may take into account matters not mentioned' in the summary it prepares for him. Accordingly, the members participating in the hearing are free to reverse any findings or inferences of fact, or any conclusions drawn from them concerning eligibility or quantum, though it would be unusual for them to come to a radically different decision. Under the 1990 revisions no application will come to a hearing that does not prima facie raise the question whether, if the members were acting as an appeal court, they would not reverse the initial or reconsidered decision on a matter of fact, or does not prima facie raise the question whether the initial or reconsidered decision was wrong in law or principle, in which case it would have to be reversed. Thus, though the conduct of the hearing will not greatly change under the 1990 revision, it will more closely resemble the appellate model.

The Scheme has always placed a substantive burden of proof on the applicant at a hearing. Both para 25 of the Scheme, and that aspect of the Statement which comments upon it, make it clear that the burden lies on him not only to prove on a balance of probabilities that his injuries were directly attributable to a crime of violence (or other victimising event), but 'also the negative ingredient that the violence was not inflicted upon him by someone acting in self-defence';[20] that is, that it was not the victim who initiated the aggression towards him. In addition, the victim is required to satisfy the hearing that compensation

---

20 Per Hodgson J in *R v Criminal Injuries Compensation Board, ex p Crangle* (1981) Times, 14 November, Lexis transcript DC/369/81.

ought not to be reduced or withheld for any other reason under para 6 or, in the case of domestic violence, under para 8. Likewise, the applicant has to satisfy the members (or a majority of them) as to the nature and consequences of the injuries sustained, and as to the loss of earnings, dependency and expenses claimed. The Working Party considered it to be entirely reasonable that this burden should lie upon an applicant.[1]

Although the application is heard afresh, the Board members at the hearing will have familiarised themselves with the factual details of the application and with its points of difficulty, and in the case of a request by an applicant, of the differences between him and the decision of the single member or the designated member of staff. Under the new procedures these points of difference should be obvious, since the applicant will have had to demonstrate them in order to satisfy the criteria in para 24(a)-(c). The Chairman for the hearing will typically commence by summarising for the applicant's benefit the events so far and the nature of his disagreement with the initial decision. This will often amount to the Chairman repeating verbatim the grounds given by the applicant in his hearing request. A copy of this request is contained in a 'Schedule of Documents before the Board' which is prepared by one of the Board's advocates for the hearing and sent to the applicant a few weeks in advance of the day on which it is listed. This Schedule contains a 'hearing summary' which in turn comprises a resume of the incident, a note of the outcome of any criminal proceedings taken in consequence, a statement of the issues to be decided, the reminder about the nature of the hearing, and a statement of the applicant's injuries and financial loss. The 'hearing summary' is followed by copies of the original application for compensation, any statements made by the applicant, the initial decision (which has sometimes been annotated by the single member to show that he took a particular fact into account), the hearing request and finally police and medical reports. Following these preliminaries the Board proceeds with expedition to the point(s) in issue, sometimes to the surprise of those practitioners unfamiliar with its practices.[2] The Board will not usually require proof of undisputed matters, and by para 23 may accept hearsay or uncorroborated evidence and attaches to it such weight as

1 Home Office (1986) para 23.6.
2 Ogden (1984-85).

it considers appropriate.[3] A corollary of its informal status is that the Board has no power to subpoena witnesses.[4]

The hearing itself is essentially inquisitorial.[5] Where the issue concerns quantum, the members usually take the initiative, asking the applicant what additional factors, for example concerning scarring or continued pain or discomfort, he thinks they ought to take into account. Also present at a hearing will be one of the Board's advocates, but they normally take an active part only in applications which raise questions of eligibility. These constitute the majority of hearing requests. In such a case the advocate will, after the preliminaries, cross-examine the applicant on his statement (and any witnesses called by him), and examine the witnesses — typically the police — called by the Board. As the advocate completes his questioning of a witness, the Chairman for the hearing will ask the applicant (or his representative) if he wishes to put any questions. Although there are no formal closing speeches, at the conclusion of this process the advocate will sum up in neutral terms the issues for the members, who in turn will ask the applicant if he wishes to make any final remarks. This completed, the members will retire to consider their decision, which, by para 25, must be made 'solely in the light of evidence brought out at the hearing.' This decision is final; the members may reject, reduce or increase an award whatever the initial or reconsidered decision; where the application is referred by a single member or a designated member of staff, the decision taken at the hearing is both the first and final decision.

By para 27 hearings are to be held in private, although the Board may permit observers to attend provided that they undertake in writing not to disclose the identity of any of the participants in any subsequent reporting. The Working Party recommended the removal of this last requirement, and that hearings should, unless the Board has no objection to an applicant's request that the public be admitted, normally be held in public,[6] but no change was introduced in the 1990 revisions. The Board itself has power to publish information about its decisions, normally in the form of press releases; however it never refers to applicants by name. The nearest the interested reader

---

3 *R v Criminal Injuries Compensation Board, ex p Lloyd* (1981) unreported decision of the Divisional Court, CICB (1981) para 20(b).
4 The Working Party considered whether the Board ought not to be given statutory powers to subpoena witnesses, Home Office (1986) para 23.7.
5 Ogden (1984–85) op cit.
6 Home Office (1986), para 24.1.

can come to an identification of individual applicants is where the Board refers to the outcome of a specific crime involving a small number of victims, such as the shooting incident at Hungerford in 1987.

Confidentiality extends also to the police reports supplied to the Board in connection with its inquiries concerning the victim or the event giving rise to the alleged criminal injury. The reports themselves are not disclosed either to the applicant or to the members participating in the hearing. They are instead retained by the Board's advocate, who will seek to elicit from the police at the hearing, the substance of what appears in the report. This may in turn be used as the basis for cross-examination as to matters of fact or opinion so expressed. Witness statements are, on the other hand, made available to the applicant, but only on the day of the hearing, and will be recovered from him at its conclusion. This practice was called in question in *R v Chief Constable of Cheshire and Criminal Injuries Compensation Board, ex p Berry*.[7] This application for judicial review arose from the refusal of the Chief Constable to make available to Berry, whose application for compensation had been rejected under para 6(c) of the Scheme and who had subsequently requested a hearing, a list of the previous convictions (if any) of the witnesses to be called by the Board. The case principally turned upon the applicant's rights as against the Chief Constable, but it was also argued that the Board's practice amounted to a denial of natural justice, inasmuch as the applicant would have access to these reports only upon the day of the hearing, and would thus be quite unprepared to meet or to challenge them. Nolan J rejected this argument, accepting the Chairman's evidence that the Board's procedures do not prejudice those with valid points to make, and observing that applicants are, when presented with such reports, always entitled to an adjournment. The point was further considered by his Lordship in *R v Criminal Injuries Compensation Board, ex p Brady*,[8] where he held that the Board was entitled to take the view that the agreement by Chief Constables to make available witness statements for the purpose of proceedings before the Board (as recorded in a memorandum to Chief Constables from the Home Secretary in May 1969), was an agreement to supply them to the Board alone. The Board's failure to supply copies until the day of the hearing did not amount to a denial of natural justice.

7 (1986) CICB para 42.
8 (1987) Times, 11 March.

Neither was the Board acting unlawfully when, in another case, it did not formally produce such witness statements at the hearing. The statements were before the Board and had been supplied to the applicant; McCowan J held that the phrase 'brought out at the hearing', while not especially clear, meant 'no more than what is before the Board at the hearing'.[9]

C. THE AWARD

Awards will either be for the full amount claimed, or, in the exercise by the Board of the discretion conferred on it under the Scheme, for a reduced amount. In fact the vast majority of applications have resulted in a full award. Though not defined this means an award which comprises compensation for all verified and allowable items of special damage, together with an appropriate sum (based on common law damages) for general damages, less any sums deductible under the terms of the Scheme. In 1988-89, of 35,971 applications resolved (after those that had been abandoned), 24,833 full awards were made by single members, with a further 2,001 made at hearings. There were 8,219 rejected applications, and 918 reduced awards.[10] Of the nil awards, 21.6% were rejected because of the victim's conduct, character or way of life, 26% did not meet the lower limit and 26.7% were not reported to the police in time.[11]

As noted in chapter 1, the applicant is entitled to payment only after he has accepted in writing the Board's offer of compensation.[12] Thus if he instead requests a hearing, he has yet to become entitled to any award, and runs the risk that at the hearing the original award may be reduced or even, though this is unlikely, denied altogether. The award is personal to the applicant, so where a personal representative (or executor or administrator) requests a hearing in respect of an award which was communicated to an applicant who died without accepting it, the personal representative divests himself of any right to receive the original award. This applies whether, as in *R v*

---

9 *R v Criminal Injuries Compensation Board, ex p Whitelock* (4 December 1986, unreported) decision of the Divisional Court, CICB (1987) para 53.
10 CICB (1989) App A.
11 Ibid, App B.
12 Supra, p 15.

Criminal Injuries Compensation Board, ex p Earls,[13] the victim dies from the injuries he received, or as in *Re Lancaster's Application*,[14] the victim dies from other causes.

Compensation is paid as a lump sum. The idea of periodical payments has never been especially attractive to the Board, which had more sympathy with the Law Commission's identification of the practical difficulties that would accompany a power to permit damages for future loss of earnings to be paid periodically,[15] than with the benefits that the Pearson Report claimed for it.[16] The Board's reservations have been prompted also by a belief that such periodical payment may act as a disincentive to a prompt return to work, and by the knowledge that it has the power to make interim awards in appropriate cases.[17]

(1)   Interim awards and the power to re-open awards

(a)   INTERIM AWARDS

With two important exceptions, awards payable by the Board have been and will continue to be final. Interim awards have been available under the Scheme since its inception, and are undoubtedly an effective way in which the Board can postpone a final judgment, while simultaneously ensuring that an applicant who has a valid claim does not go wholly uncompensated in the meanwhile. They are of particular value in cases where financial hardship will ensue if an award is delayed, yet a firm medical prognosis is unlikely to be forthcoming for some time. Earlier Reports repeatedly stressed the importance to the Board of this power.[18] It may be that the Board's reliance on interim awards will decline in response to a greater use of its power to re-open cases; while 3,917 such awards were made in 1988-89,[19] this represents a smaller percentage of all claims

13 Unreported decision of the Court of Appeal, 21 December 1982, Lexis transcript DC/456/80.
14 [1977] CLY 496 (victim committed suicide). See also Home Office (1986) para 22.17.
15 Law Commission *Report on Personal Injury Litigation - Assessment of Damages* (1973, Law Com No 56).
16 *Royal Commission on Civil Liability and Compensation for Personal Injury* (1978, Cmnd 7054) ch 14.
17 CICB (1978) paras 54-57, quoting the minority view in the Pearson Report, ibid, para 620.
18 CICB (1977) para 28.
19 CICB (1988) para 5.1.

than was the case in previous years. The availability of this power has also meant that the Board has not had to rely on the rules of the High Court made under s 32A of the Supreme Court Act 1981 permitting the award of provisional damages for personal injuries.[20]

(b) RE-OPENING AWARDS

An important power that has clearly distinguished the Scheme from the common law was introduced in the 1979-80 changes; this has enabled the Board to re-open awards in narrowly defined circumstances. In its 1978 Report the Board had indicated that it would welcome such a power, though it noted that it could achieve a similar effect by the use of 'permanent interim awards'.[1] These could be made where there was a known risk of future medical deterioration, such as epilepsy or sympathetic ophthalmia, but they afforded no discretion where unexpected complications arose. The change was recommended by the 1978 Working Party,[2] and para 13 of the Scheme provides:

'Although the Board's decisions in a case will normally be final, they will have discretion to reconsider a case after a final award of compensation has been accepted where there has been such a serious change in the applicant's medical condition that injustice would occur if the original assessment of compensation were allowed to stand, or where the victim has since died as a result of his injuries. A case will not be re-opened more than three years after the date of final award unless the Board are satisfied, on the basis of evidence presented with the application for re-opening the case, that the renewed application can be considered without a need for extensive enquiries. A decision by the Chairman that a case may not be re-opened will be final.'

As this paragraph makes clear, the desire to do substantial justice has been tempered by strong bureaucratic considerations. The Board's 1982 Report observes that while limited in number, such applications involve wholly disproportionate staff time, in particular in establishing the link between the incident and the

---

20 Home Office (1986) para 13.2. An earlier version of the Criminal Justice Act 1988 explicitly excluded this power, but the provision was subsequently dropped, Sch 7, para 8(2) to Bill no 125, as amended in Standing Committee.
1 CICB (1978) para 55.
2 Home Office *Review of the Criminal Injuries Compensation Scheme: Report of an Interdepartmental Working Party* (1978) para 4.6.

subsequent deterioration.[3] Since the power was introduced, there have been 1,344 applications, resulting in 525 being re-opened and 503 refused. As evidence of the Board's observation about the use of staff time, the Reports for the past seven years show that for each year, as many applications were under consideration as had been decided upon by the Chairman. It is clearly not just a matter of the quantity of applications to re-open earlier awards that demands so much staff time. These applications are time consuming because 'they almost invariably concern complex medical conditions', and some have been re-opened twice.[4]

Applications to re-open awards pose other problems. For the Board there has been the bureaucratic constraint implicit in the need to hold back files which would otherwise be destroyed as part of its progressive programme of file destruction.[5] Sometimes the medical prognosis will contemplate a foreseeable risk of deterioration; in other cases a judgment as to the future must be made. This obviously may generate further problems to be resolved, typically by reserving the file in case something goes wrong.[6] A second problem is that applicants may come to believe that ill-health experienced subsequent to the criminal injury is necessarily connected to it; this in turn may be productive of ill-will on their part when the Board's medical advice is that there is no causal connection.[7] The Working Party considered the administrative and other problems posed by the exercise of this discretion,[8] but its recommendation that no application to re-open a case should be contemplated more than three years after the original award has not been acted upon.[9]

(2)   The administration of awards

An award, once determined and accepted by the applicant, will normally be paid to him by cheque. Occasionally the Board may invoke the power given by para 9 to administer the award on the applicant's behalf.

---

3 CICB (1982) para 11 and (1989) paras 22.1-22.6.
4 CICB (1987) para 7.
5 CICB (1983) paras 35-36.
6 CICB (1986) para 33.
7 CICB (1982) para 11.
8 Like any other given to the Board, this discretion must be exercised reasonably, *R v Criminal Injuries Compensation Board, ex p Brown* (1988) CICB paras 50.1-50.2. See also CICB (1987) para 42.
9 Home Office (1986) para 13.3.

'If in the opinion of the Board it is in the interests of the applicant (whether or not a minor or a person under an incapacity) so to do, the Board may pay the amount of any award to any trustee or trustees to hold such trusts for the benefit of all or any of the following persons, namely the applicant and any spouse, widow or widower, relatives and dependants of the applicant and such provisions for their respective maintenance, education and benefit and with such powers and provisions for the investment and management of the fund and for the remuneration of the trustee or trustees as the Board shall think fit. Subject to this the Board will have a general discretion in any case in which they have awarded compensation to make special arrangements for its administration. In this paragraph 'relatives' means all persons claiming descent from the applicant's grandparents and 'dependants' means all persons who in the opinion of the Board are dependent on him wholly or partially for the provision of the ordinary necessities of life.'

The principal instances where this power is used is to manage an award to a minor. Where the sum is less than £10,000 it will be deposited in the National Savings Bank;[10] larger amounts will be administered by the Official Solicitor where he is appointed the child's guardian, or, for children in care, the local authority.[11] The Working Party tried to devise alternative arrangements to relieve the Board of the responsibility for administering those awards not managed by a responsible person, but were unable to reach any novel proposals.[12]

Paragraph 9 permits the Board to make arrangements for the management of the award not only where the applicant is a minor or under an incapacity, but if, simply, it is in his interests. The object is to oblige the applicant to use the money wisely, but doubts have been expressed about the justification for this power. The paternalistic ethic implicit in the judgment that an applicant is likely to dissipate the award suggests that in substance the power would be exercised for the ultimate benefit of the taxpayer, whose interests the Board regards itself as protecting.[13] Paragraph 14(1)(e) of Sch 7 to the Criminal Justice Act 1988 provides that the power to administer awards should extend only to the two specified cases, but the 1990 Scheme was unchanged in this respect.

10 Awards of less than £1,000 will normally be released to the person having parental control. See the Board's advice in its guidelines on applications concerning child abuse, CICB (1989) App E.
11 CICB (1983) para 33 (1980) para 24, and Home Office (1986) para 9.1.
12 Home Office (1986) para 23.11.
13 CICB (1977) paras 26-27, (1981) paras 32-35, and (1983) para 32.

D. COSTS

The cost of applying for compensation falls upon the applicant. An applicant who seeks legal advice may be eligible for advice under the Green Form scheme, but in common with other tribunals, legal aid is not available if he wishes to be represented at a hearing, though this will be available if he is seeking judicial review. Remarking that as the Board does endeavour, where there is a hearing, to give assistance in the formulation of the issues to be resolved and of relevant matters of evidence, the applicant is not at any particular disadvantage by not being represented, the Working Party concluded that legal aid should not be made available to applicants until such time as there was provision for representation before tribunals in general.[14]

Neither will the Board meet the costs of legal representation. However, para 25 gives the Board a discretion to reimburse the applicant's expenses in attending the hearing, together with those of any witnesses called by him or the Board. It will also contribute towards the cost of photographs (£2.70 from April 1982), for example of scarring, or of medical reports (£10.50), that it requires.[15] In its 22nd Report, the Board indicated that it was also prepared to reimburse the cost of advice (estimated in 1986 at £140 (VAT inclusive) for a straightforward claim) obtained by a parent or guardian in the case of an application made on their child's behalf.[16]

---

14 Home Office (1986) para 23.11.
15 Shapland et al (1985) p 153, and (1986) 136 New LJ 745 (complaining about the paucity of the latter figure). These were figures given by the Board at the time of writing.
16 CICB (1986) para 47.

Chapter Three

Eligibility

Assuming that the victim has sustained a criminal injury that falls within the scope of the Scheme,[1] there are a number of minimum criteria which he or his dependants must satisfy if an application for compensation is to succeed. Some of these have been alluded to in chapters 1 and 2; this chapter will examine them in detail. The criteria are:

(1) that the application must be made within three years of the incident which gave rise to the injury (para 4);
(2) that the compensation payable must be not less than the minimum amount (para 5);
(3) that the applicant must without delay take all reasonable steps to inform the police or an appropriate authority of the circumstances of the injury, co-operate with them in bringing the offender to justice, and give them all reasonable assistance in connection with the application (para 6(a) and (b)); and
(4) that the applicant's conduct before, during or after the events giving rise to the application, or his character as evidenced by his criminal convictions or unlawful conduct, do not make an award inappropriate.

Whereas non-compliance with either the limitation period or the financial minimum means that no award will be made, failure to comply with the other criteria may lead either to no award or to a reduced award. There are further provisions designed to prevent a person responsible for causing the injury from benefiting from an award to the victim and affecting intra-family violence; these are dealt with in chapter 6.[2]

---

1 Chap 4.
2 Infra, pp 153–156.

A. LIMITATION OF ACTIONS

Paragraph 4 of the Scheme provides:

> 'Applications for compensation will be entertained only if made within three years of the incident giving rise to the injury, except that the Board may in exceptional cases waive this requirement.'

There has always been a time limit on the making of an application. Under the original Scheme applications had to be made 'as soon as possible', but it was thought more appropriate that the same limitation period as is applicable to civil actions for personal injury should be required.[3] Apart from harmony with analogous areas of law, the three year limitation period introduced in 1969 has been important because stale applications cause difficulties for the Board, which would otherwise have to commence inquiries about an incident no longer fresh in the minds of those from whom it routinely seeks to verify the facts.[4]

The Chairman has discretion to waive the time limit, and has treated sympathetically applications made out of time from victims of low intelligence, who are deaf and dumb, or who are suffering from mental disability;[5] likewise where the victim was under 18 at the time of the incident or did not then know that his injury was attributable to an offence.[6] Occasionally the true extent of an injury only becomes apparent some time after it has been sustained, and in such cases the Chairman will consider accepting the application if it is made 'within a reasonable time of the applicant discovering that the injury was attributable to

---

3 Home Office, *Review of the Criminal Injuries Compensation Scheme: Report of an Interdepartmental Working Party* (1978) ch 9.
4 CICB 21st Report (1985, Cmnd 9684) para 8, and 24th Report (1988, Cm 536) para 15.3. It should also be noted that simple compliance with the three year limit was not necessarily sufficient in all cases. By para 7 of the pre-1990 Scheme the Board would have special regard to any delay that occurred in making an application arising from the commission of sexual offences, where the relationship between the victim and the offender was such that it might be difficult to establish the facts, or where it was possible that the offender might benefit. See infra p 156.
5 CICB 17th Report (1981, Cmnd 8401) para 39, and 19th Report (1983, Cmnd 9093) para 25.
6 CICB (1981) para 39, (1983) paras 22 and 24, (1988) paras 15.4-15.6, and 25th Report (1989, Cm 900) para 15.8.

a crime of violence.'[7] On the other hand, simple ignorance of the Scheme's existence or delay beyond the three year limit caused by the pursuit of a civil action will not constitute grounds for waiving the limitation period.[8]

In 1988-89 111 late applications were brought forward from the previous year for consideration by the Chairman, and a further 491 were received, more than twice the figure for the previous year. As is usual, the number of late applications refused was greater than the number accepted.[9] Despite the administrative difficulties that even this limited power to waive the time limit has generated, the 1986 Working Party recommended no change to the Chairman's discretion,[10] and none was introduced in the 1990 revised Scheme.

B. THE FINANCIAL MINIMUM

By para 5:

'Compensation will not be payable unless the Board are satisfied that the injury was one for which the total amount of compensation payable after deduction of social security benefits, but before any other deductions under the Scheme, would not be less than the minimum amount of compensation.'

There has always been a financial minimum. From 1964 until 1 March 1977, this was £50; until 1 April 1981, £150; until 1 February 1983, £250; until 6 November 1986, £400; and £550 until

---

7 CICB 22nd Report (1986, Cm 42) para 7. See also the application determined some 19 years after appalling injuries were inflicted upon the victim when she was 2 years old, whose full extent had only by then become apparent, Times, 24 March 1989.

8 To allow ignorance would introduce an infinite regress 'since to apply any time limit at all would simply result in imposing another limitation period in place of that specified in the Scheme', CICB (1988) paras 15.1-15.3 and (1989) paras 15.2-15.4. Nor would the Chairman allow a late application where the applicant, though aware of the Scheme, rejected the advice given that she should make an application, in favour of pursuing a civil action against the offender, CICB (1985) para 8. See also CICB (1989) paras 15.6-15.7. Error or negligence on the part of the victim's legal advisers will not normally constitute 'exceptional circumstances', CICB (1988) para 15.5.

9 CICB (1989) para 4.1, 141 refused and 98 accepted.

10 Home Office *Criminal Injuries Compensation: A Statutory Scheme* (1986) para 4.14.

1 February 1990, when it was raised to £750.[11] A lower limit of £500 was set in the case of applications arising from intra-family violence which were first permitted with the 1979 revisions to the Scheme; this separate figure was subsumed in the increase to £550. Paragraph 5 further provides that the lower limit shall not apply either to the payment of funeral expenses under para 15 (thus an application for such expenses in which a dependant can show no actual dependency on the victim's income will not fail for this reason), or para 16, which permits the Board to make an award to the dependants for pecuniary losses incurred by the victim prior to his death from a cause other than the criminal injury.

Paragraph 5 requires the Board not to make an award unless it is satisfied that the total amount of compensation payable after the deduction of social security benefits, but before any other deductions under the Scheme, will be more than the lower limit. By para 19, social security payments are deducted in full and without limitation of time; and under para 5 they will be deducted from the total amount payable and not merely from that item of special damage to which the benefit may be taken as referring.[12] A victim to whom the compensation payable would exceed £750 only by virtue of the addition of a sum representing, for example, income support, will therefore be ineligible for an award. However, the paragraph requires the prior deduction *only* of social security benefits. Thus, even though the Board applies para 6(c) so as to reduce an award to less than £750, or the victim is in receipt of a compensation order which, since its value has to be deducted under the terms of para 21, brings the compensation payable to less than £750, the applicant will still be compensable under the Scheme. In other words, the financial minimum does not mean that awards of less than £750 cannot be made; its effect is to preclude those applications which can be predicted to be worth less than £750 on the basis of the prior deduction of the specified benefits. The impact of this provision might be thought unfair in some cases. Suppose two victims sustain injuries identically valued at £750 before any deductions have been made. V1, who has received £100 in income support will receive no award; V2, who has received £100 by way of a compensation

---

11 163 HC Official Report (6th series) col 411 (8 December 1989). For straightforward examples of the application of this paragraph see CICB 20th Report (1984, Cmnd 9399) para 25, 23rd Report (1987, Cm 265) paras 23 and 24, (1988) paras 30.1-31.2, and (1989) paras 18.1-18.5.
12 Infra, pp 178-179.

order will have that amount deducted from his award, and will receive £650.

The financial minimum has always been an object of criticism. Both the Home Affairs Committee which sat in the 1984-85 Session[13] and the 1986 Working Party[14] received many representations about it. The hypocrisy of a government which on the one hand claims to have put the victim back 'centre stage',[15] but on the other keeps raising the lower limit and thus excluding many deserving cases was a constant theme of the debates that accompanied the 1987 Criminal Justice Bill,[16] and likewise greeted the increase in 1990 which unhappily coincided with the publication by the Home Office of the *Victim's Charter*. When criticising these increases, attention is invariably drawn to the plight of elderly victims for whom an injury, though valued less than £750, is often not trivial, especially where they have only a limited income.[17] However, in practice the Board is prepared to make at least a minimum award to the elderly applicant who, though sustaining neither pecuniary loss nor physical injury, has been put in fear by an assault upon him or upon another standing nearby.[18] Remarks by Sir Michael Ogden,[19] and by the present Chairman to the Home Affairs Committee,[20] suggest that notwithstanding further increases in the lower limit, such injuries will continue to be compensated. It is hardly necessary to underline the social importance of compensating these stereotypical victims, and it is instructive to compare the Board's less generous response to similar claims from other applicants.[1]

Increases in the minimum have a variety of implications for

13 House of Commons, Home Affairs Committee *Compensation and Support for Victims of Crime* (1984-85, HC 43) para 32.
14 Home Office (1986) para 5.2.
15 D Hurd, MP, 106 HC Official Report (6th series) col 470 (27 November 1986).
16 HC Official Report (6th series) Standing Committee F cols 731 and 793 (24 and 26 February 1987).
17 See, eg, the response to the 1983 increase, as a 'mean and niggardly act' 38 HC Official Report (6th series) cols 359-360 (3 March 1983 oral answers). The problem is aggravated in the case of the elderly where there may in fact be no loss of earnings, House of Commons (1984-85) para 32.
18 CICB (1987) para 24.
19 M Ogden 'The work of the Criminal Injuries Compensation Board' (1984-85) 52 Medico-Legal J 229-241, House of Commons (1984-85) para 32.
20 House of Commons, Home Affairs Committee *Compensating Victims Quickly: the Administration of the Criminal Injuries Compensation Board* (1989-90, HC 92) para 38.
1 T Newburn *The Settlement of Claims at the Criminal Injuries Compensation Board* (1989, Home Office Research Study 112) pp 14-15.

the Scheme; most obviously, those that significantly exceed the rate of inflation will and may be intended to lead to a decrease in the number of applications, at least for a while, but there is disagreement whether increases that only reflect the rate of inflation will have that effect. On the one hand, the Board has never been convinced that modest increases in the lower limit will have anything but a marginal impact upon the application rate;[2] critics, on the other hand, such as Victim Support, regularly deplore them as disentitling substantial numbers of formerly eligible victims. Typical was their response to the increase announced in February 1990,[3] but the difficulty lies in trying to gauge how many victims are indeed so disentitled. It is tempting, but wrong, to conclude that because 37.2% of awards (10,312) made in 1988-89 were for sums less than £800 (£750 is not used in the table),[4] the total of eligible victims has now been cut by about a third. Nor can much assistance be obtained simply by noting the number of awards made in 1988-89 that fall between the old and the new lower limits (5,700, or 20.6% of all awards).[5] As has already been noted, the lower limit does not mean that awards less than that figure cannot be made; one only has to look at the table in the 1988-89 Report to see that 5.6% of awards were for sums less than £499, and 12.6% were for sums between £500 and £599. Given that the limit governing most of these applications was £550 (there may have been a few outstanding from the £400 limit), the vast majority of these awards *must* have initially been valued above the limit, despite the final award made. What the figures in the annual table for 1988-89 cannot say is how many of the awards that were for less than £800 would, when first considered by the Board, have been ones for which the compensation payable, after the deduction of social security benefits, could have been predicted to be less than that figure. This information is simply not publicly available, though in its evidence to the Home Affairs Committee, the Home Office thought that the effect of the increase to £750 would be to disqualify less than half the number suggested by Victim Support.[6]

2 CICB 14th Report (1978, Cmnd 7396) para 2, 15th Report (1979, Cmnd 7752) para 2, (1987) para 2, and (1988) para 2.2.

3 See its evidence to the Home Affairs Committee, House of Commons (1989-90) App 4.

4 CICB (1989) para 8.1.

5 167 HC Official Report (6th series) col 907 (22 February 1990).

6 House of Commons (1989-90) Minutes of Evidence, Q 259.

It is important to be clear about what is meant by 'disqualify' in this context. On the assumption that the value of an injury remains constant in terms of the revalorisation of the lower limit, increases that do not exceed the rate of inflation disqualify no-one who would not, in the normal course of events, have been disqualifed if, instead of being adjusted every few years, the limit were index linked and adjusted annually. It is only because there is a delay in catching up with the effect of inflation that the numbers of those 'disqualified' looks so substantial. In reality, of course, the effect of the delayed adjustments is progressively to qualify for compensation *more* victims than the value of the lower limit would admit if it were adjusted annually. Supporting the Board's view, the Home Affairs Committee was of the view that, based on average earnings, the lower limit has remained reasonably constant, but it did recommend that the effects of the 1990 increase on the number of applications should be monitored and if necessary reviewed.[7]

Increases in the financial minimum also have implications for the making of compensation orders upon conviction, a point which the Magistrates' Association made in March 1984 when it recommended new guidelines for the exercise of the powers under s 35 of the Powers of Criminal Courts Act 1973.[8] Apart from the fact that CICB awards are not dependent upon a conviction, it is not clear whether applicants who would have been compensated under a previous minimum are turning instead to the courts.

At first, the sole expressed justification for the existence of the lower limit was a bureaucratic one: to eliminate applications whose administrative costs would exceed the compensation payable. Prompted by inflation, the increases in 1977 and 1981 were necessary 'to ensure that trivial cases of a kind never intended to be eligible for compensation continue to be excluded.'[9] Of more recent origin is the use of the financial limit as an explicit means of controlling expenditure on the Scheme. In 1983 the lower limit was increased above the rate of inflation in order to fund payments made under the bereavement provision

---

7 House of Commons (1989-90) para 38.
8 Times, 16 March 1984.
9 2 HC Official Report (6th series) col 52 (31 March 1981). Also 962 HC Official Report (5th series) cols 145-146 (15 February 1977) and CICB 13th Report (1977, Cmnd 7022) para 3.

introduced in that year.[10] The Home Office estimated that the increase would exclude 3,000-4,000 applicants, about double the number excluded under the previous minimum.[11] It remains to be seen whether, if the statutory sum payable for bereavement is increased from £3,500 to £7,500, as is currently being considered by the Lord Chancellor's Department,[12] the next increase in the lower limit will likewise include an element designed to pay for the sum of £4,000 × the number of bereavement awards implied by the predicted increases in applications for compensation.

As a fiscal device, the lower limit was also used to control the experimental power introduced in the 1979-80 revisions to include victims of intra-family violence within the Scheme, and has been considered as a means of holding its costs within government spending limits and of cutting the Board's workload.[13] Currently the government's intention is that the Scheme should compensate those who sustain 'an appreciable degree of injury'[14] and that increases in the lower limit are intended 'to concentrate resources on cases most deserving of compensation.'[15] Why these are the most deserving cases raises questions of social policy which have not fully been addressed.

C.   CO-OPERATION WITH THE AUTHORITIES

Paragraphs 6(a) and (b) of the Scheme provide that the Board may withhold or reduce compensation if it considers that:

(a) the applicant has not taken, without delay, all reasonable steps to inform the police, or any other authority considered by the Board to be appropriate for the purpose, of the circumstances of the injury

---

10 'The purpose of this change is to reduce the overall cost of the Scheme whilst allowing for the additional expenditure on bereavement awards.' W Whitelaw, MP, 36 HC Official Report (6th series) col 60 (1 February 1983). Also CICB (1984) para 24.
11 37 HC Official Report (6th series) col 394 (22 February 1983), and (1983) 133 New LJ 115.
12 *Damages for Bereavement: a Review of the Level* (13 March 1990).
13 House of Commons (1989-90) para 37. Besides the proposal to increase the lower limit to £1,000 as a means of reducing the cost of the Scheme, another suggestion which the then Chairman thought 'terrible' was a flat 2% cut from every award, Ogden (1984-85) op cit.
14 Home Office (1986) para 5.2, and D Hurd, MP, 106 HC Official Report (6th series) op cit, col 471.
15 163 HC Official Report, op cit, col 411.

and to co-operate fully with the police or other authority in bringing the offender to justice; or

(b) the applicant has failed to give all reasonable assistance to the Board or other authority in connection with the application.'

The Board has always regarded compliance with these requirements as crucial to establishing the applicant's bona fides: 'even where the circumstances of a particular incident are fully known and disclose no blameworthy conduct on the part of the applicant, the Board will only rarely excuse an applicant's failure in his obvious duty to report crimes of violence to the police with a view to bringing the offender to justice';[16] *a fortiori* where the circumstances of the incident were obscure and there was no corroboration of the applicant's version of events. The 1986 Working Party proposed no change to these requirements. In 1988-89 2,192 of the applications resolved were rejected for failure to comply with one or other of these requirements.[17] The two paragraphs create three requirements which are considered separately in the following sections.

(1) Reporting the circumstances of the injury

Under the original Scheme, the report could only be made to the police, although the Board occasionally waived this requirement where it was made to another responsible body, for example to educational or hospital authorities, or to the Health and Safety Executive.[18] These other possibilities were later expressly permitted, but the Statement clearly indicates the Board's preference: 'It is the police to whom matters should be reported. Reports made to employers, trade union officials, social workers and the like may not be acceptable.'[19] Containing an extended discussion of this requirement, the 1987 Report also emphasises the importance which the Board places upon the

16 CICB (1983) para 27. See also (1977) para 16 and D Williams *Criminal Injuries Compensation* (1986, Waterlow) paras 7.11-7.15 and 7.17.

17 CICB (1989) App B.

18 This was permitted only in exceptional cases, for example where the victim was too young or could not be expected to report the incident, or believed that someone else had, where he was unaware that a crime had occurred, or where his injuries did not at the time seem sufficiently serious to merit such attention. See CICB 8th Report (1972, Cmnd 5127) paras 8 (2) & (3), 11th Report (1975, Cmnd 6291) para 7(1), and 12th Report (1976, Cmnd 6656) paras 8(1) and (6).

19 The Statement, para 6A.

reporting requirement as a primary safeguard against fraudulent applications.[20]

The report must be made without delay, but here again the Board is prepared to exercise some latitude. It will, for example, accept a delayed report if the reason was that the victim was mentally handicapped, concussed or unconscious in hospital, or because the impact of the crime upon an elderly victim restricted her movements and made her fearful about going out.[1] Similarly, if in the circumstances, the victim does all he can to inform the authorities (though this turns out to be inadequate information), he will have taken the reasonable steps that the Scheme requires. Where the police are present at or after an incident, there will seldom be circumstances that can justify delay, though where it was a large-scale incident such as a riot, the applicant's explanation that he thought that he did not personally have to report what the police had obviously seen, might suffice.[2] Clearly, however, any delay for which the Board thinks the explanation given by the applicant is unsatisfactory will be fatal to the application.[3]

(2) Co-operating in bringing the offender to justice

In its Report for the year 1982-83 the Board justified its uncompromising attitude towards this requirement on the grounds that 'if the rising tide of crime is to be stemmed' and that 'if we are to walk our streets free from fear and injury', then 'victims should co-operate fully and fearlessly in the process of justice.'[4] These remarks may be thought a shade melodramatic given that the number of notifiable offences of violence against the person, robbery and sexual offences recorded by the police in 1982 was 305 per 100,000 head of population,[5] but their tenor has since been endorsed by the Court of Appeal in *R v Samuda*.[6] It is absolutely clear that an application by a victim who deliberately misleads the police, either by withholding or giving false information, will be rejected. Likewise, refusal to make a

20 CICB (1987) paras 25-36, 25. Also CICB (1984) para 26, and (1989) para 19.1.
1 CICB (1988) paras 33.1-33.4.
2 CICB (1987) para 28.
3 CICB (1988) paras 32.1-32.2, and (1989) paras 19.2-19.4.
4 CICB (1983) para 27. Also CICB (1986) para 25.
5 Home Office *Criminal Statistics England and Wales 1982* (1983, Cmnd 9048) Table 2.3.
6 (1989) 11 Cr App Rep(S) 471, CA.

statement, to attend an identification parade, to name the assailant where he is clearly known to the victim, or to give evidence, have all been treated by the Board as instances of non-compliance with this aspect of para 6(a).[7] Nor will the fact that he has been threatened by reprisals necessarily excuse an applicant.[8] However, the Board has been careful to distinguish from these cases a refusal to press charges. Provided that a victim co-operates with the authorities, his express wish that there should be no prosecution or his refusal to make a formal complaint should not preclude him from compensation.[9] Where the victim does refuse to press charges, the Board will specifically ask the police whether, in all other respects, he co-operated with them.[10]

(3) Giving assistance in connection with the application

The rejection of an application on the ground of non-compliance with para 6(c) is a rare event.[11] The reasonable assistance required by the Board may relate to matters other than the immediate circumstances giving rise to the injury, for example, failing to disclose details of a prior conviction, or failing to give a convincing explanation as to why a claim for pecuniary loss includes a holiday in the West Indies on which the applicant has taken his girlfriend.[12] The paragraph also requires the applicant to give reasonable assistance to other authorities involved in the determination of the application, for example, his doctor, a hospital out-patients' clinic,[13] the DSS or his employer, all of whom may be approached by the Board to verify details connected with the application.

D. UNDESERVING APPLICANTS

Paragraph 6(c) of the Scheme provides that the Board may withhold or reduce compensation if it considers that:

---

7 CICB (1984) para 27, (1985) para 25, (1983) para 28, and 18th Report (1982, Cmnd 8752) para 32.
8 CICB (1985) para 27.
9 [1976] Current Law para 426, and CICB (1986) para 20. See also *R v Townend, ex p Criminal Injuries Compensation Board* (9 June 1970, unreported) noted in Williams (1986) para 8.01.
10 CICB (1986) para 20.
11 CICB 16th Report (1980, Cmnd 8081) para 33.
12 CICB (1978) para 18.
13 CICB (1987) para 38.

'having regard to the conduct of the applicant before, during or after the events giving rise to the claim or to his character as shown by his criminal convictions or unlawful conduct — and, in applications under paras 15 and 16 below, to the conduct, or character as shown by the criminal convictions or unlawful conduct, of the deceased and of the applicant — it is inappropriate that a full award, or any award at all, be granted.'

The continuation of 'a wide power enabling the Board to reduce or refuse compensation on the grounds of the relevant conduct of the victim' was specifically recommended by the Home Office review in 1978,[14] but both the formulation and the implementation of this paragraph have occasioned criticism. The central issue turns on the varying conceptions of relevance that have been held by the Board, its supporters and its critics, in particular concerning what the Board should be able to take into account when considering the relevance of the applicant's biography to his application. The pre-1990 version of para 6(c) permitted the Board to take into account, in addition to his conduct before, during or after the incident giving rise to the injury, the victim's 'character and way of life', and in the case of applications arising from homicides, 'the character, conduct and way of life of the deceased and of the applicant'. For the Board, these phrases meant that any conduct or biographical detail that made the person, in its view undeserving, was relevant. The Board's critics, on the other hand, argued firstly that relevance implied a causal relationship between the injury and the disentitling condition; particularly objectionable in their view was the refusal or reduction of compensation to victims whose criminal records were causally unrelated to the incident giving rise to the injury. Secondly, compensation could be withheld or reduced though the applicant's 'conduct' was lawful, while the reference to 'way of life' permitted the intrusion of judgments that the Board's critics considered bore an inappropriately moralist slant.[15] In its consideration of the Scheme, the Home Affairs Committee agreed with the Board's Chairman that it

14 Home Office (1978) p 61. The interpretation of the equivalent provisions in the Northern Ireland Scheme, where victims of terrorist violence may themselves be associated with terrorist organisations, is of interest, see D Greer *Compensation for Criminal Injuries to Persons in Northern Ireland* (1990, 2nd edn, SLS Publications, Belfast) ch 3.

15 841 HC Official Report (5th series) cols 148-149 (20 July 1972), 16 HC Official Report (6th series) col 453 (29 January 1982), 401 HL Official Report (5th series) col 232 (13 July 1979), 428 HL Official Report (5th series) cols 1386-1387 (31 March 1982), and House of Commons (1984-85) para 34.

'should retain the power to refuse awards in *exceptional* cases of this kind',[16] and in 1985 the Court of Appeal upheld the Board's view that the phrase 'character and way of life' was 'not limited to matters relevant in some way to the particular incident'.[17]

Like its predecessor, the 1986 Working Party received many suggestions that para 6(c) should be more closely defined, but concluded that the Board had exercised its discretion reasonably and recommended no change.[18] However, following s 112 of the Criminal Justice Act 1988, the 1990 revision does introduce some limitations on what the Board may take into account when considering the applicant's character. First, the reference to 'way of life' has been removed. Secondly, the conduct which is disentitling of compensation must be unlawful, and thirdly, para 6(c) now specifies criminal convictions as the other ground on which the Board may regard the applicant's character as relevant to his application. However, the paragraph still permits the Board to reduce or refuse compensation on the ground of 'his character as shown by his criminal convictions or unlawful conduct' irrespective of any causal connection between them and the incident.

Though quantitatively insignificant (of the 35,971 applications resolved in 1988-89, but 2,441 were rejected on this basis[19]), this issue is qualitatively of the first importance. It is the one facet of a compensation scheme that most strikingly brings into focus the assumptions that lie behind the notion of the innocent, and hence deserving, victim.[20] Judging from conference proceedings, it is one of the most perplexing issues to be resolved in the formulation and implementation of any criminal injury compensation scheme; certainly it is an issue which the immediate past Chairman described as 'the most difficult aspect of the Board's work.'[1] The source of the puzzlements that this issue generates goes well beyond the causal problems that may arise in the analogous context of contributory negligence in personal

16 House of Commons (1984-85) para 34.
17 *R v Criminal Injuries Compensation Board, ex p Thompstone and Crowe* [1983] 1 All ER 936 at 945 per Stephen Brown J, upheld on appeal to the Court of Appeal [1984] 3 All ER 572, [1984] 1 WLR 1234.
18 Home Office (1986) para 6.2.
19 CICB (1989) App B. There are no separate figures to show how many awards were reduced on account of para 6(c).
20 D Miers 'Victim compensation as a labelling process' (1980) 5 Victimology 3-16, and 'Compensation and conceptions of victims of crime' (1983) 8 Victimology 204-212.
1 M Ogden 'Why reform matters for victims' (1977, Howard League for Penal Reform) p 4, and (1984-85) p 230.

injury actions. Whether damages should be payable to those who are victimised while they are intoxicated by alcohol, solvents or hallucinatory drugs, or who were at the time engaged in unlawful activity, are questions that rarely trouble the courts.[2] Though they arise relatively more frequently before the administrators of criminal injury schemes, they have no uniform answer. The problem firstly is that because delinquent victims resemble offenders too closely, and may have been formally so defined in the past, the possibility of their receiving compensation threatens the stereotype of the 'innocent' victim for whom such schemes are created. Secondly, this possibility subverts a prime objective of criminal injury schemes, which is to *distinguish* victims of crime from offenders where penal regimes are perceived to be too forgiving and too neglectful of the victim. The politicisation of the victim of crime requires that the taxpayer be asked to compensate only those victims who present 'deserving' characteristics, so it therefore becomes necessary to exclude the delinquent victim (however defined) from their beneficial provisions.[3]

The Board has always regarded 'clean hands' as being of primary importance. In the event of a hearing, it imposes on the applicant the obligation to make out his case, and where appropriate this extends, by para 25, 'to satisfying the Board that compensation should not be withheld or reduced under the terms of paragraph 6.' It is also instructive to note that the terms of this paragraph were gradually extended over the years so as to bring more aspects of an applicant's biography and conduct within the Board's scrutiny. These extensions both brought greater definition to the class of victims compensable under the Scheme while simultaneously narrowing it. The original provision from the 1964 Scheme read:

'The Board will consider whether, because of provocation or otherwise, the victim bears any share of responsibility for it, and in accordance with its assessment of the degree of responsibility, will reduce the amount of compensation or reject the claim altogether.'

---

2 Of the few decisions in this area, see *Hegarty v Shine* (1878) 14 Cox CC 145, CA; *Burns v Edman* [1970] 2 QB 541, [1970] 1 All ER 886; *Gray v Barr* [1971] 2 QB 554, [1971] 2 All ER 949, CA; *Ashton v Turner* [1981] QB 137, [1980] 3 All ER 870; and *Morris v Murray* (1990) Times, 17 September. See K Williams 'The wrongdoing passenger' (1990) 140 New LJ 1235-1237.
3 Miers (1983).

It will be seen that this referred neither to the victim's character and way of life nor to his conduct after the incident, nor to the character, conduct and way of life of a dependant in fatal cases. It was the fact of applications being made by victims of whom, in the then Chairman's opinion, 'it could undoubtedly be said that they had waged war on society for many years',[4] that prompted the Board to seek an extension to the terms of this paragraph, notwithstanding that there were some differences of opinion between its members.[5] The amended version, introduced in 1968-69, covered both the victim's 'character and way of life', and included his conduct after the incident. Following its introduction, the Board rather contrarily remarked on the difficulties that this new discretion had created, but the result was an immediate increase in the number of applications disallowed under this paragraph, when expressed as a percentage of all rejected applications.[6] The further extension to include the applicant's character, conduct and way of life in applications arising from the homicide of the victim was introduced in the 1979-80 changes.

Paragraph 6(c) creates two conditions under which the Board may refuse or reduce an award to an undeserving applicant:

1. because of his conduct before, during or after the events giving rise to the claim; or
2. because of his character as shown by his criminal convictions or unlawful conduct.

It will be seen that there is some overlap between these conditions. A victim injured in a fight which he initiated can be disentitled in whole or in part under either of them. It will also be seen that though cast in different terms, these conditions bear obvious similarities to those defences in tort that may preclude a claim for personal injuries or under the Fatal Accidents Act 1976, or result in a reduction in the damages ordered to be paid. A victim/plaintiff who was engaged in illegal conduct may be barred by the rule, *ex turpi causa non oritur actio*, and one who was engaged in risky, though not necessarily unlawful conduct, may be barred by the defence, *volenti non fit injuria*.

---

4 CICB (1985) para 19.
5 CICB 3rd Report (1967, Cmnd 3427) para 13 and 4th Report (1968, Cmnd 3814) para 11.
6 CICB (1976) para 15 and App D. The percentage then of all rejected cases on this ground was 29%; in 1989 the figure was hardly different, 29.7%, CICB (1989) App B.

Likewise the victim/plaintiff will fail where the defence can show that his conduct amounted to a *novus actus interveniens*. If his conduct did not break the causal link between the defendant's negligence and his injury, but nevertheless contributed to it, the court shall, by s 1(1) of the Law Reform (Contributory Negligence) Act 1945, reduce his damages to such extent as it thinks just and equitable. Though there are similarities between the Scheme and these aspects of tort law, there are also important differences between them. These differences may usefully be summarised here.

(a) The Board has a discretion to refuse or to reduce an award irrespective of which of the two conditions it invokes to disentitle the applicant. In tort law, on the other hand, only the defence of contributory negligence permits reduction in the amount of compensation (and it only permits this); the other defences completely bar any recovery.

(b) Where the application is made by the deceased victim's dependants, both conditions apply to the victim's conduct or biography. If, for example, the victim had a conviction for a serious offence, though it was unconnected with the attack on him, there may be no award if the Board think that it would be inappropriate to make one. In a fatal accident action, however, such a background would not bar the dependants. It is probably otherwise where the deceased lived a life of crime, as the dependants' claim arises *ex turpi causa*;[7] it would almost certainly be refused by the Board. Likewise, if the Board think it appropriate, compensation may be reduced or denied to the dependant because of the victim's conduct before, during or after the injury.

(c) Where the application is made by dependants, both conditions also apply to them. A dependant with criminal convictions or who had engaged in unlawful conduct may be disentitled, and the Board can also take into account his conduct before, during or after the events giving rise to the victim's death. This would not be the case in a fatal accident action.

(d) The Board may refuse or reduce an award because of the applicant's character as disclosed by his criminal convictions or unlawful conduct, irrespective of the absence of any connection between them and the injury. In tort law, the mere fact that the victim/plaintiff was a wrongdoer will not be a defence.

(e) The Board may take into account the applicant's convictions and unlawful conduct whenever they occurred, including a time

7 *Burns v Edman*, op cit.

after the injury or death, and the Scheme expressly allows it to consider his conduct before, during and after the events giving rise to the claim. Tort law may take into account the refusal by a victim/plaintiff to accept medical treatment following an injury, but would count as irrelevant subsequent convictions or unlawful conduct.

(f) In tort law, the defences *ex turpi causa* and *volenti* appear not to apply in the case of an unlawful fight initiated by the victim where the defendant's response is disproportionate to the provocation; for the Board, however, proportionality is not the determining factor.

(g) In invoking these two conditions, similar though aspects of them are to the defence of contributory negligence, the Board is not obliged to apply the common law's interpretation of that notion.

These differences between the Scheme and tort law all flow from one crucial factor: for criminal injury compensation it is the taxpayer who foots the bill. This alone seems to demand that compensation should not be given to those with unclean hands, no matter that the act which caused the injury is unconnected with the victim's behaviour, or if it is, goes beyond the risk of injury entailed in that behaviour. This consideration was instrumental in the 1986 Working Party's recommendation that the Board's discretion in this matter be unchanged:

> 'It is important to remember . . . that the justification for compensation by the state is that it is paid on behalf of the community as a practical expression of public feeling reflecting the sense of responsibility for and sympathy with the innocent victim which is felt by the public at large. Clearly it would not reflect this public feeling to make awards from public funds to those who have themselves led a life of serious crime, preying upon persons and property of fellow citizens, irrespective of whether their injuries are attributable to their own offences.'[8]

If a compensation scheme were, on the other hand, funded by some system of offender reparation, then arguably the issue of victim participation would diminish in importance. With the possible exception of bars equivalent to the defences of provocation and self-defence as understood in the criminal law, there would be few occasions on which the conduct of the victim would be relevant. This would be so precisely because the very

8 Home Office (1986) para 6.2.

powerful shaping influence on a compensation scheme, namely the fact of public funding, would be absent. It is this factor which has been largely instrumental in the development of the rules justifying the reduction or rejection of applications, and of the practices followed under them. These rules, and the moral censure that they encourage, additionally perform important social functions which go beyond the particular context of criminal injury compensation. They satisfy one of the basic tenets of the pro-victim (or the anti-offender) lobby: the corollary of the argument that less money should be spent on offenders or alternatively, more on 'deserving' people, is that a compensation scheme does not exist to give money to delinquent victims. Often such victims are simply getting what they deserve. Second, there is a pervasive socialising and educative role implicit in the judgments that have been made under para 6(c). Such a role is of course a feature of many decisions taken by legal institutions; in this instance, however, the decisions do themselves deviate from those which would be reached in analogous restitutive and penal contexts.

(1)   The applicant's conduct before, during or after the incident

In determining whether it is appropriate to disentitle the applicant wholly or partly from compensation in view of his conduct before, during or after the events giving rise to the claim, the question arises, what characteristics of that conduct should the Board take into account? One possibility is that it should reduce or refuse compensation commensurate with the degree to which the applicant's conduct contributed to the occurrence of the events or to the severity of the injuries he sustained. This approach, which reflects the operation in tort law of the defences of *volenti* and contributory negligence, was emphatically discounted by the Court of Appeal in *R v Criminal Injuries Compensation Board, ex p Ince*.[9] The applicant's husband, who was on duty in a police car, was killed when, in answer to a general police message, he ignored a set of traffic lights en route to the scene of the suspected offence, and collided with another police car (travelling in response to the same message) crossing with the lights. Subsequently it was discovered that this was a false alarm. The Board rejected the application on the grounds

9 [1973] 3 All ER 808, [1973] 1 WLR 1334.

first, that he was not at the material time actually engaged in the prevention of a crime, and second, that his death was attributable to his own foolhardiness.

Whereas the Divisional Court refused *certiorari*, the Court of Appeal allowed it. As to the analogy which the Board drew between contributory negligence (which it held was applicable to the policeman's driving — albeit at 20 mph — across a set of traffic lights set at red) and the terms of the Scheme, the Court of Appeal was firmly of the view that this was mistaken.[10] Scarman LJ, whose judgment is confined to this point said:

> 'There is no limitation on the sort of conduct that may be taken into consideration and the clause places on the Board the responsibility to decide whether the conduct of the victim is such that a reduction or rejection would be appropriate. Nevertheless it is important that the Board should not think in terms of contributory negligence when acting under the clause. Clearly a policeman may have to take great risks often with his own safety, and sometimes with the safety of others, in the pursuit of a criminal and in the suppression of violent crime. If he subsequently becomes a claimant for criminal injuries compensation, he is entitled to have his conduct viewed in all the circumstances of his case and the Board must have a complete discretion, unhampered by any concepts borrowed from another part of the law, to determine whether or not it is appropriate to make a full award or to diminish the amount of compensation or to reject his claim altogether.'[11]

The importance of this judgment in the development of the Board's interpretation of para 6(c) cannot be exaggerated. It both justifies the broad view the Board takes of an applicant's conduct (and, in fatal cases, the conduct of the deceased) and indicates what characterises the Board's attitude to it: whether it is appropriate to withhold or reduce compensation depends on the Board's perception of its social value. The Board's Reports disclose a continuum of conduct from the delinquent to the altruistic. Some conduct is so socially valueless, such as initiating or agreeing to a fight, that the Board will seldom compensate the loser, even where the injuries are quite disproportionate to what the victim did or said. There is then a range of conduct, such as being intoxicated or engaging in other risky activity, whose social value is questionable and which may result in refusal

---

10 As to the first point see infra, pp 119–120.
11 [1973] 3 All ER 808 at 816.

or reduction; sometimes, though questionable, conduct that is only the consequence of stupidity or carelessness may be ignored, but only after careful consideration by the Board. Some conduct, though it undoubtedly contributes to the severity of the victim's injury, for example where he refuses medical treatment, will be discounted because the Board perceives the social value of the victim's choice to outweigh his contribution to the injury,[12] and at the positive end of the continuum is helping behaviour. In tort the question whether a negligent defendant should be liable for the injuries suffered by a rescuer will largely turn on the foreseeability of someone attempting a rescue and of the kind of injury he sustains when carrying it out;[13] as *Ex p Ince* emphatically demonstrates, the question for the Board turns on the social value of the (exceptional) risk taken by the rescuer/ victim.[14]

The Board's decisions on para 6(c) typically concern delinquent or questionable behaviour. Though they often speak of a causal connection between the victim's conduct and the incident in which he was injured, such a relationship is not the determining factor. The Board can regard as disentitling of compensation conduct that has no causal connection with the events giving rise to the claim, provided only that it occurred 'before, during or after' them. So far as any conduct occurring during those events is concerned, the only question is whether the Board considers it disentitling of compensation, but in the case of conduct occurring before or after them, the prior question arises, what is the limit to the lapse of time between that conduct and those events? As to conduct occurring after the events, the final decision upon the application will be the limit, though because

---

12 *R v Blaue* [1975] 3 All ER 446, [1975] 1 WLR 1411, CA. It is very unlikely that the Board would apply para 6(c) in such a case (private correspondence between Sir Michael Ogden and the author).

13 'A negligent defendant can only escape liability if the damage can be regarded as differing in kind from what was foreseeable,' per Lord Reid, *Hughes v Lord Advocate* [1963] AC 837 at 845, held by Lord Bridge in *Ogwo v Taylor* [1988] AC 431 at 444 to be 'the proper question to be asked'. See J Fleming *The Law of Torts* (1987, 7th edn, Law Book Co) pp 155-157, and P Cane, *Atiyah's Accidents, Compensation and the Law* (1987, 4th edn, Weidenfeld and Nicolson) pp 82-93. Since the decision in *Ex p Ince*, developments in tort law have probably eroded any difference in the results likely to be achieved by the two systems of compensation in cases like this. A policeman who is negligent (shooting the lights, speeding) while chasing a car driven by a suspected offender will almost certainly be compensated under the Scheme, and would recover also in an action against the negligent driver.

14 Infra, pp 139-143.

of the increasing delay in processing applications this limit has moved further in time from the events giving rise to the claim. Thus it is open to the Board to take into account conduct occurring many months after the events, for example, if at a later stage in the process the applicant makes a fraudulent statement about the losses caused by the injury or death (though he might alternatively be disqualified in such a case because of his unlawful conduct). However, it is less easy to identify a temporal limit to the question how long before those events may the conduct occur that the Board now wishes to take into account. The phraseology of para 6(c) suggests a closer rather than a more distant connection, but subject to the Board's duty when determining a question of fact and degree not to reach a conclusion that no reasonable tribunal could reach, it seems clear that proximity may shift according to the Board's view of the social value of the conduct in question. The less valuable, the more distant from the event the disentitling conduct may be. These various points may be illustrated by reference to the Board's decisions.

Intoxication, whether through drink, drugs or other substances, is pre-eminently the kind of conduct that may disentitle an applicant. In its 20th Report the Board observed that its members were 'regrettably familiar with incidents in which drink is a substantial factor in causing or triggering violence which often leads to serious injury'.[15] The excessive consumption of alcohol has played a significant part in a substantial number of the applications arising from intra-family violence, and in these and other applications it has constituted a ground for applying para 6(c). It should be noted that the Board's Reports, while giving bare statistics on the number of applications that have been rejected under this paragraph, neither indicate the particular ground for rejection (which, it must readily be admitted would be difficult to accomplish since many such cases will disclose, as do the claims arising from intra-family violence, a variety of disqualifying factors thought relevant by the Board), nor indicate how many applications resulted in reduced awards. Reflecting the increase in solvent abuse among the young, 'applications involving assailants whose violence and viciousness can be attributed to glue sniffing and applications from victims who have made themselves vulnerable through being involved

---

15 CICB (1984) para 45.

in glue sniffing or because of their lack of control'[16] became matters of specific mention by the Board in its Reports during the early 1980s. In cases where the victim had been participating in the glue sniffing with those who became his assailants, an application could well be rejected altogether.[17]

In its 22nd Report, the Board set out at length what it then regarded as the relevant considerations in these cases.

'The Board continues to receive a large number of applications in which drink, drugs or solvent abuse, or a combination thereof, have been a substantial cause of the victim's misfortune. Many of the incidents occur at weekends and often in places and situations which the victim might have avoided had he been sober or not willing to run some kind of risk. Occasionally it is plain that the incident occurred solely as a result of the victim's own aggressive behaviour. In these cases the Board will make no award. In other cases the most that can be levelled at the victim is his or her own lack of judgment or stupidity. In this situation the Board may make an award but only after looking very carefully at all the surrounding circumstances to establish whether the applicant's conduct 'before during or after the events giving rise to the claim' was such that it would be appropriate to make a payment from public funds. In particular the Board will look critically at any provocative, annoying or loutish behaviour which can clearly be seen to be attributable to the applicant's own over-indulgence in alcohol or the misuse of drugs. Such conduct will often be grounds for complete rejection of the application or at the least some reduction in the amount of compensation awarded.'[18]

If the 'provocative, annoying or loutish behaviour' constituted an offence under s 5 of the Public Order Act 1986, or more simply constituted a common assault, then some of this conduct would be disentitling because it is unlawful. Other aspects are disentitling because, as the quotation clearly shows, the Board regards such conduct as socially valueless; but it is also clear that not all questionable conduct will result in the refusal or reduction of compensation. Often the issue is what the conduct leads to; thus conduct that the Board perceives only as immoral, though 'not by itself a reason for reducing an

16 Id.
17 CICB (1984) paras 46 and 47. See also CICB (1985) para 26.
18 CICB (1986) para 23.

award',[19] may have that result if it provokes an injurious response.

This consequence is not infrequently cast in terms of what the applicant risks by his conduct. Where the Board perceives it as being of low social value, its Reports suggest that it applies a robust sense of justice involving an equation between the risky conduct (broadly conceived) of the victim, and the injury he sustained. If a victim assumes a risk of criminal violence which is unjustified and unreasonable in the circumstances (that is, of little or no social value), he cannot subsequently complain if that risk is realised. This equation is exemplified by the Board's earlier approach to consensual fighting, though it has in recent years adopted a very much tougher stance in these cases, but continues to be exemplified by its approach to applications in which the victim has voluntarily assumed a risk of injury, for example by participating in a dangerous activity. The issue typically arises where injuries are caused by the use of air rifles and pistols in children's games. In tort, the question would be whether an ordinary child of the victim's age would have taken any greater care, but this is clearly more difficult to answer where both victim and perpetrator are children. The Board's approach has been to make no award if there were nothing to choose between the conduct of the child who inflicted the injury and that of the victim in the context of their respective understanding of the risks involved.[20]

The decisions that most vividly illustrate the development of the Board's conception of the social value of the victim's conduct and its relevance to the subsequent application concern injuries sustained in fights in which the victim was, at least initially, a willing participant. In tort law, a plaintiff who picks a fight

---

19 The Statement, para 6G. One application involving a violent incident arising from a homosexual relationship is noted in CICB (1985) para 27. A reduction of 50% was made to the award, but this was attributable to the applicant's admission to the Board that he had lied to it, and to the police, in connection with an earlier alleged homosexual affair. The result was that the Board had then made an award, and his assailant had been exposed to a more severe sentence than would otherwise have been the case. See also Ogden (1984–85) p 230, CICB (1989) para 20.3 and Legal Action June 1987, p 16. Likewise, conduct that is deeply offensive may, if it carries with it a risk of injury, be disentitling of compensation, CICB (1988) para 36.1 (15 year old school boy having been asked to give a talk to his class about a favourite pastime, described various ways of torturing cats; one of his classmates took objection and punched him in the face).

20 The Statement, para 6J. CICB (1982) para 35 and (1978) paras 29-31. As to the fault element, infra, pp 129–130.

in which he comes off worse may be denied a remedy either because of the application of the *volenti* doctrine, or because his claim arises *ex turpi causa*. Their application is, however, substantially tempered where the defendant's response is disproportionate to the plaintiff's conduct. The Board's initial response to such applications was very similar; if a 'fair fight' ensued from the victim's conduct, the application was to be rejected, but where the offender's response was out of the ordinary, a reduced award was appropriate.[1] The notion of proportionality implicit in the fair fight rule also has significant parallels in areas of the substantive criminal law and in sentencing practice,[2] but, in time, the Board adopted an increasingly tough stance; precipitation by the victim became the determining factor.

> 'Our experience leads us to believe that there is seldom such a thing as a fair fight, particularly where the participants are inflamed by drink, passion, greed or aggression, and unless we adopt a realistic approach we could well end by making a full or reduced award to the one who comes out of the incident with injuries.'[3]

This 'realistic approach' to fights, encouraged by the recommendations of the 1978 Working Party,[4] means that compensation will not normally be awarded 'if the victim, without reasonable cause, struck the first blow, regardless of the degree of retaliation; where the conduct of the victim was calculated or intended to provoke violence; if the injury or death occurred in a fight in which the victim had voluntarily agreed to take part; if the crime of violence formed a pattern of violence in which the victim or the applicant had been a voluntary participant; or where the victim or the applicant had attempted to revenge himself or herself against the assailant.'[5]

An application which well illustrates the rejection of the notion

---

1 CICB 2nd Report (1966, Cmnd 3117) para 25, (1968) para 11(4) and 6th Report (1970, Cmnd 4494) para 5(1), and the Statement para 6E: 'the Board may consider how the amount of provocation offered by the victim compares with the amount of violence used by the offender.' Compare *Lane v Holloway* [1968] 1 QB 379, [1967] 3 All ER 129, CA.

2 Eg in self-defence and provocation, and see A Ashworth *Sentencing and Penal Policy* (1983, Weidenfeld and Nicolson) passim.

3 CICB (1980) para 26, repeated in (1983) para 29.

4 Home Office (1978) para 17.5.

5 The Statement, para 6D. For examples of the application of this aspect of para 6(c), see CICB (1980) para 26, (1986) paras 22, 23 and 32, (1987) para 40, (1988) paras 38.1-38.2, and (1989) paras 20.4-20.7.

of proportionality in cases of victim-precipitated injury is *R v Criminal Injuries Compensation Board, ex p Comerford*.[6] The victim had been annoying other customers in a public house. He was butted by a man who had been singled out by the victim's provocative and offensive behaviour, and who thought that the victim was about to attack him. The victim fell, and sustained such severe head injuries that his affairs had to be put into the hands of the Official Solicitor. In the Board's account it appears that the assailant was prosecuted under ss 18 and 20 of the Offences against the Person Act 1861, that the trial judge withdrew the former charge from the jury, and that the assailant pleaded self-defence to the latter. It is not clear whether he was convicted on this charge. The Board decided that the assailant was acting in reasonable self-defence, and that even if he was not, the victim's conduct was such as to make it inappropriate that any award should be made.

The Board's decision on the first point creates some difficulty, even though its account of the outcome of the trial is not explicit. If the assailant was convicted under s 20, there is an inconsistency between the jury's necessary rejection of the assailant's evidence as raising a reasonable doubt in their minds as to whether he did not in fact act in self-defence, and the Board's view that on a balance of probabilities (the standard of proof applied by the Board), he did so act. Even if he were acquitted there is still room for some tension, since the jury's decision is consistent with the view that they *only* entertained a reasonable doubt as to whether he had acted in self-defence, but that they were not satisfied on a balance of probabilities (although this is possible but unknowable) that he did so act.[7]

As to the second point, the Board argued that it was 'neither acceptable nor in accordance with the words' of the Scheme,[8] that compensation should be dependent on the severity of the victim's injuries. As between two equally provocative acts on the part of a victim, it would, in the Board's judgment, be wrong that slight injuries would merit no award, but that serious ones would. The Divisional Court agreed. If the victim asked for it, said Lord Lane CJ, then it is irrelevant that what he got was not what he asked for, but injuries that were 'unforeseen and

---

6 (1981) CICB para 20(a).
7 Conversely, there is also an instructive comparison to be made between an acquittal and a finding that the victim was nevertheless a victim of a crime of violence, infra, pp 131–132.
8 CICB (1981) para 20(a).

unforeseeable'.[9] This reasoning is hardly satisfactory. Lord Lane invited us to answer the question, 'why it was that the applicant got hit?' with the proposition, 'because "he asked for it"'; but it had already been agreed that the 'it' for which he asked 'of course' (sic) did not include a fractured skull or brain damage. *Ex hypothesi*, a consequence not within the victim's contemplation cannot be something for which he has 'asked'. Such talk is, of course, metaphorical; what it disguises is the simple proposition that a victim who precipitates a risk of injury cannot complain when that risk is realised, and to whatever extent. This goes some way beyond the civil law's response. In *Murphy v Culhane*,[10] the Court of Appeal, on an interlocutory appeal, thought that notwithstanding a guilty plea by a defendant, it would still be open to him to raise the defences of *ex turpi causa, volenti*, or possibly contributory negligence in civil proceedings by a victim (or his dependants) where the victim initiated the incident that resulted in his injury (or death); but as *Lane v Holloway*[11] and *Barnes v Nayer*[12] show, a trivial assault by the victim will not preclude full damages where the retaliation is savage. Moreover, as Lord Denning observed in *Murphy v Culhane*, the plaintiff's conduct would have to be serious before he could be regarded as even partly responsible for his injury.[13] This, in Hudson's view, suggests that these defences would only be applicable in cases of well-matched fighting;[14] the 'fair fights' once recognised by the Board, but subsequently abandoned in cases where the victim precipitated the incident through his own provocative conduct.

Ex p Comerford gives expression to a corollary of the well established principle of both tort and criminal law, that the defendant must take his victim as he finds him: the victim must take his defendant as he finds him. A negligent/reckless defendant cannot complain if the plaintiff/victim has a particular sensitivity

9 Quoted by the Board, id.
10 [1977] QB 94, [1976] 3 All ER 533; *A-G's Reference (No 6 of 1980)* [1981] QB 715, [1981] 2 All ER 1057, CA. A police officer driving a vehicle in pursuit of a person whom he rightly suspects of having committed an arrestable offence owes the same duty of care to him as he does to any other road user, *Marshall v Osmond* [1983] QB 1034, [1983] 2 All ER 225, CA.
11 Op cit.
12 (1986) Times 19 December. A householder who shoots and injures a plaintiff burgling his house may be liable in damages if that is an unreasonable use of force in the circumstances, *Sharpe v Greenwood* (1983) Times, 30 September.
13 Op cit, p 98.
14 A Hudson 'Contributory negligence as a defence to battery' (1984) 4 Legal Studies 332-342.

that aggravates the injury; *a fortiori* where some injury was intended. Neither it seems can the provocative victim complain if the offender has a particular sensitivity which aggravates the severity of his reaction, or merely reacts disproportionately to the provocation offered. As Atiyah has argued,[15] it is difficult to formulate satisfactorily a rationale for the 'egg-shell skull' exception to the principle that a defendant's liability for a negligently inflicted injury is limited to what could reasonably have been foreseen; but where the defendant intended harm, the argument that he should not be able to rely on what was unknown to him as limiting his liability, seems stronger both in tort and criminal law. The relevant distinctions might be formulated in this way.

First, we may distinguish from the physiological or psychological characteristics of the victim that aggravate an injury, those behavioural characteristics that enhance, or expose him to, a risk of harm. Second, we may distinguish from cases in which the liability of a defendant is in issue (which will be further complicated by the nature of the fault element, if any, required to establish liability), those cases in which the victim is seeking a remedy, either from the defendant or, in the case of criminal injury compensation, from the state. The law may therefore consistently deny or limit any argument concerning the existence or extent of the defendant's criminal liability where the victim's behaviour has enhanced or exposed him to a risk of injury, while at the same time permitting the defendant to rely on it to deny or reduce his civil liability, and further, precluding the victim from recovering from funds other than those controlled by the defendant.[16] So much of these distinctions between states and actions, and between penal and restitutive law are dependent on policy considerations, it is unsurprising that the law should also distinguish between the sources from which compensation may be sought by the victim.

(2) The applicant's character

(a) AS SHOWN BY HIS CRIMINAL CONVICTIONS

The first condition under which the Board may refuse or reduce compensation because of the applicant's character is where he has a criminal record. As with the other disentitling conditions,

---

15 (1987) pp 112-114.
16 Eg *Pitts v Hunt* [1990] 3 WLR 542, CA.

the convictions may be those either of the victim or, where he died, of a dependant. Where the application is made on behalf of the victim, such as a child or a person mentally handicapped, the applicant's convictions will not be taken into account (though the victim's might); but the Board will have to be satisfied that any award it makes will not benefit anyone responsible for the injury, as might occur, for example, where a parent with a criminal record brings an application on behalf of his child who has been injured by a someone else living in the same household.[17] There is no requirement that the convictions be causally connected with the injury, though the wording of the paragraph clearly gives the Board discretion to discount some convictions. A conviction which is connected with the injury complained of has nevertheless always been an obvious case for rejection or reduction, although the nature of the connection will be a matter of degree for the Board to determine.[18] Such convictions could as well be disentitling because the conduct was unlawful, or because the Board applies the first limb of para 6(c).

It has been an article of faith for the past 25 years that the Board should have discretion to refuse or reduce an award where applicants have convictions which it regards as being qualitatively or quantitatively 'serious', irrespective of the absence of any causal connection between those offences and the injury sustained. One conviction for a serious crime of violence (unspecified by the Board but contemplating a serious offence under s 20 of the Offences against the Person Act 1861 as the threshold) or for 'some other very serious crime' (again unspecified, but presumably including such offences as aggravated burglary, arson, poisoning, robbery, conspiracy to rob and firearms offences) would be sufficient for the Board to reject an application. More than one recent conviction for less serious crimes of either kind, or numerous convictions for dishonesty of a serious nature, likewise have been sufficient ground. On the other hand, petty offences, for example, of drunkenness or minor breaches of the peace, have prompted the Board only to reduce any award payable.[19] More positively, the

---

17 Infra, p 156.
18 *R v Criminal Injuries Compensation Board, ex p Blood* (1983) CICB para 16. Also CICB (1980) para 18.
19 The Statement, para 6K2 and 3. For examples of the application of para 6(c) to applicants with convictions, see CICB (1984) paras 29 and 53, (1988) paras 34.1-35.2, and (1989) paras 20.2-20.3. See also J Shapland et al *The Victim in the Criminal Justice System* (1985, Gower) pp 160-162.

1986 Working Party approved the Board's policy of looking favourably on the applicant's attempts to 'go straight'.[20] However, while the guidelines given in the Statement are tolerably clear, research conducted in the mid 1980s suggests that in practice differentiation in the outcome as between those who do and those who do not have prior convictions will be difficult to predict. Allowing for the small number of applications sampled, Newburn's findings show a disquieting variation in the Board's exercise of this controversial discretion.[1]

The propositions set out in the Statement represent the Board's current thinking, but its views about the relevance of prior convictions were reached only after a good deal of reconsideration and amendment of the Scheme. The variations in the way in which the Board has approached this matter over the years are indicative of the difficult and controversial issues that it has generated, and no doubt will continue to generate.

Initially the Board took the view that a criminal record was irrelevant unless it was in some way causally connected with the incident in which the victim was injured.[2] That only a tenuous link might suffice is illustrated by the application made by a man who had numerous convictions for dishonesty recorded against him over a period of 18 years. It appeared that his assailants were known to him and that 'there was some suggestion of an earlier incident to which the assault may or may not have been related';[3] despite the uncertainty, the Board thought it inappropriate that public money should be paid in respect of injuries received in an assault 'for which no satisfactory explanation exculpating [the victim] was given.'[4] Even after the introduction of the 1968-69 amendments to the Scheme (which specifically extended the Board's discretion to take the victim's character and way of life into account), the Board reiterated the view that 'applicants with previous convictions are not disqualified from receiving compensation if they can satisfy the Board that the incident in which their injuries were received was unconnected with their criminal offences',[5] but the disposal of subsequent applications suggest that the Board assumed a

---

20 Home Office (1986) para 6.3.
1 Newburn (1989) pp 18-19.
2 CICB (1967) para 13.
3 CICB 6th Report (1970, Cmnd 4494) para 5(5)(a).
4 Id.
5 CICB 7th Report (1971, Cmnd 4812) para 11.

tougher stance during the 1970s. Thus one applicant who had been sentenced to terms in Borstal and prison on 19 occasions, and altogether had appeared in court on 26 occasions for 65 offences was made a 50% award although at the time of the incident he had been in continuous employment for a substantial period, was considered satisfactory and reliable by his employer, and had favourable reports from his probation officer.[6]

The 1978 Review was but slightly critical of the Board's somewhat unforgiving response to a history of prior convictions.[7] Under the Rehabilitation of Offenders Act 1974, enacted after the introduction of the 'character and way of life' provision in the 1968-69 amendments, information about spent convictions would not be made available to the Board, though being a judicial body, it could take them into account if it considered that it could not reach a just decision without that information. The Review considered that the Board should take into account any meritorious conduct on the applicant's part, and this was later reflected in the Statement, which indicates that the Board will give credit for attempts by the victim to reform himself or, if the injury arose out of an incident in which he or a policeman were trying to prevent crime or to apprehend an offender, for such efforts to promote law enforcement activity.[8] Nevertheless, any concession on this point was more than matched by the Board's quite emphatic rejection of the suggestion that the terms of para 6(c) should be amended so as to require some causal relationship between the victim's criminal past and his present criminal injury. In his evidence to the Home Affairs Committee, the then Chairman said:

'It is sometimes useful to consider extreme examples. Suppose that Peter Sutcliffe ('The Yorkshire Ripper') had been awarded compensation by the Board for an injury which was wholly unrelated to his crimes, or that an award had been made to the criminal who put a bomb on a coach containing women and children, or made an award to the man who is at the time of writing being hunted by the police in the Dunstable area in connection with extremely nasty offences of rape and other crimes. I would expect that there would be a howl of public outrage; in my view rightly so.'[9]

6 CICB 10th Report (1974, Cmnd 5791) para 8(7).
7 Home Office (1978) para 17.9.
8 The Statement, para 6K1 and 4. CICB (1987) para 39.
9 CICB (1985) para 19. Also Ogden (1984–85) p 230. Similarly the Board will very 'rarely' compensate anyone who has been engaged in terrorist offences

Public hostility is often expressed about decisions taken by legal bodies; a measure of compatibility between popular sentiment and what the law decides, permits or punishes, is an important factor in the success of any legal system to command the support of those affected by it, but it would be a poor system that used public approval or disapproval of its activities as the determining factor in its decisions. The question is whether it is defensible to refuse compensation to a person because he has a criminal record, but one which is unconnected with the injury complained of. Thousands of people remain eligible for state benefits notwithstanding prior convictions; and if those who are injured in incidents unconnected with their criminal history have been convicted and punished by due process of law, is it right that they should be so disqualified in the future? The Board's answer simply is, that it is: that where offenders commit serious offences, they put themselves, so to speak, beyond the pale of criminal injury compensation. In any event, the Board's interpretation of the terms of para 6(c) was vindicated both by the Divisional Court and the Court of Appeal in *R v Criminal Injuries Compensation Board, ex p Thompstone and Crowe.*[10] The Board had denied compensation to two applicants, both of whom had long lists of previous convictions. The attacks were unprovoked, and had no connection with these convictions; the applicants sought judicial review, contending that the Board had no jurisdiction to withhold compensation where there was no connection between the injury complained of and their 'character'. Following an extensive review of the history of the Scheme and in particular of para 6(c) and its earlier variants, Stephen Brown J said:

> '. . . the Scheme, as published, is intended to afford the widest possible discretion to the Board in its administration of the Scheme. Paragraph 6(c) gives the Board discretion to withhold or reduce compensation, both having regard to the conduct of the applicant in relation to the incident and, furthermore, having regard to his character and

or is a member of a violent gang. The inclusion of the word 'rarely' in para 6F of the Statement was made in response to criticism by the Divisional Court that an earlier version which had said that such a person 'will not receive' an award could be read as depriving the Board of its discretion; *R v Criminal Injuries Board, ex p RJC (an infant)* [1978] Crim LR 220.

10 [1983] 1 All ER 936, [1984] 1 WLR 422, DC; affd [1984] 3 All ER 572, [1984] 1 WLR 1234, CA.

way of life. In my judgment, this latter consideration is not limited to matters relevant in some way to the particular incident.'[11]

He dismissed the application, and his decision was affirmed, in arguably more forceful language, by the Court of Appeal.[12] The Master of the Rolls was quite unable to accept the appellants' submissions; the Scheme gave the Board a discretion whether to extend public bounty to applicants in these circumstances, and was by no means limited to a consideration of those convictions only that might be connected with the injury in respect of which the compensation was sought.

We conclude this section by referring to an application recorded in the Board's 22nd Report which gives a good indication of the Board's current approach in these cases.[13] The applicant and his girlfriend were unexpectedly visited by two friends of hers whom she had not seen for two years. There was much celebration accompanied by much alcohol; later an inebriated argument developed between the applicant and one of the visitors. The visitor's boyfriend arrived, and there were some verbal exchanges between him and the applicant, but no violence. The following morning three men called at the applicant's house, attacked him with knives and an iron bar and, as they were leaving, shot him with a sawn-off shotgun. The victim, who had to have his right leg amputated, had nine previous convictions, including possessing offensive weapons and controlled drugs. The single member made an interim award and decided that the final award should be reduced by 20% on account of his convictions. Under the provisions in para 22 of the Scheme, he referred the claim to a hearing, which agreed with his decision.

(b) AS SHOWN BY THE APPLICANT'S UNLAWFUL CONDUCT

The second condition under which the Board may refuse or reduce compensation because of the applicant's character is because of his unlawful conduct. As has been noted, this part of para 6(c) overlaps with the power to disentitle an applicant because of his conduct before, during or after the events giving rise to the

---

11 [1983] 1 All ER 936 at 943. See also *R v Criminal Injuries Compensation Board, ex p Taylor* (1988) Guardian, 14 April, where Kennedy J held that the Board acted properly when it rejected an application made by a victim who had, shortly before the incident in which he had been stabbed, robbed a woman of a necklace by seizing it from her neck.
12 [1984] 3 All ER 572 at 576.
13 CICB (1986) para 22. See also id, para 25, and (1987) para 39.

claim. An applicant who strikes the first blow may be refused compensation under either provision, as may an applicant who, having made one genuine application as yet not finalised, subsequently makes one that is fraudulent.[14] Whereas the phrase 'before, during or after' implies some temporal proximity between the applicant's conduct and the events, there is no such restriction here; the unlawful conduct may, it seems, have occurred at any time before (or after) the application. This disentitling condition can therefore be seen as an important supplement to that just discussed; since the Board can take hearsay evidence into account, it may disentitle an applicant whom the police have for years suspected of committing serious offences, but against whom no convictions for these offences have been secured. It goes without saying that there need be no causal connection between the unlawful conduct and the injury.

While this provision permits the Board to refuse or reduce compensation whether the unlawful conduct is connected with the injury or not, its wording clearly covers, as has been noted, applications in which the injury arose while the victim was indeed engaged in such conduct. The Board's practice is to reject applications from victims injured in the course of committing a serious crime.[15] What constitutes a 'serious' crime is not made explicit in the Statement appearing in the most recent Report. This question was discussed in the preceding section, where it was suggested that it would include any offence against the person other than an assault,[16] the major offences under the Theft Acts 1968 and 1978 and the Criminal Damage Act 1971, sexual offences, and offences involving firearms and explosives.[17] Such conduct would likewise almost always preclude a plaintiff from recovering in a personal injury action should he be injured during its commission; conversely, neither would the Board refuse, nor would *ex turpi causa* preclude, a victim from recovering where the unlawful conduct was a minor regulatory offence.

As in other areas, however, the Board's response may differ from the common law's in some of these cases. In particular,

---

14 CICB (1988) para 36.1.
15 The Statement para 6H. See also Ogden (1984-85) p 230, and CICB (1988) para 51.3.
16 The Board would be unlikely to regard a single conviction under s 47 of the Offences against the Person Act 1861 as being sufficient to justify the denial or reduction of an award (personal communication between Sir Michael Ogden and the author).
17 Broadly speaking, the offences that constitute criminal injuries for the purposes of the statutory Scheme; Criminal Justice Act 1988 s 104.

it is likely that the Board will continue to refuse applications based on injuries inflicted on a victim engaged in unlawful conduct even where the injuries inflicted by the offender were disproportionate to that conduct, and could lead to liability in tort, or even to the conviction of the offender. In its 6th Report, for example, the Board rejected an application from a burglar who had been peppered with shot by the irate householder.[18] The Board's justification for its robust approach has been that the taxpayer should not be called upon to compensate offenders who happen to become victims at the time of their offending. Such cases are distinguishable firstly from the criminal liability of the 'victim's' assailant, since the state properly has a general interest in punishing offences against the person where these cannot be justified as instances of the reasonable use of force in the prevention of crime or in self-defence, and secondly from the civil liability of the assailant, since this will amount to a charge on private, and not public, funds. There is also, no doubt, an element of just deserts in the rejection of such applications.

Although the discussion has centred on criminal conduct, the Scheme is not so restricted. A landlord who persistently fails to comply with his statutory or contractual obligations and is criminally injured by one of his tenants may have his application refused or may receive a reduced award, notwithstanding the criminal liability of the tenant; likewise an employer or co-employee who persists in racial or sexual harassment of an employee who one day, in desperation, assaults him. However, the Board would certainly look askance at such attempts by the tenant and the employee to take the law into their own hands if they, in turn, should come off worse. So, where an applicant attempted to reprimand a schoolboy who had thrown an aerosol can into the road, and then slapped his face when the boy swore at him, the Board reduced his award by 20% when one of the boy's friends who had gathered round the two of them punched the applicant in the face, causing lacerations and subsequent numbness on his right side.[19]

The discussion has also centred only on the unlawful conduct

---

18 CICB (1970) para 5(4). But compare the award of damages in a similar case, *Sharpe v Greenwood* (1983) Times, 30 September. Another example of the Board's approach involved the victim and offender being engaged in an illegal drug transaction at the time of the incident giving rise to the injury, CICB (1984) para 34. Also CICB (1977) para 22 and (1982) para 34.

19 CICB (1988) paras 37.1-37.3.

of the victim. However, as noted earlier the unlawful conduct which the Board may take into account need not be so confined where the victim has died; in this case the applicant's unlawful conduct may equally disentitle him from a full award. Thus where the victim himself initiated a fight in which he was subsequently killed, his dependants, though blameless, may be refused compensation;[20] similarly it will be open to the Board to refuse or reduce an award, for example, to the widow of a murdered terrorist or gang member. A life of crime may therefore preclude compensation both for the victim, or in the event of his death, his dependants.[1] Conversely, though the victim cannot be in any way blamed for his death, the unlawful conduct (at any time) of the applicant may bar or reduce compensation. Suppose, in a dispute between terrorist or other violent gangs, the innocent child of one of the protagonists is killed in a kidnap attempt; even though the applicant had been once acquitted on a charge under the Prevention of Terrorism (Temporary Provisions) Act 1989, his claim might well be refused.[2] Like the Court of Appeal in *Gray v Barr*,[3] the Board is not bound to take an acquittal as indicating that the plaintiff/victim was acting lawfully at the time. In permitting the refusal or reduction of compensation in such a case, the 1990 revision provides no less than did the earlier version of para 6(c), for it would have been open to the Board to reach a similar decision on the basis of the terrorist applicant's 'way of life'. That phrase, however, allowed the Board to take into account *any* aspect of the victim's or the applicant's way of life, whether lawful or unlawful; the 1990 revision does therefore impose one significant limitation here; the conduct must be unlawful.

---

20 CICB (1986) para 27, where the claim by the victim's father was rejected, the victim having injected a fatal quantity of heroin.
1 *Burns v Edman* [1970] 2 QB 541, [1970] 1 All ER 886. Even if the dependant overcame this hurdle, there would be little loss of dependency given the intermittent nature of a burglar's income.
2 Ogden (1984–85) p 231.
3 [1971] 2 QB 554, [1971] 2 All ER 949.

Chapter Four

Criminal Injuries

Applications for compensation under the Scheme are made in respect of 'criminal injuries' as defined by para 4(a)-(c). Broadly speaking, these are personal injuries directly attributable to a crime of violence, which includes arson and poisoning (para 4(a)), to law enforcement activity on the part of the applicant or another (para 4(b)), or to an offence of trespass on a railway (para 4(c)). However, not all criminal injuries qualify for compensation; para 11 excludes, for the most part, injuries arising from road traffic offences, para 6(d) requires that where a person is accidentally injured while engaged in law enforcement activity, he should at the time have been taking an exceptional risk which was justified in the circumstances, and para 4 also imposes conditions as to the place where the injury was sustained. These qualifications will be dealt with in chapter 5. In this chapter we consider first the defining characteristics of the cause of the injury, secondly, what constitutes a personal injury, and thirdly, what is required to establish to the Board's satisfaction that a criminal injury occurred.

A. THE CAUSE OF THE INJURY

(1) A crime of violence

What constitutes a crime of violence is a problem that has long bedevilled the interpretation of para 4(a). It has been the subject of debate by the Board, by the Home Office Reviews of the Scheme, and by the courts. The judicial attention that it has received is in large measure responsible for the inclusion in the 1990 revision of injuries attributable 'to an offence of trespass on a railway', but this revision did not go by any means as far as the changes made in s 109 of the Criminal Justice Act 1988. If brought into force, the Scheme would, for the first time, have defined this phrase and have done so, unusually for a criminal injury compensation scheme, both generically and by reference to specific offences. However, given the importance of the 1990 revisions to the Scheme's procedural arrangements, it was probably thought that the extensive changes in the definition of a crime of violence would be productive of further delays in the processing of applications.

The following sections look firstly at the history of attempts to define what is meant by 'a crime of violence' in para 4(a), and secondly at how it is presently understood. The historical context is a necessary background to an appreciation of para 4(c), which is better dealt with before turning to injuries caused by law enforcement activity.

(a) THE HISTORY OF ATTEMPTS TO DEFINE 'A CRIME OF VIOLENCE'

Initially, the Scheme provided for compensation to be payable for personal injuries directly attributable to the commission of a crime,[1] without, apparently, any serious consideration being given to its potential application to regulatory offences. It was not surprising, therefore, that from the outset the Board experienced considerable difficulty in delimiting the scope of the Scheme, and it quickly requested reconsideration 'with a view to defining more precisely the type of criminal offence it is intended that the Scheme should cover.'[2] Justifying the amendment made in 1969, to 'crime of violence', the Board, reflecting the Scheme's sponsors' view that it should be confined to 'real' crimes, observed that the Scheme 'was plainly never intended to permit an application to the Board instead of an action for breach of the statutory duty imposed by the Factory Acts.'[3]

It might be thought odd that the Scheme does not define 'a crime of violence',[4] but given that the vast majority of applicants under this heading could be predicted to have sustained their injuries as the result of the commission of undisputable examples of such offences, there may have seemed little point in

---

1 CICB 3rd Report (1967, Cmnd 3427) para 7.
2 Ibid, para 8.
3 CICB 6th Report (1970, Cmnd 4494) para 7. The issue continued to pose difficulties however: CICB 10th Report (1974, Cmnd 5791) para 8(2), and 11th Report (1975, Cmnd 6291) para 7(1).
4 See Watkins LJ in *R v Criminal Injuries Compensation Board, ex p Webb* [1986] QB 184 at 192, DC.

endeavouring to do what many, including the Scheme's sponsors and subsequent Home Office Working Parties, have found to be a difficult exercise.[5] At all events, the issue was not directly confronted until *R v Criminal Injuries Compensation Board, ex p Clowes* in 1977.[6] There a policeman was injured in an explosion caused by the build up of gas escaping from a main which had been broken open by a suicide who had gassed himself. The Board rejected his application on two grounds, that the deceased had not committed a crime of violence, and that the applicant's injuries were not in any event directly attributable to any crime that the deceased had committed. As to the first point, the Board decided that if there were a crime of violence, it was a crime against property, for example s 2 of the Explosive Substances Act 1883 (maliciously causing an explosion likely to endanger life or property),[7] and being such an offence, it did not fall within para 4: 'to come within the terms of the Scheme, the crime must be one which concerned violence to the person rather than violence to property.'[8] Second, even if the facts of the applicant's injury could be regarded as being within the scope of an offence against the person, for example, s 20 or s 23 of the Offences against the Person Act 1861,[9] the Board concluded that the deceased had not formed, prior to his death, the requisite fault element of either of them.

By a majority, the Divisional Court took the view that the Board should have considered s 1(2) of the Criminal Damage Act 1971, which provides that it is an offence, without lawful excuse, to damage or destroy property being reckless as to whether the life of another would thereby be endangered. This failure was sufficient in the majority's judgment to allow the application for *certiorari* to go. The Court agreed with the Board's view that the expression 'a crime of violence' connoted violence to a person; but this, it held, was not confined to offences against the person. Where an offence against property involved violence

---

5 Home Office *Review of the Criminal Injuries Compensation Scheme: Report of an Interdepartmental Working Party* (1978) paras 5.11-5.16, Home Office *Criminal Injuries Compensation: A Statutory Scheme* (1986) para 4.6. See also Criminal Law Revision Committee Offences Against the Person (1980, Cmnd 7844) para 149, and P Duff 'Criminal injuries and "violent" crime' [1987] Crim LR 219-230.

6 [1977] 3 All ER 854, [1977] 1 WLR 1353.

7 There is also a reference to s 20 of the Gas Act 1972, but this must be an error as that refers to loans made to the British Gas Corporation by the Secretary of State.

8 CICB 12th Report (1976, Cmnd 6656) para 5(2).

9 Section 23: maliciously causing to be administered a noxious thing.

in the sense that its consequences, as opposed to its definition, involved a violent injury being caused to another, then it would fall within the Scheme, provided that the offender had, or could be inferred to have had, the requisite fault element. Thus, Eveleigh J thought that the phrase meant 'personal injury directly attributable to that kind of deliberate criminal activity in which anyone would say that the probability of injury was obvious'.[10] Lord Widgery CJ, dissenting, preferred the Board's approach. This he thought more closely gave effect to the purpose of the Scheme, which he took to compensate for acts of criminal violence directed against the person. He expressly refused any attempt to define the phrase 'crime of violence' beyond commenting that the Board's submission, that it 'should mean a crime of which violence is an essential ingredient', was 'a very neat and tidy package into which to put this problem.'[11] His Lordship instead emphasised that the question was 'very much a jury point', meaning in this context (there being no jury) that whether a particular crime is a crime of violence is a question of fact.[12]

The meaning of the phrase was later reconsidered in connection with applications for compensation made by train drivers for the psychiatric illnesses they had sustained when witnessing suicides on railway lines. This is a matter of some significance. In 1981, when such an application was first considered by the Divisional Court in *R v Criminal Injuries Compensation Board, ex p Parsons*,[13] 219 people committed suicide by jumping in front of a moving train or lying down on the track, and another 36 were severely injured in suicide attempts. By 1985 the number

---

10 [1977] 3 All ER 854 at 858. His Lordship instanced murder as the most well known crime of violence; it remains so notwithstanding that no external force can be discerned in its commission. It is a crime of violence because, eg, when poisoned or asphyxiated by gas, a person suffers death 'by violence to the human system', id. As a medical condition, this may be so, but the fact that the Scheme from its inception specified poisoning as a victimising event suggests that its draftsman did have in mind as crimes of violence, those crimes that involve violence in their execution, and not merely in their consequences. See also Wien J at 862.

11 [1977] 3 All ER 854 at 864.

12 When reconsidered by the Board, it concluded that notwithstanding that the suicide had been a gas fitter, he had not been reckless when he broke open the main. The Board was using the subjective test of recklessness overruled by the House of Lords in *Metropolitan Police Comr v Caldwell* [1982] AC 341, sub nom *R v Caldwell* [1981] 1 All ER 961. A commentator in [1982] Crim LR 299 observes that had this been the law then, the 'obvious risk' test laid down by Lord Diplock would have yielded the conclusion that the gas fitter was reckless.

13 (1981) Times, 22 May, Lexis DC/145/81.

of deaths was 390,[14] and at the time that the test case, *R v Criminal Injuries Compensation Board, ex p Webb*,[15] was being heard by the Court of Appeal, the Board was holding some 250 applications arising from such incidents.

The issue considered in *Ex p Parsons* was whether the injuries sustained in cases such as these were 'directly attributable' to the commission of a crime of violence. There the applicant stopped his train when he saw a decapitated corpse by the railway line; it transpired that the deceased had committed suicide some time earlier. The Board conceded that when he had trespassed on the railway track,[16] he committed a crime of violence, being s 34 of the Offences against the Person Act 1861:

'Whosoever, by any unlawful act, or by any wilful omission or neglect, shall endanger or cause to be endangered the safety of any person conveyed or being in or upon a railway . . . shall be guilty of a [misdemeanour] . . .'

This concession was probably attributable in part to the decision in *Ex p Clowes*,[17] but judging from the observations of the Divisional Court in *Ex p Webb*,[18] was more substantially due to the House of Lords' decision in *Metropolitan Police Comr v Caldwell*[19] as to the meaning of recklessness. After quoting the Statement which appeared in the Board's 19th Report, which itself quotes Lord Diplock's definition in *Caldwell*: 'a person is reckless if he does an act which in fact creates an obvious risk of injury to other people and, when he does that act he either has not given any thought to the possibility of there being any such risk, or has recognised that there was such risk involved and has nevertheless gone on to do the act',[20] Watkins LJ said:

'When those interpretations [ie, as contained in the Statement] are examined alongside the provisions of s 34 it becomes, perhaps, less surprising that cases such as those before us were regarded for so long by the Board as falling within the scheme. A man who deliberately lies upon a railway line, or walks upon it when a train is approaching, not only invites violent injury or death for himself, but also exposes the passengers of the train to the risk of violent

14 489 HL Official Report (5th series) col 805 (2 November 1987).
15 [1987] QB 74 at 77, CA.
16 CICB 17th Report (1981, Cmnd 8401) para 21.
17 Op cit.
18 [1986] QB 184.
19 [1982] AC 341, sub nom *R v Caldwell* [1981] 1 All ER 961.
20 Ibid, p 354.

injury. Thus the former practice of the Board may be explicable, not on the basis that an offence under section 34 is by definition a "crime of violence", but on the basis that the particular criminal offences under s 34 . . . were carried out in an undeniably violent manner; that is to say, in a manner which involved not only the certainty of violent injury or death for the criminal, but the danger of violent injury for others.'[1]

The violent injury for others would be occasioned by the driver braking suddenly, causing the passengers to fall against each other or against the compartment's fittings. The concession that was made in respect of the cause of the applicant's psychiatric illness in *Ex p Parsons* was however questioned by Glidewell J who, while acknowledging that he did not have to decide the point, thought that it was stretching the phraseology a little to describe an offence under s 34 as a crime of violence.[2] The Court of Appeal would not be drawn into obiter remarks on the matter, but Cumming Bruce LJ's repetition of Glidewell J's misgivings about *Ex p Clowes* encouraged the Board that its revised position was arguably the correct one.[3] Accordingly, the Board refused the claims dealt with in *Ex p Webb*,[4] and the issue thus came to be considered on an application, supported by ASLEF, for judicial review.

After reviewing the history of the Scheme, the Divisional Court rejected the applicants' argument, that 'in deciding whether a crime is a crime of violence what matters is the impact on the victim, not the intent of the offender', preferring the Board's submission, that a crime of violence is 'one where the definition of the crime itself involves either direct infliction of force on the victim, or at least a hostile act directed towards the victim or class of victims.'[5] This too was the conclusion reached by the Court of Appeal, which added that while this interpretation was wider than that suggested by Lord Widgery CJ in his dissenting judgment in *Ex p Clowes*,[6] the second clause in

1 [1986] QB 184 at 196.
2 His Lordship's views on this matter are dealt with by Watkins LJ in the Divisional Court's judgment in *Ex p Webb*, ibid, p 193. See also Home Office (1986) para 4.4.
3 (1982) Times, 25 November. The reservations expressed by Glidewell J in the Divisional Court encouraged the Board to argue the matter before the Court of Appeal in *ex p Parsons* but without success, CICB 20th Report (1984, Cmnd 9399) para 16.
4 CICB 19th Report (1983, Cmnd 9093) para 17.
5 [1986] QB 184 at 195.
6 Op cit.

particular was 'necessary to bring within the Scheme conduct amounting to causing grievous bodily harm even though no violence is used by the offender',[7] such as that in *R v Martin*[8] where the accused by unlawful conduct caused panic among a crowd of people as the result of which a number were injured.

On one matter the Court of Appeal disagreed with the lower court. Concluding that it was 'highly unsatisfactory' that there was no definition, nor even a reasoned explanation of what constituted a crime of violence for the purposes of the Scheme, the Divisional Court offered the following definition: 'any crime in respect of which the prosecution must prove as one of its ingredients that the defendant unlawfully and intentionally, or recklessly, inflicted or threatened to inflict personal injury upon another.'[9] While accepting the underlying distinction, that it is for the Board to decide 'whether unlawful conduct because of its nature, not its consequence, amounts to a crime of violence', Lawton LJ did not however think it prudent to attempt a definition, preferring Lord Widgery's view, that the question is essentially one of fact for the Board.[10]

The Home Office Working Party preferred the Divisional Court's approach, accepting 'the need for a clear definition of a crime of violence'[11] as a way of indicating that the Scheme 'should not be regarded as underwriting any injury loosely connected with a breach of the criminal law.'[12] Like its predecessors, the Working Party quickly found that the task was easier stated than accomplished. A list, to or from which offences could be added or removed by statutory instrument, would suffer from the problem both of exclusivity (eliminating meritorious and otherwise eligible applicants) and of inclusivity (arousing false expectations by specifying offences that were 'too wide' for

---

7 [1987] QB 74 at 79.
8 (1881) 8 QBD 54, CCR.
9 [1986] QB 184 at 198.
10 [1987] QB 74 at 79-80.
11 Home Office (1986) para 4.4.
12 Ibid, para 4.5, rejecting the proposal advanced by JUSTICE that any criminal offence should be covered, as this would lead to a 'vast and unjustifiable extension' of the Scheme into such areas as industrial injuries and health and safety at work, ibid, para 4.2. Think of the cost! The idea of using a list had been rejected when the Scheme was first introduced as being too restrictive, 694 HC Official Report (5th series) col 1131 (5 May 1964), and was considered by the 1978 Working Party to be impracticable and unhelpful, op cit, para 5.11.

the Scheme's purpose).[13] The Working Party was clearly of the view that 'a crime of violence' should include an offence which was intended to cause death or personal injury, and one which caused the death or injury of any person, the offender being reckless as to whether death or injury was caused. Such a formulation would exclude the psychiatric injuries sustained by train drivers in the railway suicide cases, but the government gave way, specifically adding to the list of offences in s 109(1), trespass on a railway, now in turn incorporated as para 4(c) of the non-statutory Scheme.

(b)   THE CONSTITUENT ELEMENTS OF A CRIME OF VIOLENCE

There is, as indicated, no definition in the Scheme of what is meant in para 4(a) by the phrase, 'a crime of violence'. However, the definition given in s 109(1)(a)(ii) of the 1988 Act can be taken as capturing the essence of the Board's approach. A personal injury is a criminal injury when it is directly attributable to conduct constituting an offence which requires proof of intent to cause death or personal injury or recklessness as to whether death or personal injury is caused. An attempt to commit a crime of violence is also a 'crime of violence' for the purpose of para 4(a).

(i)   The external elements of a crime of violence

Personal injuries are not criminal injuries even though they are caused by a breach of rules under which the 'offender' may be punished, if that breach cannot be construed as constituting the external elements of a crime of violence. If a prison officer strains his back trying to carry a heavy and unco-operative prisoner, there is no act or omission on the part of the prisoner that can render this a criminal injury, no matter how much he may desire the officer to hurt himself in the process, and irrespective of the fact that his refusal to comply with the officer's instruction

---

13 Home Office (1986) para 4.6. Compare the position in Northern Ireland, whose provisions employ only a generic definition, Criminal Injuries (Compensation) (NI) Order 1988 article 2(2). See D Greer *Compensation for Criminal Injuries to Persons in Northern Ireland* (2nd edn 1990, SLS Legal Publications, Belfast). Because it thought it would 'assist in eliminating uncertainty at the borders of the scheme', the government specified in s 109(3) of the Criminal Justice Act 1988 offences from which criminal injuries could arise. The debates that accompanied these provisions are ample evidence of the difficulties identified by the Working Party, 489 HL Official Report (5th series) cols 784-793 (2 November 1987).

to move was itself a breach of the Prison Rules.[14] These external elements must also by definition be attributable to human action or inaction. The Board regularly receives applications arising from injuries caused by dog bites.[15] These, like injuries inflicted by other animals, may constitute offences if the owner intended them to be caused. Where he was reckless as to whether personal injury was caused, a jury would have to be meticulously directed both as to the external and internal elements of the offence charged, as well as to causation.[16]

Conduct may prima facie constitute the external elements of a crime of violence, but be rendered lawful by the consent of the applicant, as where a professional escapologist sustained injury when he was unable to free himself from the rope with which two volunteers from the audience, one a climber and the other himself an escapologist, had bound him.[17] Another example, though rather more bizarre, is recorded in the Board's 1988 Report. The victim allowed the offender, who was completely unqualified as a doctor, to perform 'surgical' operations upon his penis, including the removal of part of the foreskin. The victim consented, it appears, because of the offender's plausible manner and his collection of surgical instruments. On a later occasion he consented to being placed under a general anaesthetic. The offender was ultimately convicted of administering an overpowering drug with intent to assault; but the victim's application was disallowed because 'what was done was done with his consent'.[18] Comment is speculative in the absence of a full statement of the circumstances, but even on the assumption that it was freely given, a victim's consent to bodily harm does not in general relieve the person inflicting it of criminal liability.[19] Irrespective of the criminal liability of the person causing the harm, however, it would always be open to the Board to deny or reduce compensation by the application of para 6(c), for example if the injury were sustained as the result of sado-masochistic practices.

---

14 *R v Criminal Injuries Compensation Board, ex p Penny* [1982] Crim LR 298, DC; upheld on appeal (18 November 1982, unreported), decision of the Court of Appeal (Lord Lane CJ).
15 CICB 15th Report (1979, Cmnd 7752) para 18, and 25th Report (1989, Cm 900) paras 16.5-16.6.
16 *R v Dume* (1986) Times, 16 October, CA. CICB 18th Report (1982, Cmnd 8752) para 30, and 21st Report (1985, Cmnd 9684) para 43.
17 CICB (1989) paras 16.7-16.9.
18 CICB 24th Report (1988, Cm 536) paras 18.1-18.4.
19 J Smith and B Hogan *Criminal Law* (1988, 6th edn, Butterworths) pp 383-386.

Personal injuries directly attributable to the commission of a 'crime of violence' do not obviously include those attributable to crimes against property, notwithstanding that, in Eveleigh J's phrase in *Ex p Clowes*, they cause 'violence to the human system'.[20] A person who suffers a psychiatric illness upon returning from holiday to discover that his house has been criminally damaged or that his possessions have been stolen does not sustain a criminal injury.[1] Likewise, no compensation could be awarded on the following facts. Upon her arrival at work, the applicant found the alarm bells ringing. The policeman who arrived in answer to her call asked her to accompany him onto the premises. In one room they found a man, later convicted of burglary, hiding in the roof space, behind some ceiling tiles. As the first tile was removed, his leg fell limply down, causing the applicant to believe that there was a dead body there. Subsequently she developed alopecia, a condition often diagnosed as being induced by shock.[2]

Some crimes against property involve violence, for example, an offence under s 2 of the Explosive Substances Act 1883 or under s 1(2) of the Criminal Damage Act 1971; but these can constitute crimes of violence for the purpose of para 4(a) precisely because their definition includes the possibility of death being caused to another. If the conduct of the suicide in *Ex p Clowes* could, when he broke open the gas main in order to gas himself, be construed (on a *Caldwell* test) as recklessness as to whether the life of another would be endangered, the injured policeman would have sustained a criminal injury. It would be otherwise if the offence committed were under s 1(1) of the 1971 Act, as this is confined to the destruction of or damage to property. Where criminal damage under s 1(1) is caused by fire, it will be charged as arson, which is specifically included in para 4(a). Thus, to destroy a person's property by fire may constitute a criminal injury if that causes personal injury, but where the destruction is by other means, though it has the same effect, it will not be. Suppose a defendant, angered by some aspect of the victim's behaviour, drives a JCB into his front garden, knocking down the front wall and destroying his garden. This is witnessed by the victim standing at his front door, but so long as the defendant makes no attempt to assault the victim (for example, by driving the JCB at him), there is no crime of violence which could support an application should the victim suffer nervous shock.

---

20 Op cit, p 858.
1 The Statement, para 4B2.
2 CICB (1985) para 21.

It is important in such cases to be clear as to what aspect of the offender's conduct may suggest an intention to cause death or personal injury, or recklessness as to either of these. In *R v Steer*,[3] the offender shot at the victim through the windows of his house, breaking them. The victim was physically unhurt. The House of Lords dismissed the appeal from the Court of Appeal, which had allowed an appeal against a conviction under s 1(2) of the Criminal Damage Act 1971. The danger posed to the victim came not from any damage to the property, but from the bullets being discharged from the offender's gun; s 1(2) requires that it is by the damage to the property that another's life is endangered. Thus if the victim in this case had suffered harm to his mental condition as a consequence of the shock of being shot at, he would have sustained a criminal injury not because the offender had intended to endanger his life or had been reckless as to whether or not it was endangered in the terms of s 1(2) of the Criminal Damage Act, but because he had committed some other crime of violence, such as an attempt to inflict grievous bodily harm.

The absence of any definition of 'crime of violence' from the Scheme has necessitated the specific inclusion of arson and poisoning as criminal injuries in para 4(a), since these are both offences that can be committed without violence being directed against an individual, though their fault elements do contemplate death or personal injury being caused to another.[4] Although the point never appears to have arisen and although, according to its guidelines on child abuse, the Board has no doubt about the matter, there must be some doubt as to whether rape is a crime of violence within para 4(a). Clearly rape can be committed violently, but such cases pose no difficulty for the Scheme, since the infliction of force by the rapist will constitute an offence under ss 18 or 20 of the Offences against the Person Act 1861. But where the rapist obtains the woman's consent by fraud, it is difficult to see how the unquestionably illegal act is a crime of violence. The 1988 Act is of interest here. It creates two definitions of 'criminal injury'. One, by s 109(1)(a)(ii), includes conduct constituting 'an offence which requires proof of intent to cause death or personal injury or recklessness as to whether

---

3 [1988] AC 111, [1987] 2 All ER 833.
4 There has been some doubt whether the fault element in s 23 of the Offences against the Person Act 1861 requires an intention to cause death or serious injury, Smith and Hogan (1988) pp 404-405, Criminal Law Revision Committee, *Offences against the Person* (1980, Cmnd 7844) paras 184-191.

death or personal injury is caused'. The other is a list of specified offences. This list includes, by s 109(3)(a), rape. It also includes two other offences whose commission need not involve violence, kidnapping and false imprisonment. Although the definition in s 109(1)(a)(ii) is not conterminous with 'crime of violence', the inference is that the draftsman thought it necessary to specify these three offences because they are not, per se, within this category.

(ii) The fault elements of a crime of violence

As the Court of Appeal made clear in *Ex p Webb*, what makes an offence 'a crime of violence' lies not in the impact which it has on the victim, but in its nature. It is not possible to state exhaustively what offences are included in this category; this remains a matter for the Board to determine, but indisputably included are all offences of homicide and offences under ss 18, 20 and 47 of the Offences against the Person Act 1861. These constitute the bulk of criminal injuries dealt with by the Board.[5] Thus, as suggested at the beginning of this section, a crime of violence is typified by an offence whose fault elements include any one of an intention to cause death or personal injury or recklessness as to whether death or personal injury is caused.

Recklessness is the minimum level of fault acceptable to the Board. This is clear from the Statement, which incorporates Lord Diplock's definition in *Caldwell*, and expressly states that 'it is not enough for the person who caused the injury to have acted very carelessly.'[6] Thus, though an injury is clearly consistent with conduct constituting the external elements of an offence such as s 20 or s 47 of the Offences against the Person Act 1861, for example, being struck by a javelin thrown during a school sports day,[7] or being knocked over by another skater and breaking one's leg on the ice,[8] these will not constitute criminal injuries if they were only negligently inflicted. So far as the Board relies on the *Caldwell* test, what constitutes a crime of violence will also reflect the law's uncertainties in this area,[9] but what makes the Board's task more difficult is that it often has to deal with applications in which no conviction for an offence requiring

5 Home Office (1986) para 4.3
6 The Statement, para 4D.
7 CICB (1985) para 20.
8 CICB 22nd Report (1986, Cm 42) para 16.
9 Smith and Hogan (1988) pp 61-69. See further *DPP v K (a minor)* [1990] 1 All ER 331 and *R v Spratt* [1990] 1 WLR 1073, CA.

proof of the fault elements identified above has been reached. In such cases the Board has to determine whether recklessness can be inferred from the factual circumstances disclosed in the application and in the police report of the incident. We return to this point in the discussion on proof in a later section, but one example may be given here as an illustration of this difficulty. An application was brought on behalf of an eight year old girl who had developed foetal alcohol syndrome and cerebral palsy as the result of her mother's alcohol abuse during pregnancy. Such conduct could amount to a crime of violence for example if it were the mother's intention to harm the child while in the womb; but the single member concluded that no fault element consistent with such an offence could be inferred from the facts.[10]

As consent may render lawful conduct that prima facie constitutes the external elements of an offence, so the 'offender's' belief that he is entitled to use reasonable force in self-defence or to effect an arrest may negative the fault elements. A victim who is injured while being lawfully arrested does not sustain a criminal injury; but the matter is less easy where the person causing the injury was operating under a mistake. Suppose a wholly innocent applicant is mistaken by a store detective for a person whom he has reasonable grounds to suspect is committing theft, and in the struggle between them, as the applicant seeks to break free from what, from his point of view, is an unlawful arrest, he is struck and injured by the detective. In *R v Williams*,[11] the Court of Appeal held that if a defendant were labouring under a mistaken view of the facts, for example that his victim was consenting to the use of force, that it was necessary to defend himself, or that a crime was being committed, then he is entitled to be judged on the facts as he believed them to be. Accordingly the store detective would, assuming that he had reasonable grounds for his suspicion and that his use of force was reasonable, be entitled to be acquitted on a charge arising from the injuries caused to the applicant. Thus there would be no offence upon which to sustain an application. This may seem harsh from the innocent applicant's perspective, but his position is no different from that which obtains in civil law, since an action against the store detective would (leaving aside ss 44-45 of the Offences against the Person Act 1861) fail for the same reason.

However, he may think himself unfairly treated by comparison

10 CICB (1988) paras 16.1-16.4
11 [1987] 3 All ER 411.

with the following outcome, based on the facts of that case. There the victim saw a youth attempt to rob a woman. He gave chase, knocked the youth to the ground and attempted to immoblise him. The offender, who had not witnessed the attempted robbery, came upon the scene. The victim told him that he was a police officer, which was untrue, and that he was arresting the youth. When he failed to produce a warrant card the offender punched him in the face. The offender's conviction under s 47 of the Offences against the Person Act 1861 was quashed for the reasons given above. If para 4(a) were the only class of criminal injury, then the victim would be unable to sustain an application for compensation on these facts, there being no crime of violence. However, assuming that the Board did not regard his pretending to be a policeman as disentitling him under para 6(c), it seems clear that the victim's injury was caused by the apprehension or attempted apprehension of an offender or suspected offender, and it thus would constitute a criminal injury under para 4(b). There is nothing in this paragraph which requires that the injury be caused by conduct constituting an offence, or indeed, even by a human agency.[12] If it is fair that these facts should give rise to a successful application for compensation, whereas the innocent victim injured by the mistaken store detective will fail, then the distinction must lie in the pro-social behaviour of the victim who seeks to enforce the law.

As in the case where the person causing the injury may mistakenly believe he is entitled to use force in self-defence against the victim, or to arrest him, the offender may mistakenly believe the victim to be consenting when he is not. Suppose, for example, a victim such as the wife in *R v Cogan and Leak*[13] were to make an application under the Scheme. There it was held that as the husband's accomplice need only honestly believe that the woman was consenting to sexual intercourse, he would not commit rape despite the fact that he had no reasonable grounds for so believing.[14] On the assumption that rape is a crime of violence, an application under the Scheme would surely succeed, for the Board, like the Court of Appeal's robust confirmation of the husband's conviction for aiding and abetting, would never deny that the victim was indeed raped, whatever the 'rapist's' state of mind. The difference between an application arising on these facts and one arising from the mistaken actions of the store

12 Infra, pp 116–117.
13 [1976] QB 217, [1975] 2 All ER 1059, CA.
14 *DPP v Morgan* [1976] AC 182.

detective is that the rapist's beliefs merely served to excuse him from liability for what remained throughout an unlawful act; the store detective's beliefs however constituted a justification for his actions.

A case in point was decided by the Board in 1987. The victim and the offender had smoked some cannabis together in the house occupied by the victim. Later she was accosted by the offender outside the toilet, but following her protestations, he was ejected by the householder. The offender was later readmitted by him and allowed to sleep in the house in a room separate from the victim's. Two days later she reported to the police that she had been raped, but at his first trial, where the defence was that she consented, the jury could not agree and was dismissed. At the second trial, with the same defence, the offender was acquitted. The victim made a claim which was initially denied because the single member was not satisfied that she had not consented. At the hearing, however, the Board held that the outcome of the two trials was irrelevant, and on the basis of her evidence and that of the householder, made a full award.[15]

(2) An offence of trespass on a railway

Paragraph 4(c) represents the government's concession to the train drivers over the matter of railway suicides. When first published, the Criminal Justice Bill 1986, following the Court of Appeal's decision in *Ex p Webb*,[16] excluded the drivers' injuries from the Scheme. However, under pressure from the railway unions, the government gave way to an Opposition amendment, and the substance of it was included in the 1990 revision of the non-statutory Scheme. A train driver (or any other railway worker or any one else) who suffers nervous shock as a result of coming across the body of a person who had committed suicide by walking or lying on a railway track, or as a result of endeavouring to save such a person, whether successful or not, for example by applying the brakes to the train that he was driving, sustains a criminal injury within para 4(c).

This one item well illustrates the underlying problems of justifying criminal injury compensation schemes. For the drivers' union ASLEF, it was argued that it would be a grave injustice that those who had been completely blameless should receive

15 *Legal Action*, June 1987, p 16.
16 Op cit.

no compensation for the mental and physical pain that could haunt them for the rest of their lives.[17] As an example of special pleading, this applies equally of course to any child born with a physical or mental handicap, to the victims of the fire at Bradford City Football Club ground in 1985 or of the overcrowding at the Sheffield Wednesday ground in 1989, to those who survived the fire at King's Cross underground station in 1987, and so on and so forth. Since there has never been any basis for criminal injury provision other than, as the Home Office Working Party put it, 'a narrow and rather specific one: to reflect the strong public sympathy for the innocent victims of violent crime, who are unlikely to be able to obtain redress against the offender',[18] it is difficult either to draw anything but an arbitrary borderline between one victim and another, or to resist (upon what grounds?) yet another group of victims being included in the Scheme's ambit.[19] As Duff puts it:

'The difficulty is that public sympathy is a crucial element in justifying the Scheme but non-eligible victims may also attract it and there is no other cogent reason which can be given to explain compensating only the victims of "violence".'[20]

Railway suicides are not, of course, the only kind of conduct constituting a trespass on a railway that can cause personal injury. More obvious examples are cases where the offender leaves planks of wood across the track to derail the train, or stands on an embankment at the side of the track and throws stones at the train's windows. However, injuries caused to train drivers or passengers by a person standing on a bridge over the railway and dropping objects onto the train are criminal injuries under para 4(a), not para 4(c).

When the concession was initially made, the Bill was amended so as to extend to offences under s 34 of the Offences against the Person Act 1861. The difficulty with this was that as the fault element of the offence includes negligent conduct, a passenger injured by a suitcase negligently placed in a luggage rack would have sustained a criminal injury. To preclude the possibility of victims of negligence being given 'a specially privileged position if they happen to be railway passengers,'[1]

---

17 Duff (1987) p 229.
18 Home Office (1986) para 4.1.
19 Lord Irvine, 489 HL Official Report, op cit, col 788.
20 Duff (1987) p 229.
 1 489 HL Official Report, op cit, col 788.

the Scheme, like the 1988 Act, refers only to trespass on a railway. On the assumption that trespass can only be committed intentionally,[2] injuries caused by a train driver braking suddenly to avoid hitting a person (perhaps a child) whose presence on the railway was negligent, will not be criminal injuries.[3]

(3) Law enforcement

'Compensation for injury incurred accidentally in attempting to apprehend an offender or prevent an offence (whether or not a crime of violence) has been a feature of the Scheme since it was introduced.'[4] This feature is maintained in the 1990 revision which, by para 4(b), provides that personal injury directly attributable:

'(b) to the apprehension or attempted apprehension of an offender or suspected offender or to the prevention or attempted prevention of an offence or to the giving of help to any constable who is engaged in any such activity'

is a criminal injury. The Scheme further provides by para 6(d) that accidental injuries sustained by the victim in these circumstances will qualify for compensation only where the Board is satisfied that the risk that he was taking when he was injured was an exceptional risk which was justified in all the circumstances.

As the definitions of what constitutes a criminal injury are alternatives, it is quite possible that a victim who sustains a personal injury while trying to apprehend an offender, to prevent an offence, or to assist a constable engaged in one of these activities, will be able to support an application for compensation under this or para 4(a). This is of importance, as it is only in respect of criminal injuries caused by any of the activities mentioned in para 4(b) that the qualification in para 6(d) applies. Thus if in the struggle to apprehend an offender the victim is, for example, stabbed or struck by him, or by his accomplice, his personal injury will have been caused by a crime of violence, and there is no further requirement associated with the law enforcement activity to make it a qualifying injury. If however

2 F Trindade 'Intentional torts: some thoughts on assault and battery' (1982) 2 Oxford J Legal Studies 211–237.
3 *Ex p Webb* [1987] QB 74 at 79, CA.
4 Home Office (1986) para 6.8.

the injury is 'accidental', for example where the victim trips and falls while trying to restrain or to pursue the offender, it may still be a criminal injury though there is no crime of violence, but it will not be a qualifying injury unless the applicant meets the exceptional risk condition. The following paragraphs consider the interpretation of para 4(b); the exceptional risk qualification is discussed in chapter 5.

Most of the small number of applications based on para 4(b) are, not surprisingly, made by policemen injured on duty; in 1987-88 there were 1,930 (6.6% of resolved cases).[5] The Report does not give the number made by private citizens, but in 1986-87 there were 258 applications made by citizens injured while attempting to apprehend an offender and a further 24 applications made by those injured while assisting the police.[6] Of the total of 29,605 applications resolved that year, 2,220 fell under the law enforcement category. The number of applications made by policemen has nearly doubled since the figure of 1,017 in 1983-84,[7] largely as the result of such events as the riots in Toxteth and Brixton, and the public disorder that accompanied the miners' strike.

Three matters which have posed some difficulty require attention. These are, the significance of the words 'apprehension' and 'offender', and of the words 'the prevention of an offence'.

(a)   THE *APPREHENSION* OR ATTEMPTED *APPREHENSION* OF AN OFFENDER

Prior to the 1979-80 changes to the Scheme, this aspect of law enforcement was described as the 'arrest or attempted arrest' of an offender or suspected offender. The change was made in response to the Divisional Court's decision in *R v Criminal Injuries Compensation Board, ex p Carr*,[8] where the applicant witnessed a motor cycle collision and was injured while trying to prevent one of the motor cyclists from leaving the scene of the accident. With 'extreme reluctance',[9] the Board held that there could be no attempted arrest, since the applicant had no power of arrest in the circumstances, and that there was no attempt

5 CICB (1988) para 7.1. No figures are given in the Report for 1988-89.
6 CICB 23rd Report (1987, Cm 265) para 8.
7 The number of policemen compensated under this provision from 1976–77 to 1987–88 is: 2,930, 2,607, 3,065, 2,807 (the year the change was introduced), 2,652, 1,974, 1,494, 1,017, 1,755, 1,948 and 1,930.
8 [1981] RTR 122.
9 Donaldson LJ's observation, ibid, p 124.

to prevent the commission of a crime (namely, failure to stop after an accident contrary to s 25 of the Road Traffic Act 1972) since the offence had been committed when the motor cyclist sought to leave the scene and before the applicant unsuccessfully chased after him.[10] The Divisional Court held that albeit the motor cyclist had intended to leave the scene of the accident and had started to do so, he had not completed that process when the applicant began his pursuit, and thus the motor cyclist had not completed the offence under s 25 at the time when the applicant was injured. When reconsidered by the Board, an award was made, presumably on the basis that the applicant was injured while attempting to prevent the commission of a crime;[11] but the Scheme was also amended so as to make it clear that even if the Divisional Court had upheld the Board's view as to when the offence of failure to stop was completed, the applicant would still have sustained his injuries while attempting to apprehend an offender.[12]

'Apprehension', then, has no specifically legal connotation: an applicant may, for the purposes of the Scheme apprehend or attempt to apprehend an offender or suspected offender although he has no power to arrest or detain that person. The Statement also makes it clear that an 'apprehension' can begin when a police officer is first told of an offence or suspected offence; neither does it cease merely because the offender has been arrested or taken into custody.[13]

(b)   AN *OFFENDER* OR SUSPECTED *OFFENDER*

In *R v Criminal Injuries Compensation Board, ex p Lawton*,[14] the question arose whether an application could be sustained where the offender, at the time when the applicant was injured trying to apprehend him, had in fact ceased to be detained as having committed an offence, but was instead being detained under different statutory powers. In this case the Board refused an application by a policeman who had accidentally injured his back when he jumped through a police station window to prevent the escape of a man being detained under the emergency provisions of the Mental Health Act 1959. The detainee had initially been brought in on suspicion of theft, but had

10 CICB 13th Report (1977, Cmnd 7022) paras 12-13.
11 CICB (1981) para 20(1).
12 The Statement, para 4F.4.
13 Ibid, paras 4F.1-3.
14 [1972] 3 All ER 582, [1972] 1 WLR 1589.

subsequently been identified as a former in-patient at a mental hospital, and was consequently detained with a view to his being seen by a doctor and re-admitted to hospital. The Board took the view that as at the material time the detainee was being held under non-criminal regulations, he committed no offence by attempting to escape custody and was thus not an offender or suspected offender.[15] The Divisional Court decided however that the initiation by the police of procedures under the Mental Health Act did not terminate the original ground for the man's detention, and thus

'where, as here, the police officer had authority . . . to act in one of two capacities, it seems to me to be wholly unreal and quite unnecessary to pause and consider whether at the moment when he jumped through the window he had in mind one or the other. I think if it were necessary to make fine distinctions of that kind we should be introducing an unduly legalistic note into this essentially informal procedure. It is quite impossible to suppose that any officer in his situation would even apply his mind to the situation as to which of his hats he was wearing or which authority he was exercising.'[16]

The court accepted the Board's argument that an injury would not be compensable where the only hat the policeman was wearing meant that the person he was attempting to place into custody was not in law an offender or suspected offender. However, as is clear from Widgery LJ's dictum, where there is a multiplicity of hats, one of which includes the possibility that there was an offender or suspected offender, then the injuries he sustains will constitute criminal injuries.

(c) THE *PREVENTION OF AN OFFENCE*

A third difficulty was considered in *R v Criminal Injuries Compensation Board, ex p Ince*.[17] This was whether an application could succeed under the heading, 'prevention of crime', if at the time when the applicant was injured in trying to prevent it, there was actually no crime being, or about to be, committed. There, it will be recalled, the applicant's husband, who was on duty in a police car, was killed when, answering a general alarm, he shot a set of traffic lights and was killed

15 Ibid, p 584.
16 Id, per Widgery LJ.
17 [1973] 3 All ER 808, [1973] 1 WLR 1334.

in a collision with another police car crossing with the lights. Subsequently it was discovered that this was a false alarm. Beside its decision that he was guilty of contributory negligence, the Board also held that the deceased was not at the material time actually engaged in the prevention of a crime. Both the Divisional Court and the Court of Appeal held that this second decision, like the first, was in error.[18]

The Court of Appeal held that it was unduly restrictive to interpret the relevant words of the Scheme as implying that a precondition of compensation was that an offence must have been committed, for, as Lord Denning MR said:

> 'If it has been *prevented*, it never has been committed, and never will be committed. The words must cover an offence which it is anticipated *may* be committed unless prevented.'[19]

Neither, the court held, would it matter if the offence never could be committed because the circumstances in reality did not disclose an offence, provided that the policeman believed that they could. If, as was the case in *Ex p Ince*, the policeman was acting in response to a false alarm, his injury would be a criminal injury provided that he was actually engaged in preventing an offence, albeit one about whose existence he was mistaken:

> 'His claim to compensation should be tested in the light of the situation as it appeared to him at the time, and his claim or rather his widow's claim, should not be taken away by the mere circumstance that the message was afterwards discovered to be a mistake.'[20]

Had the alarm been genuine, then the applicant would on Lord Denning's interpretation have been compensable, and of course it would therefore be capricious to deny such an application where the information upon which the policeman acted was erroneous.

Paragraph 4(b) is generally intended to treat as criminal injuries personal injuries sustained by policemen or citizens while engaged in law enforcement activity, notwithstanding that the injury is not caused by a crime of violence. It is also important to note that the offence to which the apprehension, prevention or assistance is related, can be *any* criminal offence, even one triable only summarily. The three decisions just discussed show

18 Supra, p 83.
19 [1973] 3 All ER 808 at 814.
20 Ibid, p 812.

that such 'accidental' injuries may be criminal injuries notwithstanding that the victim has no power of arrest or that he was mistaken about the existence of an offence, and that the offender was escaping a custody which was not exclusively justified by reference to his suspected or proven offending. These decisions stand in contrast to the liability that a citizen bears should he arrest or attempt to arrest someone he has reasonable grounds for suspecting has committed an arrestable offence, no such offence having been committed. Personal injury sustained in such circumstances is apparently a criminal injury (though it would only be a qualifying injury if he were taking an exceptional risk); but not complying with s 24(5) of the Police and Criminal Evidence Act 1984, the arrest is unlawful, and the citizen will also be liable in an action for false imprisonment brought by the person he arrested.

B. THE DEFINITION OF PERSONAL INJURY

The Scheme contains no definition of 'personal injury'; however, as it is, unless otherwise stated, to be interpreted according to common law principles, this phrase will cover any actionable personal injury. The definition given in s 109(1) of the 1988 Act, that it includes 'any disease, any harm to a person's physical or mental condition and pregnancy', captures the scope of the phrase as interpreted by the Board.

(1) Physical injury

The vast majority of applications to the Board have involved physical injuries to the person,[1] and call for little further comment. Most of these injuries will have been occasioned directly by the offender inflicting them with a weapon or an object used for the purpose — often bottles and drinking glasses[2] — or with his fists, head or feet. In some instances the injury may be indirect, for example where victims injure themselves while making an escape. A common instance is being struck by a vehicle when running into the road,[3] perhaps to avoid the threat of rape.[4]

1 T Newburn *The Settlement of Claims at the Criminal Injuries Compensation Board* (1989, Home Office Research Study 112) pp 10-11.
2 Times, 16 March 1990.
3 CICB (1989) para 25.9 and (1987) para 51. See D Elliott 'Frightening a person into injuring himself' [1974] Crim LR 15-25.
4 CICB (1988) para 10.1.

In an unusual application the Board awarded compensation to a young and simple girl who had been forced into prostitution by threats of violence.[5] Personal injury may also be sustained where, though there is no immediate physical injury arising from the victimising event, the victim subsequently suffers such injury. For example, in *R v Dawson*, the victim was working at the cash till in a petrol station when he was threatened with a shotgun and robbed.[6] The victim had a weak heart and a short while later suffered a heart attack and died. Assuming this to be directly attributable to the crime of violence, the victim's death was a criminal injury.[7] The Board's 1984 Report records a rare instance of an award being made in respect of injuries sustained by a child in the womb following an attack upon its mother, who was also compensable for her own injuries.[8] A woman who contracts a venereal disease or becomes HIV positive as a result of rape will suffer a personal injury even if no other physical harm is caused to her, and any resulting pregnancy will likewise constitute a criminal injury, though no compensation is payable for the maintenance of the child when born.[9]

A victim who suffers any disease, pregnancy or harm to his physical condition as the result of a victimising event as defined by para 4 may also suffer mental distress in consequence. Examples recorded in recent Board Reports include a woman's acute depression consequent upon the knowledge that following her rape she is now pregnant with the offender's child or has contracted AIDS,[10] the anxiety suffered by the elderly following a physical or sexual attack,[11] and the psycho-sexual damage caused to a child sexually abused by a close relative.[12] The compensation payable for these psychological effects will be 'but another part of the scrambled strands composing the conventional item of pain and suffering',[13] the criminal injury upon which the application is based being the disease, the pregnancy or the harm to the victim's physical condition directly attributable to the victimising event.

---

5 CICB (1983) p 20.
6 (1985) 81 Cr App Rep 150, CA.
7 CICB (1987) paras 43 and 44. See also *R v Watson* [1989] 2 All ER 865, [1989] 1 WLR 684, CA.
8 CICB (1984) para 21.
9 Infra, p 149.
10 CICB (1988) paras 21.2-21.3 and 22.
11 Ibid, paras 21.1, 26-27 and 44-45.
12 Ibid, paras 20, 24-25.
13 J Fleming *The Law of Torts* (1987, 7th edn, Law Book Co) p 145.

(2) Mental injury

The 1986 Working Party was of the view that over the years the Scheme had come to include injuries that it was not originally intended to cover. In the case of injuries caused by nervous shock, it recommended that the terms of the Scheme should 'restrict compensation to those persons actually present at the scene of a crime of violence and put in fear of immediate physical injury to themselves or another person.'[14] This was given effect in an earlier version of the Criminal Justice Bill 1987, providing that if a criminal injury were caused by shock, it would not be a qualifying injury unless the two requirements of presence and fear were simultaneously met. This caused considerable controversy, in part because the clause excluded train drivers who came upon the aftermath of a suicide; but although the Bill was amended so that the requirements of fear and presence became alternatives,[15] neither a rescuer nor a bystander coming upon the aftermath of a victimising event as defined in s 109(1) of the 1988 Act would have sustained a criminal injury where he suffered harm to his mental condition, unless he was put in fear for himself or another, since by definition he was not present when the conduct or activity occurred.

A second feature of the 1987 Bill as initially drafted, was that it sought to draw a distinction between the normal emotions of grief and distress that a person may experience when witnessing death or injury to a relative, which are not compensable at common law, and the psychiatric illness that such events may cause, which are.[16] The Working Party specifically drew on Lord Bridge's remarks in *McLoughlin v O'Brian* as the basis upon which the Act would distinguish compensable from non-compensable harm to a person's mental condition:

'The common law gives no damages for the emotional distress which any normal person experiences when someone he loves is killed or injured. Anxiety and depression are normal human emotions. Yet an anxiety neurosis or a reactive depression may be recognisable psychiatric illnesses, with or without psychosomatic symptoms. So, the first hurdle which a plaintiff claiming damages of the kind in

14 Home Office (1986) para 4.11.
15 Section 109(2). See 490 HL Official Report, op cit, col 433.
16 See H Teff 'Liability for negligently inflicted nervous shock' (1983) 99 Law Quarterly R 100-112, F Trindade 'The principles governing the recovery of damages for negligently inflicted nervous shock' (1986) 45 Cambridge LJ 476-500.

question must surmount is to establish that he is suffering not merely grief, distress or any other normal emotion, but a positive psychiatric illness.'[17]

The government was also emphatic that the Scheme should reflect this distinction, and gave effect to it by providing that where a criminal injury caused by shock consisted of harm to a person's mental condition, it would only be a qualifying injury if it amounted to a 'psychiatric illness'.[18] However, this too prompted considerable disquiet, and the government ultimately withdrew the clause, thus leaving the Board to determine what constitutes harm to a person's mental condition, as distinct from the normal emotions of grief or distress.[19] This will be a matter of medical evidence with which the Board is, in the government's view, well able to deal.[20]

Neither of these two features of the Act was included in the 1990 revisions; thus, while the phrase 'psychiatric illness' is, as Dillon LJ observed in *Attia v British Gas plc*, not readily amenable to definition,[1] the Board will continue to follow the common law's understanding of its scope in its determination of those harms to an applicant's mental condition that will be compensable.

Broadly speaking, psychiatric illness directly attributable to a victimising event as specified in para 4 may arise in one of two ways. Firstly, it may arise as an incident of a victimising event. Typical examples are where the applicant is the victim of a failed stabbing or of an attempt to run him down in a car,[2] where 'a parent witnesses the murder of a child or a husband, the rape of his wife'[3], and where a parent learns that a child has been the victim of sexual abuse. Besides crimes of violence, a person may suffer psychiatric illness when witnessing law enforcement activity as defined in para 4(b), perhaps an elderly person who is present while the police are attempting to arrest a number of persons who have committed offences of riot, violent disorder or affray. Though, as Lord Wilberforce said in *McLoughlin v O'Brian*:

17 [1983] 1 AC 410 at 431, HL.
18 489 HL Official Report op cit col 803.
19 Ibid, cols 802-804.
20 Ibid, col 806.
1 [1987] 3 All ER 455 at 457-458, CA.
2 D Williams *Criminal Injuries Compensation* (1986, 2nd edn, Waterlow) para 7.06.
3 489 HL Official Report (op cit) col 803.

'. . . a claim for damages for "nervous shock" caused by negligence can be made without the necessity of showing direct impact or fear of immediate personal injuries for oneself,'[4]

a person who is put in fear by the proximate commission of offences, for example, under ss 1-3 of the Public Order Act 1986 would almost certainly be compensable if that fear prompted a psychiatric illness. Such illness may of course be suffered by rescuers. If the nurse or those in the fire, ambulance or police services who sustain harm to their mental condition when dealing with the aftermath of a bomb explosion could sustain a civil action against the defendant who planted the bomb, then they will also sustain criminal injuries within the Scheme.[5] Rescuers of those who attempt to commit or succeed in committing suicide on a railway line suffer criminal injuries if they sustain psychiatric illness, as of course do the train drivers who come across the suicide's body or are driving the train that kills or maims the person.[6]

The second principal way in which psychiatric illness may be suffered is where it is the offender's particular intention to cause such harm.[7] An assault which causes a hysterical and nervous condition in another is an offence under s 47 of the Offences against the Person Act 1861,[8] which is clearly within para 4(a) of the Scheme. Threats of harm not amounting to an assault may also cause a criminal injury, provided that they constitute a crime of violence. Such an offence is s 16 of the Offences against the Person Act, which is well illustrated by an application discussed in the Board's 1986 Report.[9] The applicant was a divorced woman who, between 1981 and 1984, had been the victim of a series of incidents including death threats, burglary involving criminal damage to her furniture and clothing, phone calls to her son's school saying that he was ill, and the fatal poisoning of her dog. During this time she entered a psychiatric

---

4 Op cit, p 418.
5 Compare the applications decided under the Northern Ireland arrangements, where in 1977, 42% of all applications were applications in respect of psychiatric illness caused by nervous shock, D Greer 'A statutory remedy for nervous shock?' (1986) XXI Irish Jurist 57-94.
6 See *Wigg v British Railways Board* (1986) Times, 4 February; *Chadwick v British Transport Commission* [1967] 2 All ER 945, [1967] 1 WLR 912.
7 See F Trindade 'The intentional infliction of purely mental distress' (1986) 6 Oxford J Legal Studies 219-231.
8 *R v Miller* [1954] 2 QB 282, [1954] 2 All ER 529.
9 CICB (1986) para 15. Compare *Wilkinson v Downton* [1897] 2 QB 57.

hospital on three occasions, the last as the result of a nervous breakdown. The Board concluded that as the offender (who was thought to be her former husband) was committing offences under s 16, she was the victim of a crime of violence.

C.   ESTABLISHING THE CRIMINAL INJURY

For a personal injury to be a criminal injury it must be directly attributable to one of the victimising events defined in para 4(a)-(c). The two matters considered in this section are firstly, what is required to prove to the Board's satisfaction that such an event occurred, and secondly, the question of causation.

(1)   Proof of a victimising event

As it constitutes by far the most common victimising event considered by the Board, this matter will be considered in connection with the need to prove that the injury was sustained as the result of the commission of a crime of violence.

The Scheme has never required a conviction to be recorded against an offender; neither is the nature of the sentence relevant to its decision whether the conduct of the alleged offender falls within para 4.[10] Nor, except in the case of applications arising from intra-family violence, is a prosecution necessary. What is required is that the alleged offender's conduct is capable of being shown, on the evidence available to the Board and on the balance of probabilities, to amount to a crime of violence. Formal evidence of such an offence is essentially supplied by the requirement that the victim report the circumstances to the police. A conviction for a crime of violence, which occurs in 40–50% of the applications the Board receives,[11] will almost invariably constitute compelling proof of this aspect of an application. Nevertheless, the Board must exercise its discretion, and unlike some other jurisdictions, a conviction is not conclusive.[12] Moreover, even where the Board is satisfied by the conviction

---

10 Williams (1986) para 7.08.
11 House of Commons, Home Affairs Committee *Compensating Victims Quickly: the Administration of the Criminal Injuries Compensation Board* (1989–90, HC 92) Minutes of Evidence, Q 261, Newburn (1989) p 10.
12 Eg under the Northern Ireland scheme, Greer (1990) pp 284–294.

that the injury was a criminal injury, its hands are not tied concerning the application of para 6(c). Thus, notwithstanding that a jury has by its verdict rejected evidence of self-defence, the Board may reduce the award if it thinks it appropriate in view of the victim's unlawful conduct, or his conduct before, during or after the injury. However, it would be incongruous for the Board to reject an application altogether on the basis that the victim was entirely to blame in such a case.[13]

A conviction for an offence other than a crime of violence, though obviously not directly to the point, may nevertheless assist the Board to conclude that the conduct complained of does fall within para 4(a). Such was the case where it held that a crime of violence had occurred when some factory workers, as a practical joke, pushed an apprentice into a tank of caustic solution causing him 58% burns, and for which they were convicted under s 7(a) of the Health and Safety at Work etc Act 1974.[14] Though the Report is not explicit, the Board would have been able to conclude that the workers had committed a crime of violence, s 47 of the Offences against the Person Act 1861 being an obvious possibility. The burns would certainly have constituted actual bodily harm, and it would not be difficult to regard the workers' behaviour as being, on a civil standard of proof, reckless.

Neither is it relevant that the alleged offender is immune from conviction. Although originally interpreted so as to exclude injuries caused by children below the age of criminal responsibility (on the ground that as there could be no conviction in law, there was in law no crime)[15] the Scheme was quickly amended to provide that 'in considering . . . whether any act is a criminal act, any immunity at law of an offender, attributable to his youth or insanity or other condition, will be left out of account.' The scope of this provision was considered in *Ex p Webb*.[16] In one of the applications heard in that case, the deceased was an 84 year old man whom the coroner's jury evidently considered was not capable of knowing what he was doing, since they returned a verdict of accidental death rather than suicide. The Board dismissed the train driver's application. It argued

13 Supra, p 89.
14 CICB (1982) para 28. Compare the application noted in CICB (1981) para 22: a fireman was injured by an explosion at a petrol station negligently caused by a defective blowlamp; despite a conviction for a regulatory offence, there was no crime of violence.
15 CICB 2nd Report (1966, Cmnd 3117) para 20.
16 Op cit.

that 'immunity' in the Scheme meant immunity from prosecution, and that therefore, since there was nothing in the deceased's condition to preclude a prosecution, the fact that he would not have been convicted of a s 34 offence had he been prosecuted meant that there was no crime of violence. The Board further argued that it could not proceed as though he were in full possession of his faculties. This leads to a difficult problem. The suicide would not have been convicted presumably because his mental state would have precluded him from satisfying the fault element of s 34. What then of a person of low intelligence who makes a mistake about facts which, if true, would justify his actions? Or indeed, what of any offender who could not be convicted because he has available to him an excuse which, if sufficient to raise a reasonable doubt in the mind of a jury, is incompatible with any one or more of the fault or external elements of a crime of violence? As was suggested earlier, the fact that the defendant in *DPP v Morgan*[17] honestly believed the victim to be consenting would never stand in the way of the Board's concluding that she was indeed raped, though her 'rapist' may be acquitted. The difficulty in *Ex p Webb* was not that the deceased was immune either from prosecution or conviction, but that he may simply have been unable to form the appropriate fault element of a crime of violence.

On the facts of the particular application the Court of Appeal affirmed the Divisional Court's decision that the words 'or other condition' were apt to include a lack of mental capacity due to old age.[18] Accordingly the question for the Board in this case was whether a crime of violence had been committed assuming the deceased was in full possession of his faculties. On this basis the Divisional Court held that there was no apparent reason to suppose he would have escaped conviction,[19] but as we have seen, it also held that there was no compensable injury because s 34 of the Offences against the Person Act is not a crime of violence. The difficulty encountered in *Ex p Webb* is present also in applications by nurses and others working in psychiatric and geriatric hospitals who may be injured by a patient.[20] To remove any doubt about the possibility of concluding that there

17 Op cit.
18 [1987] QB 74 at 80.
19 [1986] QB 184 at 197.
20 Eg where the offender is epileptic and strikes the victim during a grand mal fit, M Ogden 'The work of the Criminal Injuries Compensation Board' (1984–85) 52 Medico-Legal J 227–241, 227. See also Williams (1986) para 7.17.

was a crime of violence in such cases, para 4 was revised in this respect to read:

> 'In considering for the purposes of this paragraph whether any act is a criminal act a person's conduct will be treated as constituting an offence notwithstanding that he may not be convicted of the offence by reason of age, insanity or diplomatic immunity.'

It will be seen that the phrase 'immunity at law' has also been changed. Its inclusion allowed the Board to treat as criminal injuries, personal injuries caused, apart from those under the age of criminal responsibility, by alleged offenders who were unfit to plead, or who possessed diplomatic immunity or an immunity offered to a prosecution witness. The Court of Appeal held that 'immunity' meant 'immunity from conviction', a decision which prompted the Working Party to recommend that the statutory Scheme specifically cater for diplomatic immunity.[1] The 1990 revision is substantially identical to s 109(4) of the 1988 Act. Accordingly, in the case of an offender who is, as a matter of fact or law, immune from conviction for one of the reasons specified in para 4, the Board will be required to consider whether, had he not been so, he could, on a balance of probabilities, have been convicted of a crime of violence. Because it does not include 'or other condition', the 1990 revision seemingly does not cover applications in which the alleged offender is offered immunity by the prosecution; but cases of this sort surely pose no real difficulty. A decision by the Crown Prosecution Service not to prosecute in exchange for the offender giving evidence against others does not deny that an offence was committed nor that the offender might be convicted of it. Unlike cases in which the alleged offender is below the age of legal responsibility or is in law insane or unfit to plead, such a decision is only an exercise of the CPS's prosecutorial discretion, and that decision, if it results in no prosecution being brought, will never preclude the Board from holding that a crime of violence was committed if it is satisfied by the evidence that one was.

Convictions for crimes of violence figure in approximately half the applications made to the Board. For the rest, the failure to secure a conviction is principally due to the fact that the assailant is unknown. In a small number of cases, though known, the

---

1 Home Office (1986) para 4.15. Between 1974 and 1984, 546 serious crimes had been committed by diplomats in London who had later claimed immunity; Times, 27 June 1984.

alleged offender was not charged. Where there is no conviction, the question for the Board is whether the requisite fault and external elements of a crime of violence can be inferred from the facts as reported to and verified by the police.[2] The Board's Reports are replete with examples of applications which have been dismissed because they did not satisfy these criteria. Sometimes they simply disclose no offence;[3] sometimes the offence could only be construed as being a crime against property, notwithstanding some harm to an individual.[4] A third type of case is where the injury could clearly constitute the external elements of a crime of violence, the question being whether the offender had the requisite fault element. Where that includes recklessness, the question must be determined according to the objective test laid down in *Caldwell*.[5] This has posed some difficulties for the Board, in particular where children injure each other when firing airguns[6] or playing with fireworks,[7] and where injuries are sustained as a consequence of over-robust tackling in football, rugby and other contact sports.[8] If all that can be inferred is that the children or the participants were negligent, then the injury is not a criminal injury.[9]

In a minority of applications heard by the Board a prosecution

2 For examples of this kind of reconstruction, see CICB (1979) para 20 (woman pushing her hand through the glass door to her home after being tapped on the shoulder by the offender: assault occasioning actual bodily harm) and compare CICB (1988) paras 17.1-17.3 (woman passing out and hurting herself in the fall as she went to phone the police after the glass window in her front door was smashed in a 'reckless act of violence'), (1983) para 19 (victim a passenger in a light aircraft killed when the pilot recklessly attempted a barrel roll: manslaughter) and para 20 (victim being stuck to objects by prior application of 'superglue' causing injury to the skin and underlying flesh when removed: assault occasioning actual bodily harm).

3 CICB (1986) para 18 (victim alleging that a group of people were using radio equipment to injure her) and (1985) para 22 (victim pushing her hand through the kitchen window to scare away a man peering through it at her).

4 CICB (1980) para 16 (victim suffering bronchitis from inhaling butane gas fumes emitted by a blowlamp left in the fridge by a burglar) and (1987) paras 19-21.

5 Op cit. Cf assault and assault occasioning actually bodily harm, where recklessness implies that the defendant did himself advert to the risk of harm, see Smith and Hogan (1988) p 379, *R v Cunningham* [1957] 2 QB 396, [1957] 2 All ER 412, CCA; *R v Venna* [1976] QB 421, [1975] 3 All ER 788, CA; and *R v Pratt*, op cit.

6 CICB (1986) para 17, and the Statement, para H.

7 Williams (1986) paras 7.02 and 7.16.

8 CICB (1987) para 37. See also CICB (1986) paras 34-37 on injuries sustained on the way to sporting events.

9 CICB (1989) paras 16.3 and 16.5.

has resulted in the acquittal of the 'offender'. Where the acquittal follows a successful defence, for example, of alibi, there can be no objection to the Board's concluding that there was nevertheless a crime of violence; it was committed by someone else. Likewise where the acquittal is the consequence of the application of evidential or procedural rules particular to the criminal trial, there need be no incompatibility between that verdict and the Board's decision that on the balance of probabilities the injury was a criminal injury. Besides operating to the lower standard of proof, the Board is not constrained by the rules of evidence precluding, for example, hearsay or evidence of the offender's prior convictions.[10]

There remains a small number of applications that pose a slightly different problem, namely where the substantive criminal law of excuses will preclude a conviction, and may indeed have resulted in an acquittal. Instances of such applications were discussed earlier in this chapter. Clearly there does not have to be a conviction for there to have been an offence; yet if someone has been acquitted precisely because he believed in facts which negatived a necessary element of a possible offence under para 4(a), can we say that the personal injury is a criminal injury? It surely seems perverse that where the offender is never tried the Board is free to determine that there was, though the offender's beliefs are never examined and might indeed have resulted in an acquittal; yet where they are and there was, there would be no criminal injury. Nor need the perversity apply only in respect of a failure to satisfy the fault element of a crime of violence. The injury may have been sustained in circumstances which would support a defence of automatism, thus negativing a necessary aspect of its external elements.[11] Here too, the victim seems better placed if the offender is never prosecuted.

One way out of this apparent dilemma is simply to acknowledge that while there has been an acquittal on one charge, other offences that would satisfy para 4(a) have, on the balance of probabilities, been committed. Where, on a charge of rape, the offender honestly believes that the woman was consenting, there may still be an offence, for example, under s 47 of the Offences against the Person Act 1861. But this analysis would only hold good so long as there was another possible offence of which an offender could have satisfied its fault and external elements.

10 CICB (1981) para 49 and (1984) para 43.
11 *R v Hennessy* [1989] 2 All ER 9, [1989] 1 WLR 287, CA. P Alldridge 'Rules for courts and rules for citizens' (1990) 10 Oxford J Legal Studies 487-504.

A second approach is to attend to the differing standards of proof employed by the Board and within the criminal trial. A jury must acquit if there is a reasonable doubt that the offender believed that there was consent, but this doubt is quite compatible with their taking the view that, on a balance of probabilities, he did not have this belief. Thus although the facts cannot satisfy the demands of the criminal standard of proof, they may be sufficient to satisfy the civil standard. The conclusion which follows, that there was a criminal injury, is analogous to the Court of Appeal's decision in *Gray v Barr*, where, notwithstanding the defendant's acquittal, he was repeatedly said by Lord Denning to have committed manslaughter.[12] Only if the Board concludes that the facts will not sustain, on a balance of probabilities, the fault and external elements of a crime of violence, can we say that the personal injury was indeed not a criminal injury.

But this resolution is essentially flawed, since it is dependent on standards of proof, and if they were to change, then an acquittal would surely also require the conclusion that the victim did not sustain a criminal injury. To maintain the view that a victim may sustain a criminal injury notwithstanding the mutual incompatibility of the offender's beliefs or ability to control his behaviour, and the requirements of the offence charged, it is necessary to adopt the view that, whatever the outcome of the prosecution, the prima facie illegality of the conduct complained of remains. As was noted earlier, this was in essence the view taken by the Court of Appeal in *Cogan and Leak*.[13]

(2) Causation

The test of causation under the Scheme is that the injury has to be 'directly attributable' to the victimising event. This phrase was considered in *R v Criminal Injuries Compensation Board, ex p Schofield*[14] and in *R v Criminal Injuries Compensation Board, ex p Ince*.[15] In the former, the applicant was knocked down and injured either by a store detective or the man whom he suspected of theft and was chasing. The Board dismissed the application on the ground that the Scheme was not intended to compensate injuries to bystanders accidentally injured by someone else engaged in law enforcement activity, but Lord

12 [1971] 2 QB 554 at 568.
13 [1976] QB 217 at 223.
14 [1971] 2 All ER 1011, [1971] 1 WLR 926.
15 Op cit.

Parker CJ held that the Scheme was not so limited. As to the question whether the applicant's injuries were directly attributable to the law enforcement activity, his Lordship said that the phrase meant that the victimising event must be a *causa causans* of the injury, and not merely a *causa sine qua non*.[16]

The decision on this issue signifies no more perhaps than that a but-for test is a precondition of any test of remoteness; of much greater significance was the Court of Appeal's decision in *Ex p Ince*. The court held that 'directly attributable' did not mean 'solely attributable' but directly attributable in whole or in part to a state of affairs which existed or which the victim believed to exist, even where the intervening cause was the wrongful act of the injured person or of a third party. On the ' st point Megaw LJ said:

> 'personal injury is directly attributable to any of the matters [in para 4(a) and (b)] if such matter is, on the basis of all the relevant facts, a substantial cause of personal injury. It does not need to be the sole cause. By the word "substantial" I mean that the relationship between the particular cause and the personal injury is such that a reasonable person, applying his common sense, would fairly and seriously regard it as being a cause.'[17]

As in negligence, an intervening cause will not necessarily extinguish a plaintiff/victim's eligibility; but Lord Denning's dictum that it will only do so where it is 'so powerful a cause as to reduce the original offence to a piece of history',[18] merely begs the question, and arguably entitled applicants to compensation from the Board which, on the causal rules employed in the law of tort concerning a *novus actus interveniens* comprising the plaintiff's (or a third party's) wrongful acts, would not be available in civil law.[19]

The Working Party was critical of this decision which it considered to have extended the Scheme 'to cover injuries sustained in a much wider range of circumstances than was originally intended',[20] and recommended 'that the statutory

---

16 [1971] 2 All ER 1011 at 1013. CICB (1987) para 17.
17 [1973] 3 All ER 808 at 815, CA.
18 Ibid, p 812.
19 See H Hart and A Honore *Causation in Law* (1985, 2nd edn, Oxford UP) chs 4-5, *Winfield on Tort* (1984, 12th edn, Sweet & Maxwell) 141-147. Compare the position under the Northern Ireland Scheme, Greer (1986) pp 63-77.
20 Home Office (1986) para 4.9.

scheme should include a more stringent test of remoteness which clearly conveys the need for a very close and immediate link between the offence and the consequent injury.'[1] It was sufficiently exercised by this matter to set out in Appendix 4 to its Report, a series of injuries caused by a bomb explosion at a hospital which it considered illustrated the proper limits to eligibility. Those who should be eligible included:

1. Patient dies of injuries received in the explosion.
2. Hospital worker in basement at the time of the explosion. Uninjured by the blast but trapped by rubble. Water pipe is broken by the blast and several hours later the trapped worker drowns in the flooded basement.
3. Patient buried in rubble is uninjured by the blast but several hours later when rescued his leg is broken by a fireman taking a justifiable risk.
4. The explosion destroys the electricity supply and the hospital's emergency generator. Patient on life support machine dies when his machine stops functioning and cannot be restarted.
5. Girl riding horse immediately outside hospital. Uninjured by the blast but the horse bolts and the rider suffers injuries when she is thrown to the ground.
6. As in (5) above except that the horse and rider are 400 yards away from the blast.
7. Rescue worker injured on the day after the blast by the unexpected fall of rubble.

The Working Party prefaced these examples with the cautionary statement that some of them were borderline about which people might disagree, but assuming the person who placed the bomb was at least reckless as to whether death or personal injury was caused, the directness test applicable in criminal law would surely establish a sufficient link between the conduct and the injury in cases 1-5.

The series of examples continued with injuries that the Working Party considered should be ineligible:

8. As in (3) above except that injury is caused by foreman's negligence.
9. As in (4) above except that emergency generator is not destroyed in the blast but fails to function owing to poor maintenance.
10. Pedestrian killed by a hammer dropped by a workman on scaffolding further down the street who is jolted by the explosion.

1 Ibid, para 4.10.

11. A special drug intended for a patient in another part of the country is destroyed in the blast. No further supplies can be obtained in time and the patient consequently dies.

Example 8 is intended to restore a more rigorous application of the *novus actus interveniens* principle, while the others are intended to indicate injuries that do not show the 'very close and immediate link' the Working Party thought desirable.

The Criminal Justice Bill 1986 attempted to express this link by requiring that the injury be 'immediately caused or closely connected' to the offence, but this generated some doubt as to how it might be interpreted,[2] and the Act merely says that the injury must be 'caused by' the victimising event, which phraseology was intended to do no more than to import the normal civil law.[3] There is no change, however, in the non-statutory Scheme. Thus the apparent anomaly that arose in *R v Criminal Injuries Compensation Board, ex p Parsons*[4] may still recur. There a train driver suffered nervous shock when he found a decapitated body of a suicide lying by the railway line. Given, as was discussed earlier, that the Board had conceded that the original act of the deceased constituted a crime of violence, the question which arose was whether the shock suffered by the train driver was directly attributable to that offence. Both the Divisional Court (with some misgivings) and the Court of Appeal disagreed with the Board, and held that it was. The Board considered it anomalous that the Scheme's test could produce a sufficient causal link between the suicide and the shock, but that this would not be so on the foreseeability test applicable in the law of negligence. Whether this would always be anomalous is debatable. An offence under s 34 may be committed negligently; but crimes of violence typically require intention or recklessness and are for civil purposes akin to assault, battery and the other intentional torts, whose test of remoteness is also one of directness. In any event para 4(c) only extends to trespass on a railway, thus excluding the possibility of personal injuries being caused by negligent conduct constituting criminal injuries. Accordingly, in most cases there would be no difference in the test applicable to applications under the Scheme and those available in an action in tort.

2 486 HL Official Report (5th series) col 1315 (27 April 1987).
3 489 HL Official Report (op cit) col 800.
4 Op cit.

Chapter Five

Qualifying Injuries

The 1988 Act provides that while a personal injury is a criminal injury if it is caused by one of the specified victimising events, it will not qualify for compensation if it does not satisfy the conditions set out in s 110. These qualifications concern the place where the injury was sustained, intra-family violence, accidental injuries sustained during law enforcement activity, and traffic offences. Though not explicitly structured in this way, the non-statutory Scheme contains all four qualifications, and it is appropriate to deal with them as matters separate from the question whether the applicant sustained a criminal injury. As the qualification concerning applications arising from intra-family violence more obviously concerns the question, who is compensable, it is considered in chapter 6. The other three qualifications are now dealt with *seriatim*.

A. JURISDICTION

By para 4 compensation may be payable where a criminal injury was sustained:

'in Great Britain, or on a British vessel, aircraft or hovercraft or on, under or above an installation in a designated area within the meaning of s 1(7) of the Continental Shelf Act 1964 or any waters within 500 metres of such an installation, or in a lighthouse off the coast of the United Kingdom.'

The Scheme thus extends firstly to the land borders of England, Wales and Scotland. In Northern Ireland criminal injury compensation was governed prior to the introduction of direct rule by the Criminal Injuries to Persons (Compensation) (NI) Act 1968 and is now governed by Order in Council.[1] Though the Scheme is not explicit, a criminal injury sustained, in the words of s 110(2) of the 1988 Act, 'within the limits of the territorial waters adjacent to the United Kingdom' will also qualify. Whereas the land border between Northern Ireland and the Republic may generate some jurisdictional difficulties arising from the territorial extent of the criminal law,[2] there do not appear to have been any difficulties created by the fact that the Scheme extends to marine areas within the United Kingdom's jurisdiction. A criminal injury sustained in a lighthouse off the coast of Northern Ireland falls within the scope of the Scheme, and not, it seems, within the scope of the Criminal Injuries (Compensation) (Northern Ireland) Order 1988. Even if the injury were compensable under both sets of arrangements, there can be no double recovery of compensation since each set contains a provision requiring deduction of other moneys received from the state in respect of the injury.[3]

The Scheme's extent is thus defined by reference to the place where the injury is sustained, and not by reference to British nationality or citizenship: a British passenger on a Danish North Sea ferry who is criminally injured by another passenger will not qualify under the Scheme.[4] Such injury would however qualify if it were sustained on a British cross-channel ferry, or on a British aircraft, hovercraft or oil rig. The terms of the European Convention on the Compensation of Victims of Violent Crimes, which the United Kingdom ratified on 11 January 1990, eliminates this discrepancy. The Convention includes a provision whereby British citizens will be eligible for compensation under the arrangements established in any other state which is a party to the Convention and within whose jurisdiction a criminal injury was sustained.[5] It also appears that British citizens will

---

1 Criminal Injuries to Persons (Compensation) (Northern Ireland) Order 1977 as amended in 1988. See D Greer *Compensation for Criminal Injuries to Persons in Northern Ireland* (1990, 2nd edn, SLS Legal Publications, Belfast).
2 Greer (1990) pp 51–54.
3 Infra, p 185.
4 CICB 20th Report (1984, Cmnd 9399) paras 19 and 20, and 24th Report (1988 Cm 536) paras 19.1-19.2. A British national criminally injured by a letter bomb delivered to a British Embassy abroad did not qualify because the Embassy was not British territory, D Williams, *Criminal Injuries Compensation* (1986 Waterlow) para 5.10.
5 *European Convention on the Compensation of Victims of Violent Crimes* (1983) Art 3, European Treaty Series No 116. See D Miers, 'The provision of compensation for victims of violent crime in continental Europe' (1985) 10 Victimology 662-671.

be able to benefit under any such arrangement made by a member state of the European Community. In *Cowan v Le Trésor Public*,[6] a British citizen was seriously injured in a robbery on the Paris Metro. His application to the *Commission d'indemnisation des victimes d'infraction*[7] was turned down on the basis that Article 706-15 of the French Code of Criminal Procedure provides that compensation shall be payable to foreign nationals only if there is a reciprocal agreement with the other state, or the foreign national has a residence permit. Neither applied in his case. The applicant then referred to the Court of Justice of the European Communities for a preliminary ruling on the question whether the conditions attached to the eligibility for compensation of foreign nationals constituted a breach of Article 7 of the EC Treaty, which prohibits discrimination on the grounds of nationality. The court ruled that as it had previously held that tourists are recipients of services and are free to move from one member state to another to receive those services, so the protection afforded to each person as a corollary of that freedom of movement could not be qualified by reference to nationality. Thus compensatory arrangements for acts of criminal violence could not be made dependent on such conditions as reciprocity with another member state, or the possession of a residence permit.

Since the geographical extent of the Scheme is defined by reference to the place in which the criminal injury was sustained, foreign nationals visiting Great Britain have always qualified.[8]

Within Great Britain the Scheme applies for the most part uniformly. To the extent that it is based upon the common law or upon statutory provisions particular to England and Wales on the one hand, and to Scotland on the other, there will continue to be differences in its detailed application. One example is that in the event of a qualifying injury occurring in Scotland and resulting in the death of the victim, the statutory award to the dependants for loss of society includes an award for the benefit of any person regarded by the deceased as a child of his or her family, whereas no bereavement award may be made in England and Wales to the deceased's children. Were it not for para 4 discounting the relevance of age in considering whether any act is a criminal act, the differing minimum ages of criminal

---

6 Case 186/87: (1989) Times, 13 February.
7 M Boland and D Martin 'Victim compensation schemes: a comparative approach' (1985) 10 Victimology 672-679.
8 Williams (1986) paras 7.07 and 9.01.

responsibility in the two jurisdictions would create a serious anomaly in the Scheme's application.

B. ACCIDENTAL INJURIES SUSTAINED IN LAW ENFORCEMENT ACTIVITY

The treatment of accidental injuries sustained while a citizen or policeman is attempting to apprehend an offender or prevent a crime has always been a problematic aspect of the Scheme. Some of the early decisions show some inconsistency in the application of the entitling provision,[9] but the Board did seek to draw the line at compensating bystanders who were accidentally injured while an arrest was taking place:

> '. . . the purpose of the Scheme was to compensate those who try to arrest an offender or who try to prevent the commission of a crime, or who assist a constable to do either of these things; [but] it did not, in our view, cover bystanders who are accidentally injured by anyone who is engaged in the task of arresting an offender.'[10]

One of the obvious difficulties is the systematic ambiguity of the word 'accident';[11] it is not a term of art, and clearly carries many conflicting nuances of meaning. In the context of the Scheme, it appeared initially to mean any injury directly attributable to law enforcement activity which the offender had caused in fact, for example, by wrestling free of the person trying to detain him, but where he had no intention to cause injury, nor was reckless as to whether it would be caused. Later it appeared to cover any injury sustained by a would-be enforcer of the law not attributable to a crime of violence.

Despite the caution that the Board expressed in its early years, the Court of Appeal significantly extended the scope of the Scheme in *R v Criminal Injuries Compensation Board, ex p Schofield* to include bystanders accidentally injured while

---

9 The Board rejected the applications of a policeman who injured his hand on the glass exit door to the police station as he left in answer to an emergency call, and of another whose car was hit by the one he was chasing, CICB 4th Report (1968, Cmnd 3814) para 6, but allowed those of a policeman whose car skidded as he was answering a general call, CICB 5th Report (1969, Cmnd 4179) para 6(7) and another who, while chasing an offender, slipped and broke his jaw, CICB 7th Report (1971, Cmnd 4812) para 7(5).

10 CICB (1971) para 8.

11 See P Cane *Atiyah's Accidents, Compensation and the Law* (1987, 4th edn, Weidenfeld and Nicolson) 1-7.

someone else was attempting to prevent a crime, effect an arrest or assist a constable to do either of these things.[12] The majority of the court took the view that there was nothing in the relevant paragraph to limit an award of compensation to those who were actually engaged in the law enforcement activity. According to Lord Parker CJ, the paragraph created four separate occasions for compensation:

'(i) where the injury suffered was directly attributable to a criminal offence; (ii) where the injury suffered was directly attributable to an arrest or attempted arrest of an offender or suspected offender; (iii) where the injury suffered was directly attributable to the prevention of an offence; and (iv) where the injury suffered was directly attributable to the giving of help to any constable who is engaged in arresting or attempting to arrest an offender or suspected offender or preventing or attempting to prevent an offence.'[13]

His Lordship was unconvinced by the argument that if categories (ii) and (iii) were not taken to presuppose that the applicant was himself actively engaged in law enforcement, category (iv) became otiose. The purpose of category (iv) was, he thought, merely to identify a 'typical case in which an applicant would be entitled to receive compensation',[14] and its inclusion should not interfere with the plain construction of the other categories.

This decision extended the Scheme to compensate bystanders accidentally injured while others were engaged in law enforcement activity; a further substantial extension followed the Court of Appeal's decision in *Ex p Ince*.[15] Concerning the word 'attempt' in the phrase 'attempted prevention of an offence,' Megaw LJ thought that it should not be confined to the meaning commonly attached to it in the criminal law, but should be interpreted more widely, so that where a:

'police officer goes towards the place or supposed place of the supposed offence, he is, in the ordinary sense of the words, at least unless there are some special features, attempting to prevent an offence.'[16]

Combined with the Court's interpretation of the phrase 'directly attributable' as meaning not solely attributable, but attributable

12 [1971] 2 All ER 1011, [1971] 1 WLR 926.
13 Ibid, 1012.
14 Ibid, 1013.
15 [1973] 3 All ER 808. [1973] 1 WLR 1334, Supra, pp 119–120.
16 Ibid, 815.

in whole or in part to the offence or supposed offence (or to a crime of violence), this decision meant that:

'compensation was likely to be payable not only to a police officer injured at the scene of a crime while taking active steps to prevent its commission, but also to any officer who believed that an offence was about to take place and took some action to prevent it; in the case of an attempted arrest, any injury accidentally sustained from the time that a police officer received instructions and responded to them was likely to be within the scope of the Scheme.'[17]

The Board became increasingly concerned about these judicial extensions to the Scheme. In 1977 the Chairman remarked that as the Scheme then stood:

'a police officer who slipped and fell in a police station when about to go and arrest an offender at his home some miles away would be entitled to compensation. I doubt whether the draftsman of the Scheme even contemplated that such an application should be within the Scheme.'[18]

It was in response to this unease that the 1978 Working Party proposed that such injuries should only be compensable if the applicant was at the time taking an exceptional risk which was justified in all the circumstances.[19] Following the introduction of this qualification as para 6(d) of the Scheme, the Board sought to give guidance on what it would regard as an exceptional risk. Injuries sustained while walking or running towards an incident or going to apprehend an offender, or escorting a non-violent prisoner are not within the Scheme;[20] neither are those sustained when climbing, or jumping over walls, fences, parapets or other

---

17 Home Office *Criminal Injuries Compensation: A Statutory Scheme* (1986) para 6.9. Also 489 HL Official Report (5th series) col 798 (2 November 1987) where it is observed that as then interpreted, the Scheme might even have compensated a policeman who walked into a lamp post in answer to a call.

18 M Ogden 'Why reform matters for victims' (1977) *Howard League for Penal Reform* 2. See also Cane (1987) pp 300-301, CICB 8th Report (1972, Cmnd 5127) para 7 (woman held within the Scheme when she was accidentally knocked down onto the pavement by an unknown man who had run out of a bank being robbed by armed men, the Board presuming that the man's intention was to raise the alarm), and the dissenting judgment of Bridge J in *Ex p Schofield*, 1015.

19 Home Office *Review of the Criminal Injuries Compensation Scheme: Report of an Interdepartmental Working Party* (1978) para 5.23, the Scheme para 6(d).

20 The Statement, para 6L.1. Also CICB 18th Report (1982, Cmnd 8752) paras 31, 36 and 37 and (1988) paras 28.1-28.5 (policemen tripping and falling while chasing offenders/answering calls: no exceptional risk).

obstructions, unless the applicant cannot see what is on the other side, or the incident occurs at night.[1] Falling from a height, or through a roof or a skylight will normally be regarded as taking an exceptional risk.[2] Answering a 999 call concerning intruders in an unoccupied building will not normally be within the Scheme, although the Board will consider the nature of the premises in question; chasing or trying to intercept a car which has refused to stop has been accepted as being within the Scheme.[3]

The exceptional risk requirement also disqualifies a bystander such as the applicant in *Ex p Schofield*, as it is he, and not the person enforcing the law, who has to be taking such a risk. Thus a bystander who, judging himself incapable of giving direct help to a policeman struggling with an offender, slips and is injured while running to a phone box to make a 999 call does not sustain a qualifying criminal injury. It might be otherwise if the route he took were hazardous. In its review, the Home Office Working Party acknowledged that this requirement had restored to the Scheme 'something of its original intention and effect',[4] but also noted the difficulty which the Board had experienced in practice in applying it.[5] Neither was the police lobby happy with the qualification and argued its repeal. After lengthy consideration the Working Party recommended that where accidental injuries are incurred 'within the scope of employment within the law enforcement field', they should not fall within the Scheme at all.[6] Accordingly, since that would leave only private citizens to benefit from the Scheme where they

---

1 The Statement, para 6L.2. Also CICB (1982) para 38 (policewoman cutting thigh while climbing through barbed wire not an exceptional risk); but 'acts which would not be regarded as constituting an exceptional risk in daylight, may well be so at night', ibid, para 6L.5, CICB (1988) paras 29.1-29.3 and 25th Report (1989 Cm 900) para 17.3, unless perhaps the area is well-lit, CICB (1989) para 17.2.
2 The Statement, para 6L.3. Also CICB (1982) para 41 (policeman falling off a roof in daylight was an exceptional risk), and paras 39 and 40, and CICB 19th Report (1983, Cmnd 9093) para 30 (policemen falling into an inspection pit in a lorry depot at night, through a skylight in poor light and from a high wall by a canal, also at night, were exceptional risks).
3 The Statement, para 6L.4, and CICB 22nd Report (1986, Cm 42) paras 24 and 28. The Board has also taken into account 'factors such as the gravity of the incident and suspected danger to the public', the Statement, para 6L.6.23
4 Home Office (1986) para 6.11.
5 489 HL Official Report, op cit, col 797.
6 Home Office (1986) para 6.12, and chapter 26. Cf the House of Lords' refusal to extend the American doctrine that professional rescuers such as firemen must be taken to have accepted that they may sustain injuries dealing with risky situations created by negligent defendants, *Ogwo v Taylor* [1988] AC 431.

engaged in law enforcement activity, the Working Party saw no need to retain the exceptional risk requirement, since for them such activity is almost always exceptional.[7]

The government did not adopt this recommendation, preferring, to the satisfaction of the Police Federation, the status quo.[8] No change was made to para 6(d) in the 1990 revisions to the non-statutory Scheme. The position is thus as it has been since the introduction of the exceptional risk qualification ten years ago. Whether the risk the policeman or citizen was taking was exceptional and was justified in all the circumstances is for the Board to decide, and the earlier guidance it has given on this matter will continue to be relevant. The Board may employ different standards as between different law enforcers; what is exceptional for a citizen, for example, tackling a man armed with a knife, may not be so for a policeman.[9] In this way the Board could go some way to reflect the reservations the Working Party expressed about the extension of the Scheme to those who are paid to enforce the law and who are, if injured in the course of their employment, eligible for industrial injury benefit.

C. TRAFFIC ACCIDENTS

Paragraph 11 of the Scheme disqualifies applications based on injuries attributable to traffic offences, except where they are 'due to a deliberate attempt to run the victim down.'[10]

7 Home Office (1986) para 6.13. The Working Party could see no justification for permitting bystanders accidentally injured to recover compensation under the Scheme: 'although instances of accidental injury are undoubtedly deserving of sympathy, accidental injury can, of course, arise in many ways in the course of everyday life; the question is whether compensation from public funds for injury incurred accidentally is appropriate under a scheme which exists for the purpose of compensating the victims of violent crime,' Home Office (1986) para 6.8.

8 Opposition MPs became very indignant about the inclusion of the exceptional risk requirement which they regarded as being an indefensible sell-out of the government's duty to ensure that the police are properly rewarded for performing their duties. Given the Police Federation's acceptance of the government position, this high dudgeon, which was ventilated mostly on the 1986 Bill, rather took the form of beating the air, 106 HC Official Report (6th series) cols 470 and 479-480 (27 November 1986), and 113 HC Official Report (6th series) cols 1012-1018 (31 March 1987).

9 Even then, it is not enough that there is a risk of injury, it must be exceptional. CICB 23rd Report (1987, Cm 265) para 22.

10 Clear examples of the deliberate use of a car to cause personal injury are CICB (1984) para 33 and (1988) para 41.1; by contrast, CICB 15th Report (1979, Cmnd 7752) para 23 and (1988) paras 40.1-40.2. See also J Spencer 'Motor vehicles as weapons of offence' [1985] Crim LR 29-41.

The justification for the exclusion of road traffic offences, even where they constitute crimes of violence, as in the case of causing death by reckless driving or of causing bodily harm by wanton or furious driving, does not arise 'from the nature of the offences, but from the purely practical consideration of avoiding the need for the Board to embark upon detailed consideration of cases which are eligible for compensation under motor insurance arrangements, including the agreements between the Motor Insurers' Bureau and the Secretary of State for Transport.'[11] Accordingly, where an injury is directly attributable to the commission of such an offence under ss 1 or 2 of the Road Traffic Act 1988 or s 35 of the Offences against the Person Act 1861, compensation will be payable under the Scheme if the circumstances of the injury fell outside the terms of the MIB agreements, for example if the injury occurred on private land, or in the case of the untraced drivers agreement, the vehicle was being deliberately used as a weapon.[12] In the latter case, dispute could arise between the Board and the MIB precisely as to the question whether the vehicle was being so used; the MIB arguing that it was, the Board that it was not. What is at stake, of course, is the financial liability that follows from the answer; but remarks by the Board's Chairman indicate that it would not let a victim go uncompensated on the ground only that the two could not agree an answer.[13] Whereas offences under ss 1 and 2 of the Road Traffic Act 1988 can constitute crimes of violence, in *R v Criminal Injuries Compensation Board, ex p Letts*, the Court of Appeal doubted whether an offence of careless driving (s 3) could ever satisfy para 4(a), though it was not prepared to rule out the possibility altogether.[14]

Clause 1(e) of the untraced drivers agreement eliminates liability where the vehicle was being deliberately used as a weapon; in such cases the MIB and the Scheme are mutually

---

11 Home Office (1986) para 11.1. Also CICB (1984) para 32. D Williams *Hit and Run and Uninsured Personal Injury Claims* (1988, Barry Rose). A revised agreement with the MIB taking effect from 21 December 1988 was published in January 1989.

12 CICB 16th Report (1980, Cmnd 8081) paras 19-20. See Williams (1986) para 7.03.

13 M Ogden 'The work of the Criminal Injuries Compensation Board' (1984-85) 52 Medico-Legal J 227-241. Also CICB (1984) paras 32 and 34.

14 Unreported, CICB (1989) para 26.2. According to *R v Seymour* [1983] 2 AC 493, [1983] 2 All ER 1058, HL, causing death by reckless driving may be equivalent to manslaughter, but if the death is occasioned by what constitutes an offence under s 1 of the Road Traffic Act 1988, it will be excluded from the Scheme if it is covered by the MIB.

exclusive. This is not so, however, under the uninsured drivers agreement, which deals with injuries caused by identified but uninsured drivers. Here the MIB and the Scheme overlap, and the relationship between them was considered by the House of Lords in *Gardner v Moore*.[15] The driver was convicted under s 18 of the Offences against the Person Act 1861 when he deliberately drove his car at the plaintiff causing him serious injury. The plaintiff brought an action against the driver and, as second defendants, the MIB, seeking a declaration that, under the uninsured drivers agreement, they were liable to indemnify him for any unsatisfied judgment against the driver. The issue to be determined by the House of Lords was whether the driver could, notwithstanding his deliberate use of the car as a weapon, rely upon this agreement. The MIB argued that the well-established principle of insurance law that a person was not entitled to profit from his own wrong should be applied in this case. The House of Lords rejected this, holding that since the satisfaction of the driver's liability to the plaintiff was incidental to the main purpose of the MIB agreement, which was the protection of innocent victims, the principle was not compromised by such a declaration. In argument, the MIB suggested that as the facts showed a deliberate hit and run, the proper source of compensation was not the MIB, but the Board. Lord Hailsham LC rejected this: 'the two remedies are not necessarily mutually exclusive alternatives and were not designed to be so.'[16]

While uncertain why deliberate hit and run cases were excluded from the untraced drivers agreement, but not from that governing uninsured drivers, the Working Party did not see it as its function to review their terms; what it sought was clarity in the relationship between those agreements and the terms of the Scheme, whose task it is to act only 'as a back-up provision' in the event that an injury is not met from other sources. Accordingly, the Working Party recommended that, so far as the uninsured drivers agreement is concerned, the Act should make it clear that deliberate hit and run cases should not qualify, on the assumption that they would be covered by that agreement.[17] On the other hand, it recommended no change in the provision for deliberate hit and run injuries under the untraced drivers agreement. The Board had argued that all such cases should be dealt with by the MIB;

---

15 [1984] AC 548, [1984] 1 All ER 1100, HL.
16 Ibid, 1107.
17 Home Office (1986) para 11.4.

the MIB, taking the view that 'there is a clear moral dividing line between injuries caused accidentally and injuries caused intentionally as a result of use of a vehicle as a weapon, in the same way as a brick or a bottle, to commit a violent crime',[18] that such injuries were properly to be met under the Scheme. The Working Party's recommendation, that the statutory arrangements 'should exclude applications arising from traffic offences, except where the offence constitutes a crime of violence and compensation is not payable under motor insurance arrangements or one of the MIB agreements',[19] was enacted as s 110(7), but no changes were made to para 11 in the 1990 revision.

It should be noted that where criminal injuries caused by untraced or uninsured drivers have qualified under the Scheme, they have attracted a smaller quantum of compensation than where they have fallen under the MIB's agreements. This is so, and as Lord Hailsham LC observed in *Gardner v Moore* has been to the victim's disadvantage, because unlike the MIB, the Board has always been required to deduct in full and without limitation of time virtually all benefits that have accrued as a result of his sustaining the injury.[20] Where he was injured by an uninsured driver, the victim could apply both to the Board and to the MIB, though as the Working Party remarked, this would not advantage him as any compensation payable by the Board would invariably be cancelled out by the payment under the MIB agreement, 'because the MIB follow civil law practice without the limitations built into the . . . Scheme'.[1] However, the change introduced by s 22 of the Social Security Act 1989, which requires the full deduction of all state benefits from an award of damages, substantially reduces the differences between the two systems of compensation. Nevertheless, there remain different assessment rules, and thus similar injuries will continue to attract different amounts of compensation, which will in turn be dependent on such irrelevant (to the assessment of the victim's injury) factors as where the injury took place, and whether the driver was identified. These differences may be seen as yet further evidence of the need to deal with the consequences at least of automobile accidents in a uniform manner.

One final matter requires comment. The Board receives applications arising from injuries sustained on the road, but

---

18 Ibid, para 11.2.
19 Ibid, para 11.5.
20 [1984] 1 All ER 1100 at 1107. Infra, pp 177–181.
1 Home Office (1986) para 11.3.

where the victim was, for example, pushed or forced into the path of an oncoming vehicle whose driver is entirely blameless for the ensuing injury.[2] These are not excluded under para 11; indeed such injuries are materially indistinguishable from a case where the offender pushes the victim into a canal or river, or over a cliff or other natural or artificial embankment intending to cause death or personal injury, or being reckless as to whether these are caused. The Board's 1986 Report gives such a case. A motorcyclist was caused to fall off his machine and into the path of a following vehicle by a length of strong tape that had been stretched taut across the road between two lamp posts.[3] The victim's claim succeeded, but the side note in the Report is misleading in its reference to 'traffic offences'; this was a straightforward example of a crime of violence.

2 CICB (1983) para 25.
3 CICB (1986) para 26. Also (1979) para 22 (cyclist injured when colliding with an obstruction deliberately placed in the road), and (1982) para 29 and (1988) paras 43.1-43.2 (victim riding on a moped/motorcycle bumped and pushed by offenders riding alongside him on motorbikes). However, where the stolen car a police driver was chasing stopped in the middle of the road, forcing the applicant to come to a halt, and who was then struck by a third car, the Board held that the application failed under para 11, *R v Criminal Injuries Compensation Board, ex p Emmett* unreported, CICB (1989) para 26.3

Chapter Six

Eligible Persons

Paragraphs 4, 15 and 16 of the Scheme specify those to whom awards of compensation may be made by the Board. The heads of compensation payable and the method by which compensation is assessed will be the subject of the next chapter. Besides any restrictions mentioned in these paragraphs, there is a further group of persons to whom the Board may refuse to make an award, notwithstanding that they have sustained criminal injuries. This group comprises those who, broadly speaking, have been victimised by intra-family violence. Where the victim was under the age of 18 when the injury was sustained the Board shall, by para 8(c), consider whether it is in his interests to make an award; if it is, and in all cases where the victim was over 18 at the time the injury, compensation will not be payable unless the Board is satisfied on the other matters specified in para 8(a)-(b). This class of excluded victims is considered in section B below.

A. THE CLASSES OF COMPENSABLE PERSONS

(1) Non-fatal injuries

(a) THE ORIGINAL INJURY

Paragraph 4 provides that the Board will entertain applications for ex gratia compensation in any case where the applicant sustained a criminal injury. The vast majority of applicants have comprised those who themselves sustained a personal injury arising from a crime of violence, an act of law enforcement or trespass on a railway. In cases in which the victim is a child, the application will be made by its parents or by the person in loco parentis.[1] Applications made by Directors of Social Services in respect of physical or sexual abuse of children now in their care have risen substantially in recent years as local authorities have become aware of the Scheme. In 1989 the Board received 1,300 applications arising from child sexual abuse, of which approximately 800 were non-stranger offences. To assist applicants in such cases the Board has prepared a separate leaflet outlining its procedures and the relevant provisions of the Scheme.[2]

A rather less usual application would be one made on behalf of a child born disabled as the result of its sustaining a qualifying injury while in the womb, which was directly attributable to a crime of violence being committed against its mother.[3] There seems no reason in principle why the qualifying injuries that may be sustained by an unborn child should not be as extensive as those that give rise to liability under the Congenital Disabilities (Civil Liability) Act 1976.[4] If an offender gives a pregnant woman a drug in circumstances constituting an offence under ss 23 or 24 of the Offences against the Person Act 1861 which causes no harm to her, but which causes the child to be born disabled, there should be a qualifying injury under the Scheme.[5]

Applications on behalf of a child injured *en ventre sa mere* are of course quite separate from any application that the mother may have for a qualifying injury that she sustained at the time. If she also suffered an injury by being given a drug under the circumstances outlined above, or from a physical assault, she will sustain a qualifying injury. Where a woman is raped, she will be eligible for compensation for that injury, but should she also keep the child conceived thereby, she may make a separate application under para 10 of the Scheme, which permits compensation to be paid 'in respect of pain, suffering and shock and in respect of loss of earnings due to consequent pregnancy'.

---

1 Where the child is a ward of court, a *Practice Direction* issued by the Family Division provides that application must be made by the guardian ad litem for leave to apply and to disclose to the Board such documents on the wardship proceedings as are considered necessary to establish eligibility and quantum. Provision is also made where the judge has not given leave at the wardship hearing, and for the management of the award; [1988] 1 All ER 182.
2 CICB 25th Report (1989, Cm 900) paras 21.4-21.5 and App E.
3 CICB 20th Report (1984, Cmnd 9399) para 21.
4 *Winfield on Tort* (1984, 12th edn, W Rodgers, Sweet & Maxwell) 685.
5 Cf HC Official Report (6th series) Standing Committee F col 796 (26 February 1987) where the Minister of State indicated that he thought that a child contracting AIDS as a result of rape would not be eligible under the Scheme in the Criminal Justice Bill 1986.

At common law there has been a division of opinion as to whether damages are recoverable by the parents for the costs and expenses associated with the upbringing of a child whose birth was unwanted, the current position being as established in *Thake v Maurice*,[6] but the Scheme has always provided that no compensation will be payable for the maintenance of a child born as a result of a sexual offence. The continued exclusion of this head of compensation was justified by the Working Party on the grounds that while it was right that the Scheme should make provision for the injury directly resulting from the rape, including the birth of the child, 'for the Scheme to accept full responsibility for [its] upkeep until it reaches economic independence would be tantamount to accepting that the whole life of the child was attributable to the original crime.'[7] There are, additionally, the practical objections that arise from the considerable problems associated with any assessment of such maintenance. Nevertheless, the Working Party thought that the Scheme should recognise, 'in a more limited way, the difficulties faced by a woman who bears a child conceived as a result of rape',[8] and recommended the specific provision in the Scheme of a conventional sum. This is given effect by the 1990 revision to para 10, which provides that:

'Compensation will not be payable for the maintenance of any child born as a result of a sexual offence, except that where a woman is awarded compensation for rape the Board shall award her the additional sum of £5,000 in respect of each child born alive having been conceived as a result of the rape which the applicant intends to keep.'

This is similar in substance to s 111(11) of the 1988 Act, which also provides that the sum may be varied by order by statutory instrument.

(b) DETERIORATION FOLLOWING A SUCCESSFUL CLAIM FOR THE ORIGINAL INJURY

Following the 1979-80 revisions to the Scheme, the Board was given discretion in para 13 to re-open cases where there had been 'such a serious change in the applicant's medical condition that

---

6 [1984] QB 644, [1984] 2 All ER 513.
7 Home Office *Criminal Injuries Compensation: A Statutory Scheme* (1986) para 10.3.
8 Ibid, para 10.5.

injustice would occur if the original assessment were allowed to stand.' There is no limit to the number of such applications that can be made, save that on the first occasion it must be brought within three years of acceptance of the final award (there may have been interim awards), though the Chairman has discretion to accept applications to re-open cases that are made out of time. As we saw in chapter 2, such cases impose substantial administrative and judgmental burdens on the Board.[9] In determining whether the deterioration requires reconsideration, the Board must be satisfied both as to the causal link between that and the injury, and as to the injustice of a refusal of further compensation, given the extent of that deterioration. This allows the Board not to entertain applications where the deterioration is attributable, for example, simply to ageing, or is slight.

(2) Fatal injuries

In tort law, death creates a cause of action for the victim which, by virtue of the Law Reform (Miscellaneous Provisions) Act 1934 survives for the benefit of his estate and, independent of this, a cause of action for those of his dependants as can establish a loss of dependency or eligibility for the bereavement award under the Fatal Accidents Act 1976, s 1A. At common law the primary significance of the survival of the victim's cause of action was to give the estate the benefit of the conventional sum for loss of expectation of life, abolished by s 1(1)(a) of the Administration of Justice Act 1982. When the Scheme was first devised, it was thought inappropriate that this benefit should be payable from public funds and so it was excluded,[10] limiting compensation in fatal cases to dependants (though this class was more narrowly drawn than under the Fatal Accidents Act 1976 or the Damages (Scotland) Act 1976) and to those non-dependants who incur reasonable funeral expenses.

Paragraph 4 provides that the Board will entertain applications for ex gratia payments of compensation from a spouse or dependant of a person who sustained a criminal injury and who later died. The Scheme then distinguishes between those cases in which the victim died in consequence of the injury (para 15), and those in which he died from other causes (para 16). It should be recalled that even where the victim sustained a qualifying

9 Supra, pp 61-62.
10 839 HC Official Report (5th series) col 150 (22 June 1972).

injury in respect of which the Board does not exercise its discretion under para 6(c), it may nevertheless refuse or reduce compensation if it considers the dependant(s) to be undeserving as defined in those ways.[11] For the purpose of paras 15 and 16 the words 'dependant' and 'relative' have the same meaning as they are given respectively by the Fatal Accidents Act 1976 and the Damages (Scotland) Act 1976.

A change made in the 1990 revision is that cohabitees may now make an application to the Board for loss of support. When the Administration of Justice Act 1982 extended the class of dependants to persons who had been living with each other as husband and wife for at least two years immediately before the death, the Scheme was amended so as to maintain their non-eligibility.[12] The Working Party, which recommended that the conditions attaching to applications arising from domestic violence (considered below) should apply also to cohabitees, did not believe that the factors that had prompted the imposition of those conditions 'justify the exclusion of people who have enjoyed a stable relationship as unmarried husband and wife of which there is ample evidence'.[13] However, as in tort law, there is no change in the non-eligibility under the 1976 Act of cohabitees for the bereavement award.[14]

(a)   WHERE THE VICTIM DIES AS A RESULT OF THE
QUALIFYING INJURY

Arising from a homicide or from a death occasioned by law enforcement activity or by an offence of trespass on a railway, those who are dependants within s 1(3) of the Fatal Accidents Act 1976 may be awarded compensation under para 15, which will be assessed on the basis of the principles that apply to fatal accident actions. This includes compensation for bereavement, and in Scotland, loss of society. This is payable to any person falling within s 1A(2) of the Fatal Accidents Act 1976 or s 10(2) of the Damages (Scotland) Act 1976, which, as just noted, maintains the exclusion of cohabitees from this award. Their compensation will otherwise be assessed on the same principles

11 Supra, pp 79-81. CICB 14th Report (1978, Cmnd 7396) para 55, 17th Report (1981, Cmnd 8401) paras 9-12, 18th Report (1982, Cmnd 8752) para 11, 19th Report (1983, Cmnd 9093) paras 35-36, 969 HC Official Report (5th series) cols 59-61 (25 June 1979).
12 36 HC Official Report (6th series) col 60 (1 February 1983).
13 Home Office (1986) para 15.6.
14 Ibid, para 15.7.

as apply to actions under the 1976 Act, which will principally concern loss of support. Besides these, para 15 further provides that a reasonable amount of compensation for funeral expenses may be awarded to any person 'even where the person bearing the cost of the funeral is otherwise ineligible to claim under this Scheme.'

Occasionally the victim may survive the immediate injuries caused by the victimising event and die from them some time later. If, while he was still alive, he became entitled to compensation from the Board, any award payable to his dependants for the same injury will be reduced by the amount of his compensation. Such applications are subject to the conditions set out in para 13.

(b) WHERE THE VICTIM DIES OTHERWISE THAN AS A RESULT OF THE QUALIFYING INJURY

By para 16, where the victim dies otherwise than in consequence of the injury, the Board may make an award to a dependant (or relative) for loss of wages, expenses and liabilities incurred by the victim before his death. It is implicit in para 16 that if the victim had made a successful application for compensation during his lifetime, no compensation will be payable to the dependants since the award to him would have fully covered these items up to the time of death. If an interim award only was made prior to the victim's death, a dependant may be made an award under the terms of para 16, though it too will be reduced by the amount of the interim award. This is standard practice where the victim survives.

B. THE CLASSES OF NON-COMPENSABLE PERSONS

Despite a qualifying injury, para 8 of the Scheme gives the Board discretion not to make an award where the injuries were sustained as a result of domestic violence. By para 8(c), where the victim was, at the time of his sustaining the injury, under 18 and living in the same household and as part of the same family as the person(s) responsible for it, the Board shall not make an award unless it is satisfied that it is in his interests. Where the victim is over 18, the conditions set out in para 8(a)-(b) must be met before compensation will be awarded.

In Great Britain, as elsewhere, compensation (or the denial thereof) for victims of intra-family violence has always been a controversial matter. Attention has been drawn to the difficulty of establishing the facts and of distributing blame, of the possibility of fraud, and of the administrative problem of ensuring that the offender does not benefit. Where the victim is a minor, there is the additional potential for subsequent harm should the award be managed outside the family, later to be released to the now adult beneficiary who perhaps for the first time discovers that he was physically abused by his family.[15] There are matters of genuine concern here, though they should not be overstated. On the matter of fraud, for example, as Trobiner J remarked in *Dillon v Legg*, 'the possibility that fraudulent assertions may prompt recovery in isolated cases does not justify a wholesale rejection of the entire class of claims in which that potentiality arises.'[16]

The original Scheme excluded such cases, but at the Board's initiative, the question was considered by the Home Office Working Party in 1978, which recommended that the rules be changed to permit such applications, subject to strict qualifications.[17] Currently, these are that:

> '(a) the person responsible has been prosecuted in connection with the offence, except where there are practical, technical or other good reasons why a prosecution has not been brought; and
> (b) in the case of violence between adults in the family, the Board are satisfied that the person responsible and the applicant stopped living in the same household before the application was made and seem unlikely to live together again.'

When first introduced there was a further condition, that the injury met a higher (£500) minimum loss than the normal case.

Though regarded as an 'important advance' by the Board,[18] there was a limited response to this change.[19] In the five years following the introduction of the amended Scheme, 781 applications under para 8 were finalised, yielding 415 awards. Given the preconditions to compensation and the circumstances of much family violence, there was, not surprisingly perhaps, a very high proportion of rejected applications: 342 (44%) out

15 Ibid, ch 8.
16 (1968) 29 ALR 3d 1316 at 1323. See further Stephenson LJ, *McLoughlin v O'Brian* [1981] 1 QB 599 at 616.
17 Home Office *Review of the Criminal Injuries Compensation Scheme: Report of an Interdepartmental Working Party* (1978) ch 7.
18 CICB 16th Report (1980, Cmnd 8081) para 9.
19 CICB (1981) paras 7-8.

of the five year total. The main reasons for rejection were (and often more than one reason might apply): a failure to reach the £500 threshold,[20] the victim and offender continuing to live together,[1] a failure to report without delay,[2] and want of prosecution. A notable feature of the rejected applications to which the Board has drawn attention is the role played in these cases by the excessive consumption of alcohol; it is also unsurprising that such applications often disclose a history of violence.[3]

These application figures are not only low, but also were, in the first two to three years following the 1978-79 amendments, lower even than the number that were formerly rejected each year. Wasik has argued that such factors as fear of reprisal and public embarrassment would continue to deter women (who are the main but not the only victims who fall within this category) from reporting acts of violence to the police.[4] A further disincentive is that the requirement of a prosecution conflicts with any policing practice which seeks to decriminalise domestic violence, although para 8(a) does give the Board a discretion to compensate (assuming the other conditions were met) where it considers that there are good reasons why a prosecution has not been brought. Another factor deterring applications until 1986, when the lower limit was raised to £550, was the higher financial threshold applicable in these cases. The reason for this variation, which Wasik called 'arbitrary and anomalous' was, indeed, apart from its function as a crude quantity control, hard to see. Certainly, it could not be defended on any qualitative basis; a woman who, before the last but one increase, sustained at the hands of a stranger an injury valued at £450 would have

20 CICB 21st Report (1985, Cmnd 9684) para 6.
1 For the purposes of para 8, 'a man and a woman living together as husband and wife shall be treated as members of the same family', *R v Criminal Injuries Compensation Board, ex p Staten* [1972] 1 All ER 1034, [1972] 1 WLR 569. An applicant divorced from the victim but living with him when he was murdered was not entitled to compensation under the Scheme, the Board applying *Payne-Collins v Taylor Woodrow Construction Ltd* [1975] QB 300, [1975] 1 All ER 898, CICB (1980) para 22. For other examples see CICB (1982) paras 43 and 44, (1984) paras 30 and 31, 22nd Report (1986, Cm 42) paras 25 and 29 and 24th Report (1988 Cm 536) paras 39.1-39.3. See also *Jones v Jones* [1976] Fam 8, [1975] 2 All ER 12, CA and *Hoskyn v Metropolitan Police Comr* [1979] AC 474, [1978] 2 All ER 136, HL.
2 CICB (1982) para 42.
3 CICB (1980) para 9, (1981) paras 7-8, (1982) paras 9-10 and 42-44, and (1983) paras 7, 31 and 33a.
4 M Wasik 'Criminal injuries compensation and family violence' [1983] J Social Welfare Law 100-108.

been entitled to compensation, but not if the offender lived with her, even if all the other conditions in para 8 had been satisfied. At the time of its introduction it was twice the threshold applicable in all other cases, which made the discrepant treatment of this class of victim the more acute.

The Working Party was satisfied with the approach taken by the Board, and saw little scope for amendment.[5] One recommendation was that the Act should make it clear that the phrase 'in the same household' covered homosexual as well as heterosexual liaisons, and also included persons merely sharing accommodation.[6] This was enacted in s 109(1)(a), and the revised para 7 of the Scheme creates the same effect. This provides that:

> 'Compensation shall not be payable unless the Board are satisfied that there is no possibility that a person responsible for causing the injury will benefit.'

This paragraph used to be concerned with applications arising 'in respect of sexual offences or other offences which arise out of a sexual relationship or where the relationship between the victim and the offender is such that there may be difficulty in establishing the facts or it seems possible that the offender may benefit from any award of compensation to the applicant.' The Board was enjoined to scrutinise such applications 'with particular care'. As amended, para 7 may be read as a specific postscript to the conditions set out in para 8, but it must be emphasised that its effect is not so limited; it clearly applies to every application made to the Board.

5 Home Office (1986) para 8.1. A typical case is CICB (1989) para 21.2.
6 Home Office (1986) para 8.5.

Chapter Seven

The Assessment of Compensation

With the exception of the survival of a deceased victim's action, and a few other variations, the assessment of compensation under the Scheme has always been based on the principles applicable to an action under the Fatal Accidents Act 1976 or to a personal injury action. Thus by para 12: 'Subject to the other provisions of this Scheme compensation will be assessed on the basis of common law damages . . .' Whether these principles are appropriate to a criminal injuries compensation scheme is arguable. The 1961 Working Party canvasssed the alternatives of loss and need as the basis for the assessment of compensation, and set out an option modelled on the industrial injury scheme which emphasised its characteristic features: awards payable by pension and not as a lump sum, thus allowing variation for deterioration in the victim's condition, adjustment for inflation and protection against dissipation; flexibility and easy dovetailing with social security benefits and payments by the offender; and administrative convenience.[1] The common law model was however, with some modifications, preferred, and it has not seriously been questioned since either by the Board or by its parent department. Nor, with one or two exceptions has it been much questioned by others who have commented upon the Scheme.[2] Like the Pearson Commission,[3] the 1986 Working Party considered the common law model to be 'the best available

---

1 Home Office *Compensation for the Victims of Crimes of Violence* (1961, Cmnd 1406) paras 12-13. Also JUSTICE *Compensation for Victims of Violence* (1962).
2 Cf P Cane *Atiyah's Accidents, Compensation and the Law* (1987, 4th edn, Weidenfeld and Nicolson) pp 290-297. Those favouring the introduction of the Scheme were almost uniformly of the view that common law damages was the appropriate basis; 694 HC Official Report (5th series) col 1132 (5 May 1964). Cf Baroness Wooton 257 HL Official Report (5th series) col 1379 (7 May 1964).
3 *Royal Commission on Civil Liability and Personal Injury* (1978, Cmnd 7054) para 1591.

157

basis for the compensation of victims by the state', but offered no reasons why this should be so.[4]

Despite the implication that it is self-evident that the Scheme ought to start from the proposition that the loss to the victim or his dependants ought to be compensated in full, this unquestioning stance cannot disguise the very real difficulties that this basis can create. A good illustration is the continuing difficulty that the Scheme has when dealing with victims who earn high salaries. Though the adoption of the common law model necessarily implied that high earners should be compensated to the full extent of their loss, the Scheme's progenitors thought it inequitable that this should be met from the public purse:

'A state scheme which resulted in two different persons, because they followed different employments, being paid different amounts in respect of identical injuries, received in respect of identical offences, might be regarded as unfair.'[5]

This view persists; the 1986 Working Party observing:

'public feeling demands that innocent victims should be able to maintain a reasonable standard of living compared with that which they enjoyed previously, but this does not extend to compensating in full from public funds the loss of earnings incurred by very highly paid employees.'[6]

The Working Party further endorsed its predecessor's view that high earners are more likely to make some provision against the possibility that their earnings or earning capacity will be interrupted by injury, whether accidental or otherwise, but this assertion has not been matched by any published data showing whether those who apply to the Board have indeed made such provision. Accordingly, the Scheme's solution to this matter, which is the imposition of an arbitrary ceiling on compensable loss of earnings, amounts to a penalty against those who have not taken out such insurance. Moreover, this solution stands in marked contrast to that provision of the Scheme which excludes from the rules requiring the deduction from the award of

4 Home Office *Criminal Injuries Compensation; A Statutory Scheme* (1986) para 12.4.
5 Home Office (1961) para 49.
6 Home Office (1986) para 14.1.

collateral benefits, any moneys payable to the victim or his dependants under an insurance policy to which the recipient was the subscriber.

A further illustration of this particular difficulty which the Working Party broached, but upon which it made no recommendation, concerned the applicability of the ceiling to victims who have two sources of income, only one of which is affected by the criminal injury, the other exceeding, or contributing to exceed, the upper limit.[7] The Working Party acknowledged that to vary the Board's current practice, which is to compensate to the limit for the criminal injury notwithstanding the other earnings, would involve a radical departure from the principle of compensation for loss to the adoption of 'a sort of means testing',[8] but given the small numbers, considered such a move too costly in administrative terms. The European Convention on Compensation for Victims of Crimes of Violence suggests the adoption of an approach such as this where victims are wealthy,[9] but it seems very unlikely that the basis of the Scheme will be altered in the absence of the kind of wider-ranging review that would accompany a change in all accident compensation provision.

A rather different approach canvassed before the Working Party was that compensation under the Scheme should be assessed according to a tariff reflecting not merely the harm to the victim, but also its 'seriousness' as evidenced by the offender's degree of fault. Such a tariff would reflect, Shapland argued, the fundamental difference between negligently and intentionally inflicted injuries:

> 'The "criminal scale" would be based on a concept of the seriousness of the offence from the point of view of the typical victim, taking into account not only the actual consequences to the victim, but also the symbolic gravity of the offence and the fact that the victim has been the victim of a crime rather than an accident.'[10]

Thus under this tariff the victim of a given injury would receive greater compensation than is available at common law where

---

7 Ibid, para 14.4.
8 Ibid, para 14.5.
9 Council of Europe *European Convention on the Compensation of Victims of Violent Crimes* (1983, Treaty Series No 116) Art 7. D Miers 'The compensation of victims of crime in continental Europe' (1985) 10 Victimology 662-671, 667-668.
10 Home Office (1986) para 12.2.

it was inflicted in the commission of an offence of high seriousness, and conversely less where an the offence was of low seriousness. Such a proposal faces formidable objections. Devising a matrix that would permit distinctions to be drawn in one dimension according to the offender's degree of fault (representing, though very crudely, the seriousness of the offence), and in the other according to the actual impact of the injury, would be profoundly controversial. Let us suppose, as is demonstrated by the Board's 23rd Report, that a victim having his two front teeth knocked out would receive £1,500 general damages.[11] What multiplier would we use to distinguish an intentional from a reckless blow or to distinguish its symbolic gravity to a 70 year old from a 20 or 10 year old victim, or a male from a female victim? And how if the injury was not caused by a crime of violence but was accidentally sustained while the victim was taking an exceptional risk, justified in all the circumstances, in an act of law enforcement? If he should therefore receive less because it was of low symbolic gravity, we should hardly be surprised if the Scheme came under a torrent of criticism. And then how would the Board have any way of judging the seriousness of a criminal injury caused by a crime of violence when the offender is unapprehended?[12] The Working Party rightly rejected this proposal while favouring the retention of common law damages as the preferred model.

In general, the principles upon which quantum is to be assessed depend on whether the application falls to be determined under the law of Scotland or of England and Wales. One major difference between the two jurisdictions is that in the case of fatal injuries, the law in England and Wales provides for the conventional sum of £3,500 for bereavement, whereas in Scotland compensation for loss of society is to be assessed in each case. To the extent that it appears anomalous that different provisions should apply to the same injury depending upon where it was sustained, the

11 CICB 23rd Report (1987, Cm 265) para 41.
12 The 'typical' victim of the kind of conduct that may lead to a criminal injury qualifying under the Scheme is, statistically speaking, a young male. It is not clear from the Working Party's discussion of Shapland's suggestion whether this is the 'typical' victim she had in mind. There are also problems, as the British Crime Survey noted, with how 'serious' the respondents sampled in its survey regarded different offences, M Hough and P Mayhew *Taking Account of Crime* (1985, Home Office Research Study 85) 20-23. See further M Levi and S Jones 'Public and police perceptions of crime seriousness in England and Wales' (1985) 25 BJ Crim 234-250.

Working Party did not think that the anomaly required rectification; in any event it was unable to find any acceptable common method of assessment to be followed throughout Great Britain.[13]

As the assessment of compensation is based on the principles applicable in personal injury and fatal accident actions, the Board will, for example, expect the victim to mitigate his loss where it would be reasonable for him to do so.[14] Nevertheless, the Scheme maintains its established variations upon those principles. These variations concern such matters as what is compensable (for example, no exemplary or punitive damages), what is deductible (for example, all moneys accruing from occupational pensions), and the finality of an award (the Board has power to reconsider cases in the event of deterioration). There are also other differences, such as the upper limit on loss of earnings, and in fatal cases, the requirement that the applicant (and not just the deceased) should himself not fall within the terms of para 6(c) disentitling him to any or full compensation. The remainder of this chapter sets out the Scheme's provisions governing these and allied matters, and discusses the Board's implementation of them. Attention is drawn to the differences between the Scheme and personal injury or fatal accident actions where appropriate, but no particular attention is paid to those aspects of the assessment of damages that go beyond the concerns of the Scheme.

A. PERSONAL INJURIES

Paragraph 17 is the sole exception to the proposition that compensation under the Scheme is payable only for personal injury. Particular differences between the assessment of damages for personal injuries at common law and under the Scheme will be observed in the text following. It is appropriate to recall at the outset that because the Board has, by para 12, power to make interim awards, it has no jurisdiction to make awards of provisional damages under s 32A of the Supreme Court Act 1981.[15]

---

13 Home Office (1986) paras 12.6-12.9 and 15.3-15.4. See also CICB 13th Report (1977, Cmnd 7022) paras 18-19 and (1987) para 45.
14 CICB (1987) para 46.
15 Nor, since the applicant's loss is determined at the date of assessment, is interest payable on awards as in a personal injury action; s 35A, Supreme Court Act 1981. On interim awards see supra, pp 60-61.

(1)   Special damages

(a)   LOSS OR DAMAGE TO PROPERTY

Under para 17 of the revised Scheme:

> 'Compensation will not be payable for the loss of or damage to clothing or to any property whatsoever arising from the injury unless the Board are satisfied that the property was relied upon by the victim as a physical aid.'

Compensation has always been payable for the cost of replacing lost or damaged personal adjuncts such as spectacles, dentures, hearing aids and artificial limbs, though not for such adjuncts as jewellery, watches or rings lost or damaged at the time of or after the incident, or in the course of medical or other treatment arising therefrom.[16] Lost or damaged clothing, on the other hand, was, prior to the 1990 revision, a compensable item. In 1986 the Board paid out approximately £800,000 a year on clothing, personal adjuncts and other out-of-pocket expenses, of which one half was attributable to claims for clothing. The Working Party took the view that whereas it was appropriate to compensate for such as hearing aids and dentures, 'upon which a person is dependent to the extent that the effect of their loss or damage is akin to personal injury', the line should be drawn there.[17] Claims for lost or damaged clothing are difficult to verify, and anyway clothes wear out in time and have to be replaced. The government likewise argued that the case for compensating lost or damaged clothing was weak, but was repeatedly subjected in debate to the criticism that the exclusion from the statutory Scheme of what had been in its predecessor was mean, in particular where the victim is poor and cannot readily afford to replace the lost or damaged item.[18] The government resisted a number of amendments seeking to restore the position under the pre-1990 Scheme, arguing that as the concession to the railwaymen to include harm to a person's mental condition arising from railway suicides as qualifying injuries would cost £800,000, there was nothing left in the kitty for clothing.[19]

---

16 The Statement, para 5(1)c.
17 Home Office (1986) para 17.1.
18 On the provision in the Criminal Justice Bill 1986, HC Official Report (6th series) Standing Committee F cols 788-793 (26 February 1987), and on the 1987 Bill 489 HL Official Report (5th series) cols 754-756 (29 October 1987) and 490 HL Official Report (5th series) cols 413-414 (2 November 1987).
19 HC Official Report (5th series) Standing Committee F, op cit, col 790.

By s 111(3) of the 1988 Act, compensation for property loss or damage is limited in two ways. Firstly the applicant may be awarded compensation only if he relied on the item as a physical aid and its utility has been impaired by the victimising event. Secondly, the amount of compensation shall only be enough, in the case of a lost item, to replace it with property of equal utility, for example, spectacles to the same prescription but not with frames other than those sufficient to make them wearable, and in the case of a damaged item, to restore their utility. The simple object is to preclude compensation being paid to replace or to restore hearing aids, spectacles, dentures and the like which are more expensive than is necessary for them to perform the task for which they were prescribed. The taxpayer should only be expected to subvent NHS equivalent costs. Paragraph 17 of the 1990 revision is not as detailed as its statutory equivalent, but the Board may be expected to apply similar guidelines in such cases.

(b) MEDICAL AND OTHER EXPENSES

On the assumption that the applicant can verify each item, the Board will routinely include in the award compensation for out-of-pocket expenses such as dental costs, fares to hospital and the cost of any treatment prescribed. Where the injuries sustained require long term care for the victim, including, for example, alterations to the victim's house or domestic arrangements where he has been disabled by the injury, expenses incurred will be compensable as at common law. The Board's Reports show awards covering the cost of rehabilitation courses,[20] blind aids, talking watches and home assistance for victims blinded by an attack,[1] for nursing care,[2] changes to the structure and layout of a house[3] including the provision of additional heating,[4] and for the provision of an adapted car for victims handicapped by paralysis.[5] The Board will endeavour to make provision for any increases in such expenses that are now foreseeable.[6] Expenses or losses incurred by others, for example, the loss of present or

20 CICB (1977) para 30.
1 CICB 20th Report (1984, Cmnd 9399) para 36.
2 CICB 18th Report (1982, Cmnd 8752) para 18, 21st Report (1985, Cmnd 9684) para 11, 22nd Report (1986, Cm 42) para 9 and (1987) para 11.
3 CICB 17th Report (1981, Cmnd 8401) paras 14-15, (1982) para 18, (1985) para 11, (1986) para 9 and (1987) para 11.
4 CICB (1987) para 11.
5 CICB 15th Report (1979, Cmnd 7752) para 6.
6 CICB (1986) para 29.

future income earned by a spouse or parent who gives up a job to nurse the victim is compensable.[7] It is assumed that the medical treatment sought by, and provided to, the victim will fall within the National Health Service; where the victim seeks private medical treatment, para 18 provides:

> 'The cost of private medical treatment will be payable by the Board only if the Board consider that, in all the circumstances, both the private treatment and the cost of it are reasonable.'

This represents the common law position, which allows the plaintiff damages for such medical expenses as are reasonably incurred by him as a result of the injury, which may include private medical and nursing care.[8]

The Working Party thought that the statutory Scheme should make it clear that the Board should not normally pay for such treatment; hence the requirement in para 9 of Sch 7 to the 1988 Act that it be not merely reasonable, but essential.[9] What constitutes 'essential' treatment was a matter of some debate during the Bill's parliamentary stages. The typical case used in support of amendments to return to a test of reasonableness, was that of a young woman waiting for many months or even years for plastic surgery to correct the facial scars left by the criminal injury. In debate on the equivalent clause in the 1986 Bill, the Minister of State indicated that, though each application was for the Board to determine, the government, expecting the provision 'to be treated fairly liberally', would consider private treatment for scarring essential in such a case.[10] The Lord Advocate, speaking for the government at the Committee Stage of the 1987 Bill was less forthcoming; despite acknowledging that being a Member of the Board, Lord Morton would have found little difficulty in deciding such a case other than in favour of the applicant, he refused to be drawn into an affirmative statement to that effect.[11] What is essential treatment is, of course, as Lord Morton observed, a difficult matter: 'what is it to be

---

7 *Donnelly v Joyce* [1974] QB 454, [1973] 3 All ER 475, CA. CICB (1981) paras 14-15, 19th Report (1983, Cmnd 9093) para 11, (1984) para 10 and (1986) para 9.

8 CICB (1977) para 30, 14th Report (1978, Cmnd 7396) para 26 and (1979) paras 6-7. See generally H McGregor *McGregor on Damages* (1988, Sweet and Maxwell) paras 1497-1500.

9 Home Office (1986) para 18.1.

10 HC Official Report (6th series) Standing Committee F, op cit, col 795.

11 489 HL Official Report, op cit, col 757.

essential to — the life of the applicant, the good temper of the applicant, or what?'[12] Essential in the light of the victim's circumstances might be an acceptable way of answering this question, but as is the case under the unamended para 18 of the Scheme, like 'reasonable', it would always be a matter for the Board's discretion.

(c) MAINTENANCE OF A CHILD BORN AS A RESULT OF RAPE

Pain and suffering experienced by a rape victim is compensable, as is any pain and suffering associated with the pregnancy and any expenses associated with the birth. The Scheme does not, however, permit compensation to be paid for the maintenance of the child; what is provided by para 10 is the additional sum, currently £5,000,[13] payable for each child born and conceived as a result of the rape which the mother, at the time of the award, intends to keep. This sum is not recoverable by the Board should she later seek to have the child adopted.

(d) LEGAL EXPENSES

Legal costs incurred by the applicant in the preparation of an application to the Board are not compensable. Neither are they compensable where they have been incurred for the purpose of representation at a hearing (even at one requested by a single member), though para 25 permits the Board to reimburse expenses incurred by the applicant and any witnesses called to a hearing. As to legal representation at a hearing, however, it was presumably thought that the taxpayer ought not to bear the costs of legal fees, at least where the applicant would himself not be eligible for legal aid; but this rule does seem harsh on those who would be. Two hours' free legal advice is available to applicants under the Green Form procedure, but the Working Party proposed no change in the basic rule excluding the cost of representation.[14]

Neither will the Board reimburse an applicant for the costs he incurred in pursuing an unsatisfied judgment in civil proceedings.[15]

---

12 Ibid, col 758. See also 490 HL Official Report, op cit, col 416.
13 The figure of £5,000 was considered to be the product of the application of a multiplier of 10 years to 17 years' maintenance of the child, HC Official Report (6th series) Standing Committee F, op cit, col 802.
14 Home Office (1986) para 23.1. Supra, p 64.
15 D Williams *Criminal Injuries Compensation* (1986, Waterlow) para 7.02.

(e) LOSS OF EARNINGS

As at common law, the applicant is entitled to damages for loss of earnings to the date of the trial and for future loss of earnings;[16] included will be compensation for the lost years in cases where the victim's life expectancy has been reduced.[17] Assuming the victim was not unemployed or unemployable, loss of earnings can generally be calculated by reference to his wage or salary slips. In any event the applicant is required to state in his application his average net earnings after tax, which figure is routinely checked with the employer. Where the applicant is self-employed, or has income from some other source, such as a share of a firm's profits, he will be asked to produce a set of accounts or a tax assessment in order to substantiate his claim for loss of earnings. As the Board observed in its 25th Report, the calculation of the applicant's loss of earnings can of course be protracted, especially where he has had to change employment or been medically retired. Extensive enquiries may have to be made to determine salary increases, promotion prospects, pension rights and entitlement to state benefits. These calculations may in turn have to take account of the cost of special care, accommodation or equipment.[18]

The net rate of loss of earnings including future loss of earnings (which is calculated by application of the multiplier appropriate to the victim's circumstances) and of earning capacity was, prior to the 1990 revisions to the Scheme, subject to the limitation set out in para 14(a):

> 'the rate of net loss of earnings or earning capacity to be taken into account shall not exceed twice the gross average industrial earnings at the date of assessment (as published in the Department of Employment Gazette and adjusted as considered appropriate by the Board)'

'Gross' average industrial earnings means earnings before deductions for income tax and national insurance contributions.[19] The upper limit was initially expressed to be calculated at the

---

16 CICB (1986) para 9. Earnings includes fringe benefits, ibid, para 30. McGregor (1988) paras 1451-1481.

17 *Pickett v British Rail Engineering Ltd* [1980] AC 136, [1979] 1 All ER 774, HL.

18 CICB 25th Report (1989, Cm 900) paras 23.3-23.9.

19 *R v Criminal Injuries Compensation Board, ex p Richardson* [1974] Crim LR 99, and CICB 10th Report (1974, Cmnd 5791) para 4.

date of the incident, but the 1978 Working Party considered this to be harsh in inflationary times (the quantum of compensation necessarily being calculated some months, and in recent years, over a year, after the injury) and was changed by the 1979-80 amendments to the date of assessment;[20] hence the exclusion of interest on awards.

The upper limit was included not so much as an economic measure, as was argued in connection with the minimum limit, but rather, as was noted earlier, to prevent the perceived inequity of the very high earner being sustained at the taxpayer's expense in the manner to which he had grown accustomed.[1] While being entirely arbitrary, the limit specified has probably adversely affected only a very small percentage of applicants to the Board. The 1978 Working Party thought the limit too high, but its recommendation that it be reduced to one and a half times the average industrial earnings was not implemented.[2] The 1986 Working Party was of the same mind,[3] and the government, more conscious now perhaps of the cost of the Scheme, included it in the 1990 revision to para 14(a).

The reduction in the upper limit has not been without its critics who consider this a further indication of the government's parsimony to victims of crime, and amendments were tabled seeking to restore the status quo.[4] In 1987, the effect of the old limit was to allow the Board to compensate for loss of earnings or earning capacity to a maximum of, in round figures, £400 a week or £21,000 a year. With the multiplier at one and a half, the annual gross limit would now be approximately £17,500. This, the Working Party estimated, would leave around 70% of full time workers unaffected,[5] but there are no published figures indicating how much the reduction will achieve in the Scheme's expenditure.

Like personal injury actions, the assessment of compensation under the Scheme has not been specifically linked to the retail

---

20 CICB (1983) para 11.
1 490 HL Official Report, op cit, col 419.
2 Home Office (1978) paras 11.2-11.4. 902 HC Official Report (5th series) col 293 (11 December 1975), and 927 HC Official Report (5th series) col 436 (7 March 1977).
3 Home Office (1986) para 14.2.
4 On the Criminal Justice Bill 1986, 113 HC Official Report (6th series) col 1015 (31 March 1987) and 486 HL Official Report (5th series) col 1316 (27 April 1987), and on the 1987 Bill, 489 HL Official Report (5th series) op cit, cols 763-65.
5 Home Office (1986) para 14.2.

price index.[6] This does not imply any erosion of awards greater than now occurs in personal injury actions, since the multipliers used by the Board, being those approved by the courts, provide for a 4-5% increase in inflation;[7] but as with common law damages, the Board's awards are necessarily affected where the rate is higher. In the case of loss of earnings and of earning capacity, the upper limit specified under para 14 is self-adjusting, being based upon the weekly average published by the Department of Employment. Similarly, no further adjustment to the multiplier should be made by the Board to take account of the fact that in a very serious case where the muliplicand is substantial, it is likely that the income generated by the investment of the award will attract a higher rate of tax. It should ordinarily be assumed that the future incidence of tax will be dealt with by the conventional assumption of an interest rate applicable to a stable currency and the selection of a multiplier appropriate to that rate.[8]

(2)   General damages

Being based on the common law, the Board can award compensation for loss of amenity and for pain and suffering, and can take into account under that heading the victim's awareness of his loss of expectation of life which, before it was abolished by the Administration of Justice Act 1982, was dealt with as a separate element of general damages. Excluded by para 14(a) of the Scheme is any 'element comparable to exemplary or punitive damages', being matters inappropriate to a state-funded compensation scheme. Exemplary damages are not awarded at common law for the injury, but as a means of punishing the defendant;[9] aggravated damages, on the other hand, are intended to be compensatory, reflecting for example the injury to the plaintiff's feelings that arises from the defendant's particularly malicious conduct, or from the unusually distressing circumstances of the injury. It is only relatively recently that

---

6   *Cookson v Knowles* [1979] AC 556, [1978] 2 All ER 604, HL; *Wright v British Railways Board* [1983] 2 AC 773, [1983] 2 All ER 698, HL. CICB (1981) para 14, 969 HC Official Report (5th series) cols 59-61 (25 June 1979) and 15 HC Official Report (6th series) col 185 (17 December 1981).

7   *Lim Poh Choo v Camden and Islington Area Health Authority* [1980] AC 174, [1979] 2 All ER 910; *Auty v National Coal Board* [1985] 1 All ER 930, [1985] 1 WLR 784, CA.

8   *Hodgson v Trapp* [1989] AC 807 at 835 per Lord Oliver.

9   *Rookes v Barnard* [1964] AC 1129, [1964] 1 All ER 367, HL; *Cassell & Co Ltd v Broome* [1972] AC 1027, [1972] 1 All ER 801, HL.

the criteria applicable to aggravated damages have been considered in detail, and Woolf J's decision in *Kralj v McGrath* indicates the difficulties that they generate.[10] The Working Party considered that the concept of aggravated damages was inappropriate to the Scheme, given that almost all criminal injuries will be occasioned by ill-will,[11] and by para 8 of Sch 7 of the 1988 Act, the statutory Scheme excludes them. Aggravated damages are not specifically mentioned in the non-statutory Scheme, but to the extent that the assessment of pain and suffering does take the matter into account, this does not mean that an award cannot be made that reflects the hurt to the victim's feelings.

The Board expresses the award for general damages as a global sum, and thus only limited assistance can be gleaned from its Reports as to how this is made up in any particular case. On the other hand, the Board does regularly publish guideline figures for pain and suffering as part of its continuing efforts to ensure that its awards are in line with common law damages.[12] Although its own members have extensive experience in personal injury litigation, and are expected to deal with 1,500 applications a year,[13] the Board has, for a number of years, conducted compensation exercises with High Court Judges and QCs. The results of the last three of these exercises updated to 1990 show:[14]

INJURY	1981-82	1983-84	1986-87	1990
undisplaced nasal fracture	375	450	550[15]	650
displaced nasal fracture	625	700	850[16]	1,000
wired jaw	1,200	1,250	1,750	2,500

10 [1986] 1 All ER 54.
11 Home Office (1986) para 14.8.
12 CICB (1978) paras 21-25 indicate that on some matters the Board will in consequence of its assessment exercises, revise the guidelines upwards.
13 House of Commons, Home Affairs Committee *Compensating Victims Quickly: the Administration of the Criminal Injuries Compensation Board* (1989-90 HC 92) para 8.
14 CICB (1982) para 46, (1984) para 35, (1987) para 41 and its *Guide to the Level of Awards* (1990). It is intended that the 26th Report shall contain a list indicating guidelines both for the Board and for compensation orders made by a criminal court, CICB (1989) para 23.1(a).
15 CICB (1989) para 25.1.
16 Ibid, paras 25.2 and 25.6.

rape (no serious damage)[17]	2,200	2,750	5,000	—[18]
loss of two front teeth (plate or bridge)[19]	1,000	1,200	1,500	1,500
male scar	4,000	4,500	5,000	6,000[20]
female scar	5,000	6,500	7,000	8,000
loss of one eye	10,000	12,000	13,000	15,000
loss of vision	45,000 (total)	—	50,000[1] (total)	15,000 (one eye)
loss of hearing	25,000 (total)	27,000 (total)	32,000 (total)	11,500 (one ear)

The Board's current *Guide to the Level of Awards* also gives other examples: loss of taste and smell as a result of a fractured skull (£12,500), simple fracture of tibia, fibula, ulna or radius with complete recovery (£2,500) and laparotomy (£3,000); guidance can also be obtained from Kemp and Kemp[2] and from the specimen awards given in the Board's Reports.[3] Despite these explicit statements, there is considerable variation in the reliance placed upon them by practitioners representing applicants at hearings.[4] There also appears, from a pilot study of the Board carried out by the Home Office, to be some variation in the general damages awards reached by single members and at hearings. We consider this more closely in chapter 12.[5]

These figures are, as the Board has been at pains to insist, guideline figures only.[6] They do not, and cannot, displace its discretion under the Scheme to assess the appropriate

17 For other sexual offences see, ibid, para 25.8 and T Newburn The *Settlement of Claims at the Criminal Injuries Compensation Board* (1989 Home Office Research Study No 112) p 25.
18 The figure for rape has been publicised, as the Board now considers this to be too unrealistic.
19 CICB (1989) paras 25.3-25.4.
20 Ibid, para 25.7.
1 CICB (1987) para 48.
2 *The Quantum of Damages* vol 2, Personal Injury Reports (Sweet & Maxwell) contains reports of CICB awards. See also Newburn (1989) pp 24-25.
3 For examples of the Board's general damages awards, CICB (1984) paras 36-39, (1985) paras 11 and 33-41, (1986) paras 29-39, (1987) paras 11 and 46-51, 24th Report (1988, Cm 536) paras 43.1-48.2, and (1989) paras 25.1-25.10.
4 Infra, pp 305-306. Care should be taken not to rely on figures more than two years old.
5 Newburn (1989) pp 22-24. Infra, p 306.
6 CICB (1985) para 35. *Guide to the Level of Awards* (1990).

compensation in each case. The Board's observations in the 1987 Report are typical:

> 'It is emphasised that in each case the figure is a starting point figure and may be increased or decreased according to circumstances. In every injury the effect which it has on the applicant in question is of great importance; if the effect on the applicant is greater than that which such an injury usually causes, a higher award will be made.'[7]

Such cautionary remarks are frequently accompanied by an illustration, again in fairly general terms, of its application to particular injuries: 'for example, most broken noses recover completely, but if there is any significant permanent disability or cosmetic defect, the award will be more, and perhaps substantially more, than the guideline figure.'[8] The 1987 Report repeats earlier observations about the differential impact on male and female victims of scarring, and the corresponding variations in the award that would be made in each case, and also observes that an elderly victim sustaining a minor assault may well be made an award higher than if the victim were young: 'in particular, hand-bag snatching cases frequently turn a self-reliant, confident, elderly person into one who is frightened and nervous.'[9]

The regular iteration of this cautionary advice has not, however, diminished the level of criticism directed, in particular, at the guideline award for rape. The figures given in the table are, according to the Board, appropriate for cases leading to no serious physical or psychological damage, and where the Board is assured that the victim has made a complete recovery from the experience. Nevertheless, the guideline figure has been widely regarded as being an insufficient recognition of the emotional significance to a woman of the unwanted invasion of her body. Although the figure will be increased where the conditions mentioned by the Board do not obtain, the group Women Against Rape, thought it 'outrageous' that the base figure in 1984 for rape was £2,750, while the figure given for a scar on an unmarried woman, 'running from left corner of her mouth backwards and downwards and ending just underneath her jaw bone' was £7,000.[10]

These criticisms were particularly heightened by the outcome of the claims for compensation, both to the Board and in civil proceedings, which arose from the injuries Christopher Meah

---

7 CICB (1987) para 41.
8 Id.
9 Id. To the same effect, CICB (1986) para 31.
10 CICB (1984) para 35.

sustained when a passenger in a negligently driven car, and from the injuries he in turn caused to two women as a consequence of the personality change he suffered.[11] Meah was awarded £45,750 general damages for the personality change and for his classification as a Category A prisoner following his violent rape and sexual assaults upon his two victims who, in their civil action against him, received respectively £10,480 and £7,080.[12] In a separate application to the Board, they were awarded £3,600 and £1,000. Many were critical of the discrepancies between these various figures, which were aggravated by the requirement that the victims would either have to repay the Board the awards from their civil action, or have those damages deducted in advance of the award being made.[13] Some of this criticism was no doubt uninformed; but two substantial points remain. Firstly, inasmuch as the Board has relied to a great extent for its guidelines on members of the Bar and on High Court judges with experience of personal injury litigation, the figure for rape may have been, as one commentator has argued, 'somewhat suspect',[14] given that personal injury actions such as *W v Meah* are very rare,[15] and thus only a handful of practitioners will ever have had direct experience of them. Secondly, and given the paucity of cases, it may be that the level suggested by the compensation exercises simply does not, if attempts are to be made to translate such injuries into money terms, adequately value the pain and suffering experienced by a rape victim.

The Working Party was particularly conscious of the sensitivity of this particular matter, a consciousness that was evident in its recommendation that there should be a fixed sum payable where the woman bears and keeps the child. It also observed that it would expect the pain and suffering award in claims arising from rape to make exceptional provision for that offence:

'an exception [to the normal assessment of pain and suffering which will take into account the injury to the victim's feelings] must be made for offences where injury to feelings caused by an abhorrent act might be of greater importance than any actual physical or mental injuries. Such an exception is in our view essential in the case, for

---

11 *Meah v McCreamer* [1985] 1 All ER 367.
12 *W v Meah*; *D v Meah* [1986] 1 All ER 935.
13 Times, 11 and 12 December 1985, Sunday Times, 15 December 1985.
14 (1984) 134 New LJ 639. See also 'Rape compensation' (1982) 132 New LJ 175.
15 See *Miles v Cain*, unreported, in which a woman sexually assaulted and raped by a physiotherapist was awarded £25,108 damages in an action for trespass to the person (1988) Independent, 26 November.

example, of sexual offences as the Board's current assessment of compensation for rape starts from a figure which would be awarded where there were no long-lasting physical or psychological injuries, and such an award must contain a substantial element in respect of injury to feelings.'[16]

Whether the Board will be publicly responsive on this issue remains to be seen, though it is of interest to note that its 1987 Report shows an increase in the starting figure for rape to £5,000 because of the woman's fear that she may have contracted AIDS.[17] Given, as has been noted, that the Board members have far more experience of dealing with damages awards for intentional torts to the person than most others dealing with personal injury litigation, it is open to them to give a lead on the matter of rape compensation.

B. FATAL INJURIES

As we saw in chapter 6, an application may be made by a dependant or, in Scotland, a relative of a person who died after sustaining a qualifying injury. The Scheme distinguishes between those cases where the victim died as a result of the injury (para 15), and those where he died otherwise than as a result of it (para 16). In the latter case, the heads of damage are restricted to 'loss of wages, expenses and liabilities incurred by the victim before death as a result of the injury'. This is in effect the compensation for financial loss sustained as a result of the injury to which the victim would have been entitled had he survived. Thus an award will be payable to a dependant in respect, for example, of the victim's medical treatment following the victimising event. In the former case, compensation will also be payable where the dependant has sustained a loss as a result of the deceased's injury, for example, a spouse who gave up a job in order to nurse the victim.[18] By para 5, the lower limit does not apply to applications

16 Home Office (1986) para 14.8.
17 CICB (1987) para 41.
18 In *R v Criminal Injuries Compensation Board, ex p McGuffie* [1978] Crim LR 160, the applicants were two aunts who had given up their jobs to foster the three children left when their father was imprisoned for the murder of their mother. They applied both on behalf of the children, and on their own behalf. The aunts received a boarding out allowance from the local authority which the Board deducted from their own claim for loss of wages. Pain J held that while the Board was right to deduct that amount of any allowance attributable to the actual cost of materials consumed in looking after the children, there should be no deduction in respect of any amount

under para 16; however, any loss suffered by a reduction in the deceased's prospective earnings is by implication excluded. Likewise any expenses or liabilities incurred by the dependant concerning the victim's death, for example, funeral expenses, are not compensable. Neither does para 16 give those dependants specified in s 1A of the Fatal Accidents Act 1976 the fixed award for bereavement, this being payable only where the victim died as a result of the injury. In this case, para 15 provides that compensation shall be assessed as though it were an action by a dependant under the Fatal Accidents Act 1976. The following sections consider its implementation.

(1) Special damages

(a) FUNERAL EXPENSES

Where the victim died as a result of the injury, compensation for reasonable funeral expenses is payable to anyone who incurred them. This is so notwithstanding that the expense is less than the minimum limit specified in para 5 or that the applicant is otherwise ineligible, for example, because the Board would apply para 6(c) either because of the victim's or the dependant's unlawful conduct or character.

The Board claims to have a sympathetic approach to applications for funeral expenses, and the Statement indicates what it regards as a reasonable expense.[19] This includes the cost of a tombstone and of conveying family mourners to the funeral but excludes memorials (if they are part tombstones, that cost has been met), newspaper announcements, wreaths and funeral breakfasts (though reflecting the more generous provision under Scots law, awards have been made for the costs incurred for these three, where the expenditure was apt and reasonable). The Working Party further indicated that the Board would be very unlikely to meet the cost of burial overseas of a victim resident

attributable to the cost of providing emotional care for the children. In reconsidering the application, the Board commented on its approach, as implicitly approved by the Divisional Court, 'that, where a fostering allowance is being paid, the financial element of the allowance intended to pay for the cost of feeding, clothing and maintaining the child is to be set against any claim for dependency, and any element there may be in a fostering allowance which is intended to compensate for the loss of care which the mother bestowed on the child is to be set against any claim for loss of the mother's services.' CICB (1978) para 13. See *Spittle v Bunney* [1988] 3 All ER 1031, [1988] 1 WLR 847, CA; *Stanley v Saddique* (1990) Times, 24 May, CA.
19 The Statement, para M.

in this country; by contrast, if satisfied that the expenditure is justified, it may be more prepared to meet the cost of a burial in his own country of a visitor here.[20]

(b) LOSS OF SUPPORT

The Scheme follows the familiar method of assessing the value of the lost dependency, which, as Lord Wright said in *Davies v Powell Duffryn Associated Collieries Ltd*, 'is a hard matter of pounds, shillings and pence'.[1] The process is similar to that which applies in a fatal accidents action to the calculation of future loss of earnings, commencing with an enquiry into the victim's gross earnings before tax as the figure from which to deduct his own expenses, and then applying the appropriate multiplier to give a figure representing what the dependant has lost.[2] In determining the value of the lost dependency, the Board proceeds, as s 4 of the Fatal Accidents Act 1976 requires, by disregarding any 'benefits which have accrued or will accrue to any person from his estate or otherwise as a result of his death.' The purpose of s 4, though broader than its predecessors in not confining 'benefits' to 'social security benefits', is, like them, 'to produce an exception to the common law rules for calculating the quantum of damages, namely to prevent the deduction of a benefit which would otherwise have to be deducted in order to arrive at the true loss on a common law basis.'[3] However, the Scheme goes on to provide that certain kinds of benefit are nevertheless to be deducted from the award that would otherwise be payable for the lost dependency. This is dealt with shortly. If there was no dependency, then no compensation is payable, or if, as in a case such as *Burns v Edman*,[4] the victim's earnings were the proceeds of criminal activity, the Board will refuse to make an award. In determining the multiplicand, para 14(a) stipulates that the rate of net loss of earnings or earning capacity shall not exceed one and a half times the gross average industrial earnings.

---

20 Home Office (1986) para 15.11.
  1 [1942] AC 601 at 617. For examples of the Board's approach see CICB (1980) para 24, (1981) para 31, (1982) para 19, (1983) para 23, (1984) paras 11, 40 and 41, (1985) para 32, (1986) para 28, (1987) para 44 and (1988) paras 42.1-42.3. McGregor paras 1551-1592.
  2 Kemp and Kemp *The Quantum of Damages* (Sweet & Maxwell) para 6-005ff.
  3 *Pidduck v Eastern Scottish Omnibuses Ltd* [1990] 2 All ER 69 at 74 per Purchas LJ. McGregor (1988) para 1594.
  4 [1970] 2 QB 541, [1970] 1 All ER 886.

The Scheme necessarily imports into the Board's assessment of the loss of support sustained by the dependants, s 3(3) and (4) of the Fatal Accidents Act 1976. These mean, firstly, that in assessing the compensation payable to a widow in respect of the death of her husband, the Board shall take no account of her remarriage or the prospects thereof. This provision does not apply where the applicant was a woman living with the deceased as his wife.[5] However, where the dependant was not married to the deceased but was living with the other as husband or wife, the Board shall, by s 3(4) of the 1976 Act, take into account the fact that the applicant had no enforceable right to financial support. Given the low incidence of homicide,[6] the Board presumably receives only a small number of applications under para 15, and they do not appear to have generated any special difficulty.

(2)   General damages

In England and Wales general damages for dependants have only been available since the introduction of the bereavement award in the Administration of Justice Act 1982. This is a fixed sum of £3,500, payable to a more narrowly defined range of dependants than are eligible for special damages, and, as noted earlier, is further qualified by s 1A of the Fatal Accidents Act 1976 to exclude 'common law' wives and husbands. By contrast, the law in Scotland is more extensive.[7] Under the Damages (Scotland) Act 1976 an award for loss of society is payable to any person who was a parent or child of the deceased, and to any person accepted by the deceased as a child of his family. Bereavement is restricted to the lawful spouse of the deceased, and to the parents of an unmarried minor if he was legitimate or to his mother if illegitimate.[8] Unlike bereavement, loss of society is not a conventional sum, but was interpreted by the Inner House in

---

5 Home Office (1986) paras 15.8-15.9.
6 In 1988 the number of homicides per million of population was 11.8, and there were 306 convictions for homicide in that year; Home Office *Criminal Statistics England and Wales 1988* (1989, Cm 847) tables 4.1 and 4.7(a).
7 The level of the award in England and Wales is under review, Lord Chancellor's Department *Damages for Bereavement: A Review of the Level* (1990).
8 Where an unmarried person is injured by a victimising event before his 18th birthday, and dies from it after he has attained that age, the parents are not entitled to damages for bereavement. This is so because the entitlement arises at the date of death, not at the date of the wrongful act, *Doleman v Deakin* (1990) Times, 30 January, CA.

Dingwall v W. Alexander & Sons (Midland) Ltd as requiring an amount representing proper compensation 'for the loss of a father's help as a member of the household and of his counsel and guidance as a husband and father and for similar, unquantifiable loss in relation to the death of a wife and mother or of a child.'[9] Examples of the application both of the bereavement award and of the assessment of loss of society are given in the Board's Reports.[10]

C. DEDUCTIONS

A distinguishing feature of the Scheme is that almost all collateral benefits have fallen to be deducted from any compensation payable, including all social security benefits without limitation of time, insurance or pension moneys payable otherwise than upon a policy subscribed to by the victim (or his parents if under 18), and any award payable by the offender to the applicant under a compensation order or a court order for damages. There can be no controversy as to the last of these; so far as the Scheme seeks to substitute for the offender, it must be right that where he can be pursued to judgment, the taxpayer's burden be correspondingly reduced. Deduction of social security benefit is 'based on the sound principle that there should be no duplication of payments from public funds',[11] while the deduction of any benefits payable by an employer by way of insurance, gratuity or pension, is justified on the basis that state compensation should not provide an income which is in effect higher than the victim (or his dependants) enjoyed before the injury.

In a number of respects the rules governing the deduction of collateral benefits under the Scheme have, from its inception, been different to those which have obtained in personal injury or fatal accident actions; these and some other differences remain following the 1990 revisions and the changes introduced by s 22 of the Social Security Act 1989.[12] These differences are, in the case of applications brought by the dependants of a person killed as a result of a qualifying injury, substantial. Although the benefits which have accrued or will accrue to any person from

9 1980 SC 64, 1979 SLT (Notes) 100. See further CICB (1985) paras 40-41.
10 Eg CICB (1989) paras 24.2-24.8.
11 Home Office (1986) para 19.1. 838 HC Official Report (5th series) col 37 (8 June 1972).
12 McGregor (1988) paras 1481-1496 (personal injuries) and 1597-1600 (fatal injuries).

his estate or otherwise as a result of his death will have been disregarded by the Board when determining the value of the lost dependency, most benefits fall to be deducted in full from the award, and some others to 50% of their value. On the other hand, the difference between the Scheme and a personal injury action has lessened significantly following the enactment of s 22 of the Social Security Act 1989. This essentially provides that the value of all social security benefits aggregated over five years are to be deducted from common law awards of damages. However, the Scheme continues to require the deduction of benefits that would, under s 22(4) qualify as 'exempt payments'.

Paragraphs 19-20 govern the deduction of collateral benefits under the Scheme. These distinguish the following benefits: social security benefits (para 19(a) and (c)), other criminal injury compensation awards (para 19(b) and (c)), insurance payments (para 19(d)); occupational insurance and pension rights (para 20); and payments made by way of damages or under a compensation order (para 21). Before turning to consider in detail the operation of these paragraphs, it should be noted that, subject to two qualifications, they operate to deduct the benefit accruing to the applicant from the full amount of any compensation payable, and not merely from that element of loss to which they may substantially relate. The operative paragraphs speak of compensation being reduced 'by the full value' of the benefit (para 19), 'to take into account' of any pension (para 20) and 'by the amount of payment received' by order of the court (para 21). The Board makes no attempt to match deductible benefits to particular losses; once it has set the aggregate value of these various benefits against its overall assessment of the compensation that would otherwise be payable, it quite simply deducts any excess firstly from any heads of special damage and secondly from any heads of general damage until the excess is exhausted. In the case of a personal injury application, this means deduction from the award of general damages, a requirement that now applies by virtue of s 22 of the Social Security Act 1989 to the deduction of social security benefits from an award or settlement of damages. In the case of an application under para 15, this means deduction from the conventional award for bereavement or from the assessed award for loss of society.[13]

The Working Party considered the argument that these sums should only be deducted from that part of the award for special

---

13 CICB (1987) para 44.

damage to which they apparently relate, as s 2(1) of the Law Reform (Personal Injuries) Act 1948 provided, for example in the case of unemployment benefit, to loss of earnings. The argument was rejected because social security benefits do not relate exclusively to pecuniary losses, and thus to allow them to go undeducted would permit some duplication of payment from public funds.[14] In the case of payments received by way of damages or compensation orders, it would be inappropriate to permit the applicant to recover twice for the same injury, since by definition these orders will have made some allowance for general damages. Similarly payments made under pension or insurance arrangements executed by someone other than the victim or his parent need not be wholly confined to loss of earnings, and even where the payment may be expressly related only to loss of earnings or of earning capacity, the Working Party could see no way in which the Scheme could draw a workable distinction between these and other collateral benefits which may be intended to meet, to some extent, the general damage suffered by the victim. In any event, to allow such differentiation would have cut across the government's acceptance of the view that in the context of personal injury actions, the state should not subsidise the tortfeasor, and that the victim should not get the windfall of double compensation.[15]

The first qualification concerns applications made under para 15 for funeral expenses. Where the application is made by a person other than the dependant who was in receipt of the specified benefits, the applicant will receive an award irrespective of the value of those benefits (and irrespective of whether his expenses exceed the lower limit: para 5). This is so simply because there is nothing to deduct from the applicant's claim. However, the Board has also made an award for such expenses where the applicant himself was in receipt of the deductible benefits specified in paras 19(a) and 20. In a case reported in 1986, though the value of the sum of DSS benefits and employer's pension totalled £17,267 as against £16,647 for the value of the lost dependency and thus no award was payable in respect of it, the Board did compensate the applicant for her funeral expenses.

---

14 Home Office (1986) para 19.2.
15 144 HC Official Report (6th series) col 719 (10 January 1989). The position that obtains under the Scheme was always favourably compared with that at common law. See 488 HL Official Report (5th series) col 943 (14 July 1987), *Royal Commission on Civil Liability and Personal Injury*, op cit, ch 13, 395 HL Official Report (5th series) col 288 (18 July 1978) and 446 HL Official Report (5th series) col 285 (14 December 1983).

These amounted to £412, less than the £620 excess of benefits over the lost dependency.[16] The basis for this differentiation appears to be para 15, which provides that an applicant may be made an award for funeral expenses who is otherwise ineligible. But this is not satisfactory, since eligibility usually relates to the question whether an applicant has a cause of action, not to the question of quantum, which necessarily supposes that he has. Moreover, if ineligibility includes cases where the applicant's para 19 and para 20 benefits exceed the compensation payable, then why should it not equally include para 21 benefits? The question arises whether the Board would make an award for funeral expenses if the dependant had succeeded in obtaining a court order for damages against the person responsible for the deceased's killing, which order specifically included the cost of the funeral. It seems unlikely; under the statutory Scheme the court order would certainly be deductible. By para 13 of Sch 7 to the 1988 Act, where the applicant has received payment, whether by way of a compensation order or damages, which compensates him for any loss for which compensation would be payable under the Scheme, his compensation shall be assessed 'on the basis that that loss is reduced by the amount of that payment'. On the other hand, paras 11 (social security benefits) and 12 (occupational insurance pensions) of Sch 7 are both expressed so as to exclude compensation for funeral expenses from this process of reduction. In this respect the Act follows the non-statutory Scheme, but in differentiating in the case of funeral expenses only between payments made by the offender and payments made by innocent third parties, the Scheme deviates from one of its principal operating premises, which is to compensate for the net loss sustained by the applicant.

The second qualification concerns the additional sum payable under para 10. A woman who has been raped and who has suffered a loss of earnings in consequence will have the value of any unemployment benefit, income support or of employer's wages or sick pay to which she is entitled deducted from the compensation payable for this head of damage and, if these exceed that loss, from general damages. Though not explicit, the use of the phrase 'additional sum' in para 10 suggests that whatever the outcome of the application of paras 19-21 to the compensation payable, the applicant will be awarded £5,000 in respect of each qualifying child.

Paragraphs 19 and 20 refer only to benefits to which the

16 CICB (1986) para 28.

applicant's entitlement, whether present or future, can be established at the date upon which his application is determined. Should he subsequently become entitled to a benefit resulting from the criminal injury that would fall to be deducted if the assessment were then to be made, the Board can do nothing to recoup the sum payable. The exception to this is a subsequent entitlement arising in pursuance of a judgment or settlement of damages, or under a compensation order. Paragraph 21 expressly requires the applicant 'to undertake to repay [the Board] from any damages, settlement or compensation he may subsequently obtain in respect of his injuries'. The Working Party recommended that the Board should 'be able to recover any other payments subsequently received which the Board would have been obliged to take into account if they had already been made',[17] and such a power is contained in s 115(4) of the 1988 Act. However, no such amendment was made in the 1990 revision of the non-statutory Scheme.

(1) Deductions under para 19

This paragraph provides:

'Compensation will be reduced by the full value of any present or future entitlement to —

(a) United Kingdom social security benefits;
(b) any criminal injury compensation awards made under or pursuant to statutory arrangements in force at the relevant time in Northern Ireland;
(c) social security benefits, compensation awards or similar payments whatsoever from the funds of other countries; or
(d) payments under insurance arrangements except as excluded below which may accrue, as a result of the injury or death, to the person to whom the award is made'.

In assessing such entitlement the Board is required to take account of any income tax liability that is likely to reduce its value. This permits the Board to adjust (upwards) an award where the unadjusted payment of it would result in the applicant losing some or all of the value of the benefit to which he is entitled. However, it does not assist applications in which the award itself has an impact upon the entitlement, as may be the case where

17 Home Office (1986) para 21.2.

a rape victim receiving income support will lose that upon being compensated by the Board, since the award is almost always going to be more than the current £6,000 limit above which such benefit ceases to be payable.[18]

In the case of applications under para 15, the Board shall not take any account of the prospects of remarriage when calculating the value of such entitlements to the surviving spouse. This maintains a provision introduced in the 1979-80 amendments, which reversed the earlier 'strange anomaly' whereby, while her prospects of remarriage were to be discounted when determining the value of the lost dependency (in conformity with s 4 of the Law Reform (Miscellaneous Provisions) Act 1971), any social security benefits payable to a widow were to be reduced in value by the prospects of remarriage.[19] This position thus gave the applicant both the benefit of not having the value of the lost dependency reduced by the prospect of remarriage and the benefit of having a smaller sum (representing any appropriate social security payments) deducted from that dependency precisely because of her prospects of remarriage. The Board will continue to disregard any reduction or withdrawal of DSS benefit consequent upon actual or impending remarriage, while the value of the lost dependency will likewise remain unaffected by that event.

If the Board considers that an applicant might be eligible for social security benefits, it can refuse to make an award until he has made reasonable efforts to claim them.[20]

(a)   SOCIAL SECURITY BENEFITS

Deduction for the purposes of the Scheme is uniform: all such benefits are deductible in full and without limitation of time. This contrasts with the position that obtained before the requirements of s 22 of the Social Security Act 1989 were introduced. In a personal injury action some benefits were fully deductible (unemployment benefit,[1] income support (supplementary

---

18 Independent, 9 March 1987, Times, 28 November 1988, Observer, 29 July 1990. By para 11(3)(b) of Sch 7 to the 1988 Act, the Board shall have regard 'to any effect the making of the award is likely to have on that entitlement'.
19 CICB (1974) para 6. See 490 HL Official Report, op cit, col 423.
20 CICB (1985) para 48, Home Office (1986) para 19.6. Cf *Eley v Bedford* [1972] 1 QB 155, [1971] 3 All ER 285, where at common law social security benefits which had not been claimed were not deductible.
 1 *Nabi v British Leyland (UK) Ltd* [1980] 1 All ER 667, [1980] 1 WLR 529.

benefit) received before trial,[2] attendance allowance,[3] family credit,[4] statutory sick pay[5] and redundancy payments that would not have been paid but for the injury[6]); some were deductible under s 2 of the Law Reform (Personal Injuries) Act 1948 to the extent of half their value over the five years following the accident (sickness benefit, invalidity benefit, non-contributory invalidity pension, industrial injury and disablement and severe disablement benefit[7]); while some were not deductible at all (constant attendance allowance and the state retirement pension). Under s 22, a 'compensator' (s 22(1)) is required to withhold compensation payable in respect of an injury under a court order or in pursuance of a settlement until the Secretary of State has provided him with a certificate stating the value of the benefits to be deducted from the payment. 'Benefits' means any benefits payable under the Social Security Acts 1975 to 1988. However, there remains an important difference between the Scheme's requirements and those of s 22. For the 1989 Act, the value of the benefits is determined over five years from the day following the day on which the injury occurred; for the Scheme, the value of the benefits payable to the applicant are aggregated over his lifetime.

We may note here that by s 22(4)(f), a payment by the Board under s 111 of the Criminal Justice Act 1988 is an 'exempt payment'. Until the relevant sections of the 1988 Act are brought into force, awards under the non-statutory Scheme do not fall within the scope of s 22, but this does not mean that there is any double recovery, since under para 21 of the Scheme the applicant undertakes to reimburse to the value of the award from any sums received in pursuance of a civil action against the offender.

In the case of an application made by a dependant of a person who died as a result of the injury, death grant and widow's benefit

2 *Plummer v PW Wilkins & Son Ltd* [1981] 1 All ER 91, [1981] 1 WLR 831; *Lincoln v Hayman* [1982] 2 All ER 819, [1982] 1 WLR 488, CA. CICB (1981) para 29 and (1982) para 48.
3 *Hodgson v Trapp* [1989] AC 807, [1988] 3 All ER 870, HL.
4 *Gaskill v Preston* [1981] 3 All ER 427.
5 *Palfrey v Greater London Council* [1985] ICR 437.
6 *Colledge v Bass Mitchells & Butlers Ltd* [1988] 1 All ER 536, CA. Redundancy payments are exempt payments under s 22(4)(k) of the Social Security Act 1989.
7 *Denman v Essex Area Health Authority* [1984] QB 735, [1984] 2 All ER 621. CICB (1984) para 48 and (1985) para 35.

are, unlike a fatal accidents action, fully deductible,[8] though as previously mentioned, no account is taken of the prospects of a widow's remarriage.

Since many applicants will be in receipt of social security benefits, these rules are of considerable importance, and may indeed have a very substantial impact upon their applications. Of particular importance is the deduction of industrial injury benefit payable to those criminally injured at work, notably the police[9] and occasionally, firemen, hospital workers and nurses.[10] The impact of full deduction for these particular victims has for some time been a controversial matter. As has been noted, the total of these (and all the other deductible collateral benefits) are deducted not just from the element of special damages but from the entire award. Accordingly, where the victim is seriously disabled as a result of his sustaining a qualifying injury and is entitled, in addition to industrial injury benefit, to such benefits as mobility allowance,[11] disablement benefit,[12] or blind person's allowance,[13] it is quite likely that the Board will be unable to make any award at all, or at least one that is not substantially reduced by the aggregated value of these benefits.[14] The Board has been criticised where this does occur,[15] unfairly perhaps considering that it is here interpreting rules which give it no discretion, and it is indeed sensitive to any alleged lack of sympathy on its part which such nil or very small awards might suggest. In its defence it has typically prayed in aid an underlying principle of the Scheme, which is that the taxpayer ought not to compensate a victim twice for the same injury.[16]

Paragraph 19(c) also requires the deduction of any analogous benefits paid to the applicant in another country.

---

8 CICB (1978) para 20, (1980) para 24, (1982) para 19 and (1984) paras 40 and 41.
9 CICB (1983) para 30.
10 M Ogden 'The work of the Criminal Injuries Compensation Board' (1984–85) 52 Medico-Legal J 227-241, 233.
11 CICB (1979) para 6.
12 Id.
13 CICB (1977) para 30.
14 CICB (1985) para 32, and (1986) para 9.
15 Eg an award which, after deductions, amounted to £2,660 to a policeman who in April 1981 had been shot at point blank range through the chest, stomach and bowels, and who continued to experience pain from these injuries some three years later, was described as 'mean recompense' by the Police Federation, Times, 5 April 1984.
16 CICB (1979) para 6, (1980) para 11 (service pension), and (1981) paras 14-15 (policemen). 838 HC Official Report (5th series) col 137 (8 June 1972).

(b) OTHER STATE COMPENSATION FOR CRIMINAL INJURIES

It is possible, though unlikely, that an applicant could be eligible under both the Northern Ireland provisions and the Scheme. Paragraph 19(b), which has been revised slightly, simply means that the Board will deduct that compensation from any award.[17]

Some countries have compensation schemes that provide for the compensation of their own nationals who sustain criminal injuries abroad. Many more, and in particular those who are signatories to the Council of Europe's Convention on the Compensation of Victims of Violent Crime, have, or propose to have, reciprocal arrangements whereby a signatory state will compensate the nationals of co-signatories who sustain criminal injuries within its own jurisdiction, if the co-signatories will likewise compensate its nationals who sustain criminal injuries in their jurisdictions.[18] It is also the case that such arrangements, where they are made by member states of the European Community, may be enforceable by nationals of other member states who are injured while engaged in conduct falling within the Treaty.[19] Paragraph 19(c) prevents double recovery under these provisions.

(c) THIRD PARTY AND PRIVATE INSURANCE ARRANGEMENTS

Paragraph 19(d) is intended to lead to the deduction from the award of any payments made under insurance arrangements effected by a third party. Where that is the victim's employer, and the payment accrues to him by virtue of his employment, the deduction is covered by para 20. Moneys payable under private insurance arrangements, such as a personal accident policy, are not, however, deductible.[20] The Board 'will disregard moneys paid or payable to the victim or his dependants as a result of or in consequence of insurance personally effected, paid for and maintained by the personal income of the victim or, in the case of a person under the age of 18, by his parent'. The Working Party agreed with the Board that it was illogical that insurance benefits accruing from premiums paid for by a spouse should be deductible;[1] and in its definition of 'private insurance

---

17 Home Office (1986) para 19.4.
18 Ibid, para 19.3.
19 Supra, pp 137–138.
20 *Bradburn v Great Western Rly Co* (1874) LR 10 Exch 1. See s 22(4)(j) of the Social Security Act 1989.
 1 Home Office (1986) para 19.3. See also 490 HL Official Report (5th series) col 422 (25 November 1987).

arrangements', the Act includes those paid for by a spouse or by a person who at the date of injury was living in the same household with the victim as his spouse, and had done so during the whole of the two years immediately preceding that date. This change has not been introduced in the 1990 revisions to the non-statutory Scheme.

(2) Occupational insurance, pensions and other employers' payments

By para 20 of the Scheme, any pension payable as a result of his injury or death under arrangements connected with the victim's employment are fully deductible unless the contributions to the funds were made wholly by the victim. For the purpose of this paragraph, 'pension' means 'any payment payable as a result of the injury or death, in pursuance of pension or other rights whatsoever connected with the victim's employment, and includes any gratuity of that kind and similar benefits payable under insurance policies paid for by employers'. The paragraph goes on to provide that where the pension is taxable, for example as an 'approved scheme' which falls to be taxed as earned income, one half of its value will be deducted, but where it is not so taxable, for example a lump sum payable upon death or injury in service, or where it is commuted for a proportion of the victim's final salary, it will be deducted in full.[2]

The Working Party recommended the retention of the deduction for pension payments accruing as a consequence of the victim's employment, but saw little justification for the continuation of the variable rate of deduction based on whether the income from the pension is chargeable to tax.[3] The Working Party's objection was that the effect of the distinction was to make an allowance for the pension contributions if the income were taxable, irrespective of whether those contributions were subscribed to by the victim. As there is little difference in practice between contributory and non-contributory schemes (since in the latter the fact will be reflected in the rate of pay), the Working Party thought it simpler to take 'an uncomplicated approach', and recommended that where such benefits are taxable, the

---

2 J Tiley, ed *Butterworths UK Tax Guide 1989-90* (1989, Butterworths) ch 30.
3 Home Office (1986) para 20.5.

allowance should be made at the the basic rate.[4] A further objection to para 20 is that the 'rough and ready'[5] approach to taking into account liability to income tax in fact means that the income is treated as being taxed at 50%, whereas some victims would have been retaining, in 1990–91, not 50% but 75% of the income after payment at the basic rate.

Paragraph 12 is intended to cover firstly insurance and pension arrangements made by an employer and payable to the victim or his dependants if death should occur while he is in that employment. Pension rights accruing solely as a result of payments by the victim or a dependant will be disregarded.[6] This reflects the common law position established in *Parry v Cleaver*[7] and emphatically reiterated by Lord Bridge in *Hussain v New Taplow Paper Mills Ltd*, that:

> 'prima facie the only recoverable loss is the net loss. Financial gains accruing to the plaintiff which he would not have received but for the event which constitutes the plaintiff's cause of action are prima facie to be taken into account in mitigation of losses which that event occasions to him.'[8]

Thus payments made to a plaintiff under occupational insurance, whether contributory or not, are deductible if they have reduced the loss he has sustained; but the Scheme goes further in requiring the deduction of a pension which, again whether contributory or not, is not deductible at common law because it is not equivalent to a loss of earnings.[9]

These deductions must be made notwithstanding that the employer provides, in addition to the pension or personal accident scheme, a further sum designed to reflect the risk of criminal

---

4 The government resisted attempts to amend these provisions so that contributory pensions and insurance arrangements would be more favourably treated, 489 HL Official Report (5th series) cols 766-68 (29 October 1987).

5 Home Office (1986) para 20.5.

6 CICB (1984) para 41. On the scope of occupational pensions see Home Office (1986) para 20.4 and CICB (1979) paras 25 and 27.

7 [1970] AC 1, [1969] 1 All ER 555, HL.

8 [1988] AC 514 at 527. His Lordship continued by drawing attention to the two well established exceptions (recovery under an insurance policy for which the plaintiff has paid the premiums, and charitable payments), but also observed (at 528) that there are a variety of borderline cases in respect of which the courts 'have been baffled by the problem of how to articulate a single guiding rule' to distinguish those receipts that are deductible from those which are not. See Lord Bridge's similar remarks in *Hodgson v Trapp* [1989] AC 807 at 819.

9 *Parry v Cleaver*, op cit.

injury when the victim is acting in the course of his employment. The British Security Industry Association argued that the blanket deduction rule acted as a disincentive to its members who have routinely provided additional lump sum benefits in the event of their employees being killed or injured as a result of a robbery, and suggested that the statutory Scheme should seek to distinguish these.[10] The Working Party could devise no formula that would permit a severance of the sums payable to an applicant in these circumstances, and indeed took the view that even if it could, such discrimination would conflict with the general principle that underlies this and the associated provisions, that state compensation should not enrich the victim:

> 'The fact remains that in determining an applicant's loss of income it is relevant and reasonable to take account of moneys which accrue as a result of his employment and, if special benefits related to criminal injury on duty are provided as an entitlement under conditions of employment, it is appropriate that these should be taken into account. Accordingly, like the previous Working Party, we favour the retention of the wide definition of "pension".'[11]

Paragraph 20 also requires the deduction of any other payments payable 'in pursuance of . . . other rights whatsoever in connection with the employment', which is apt to cover wages or sick pay paid for by an employer as a matter of contractual obligation, which are fully deductible at common law.[12] However, the Scheme goes on to require the deduction of gratuitous payments made by an employer, but which are probably not deductible at common law.[13]

On the matter of ex gratia payments made by employers, the Working Party would have liked to have been able to differentiate from a truly gratuitous sum, such as an award for bravery paid by the victim's employer, those which arise from some expectation on the part of the victim, but was unable to devise a satisfactory test. Thus it reluctantly reached the conclusion 'that the only practical means of dealing with payments by employers is to regard all such payments as benefits arising out of employment

---

10 Home Office (1986) para 20.1.
11 Ibid, para 20.2.
12 *Hussein v New Taplow Mills*, op cit.
13 *Dennis v London Passenger Transport Board* [1948] 1 All ER 779; *McCamley v Cammell Laird Shipbuilders Ltd* [1990] 1 All ER 854, CA.

which should be taken into account in assessing compensation.'[14] That has always been, and continues to be, the position under the non-statutory Scheme.

(3) Recovery of damages or of compensation by the offender

Under para 21 of the Scheme, damages obtained as a result of a civil judgment or settlement, and compensation obtained under a compensation order made upon conviction are fully deductible by the Board from any award it might make. It is of course rare that civil proceedings can be successfully pursued against an offender, and as the Board's Reports have, since 1977-78, ceased to publish figures indicating the recovery of damages, it is not possible to judge their contemporary importance.[15] On the other hand, compensation orders appear to figure more frequently among those making applications to the Board, though as we shall see in chapter 12, the number of compensation orders made by courts for personal injury compares very badly with the number made in respect of criminal damage and theft.[16] In the three years to March 1989, the Board's Reports show that 1,802, 1,660 and 2,064 applicants had such orders made in their favour following a conviction, at face value amounting to £263,194, £230,419 and £341,275 respectively.[17] If entitlement were to be treated by the Board as reducing the loss for which compensation is to be assessed, some victims would in fact fail to receive their full award then (since there might be some delay in the offender's compliance with the order), or at all (since he might default). The Board's 1989 Report shows that at the time when these applicants received their awards, the amounts received under the compensation orders totalled about 75% of their face value,[18] but this does not of course indicate how individual applicants fared.

In order to deal with the possibility of delay and default in the payment of compensation orders, arrangements have for some time been in existence whereby the award paid to the victim will be for the full sum less only so much of the compensation

---

14 Home Office (1986) para 20.3.
15 In 1975-76 five applicants had received £5,457 in damages and in 1976-77 eight had received £2,394. In 1977-78, an unspecified number shared £13,740. CICB 12th Report (1976, Cmnd 6656) para 22, (1977) para 42, and (1978) para 48. Also CICB (1981) para 20(d).
16 Infra, pp 322–323.
17 CICB (1989) para 12.2.
18 Id.

order as has been received by him; the outstanding instalments paid by the offender have then been forwarded to the Board by the magistrates' court responsible for their enforcement.[19]

The Working Party received evidence from a number of bodies proposing that the Board should be given a statutory power to recover directly from the offender, either by applying to the court before which the offender was convicted for a compensation order, or by subrogation of the victim's civil action against him.[20] It rejected the former, largely because of the inappropriateness of the court having to reconsider an issue designed to be settled at the sentencing stage, 'a compensation order being part (sometimes the whole) of the sentence imposed for the offender's crime'.[1] It also took the view that it was unnecessary for the Board to assume the victim's right of action, but that it was sufficient that it had a power of recovery where it had reasonable cause to believe that the offender has the means to reimburse the whole or a substantial part of the compensation paid. This is given effect by s 115(1)-(3) of the Act, but these powers were not included in the 1990 revision.

(4)   Non-deductible payments

A few payments that may be made to a victim or his dependants consequent upon a qualifying injury do not have to be taken into account by the Board. As we have seen, payments made under a privately financed insurance policy are expressly excluded from para 19(d), as are those made under a privately financed pension plan from para 20. In addition, payments from charitable sources,[2] perhaps as a reward for an act of law enforcement are not deductible unless they are made by the victim's employer. These are consistent with the two 'well-established' exceptions to the rule that receipts accruing to the applicant in consequence of the injury are to be set against his loss.[3] A payment made by a court in recognition of a victim's attempts to enforce the law will also escape.

19 The arrangments are set out in CICB (1984) para 55.
20 Home Office (1986) para 21.6. The Board was reluctant to have such power, Ogden (1984–85) p 233.
1 Home Office (1986) id.
2 *Redpath v Belfast and County Down Rly* [1947] NI 167.
3 *Hussain v New Taplow Paper Mills*, op cit, 527. See also *McCamley v Cammell Laird Shipbuilders Ltd*, op cit, 859-861 per O'Connor LJ.

D. THE SIZE OF AWARDS

The following table shows the distribution of final monetary awards for the three years ending in March 1989.[4] It is unsurprising that, reflecting increases in common law damage awards and the effects of inflation, the underlying trend of awards is upwards. The decreasing number of awards below £400 reflects the reduction in the backlog of cases received prior to February 1983 when the lower limit was raised to that figure.

	1988-89		1987-88		1986-87	
	No	%	No	%	No	%
under £400	520	1.9	583	2.8	639	2.9
£400-£499	1,018	3.7	2,336	11.1	2,760	12.6
£500-£599	3,499	12.6	2,271	10.8	2,362	10.8
£600-£799	5,275	19.0	3,428	16.3	3,479	15.8
£800-£999	3,489	12.6	2,250	10.7	2,256	10.3
£1,000-£1,999	7,651	27.6	5,388	25.7	5,618	25.6
£2,000-£4,999	4,418	15.9	3,245	15.5	3,570	16.3
£5,000-£9,999	1,235	4.4	915	4.4	728	3.3
£10,000 and over	647	2.3	575	2.7	513	2.4
	27,752	100.0	20,991	100.0	21,925	100.0

4 The table, and the comments, are taken from CICB (1989) para 8.1.

Chapter Eight

Compensation by the Offender: Compensable Persons and Compensable Injuries

A. INTRODUCTION

Unlike state-funded compensation, there has been relatively little controversy concerning the introduction of arrangements designed to promote a greater incidence of offender-funded compensation to victims of crime.[1] The legal and the moral norms which justify the proposition that offenders ought to recompense those whom they have harmed is typically questioned only where those norms are indeterminate (for example, as to the definition of the harm in question), or some relevant excusing condition is offered by an offender; in clear cases the obligation to compensate cannot be gainsaid. This is not to say, however, that the introduction of such arrangements is without its share of contentious issues. These centre on three sets of inter-connected questions: firstly, whose should be the responsibility to collate and to present the victim's claim for compensation at the trial and upon what quality of evidence should a sentencer proceed to order compensation; secondly, upon what basis is the level of compensation to be determined and, in particular, what ought to be the relationship between an ideal assessment of the victim's loss or injury and the amount of compensation that the offender can afford; and thirdly, what is the place of victim compensation by the offender within the full range of the penal system's objectives, and how should conflicts between them be resolved as a matter both of theory and of sentencing practice.

For many years, courts of criminal jurisdiction have possessed powers to require those convicted of offences causing personal injury to compensate their victims.[2] Until 1972, however, these

---

1 Supra, pp 3–8.
2 The earlier legislation is described in a number of sources. Advisory Council on the Penal System *Reparation by the Offender* (1970, Home Office) paras 18-19 and 47-48, I McLean 'Compensation and restitution orders' [1973] Crim

powers were limited in a number of ways. Under the principal provision, s 11(1) of the Criminal Justice Act 1948, a court could require an offender to pay 'damages for injury' but only as an order ancillary to the making of a probation order or of an absolute or conditional discharge; and in the case of a magistrates' court, the order could not exceed £100.[3] Together with the impact of such other factors as the poverty of the offender and the absence of any clear basis upon which their loss and injuries could be evaluated, few victims of criminal violence could expect to obtain compensation for their injuries as a routine incident of the sentencing process.

In its analysis of the implementation of these powers, the Advisory Council on the Penal System estimated that in 1969 for example, following 20,280 convictions of persons over 17 for malicious wounding, only 138 compensation orders (totalling £2,003 in value) were made.[4] While acknowledging the limitations of the *Criminal Statistics* then published, the Council concluded:

> 'that these powers are sparingly and unevenly used and that in practice the prospects of a victim receiving compensation in pursuance of an order of a criminal court are remote.'[5]

Beyond the total of offences for which convictions are obtained there are, of course, further offences causing personal injury known to the police (some of which may be cleared up according to other criteria employed by the *Criminal Statistics*) and an unknown number of dark figure offences. If we were to assume that the British Crime Survey's best estimate,[6] that there were

---

LR 3-6, P Softley *Compensation Orders in Magistrates' Courts* (1978, Home Office Research Study 43) pp 1-5, and the Report of the Hodgson Committee *The Profits of Crime and their Recovery* (1984, Heinemann) ch 2.

3 There was some disagreement whether this figure had by virtue of para 9 of Sch 2 to the Criminal Law Act 1967 (which increased the powers of a court to award compensation on conviction for felony under s 4 of the Forfeiture Act 1870 from £100 to £400, substituted 'any offence tried on indictment' for 'felony' and extended the reference to loss of property to damage to property), been increased to £400: see the Advisory Council on the Penal System (1970) para 18 n 4. Since the Forfeiture Act 1870 was concerned with property offences only, the Advisory Council's view, that s 11(2) of the Criminal Justice Act 1948 remained unaffected by the changes in 1967, seems correct. Softley (1978) p 2 also adopts this view.

4 Advisory Council on the Penal System (1970) para 24 and Apps C and E.

5 Ibid, para 24.

6 M Hough and P Mayhew *The British Crime Survey* (1983, Home Office Research Study 76) pp 8-10.

in 1981 five times as many wounding offences as were recorded by the police is applicable to the 1969 figure of 32,654 class 8 offences, 'it would be possible to gain . . . some indication of the extent to which even full reparation by convicted offenders would fall short of achieving complete reparation for all victims of crime against [the] person'.[7]

Not all convicted offenders are amenable to compensation orders being made against them: many have insufficient funds, are too young, or other penal objectives may dictate or suggest a sentence that precludes, in law or practice, compliance with such an order. Besides these, there were other factors identified by the Advisory Council that prejudiced the more common use of the powers conferred by s 11 of the 1948 Act. These factors survived the statutory changes introduced in 1972 and 1982 and apparently continue to exert a depressive influence on sentencers' readiness to make compensation orders in personal injury cases.

The 1972 changes were brought about following the publication in 1970 of the Advisory Council's report, *Reparation by the Offender*. Asked, inter alia, 'to consider how the principle of reparation by the offender might be given a more prominent place in the penal system',[8] the Council's recommendations for encouraging courts to consider ordering compensation in respect of the direct consequences of an offence resulting in personal injury to a victim were relatively simple: permit compensation orders to be made in conjunction with virtually any sentence, custodial or otherwise, and raise the limit applicable in magistrates' courts to £400. These recommendations were given effect by the Criminal Justice Act 1972, whose provisions were re-enacted as ss 35-38 of the Powers of Criminal Courts Act 1973.

Two amendments to these powers were made by the Criminal Justice Act 1982. The first gave statutory preference to a compensation order over a fine where the offender has insufficient means to comply with both, and the second established the order as a sentencing option in its own right. A further statutory preference was introduced by the Criminal Justice Act 1988, giving priority to compensation over a confiscation order. That Act also seeks to deal with the criticism that compensation orders have not been more frequently made simply because courts have failed to advert to the possibility of imposing them, by placing on the court a duty to give reasons why it has not made an order where it is empowered to make one. The 1988 Act further

---

7 Advisory Council on the Penal System (1970) para 24.
8 Ibid, p v. The current law is reproduced in Appendix IV.

amended the scope, effect and enforcement of compensation orders, and also introduced a power to order compensation to be paid out of the proceeds of the sale of property forfeited under s 43 of the 1973 Act.

This chapter discusses the classes of compensable persons and compensable injuries, concluding with the new power under s 43A, and begins by considering what liability it is necessary for the offender to have before a compensation order may be made. The three chapters following detail the assessment of compensation, the procedural requirements and enforcement of a compensation order, and its place in the sentencing process.

Section 35(1) of the Powers of Criminal Courts Act 1973 as amended now provides:

'(1) Subject to the provisions of this Part of this Act and to s 40 of the Magistrates' Courts Act 1980 (which imposes a monetary limit on the powers of a magistrates' court under this section), a court by or before which a person is convicted of an offence, instead of or in addition to dealing with him in any other way, may, on application or otherwise, make an order (in this Act referred to as 'a compensation order') requiring him to pay compensation for any personal injury, loss or damage resulting from that offence or any other offence which is taken into consideration by the court in determining sentence, or to make payments for funeral expenses or bereavement in respect of death resulting from any such offence, other than a death due to an accident arising out of the presence of a motor vehicle on a road; and a court shall give reasons, on passing sentence, if it does not make such an order in a case where this section empowers it to do so'.

B. THE LIABILITY OF THE OFFENDER

(1) The criminal liability of the offender

(a) THE OFFENCE FOR WHICH THE OFFENDER IS CONVICTED

The criminal liability of the offender is an absolute condition precedent to a compensation order being made in favour of a victim who has suffered personal injury as the result of the commission of an offence. The section does not, however, require that the offence occasioning the personal injury was itself an offence against the person, nor does it require that the offence in respect of which the compensation order is made is also the one for which the offender was convicted, provided that the injury is attributable to an offence taken into consideration by the court in determining sentence. This second possibility is considered in section (b) following.

Section 35(1) empowers a criminal court to make a compensation order for personal injury, loss or damage sustained by victims of crime. So far as personal injuries are concerned, such orders will normally be made consequent upon a conviction for an offence against the person; typically an assault occasioning actual bodily harm, wounding, or causing or inflicting grievous bodily harm.[9] There is, however, no statutory obstacle to a compensation order being made in respect of a personal injury sustained by the commission of a crime against property. Shock is a common reaction to burglary and, as Maguire's research shows,[10] can have a lasting impact upon the psychological well-being, in particular, of female and of elderly victims. A compensation order recognising that effect may (and independent of any element of compensation for stolen property) therefore be appropriate, provided of course that the shock experienced is sufficient to be treated in law as a 'personal injury' within the section. These points are illustrated by *Bond v Chief Constable of Kent*,[11] where the Divisional Court held that a compensation order could be made for the distress and anxiety caused by an offence under s 1(1) of the Criminal Damage Act 1971.

Assuming a sufficient causal link between the offender's behaviour and the victim's injury,[12] there is no statutory constraint in s 35(1) to a compensation order being made consequent upon a conviction for *any offence* (other than offences arising out of motor vehicle accidents to which special provisions apply, dealt with below).[13] A compensation order could therefore be apt should an elderly person suffer nervous shock as a result of being an unwilling and proximate spectator to a street fight which results in convictions under ss 1-3 of the Public Order Act 1986.[14]

---

9 See J Vennard 'Magistrates' assessments of compensation for injury' [1979] Crim LR 510-523, and T Newburn *The Use and Enforcement of Compensation Orders in Magistrates' Courts* (1988, Home Office Research Study 102) table 2, p 9.
10 M Maguire *Burglary in a Dwelling* (1982, Heinemann) pp 122-131.
11 [1983] 1 All ER 456, [1983] 1 WLR 40. The facts are recounted infra, p 206.
12 Griffiths LJ, ibid, p 458.
13 Infra, pp 207-209.
14 The victim would also sustain a qualifying injury for the purposes of the Criminal Injuries Compensation Scheme (hereafter, the Scheme), supra, pp 123-126.

Likewise, a young child who suffers emotional trauma from witnessing a man masturbating himself (or another) in public would, in principle, be eligible for compensation following an appropriate conviction. The scope of the 'offence' for the purpose of s 35(1) is, it seems, as broad as the whole canon of criminal liability. Prima facie, offences under such legislation as the Safety of Sports Grounds Act 1975, the Health and Safety at Work etc Act 1974, the Food Act 1984 and the Consumer Protection Act 1987 which result in personal injury, are instances in which compensation orders can be made.

While recognising that '[a] general power to order compensation in respect of personal injury . . . would be wide enough to cover cases where the offence did not involve the deliberate intention to do harm', the Advisory Council on the Penal System found the possibility that compensation orders might be made in respect of regulatory offences of strict liability objectionable. In its opinion, compensation was appropriate 'in respect of what might be termed 'common law' offences';[15] broadly speaking, those offences involving the intentional or reckless infliction of injury (or loss or damage) upon the victim in whose favour the order is made, and not regulatory offences. Offences of strict liability or involving no more than negligence were, where they gave rise to personal injury, thought to be better suited to civil proceedings.[16]

A number of factors combine to reduce the likelihood of compensation orders being made in these, or in the public order cases instanced above. Apart from the difficulties of establishing a sufficient causal connection between the offender's behaviour and the victim's injury, a criminal court may feel that it is inappropriate for it to endeavour to assess (assuming the offender has means) potentially controversial issues of liability and quantum, even where these issues concern the application of accepted rules governing the liability of joint tortfeasors. In practice, criminal courts have for the most part confined the making of compensation orders to those cases in which these two issues are well settled.[17] Beyond these factors, however, the Advisory Council felt that it would be:

'impracticable to deal with this point by specifically excepting certain categories of offence on the ground that the ordering of compensation

---

15 Advisory Council on the Penal System (1970) para 60.
16 Ibid, para 61.
17 Infra, pp 218–223.

for their consequences is more suitable for civil proceedings because of lack of deliberate intention to inflict injury.'[18]

Instead, the Advisory Council was content to leave the matter to the 'good sense' of the criminal courts, and judging by the reported cases at least, the courts (or prosecutors) do appear to have responded in practice to its expressed wish, that compensation orders for personal injury be confined to offences involving 'a deliberate intention to do harm'.[19]

(b)   OFFENCES TAKEN INTO CONSIDERATION

Conviction for *an* offence is a precondition to the making of a compensation order, but s 35(1) further provides that the order may be made in respect of 'any other offence which is taken into consideration by the court in determining sentence'. The possibility of a victim of an offence taken into consideration (TIC) being able to translate his eligibility for compensation into an order against the defendant has hitherto been remote.[20] The victim would have needed to know the date and venue of the trial and been able to afford to give up the time to attend in order to make representations to the court that a compensation order should be made in his case.[1] The duty now imposed on the court to give the reasons why it has not made an order in a case where it has power to do so clearly implies that if the victims of TIC offences are known to it, the court must consider whether to make orders in their cases. However, this duty does not extend to conducting an inquiry into the whereabouts of other victims; thus the victim's chances of recovering compensation from a TIC offence still depend on information concerning his injury being before the court. Changes introduced by the Home Office in 1988 mean, however, that where the victim is known to the prosecutor, the onus is no longer solely upon him to bring this information to the court's attention.[2] Nevertheless, the amount of any compensation ordered by magistrates is subject to their statutory duty to consider the offender's means and to the maximum specified by s 35(5). This

---

18 Op cit, para 61.
19 Id.
20 The Advisory Council considered at length the desirability of allowing compensation orders to be made in respect of offences taken into consideration. For the most part the discussion was concerned with offences against property, ibid, paras 71-75.
1 The victim has no right to be heard.
2 Infra, pp 257-262.

last consideration creates a substantial obstacle, in particular where there are a number of TIC offences.

These points are relevant to convictions for regulatory offences. Where, on a conviction under the Food Act 1984, there are TIC offences of marketing bad food, compensation orders can, in theory, be made in favour of all those who suffered personal injury as a result of consuming it, but the variations in procedures employed by trading standards authorities for TIC offences mean that in the normal course of events it is very unlikely that orders will be made in respect of them. In any event, as we have seen, compensation orders are not normally made for personal injuries caused by regulatory offences, the relevant enforcement agencies usually taking the view that compensation is a matter for the victim to pursue, if necessary by civil action.[3]

(c) ORDERS AGAINST YOUNG OFFENDERS

By s 55 of the Children and Young Persons Act 1933 as amended by s 27 of the Criminal Justice Act 1982, if a child or young person is found guilty of an offence for the commission of which a compensation order may be imposed and the court is of the opinion that the case would best be met by making such an order (with or without any other punishment), it shall be the duty of the court to order that the compensation be paid by the parent or guardian, unless the parent or guardian cannot be found, or if they can be found, it would be unreasonable having regard to the circumstances.[4]

When considering whether to make a compensation order the court is statutorily bound to consider the means of the person against whom the order is to be made, and in cases where it

---

3 H Street 'Offences taken into consideration: compensation orders and the Trade Descriptions Act 1968' [1974] Crim LR 345-348, Anon 'Compensation orders' (1988) 138 New LJ 288. Sheriffs applying the equivalent provisions in the Criminal Justice (Scotland) Act 1980 have expressed the view that it is highly unlikely that compensation orders would be appropriate for offences under the Trade Descriptions Act 1968 or for food hygiene offences. Apart from the difficulties of dealing with multiple claimants and of quantifying loss, one reason given was that it would be illogical to make an order where there might be no civil liability; G Maher and C Docherty *Compensation Orders in the Scottish Criminal Courts* (1988, Scottish Office) pp 35-36.

4 These provisions also apply to the payment of fines and costs by a child or young person. 'Guardian' does not include a local authority for this purpose, *Leeds City Council v West Yorkshire Metropolitan Police* [1983] 1 AC 29, [1982] 1 All ER 274, HL. If the injury the victim sustains is sufficiently serious, it may be compensable under the Scheme.

is contemplating the use of s 55, the court must therefore have regard to the parents' or the guardians' means, and not just those of the offender.[5] This quite clearly requires that no order can be made if the parents' means are inadequate, but it is unclear whether, if the parents are wealthy the court can make an order as if they were the offender, though the offender's only income is pocket money.[6] The *Criminal Statistics* show that in 1988, the number of children and the number of young persons ordered by magistrates to pay compensation for indictable offences was 918 and 7,833 respectively. In the case of the orders made against children, over half were for less than £25; in the case of young persons, 5,129 were for less than £50. A third of the orders made against children were ordered to be paid by the parents, while a fifth of the orders made against young persons were so payable. Apart from the formality of a court order against them, it is estimated that about 75% of parents pay the orders made against their children.[7]

(2)   The civil liability of the offender

Whereas the *criminal* liability of the offender is an absolute precondition to the making of a compensation order, the need for an equivalent *civil* liability for the injury caused has been less certain. It is difficult to envisage a conviction for an aggravated assault or under ss 18 or 20 of the Offences against the Person Act 1861 not giving rise to a liability for which the offender could be ordered, in civil proceedings, to pay damages. Certainly it was envisaged that compensation orders would

---

5 Infra, pp 233–236. See *Lenihan v West Yorkshire Metropolitan Police* (1981) 3 Cr App Rep (S) 42; *R v Parker* (1981) 3 Cr App Rep (S) 278 and *R v Crown Court at Sheffield, ex p Clarkson* (1986) 8 Cr App Rep (S) 454. The parent or guardian must be given an opportunity to be heard before the court may make an order under s 55.

6 'The compensations of parenthood' (1983) 147 Justice of the Peace 258.

7 Home Office *Criminal Statistics: England and Wales; Supplementary Tables 1988 vol 4* table S4.9(A), p 92, and *Criminal Statistics England and Wales 1988* (1989, Cm 847) para 7.43. See further the government's suggestion that parents who deliberately turn a blind eye to their children's offending should routinely be expected to make compensation to their victims; J Patten MP, Times, 31 March 1989, and the attempt to amend the Criminal Justice Act 1982 to give the court power to apportion the payment of compensation between the parents and their children, which was opposed by the government because it placed blame on parents who had not been put on trial, 434 HL Official Report (5th series) col 739 (12 October 1982).

normally be made only where an equivalent civil liability was unproblematic:

> 'Compensation orders were introduced into our law as a convenient and rapid means of avoiding the expense of resort to civil litigation when the criminal clearly has the means which would enable the compensation to be paid. One has to bear in mind that there is always the possibility of a victim taking civil proceedings, if he be so advised. Compensation orders should certainly not be used when there is any doubt as to the liability to compensate . . .'[8]

This final remark has been repeatedly affirmed by the courts, usually in connection with the issue of quantifying the extent of the victim's loss; but opinions have differed as to whether a compensation order should be made in the absence of any civil liability arising from the offender's behaviour.[9] However, in 1985 the Court of Appeal held that the existence of a civil liability is not a precondition to the making of a compensation order.

So far as orders for personal injury are concerned, this issue is relevant to injuries caused by regulatory offences of strict liability which do not give rise to actions in tort or for breach of statutory duty. The Advisory Council took the view that:

> 'In theory, a power to order compensation in criminal proceedings in respect of any offence might make it possible for compensation to be awarded in situations in which there is no civil liability, but the risk of this happening seems somewhat remote.'[10]

This pragmatism was shared by the government. Several amendments were put down in Committee to ensure that compensation orders could not be made in the absence of a civil liability, but these were resisted.[11] The government was concerned

---

8 Scarman LJ, *R v Inwood* (1974) 60 Cr App Rep 70 at 73, CA.

9 P Atiyah 'Compensation orders and civil liability' [1979] Crim LR 504-509 suggests that this inference cannot confidently be drawn from such similar general remarks as are to be found in *R v Daly* [1974] 1 WLR 133 at 134, CA; *R v Grundy* [1974] 1 All ER 292 at 294, CA and *R v Kneeshaw* [1975] QB 57 at 60, CA. See also Hodgson, pp 61-62 and M Wasik 'The Hodgson Committee Report on the Profits of Crime and their Recovery' [1984] Crim LR 707, 714. Under s 58 of the Criminal Justice (Scotland) Act 1980 establishing compensation orders in Scots law, civil liability is not a prerequisite. See further the Report of the Dunpark Committee, *Reparation by the Offender to the Victim in Scotland* (1977, Cmnd 6802) paras 7.10-7.17.

10 (1970) para 61.

11 HC Official Report (5th series) Standing Committee G cols 51, 61, 64-70 and 90-92 (7 December 1971).

that magistrates should not have to decide difficult issues of civil liability, but as Atiyah observed, this does not answer the point.[12] Three permutations arise. Sometimes the offender's behaviour will give rise to a civil liability for an injury suffered by someone as a result of it, for example, where the offender is convicted under s 24 of the Offences against the Person Act 1861 for poisoning the victim.[13] Sometimes the offender's behaviour will not give rise to any civil liability, despite the fact that someone has been injured. For example, on facts similar to those in *Smedleys Ltd v Breed*,[14] a person may be convicted of an offence of strict liability under s 2 of the Food Act 1984 where he sells to the purchaser's prejudice any food not of the nature, substance or quality demanded by the purchaser, yet the reasonable steps taken to prevent such occurrences, while affording no defence to criminal liability, may preclude a finding of negligence in civil proceedings. Finally, there may be doubt as to whether the offender's behaviour gives rise to any civil liability, as for example where a person is poisoned when he injects himself with an adulterated drug supplied by another who is convicted for an offence under the Misuse of Drugs Act 1971.[15] There is agreement that magistrates should not have to decide such issues of civil liability as are posed by the third case (and this has been repeatedly affirmed by the courts), and agreement likewise that in the first case a compensation order would be apt, but the government's response in 1971 did not resolve the question whether an order would be apt in the second case.

Dicta in *R v Lester*[16] suggested that the answer should be in the negative. There the offender was convicted of offences under ss 1 and 11 of the Trade Descriptions Act 1968; declining to make a compensation order, Bridge LJ said:

'There is some doubt in our minds as to whether in such cases as the present, where it is at least arguable whether any civil liability arises from the commission of an offence under the Act of 1968, there is any "loss . . . resulting from that offence" within the meaning of those words in s 35(1) of the Act of 1973'.[17]

However, the Court of Appeal's decision in *R v Thomson*

12 Atiyah (1979) p 508.
13 See CICB 20th Report (1984, Cmnd 9399) para 38.
14 [1974] AC 839, [1974] 2 All ER 21, HL.
15 *Berkeley v Orchard* [1975] Crim LR 225.
16 (1975) 63 Cr App Rep 144, CA.
17 Ibid, 146.

Holidays Ltd[18] was taken as indicating the opposite view. The defendant company was convicted under s 14(1) of the 1968 Act of recklessly making a false statement in its holiday brochures as to the amenities offered at one of the hotels specified in its package holidays. The proceedings were taken following complaints made by two holiday-makers, and the company was ordered to compensate them for 'the disappointment and inconvenience of [their] ruined holiday'.[19]

Assuming that the fine print would have precluded any action for breach of contract and that, as Street suggested,[20] an action in tort would be unlikely to succeed, it seems that compensation is being made although no civil liability exists (or would exist but for its exclusion) or is at best controversial. Street's reaction to this possibility was that it 'must be assumed (however surprising) that the policy of the Powers of Criminal Courts Act is to enable victims of trade description offences to be compensated by criminal courts for proved offences even though they have no civil claim for damages.'[1] Brazier, to the contrary, found this possibility not merely quite unsurprising,[2] but the dicta of the Court of Appeal in *Lester* 'misconceived. All that the 1973 Act requires, he remarked, 'is that "loss or damage" results from an offence.'[3] Atiyah, on the other hand, was less sanguine:

'to make such an order where there could be no [civil] proceedings, or where they would inevitably conclude in favour of the defendant, is to create new substantive rights; and these rights, on this view, are created by the enactment of half a dozen words which say nothing whatever about the principles on which they are to be determined beyond the fact that loss or injury must have resulted from the offence. The anomalies which would result from this view are manifest.'[4]

These anomalies exist at various levels. In practice, criminal proceedings offer limited opportunities for a reasoned assessment of the victim's injuries and consequently of what sums of money would be apt to compensate for pecuniary and non-pecuniary loss. Such opportunities as do exist are inevitably more limited where pleas of guilty are entered. For these and associated reasons,

---

18 [1974] QB 592, [1974] 1 All ER 823.
19 Griffiths LJ, *Bond v Chief Constable of Kent*, op cit, 456.
20 Street (1974) p 348.
 1 Id.
 2 R Brazier 'Appellate attitudes towards compensation orders' [1977] Crim LR 710-719.
 3 Ibid, p 718.
 4 Atiyah (1979) p 505.

there are, as will be argued in a later chapter, serious objections to the suggestion that the victim should routinely expect to be compensated at the sentencing stage.

At a more abstract level, the effect of a finding of *criminal* liability is to justify *state* action against an offender, typically in the form of the deprivation of property or liberty: a conviction does not automatically entail liability to any individual. Yet a compensation order in favour of an individual imposes liabilities upon an offender similar to those which he faces following a civil judgment and indeed, goes further, since he may be imprisoned for failure to comply with the order.[5] Instances in which civil liability has been found to exist notwithstanding an acquittal on a criminal charge are not uncommon, and since there are significant procedural differences between civil and criminal proceedings, they do not necessarily pose conceptual or practical problems: *Gray v Barr*[6] is a case in point. But there the defendant has the benefit and protection of *two* trials; this is not the case where a compensation order is made following a conviction.

There were also, as Atiyah pointed out,[7] anomalies created by the provisions of ss 37 and 38 of the 1973 Act, repealed and replaced in part by s 105 of the Criminal Justice Act 1988. In short, s 37(a) continues to provide that where civil proceedings are taken following the making of a compensation order, the order may be discharged or reduced in the event that the value of the injury is held to be less in those proceedings than it was in the order; while s 38 now provides that the victim/plaintiff may only recover, following the court's assessment of the damages payable, the amount by which they exceed the compensation ordered and paid.[8] Both sections thus contemplate some mitigation of the offender's liability to comply with the compensation order as originally made, yet neither specifically indicates what should happen if the civil proceedings conclude for the offender. In that event, it might be argued that the injury has, in the words of s 37(a) 'been held in civil proceedings to be less than it was taken to be for the purposes of the order', but this implies that there was liability, though to a smaller degree; not that there was no liability at all.

---

5 Infra, pp 266–268.
6 [1971] 2 QB 554, [1971] 2 All ER 949, CA.
7 Atiyah (1979) pp 505–506.
8 Infra, pp 253–254.

In 1982 the Court of Appeal held in *R v Chappell*[9] that the existence of civil liability is not a precondition to the making of a compensation order. The offender, a director of a company that had since ceased trading, was convicted of recklessly causing delivery of untrue VAT returns contrary to s 167 of the Customs and Excise Management Act 1979. Since, in the absence of fraud (which was admitted by the prosecution) he was not personally liable for the discrepancies, there was no one against whom the Department of Customs and Excise could proceed to recover the unpaid tax. Making a compensation order against the offender, the court held that to require civil liability as a precondition would necessitate reading the word 'actionable' into s 35(1) before the words 'personal injury, loss or damage'. The court's reasoning was as follows. A compensation order does not exactly mirror, though it may often reflect, civil liability. In civil proceedings, a court has no alternative but to make an award of damages if the defendant is liable; but a compensation order is discretionary. In the exercise of that discretion the court is statutorily bound to take into account the offender's means, but it is not bound to treat the presence or absence of civil liability on his part as crucial, this is simply a factor which it can take into account when exercising its discretion whether to make an order in a particular case. Thus it follows that even where civil liability does exist, competing sentencing considerations may require that no order be made, notwithstanding an agreed or proved injury to the victim.

While *Chappell* authoritatively resolves the question whether civil liability is a prerequisite to the making of a compensation order, it does not resolve the objections raised earlier. In particular, it may work harshly against an offender convicted of an offence of strict liability who has but minimal responsibility for the injuries sustained by the victim.[10]

C. COMPENSABLE PERSONAL INJURIES

A compensation order is made in respect of 'personal injury'. In almost all cases, this will comprise physical injury to a victim which constitutes the external elements of an offence against the person, and will also include any harm to the victim's mental

---

9 (1985) 80 Cr App Rep 31. See E Jacobs 'Compensation orders' (1985) 149 Justice of the Peace 440–443.

10 M Wasik 'Compensation orders and civil liability' (1985) Modern LR 707–711.

condition which accompanies such an offence. 'Personal injury' is also apt to cover cases where harm to the victim's mental condition is the only injury sustained. An assault which causes a hysterical and nervous condition in the victim is an offence under s 47 of the Offences against the Person Act 1861 and would constitute an 'injury' for the purpose of s 35(1).[11] Thus where, as in *Smith v Chief Superintendent, Woking Police Station*,[12] the offender succeeds, as he intended, in frightening the victim, compensation could be ordered. There the offender had frightened the victim by looking through her bedroom window at night; the shock of a firearm discharged behind the victim with the intention of frightening him could also produce a 'personal injury' within the section.

In addition, as *Bond v Chief Constable of Kent*[13] illustrates, personal injury may include distress and anxiety occasioned by a crime against property. There the occupier of a house was woken one night by noises coming from his front garden. Having ascertained that there was someone there behaving strangely (the appellant), he telephoned the police. Before they arrived the appellant threw a stone through a window of the house. Terrified, and fearing further attack, the occupier gathered his family together in one room for safety, and when the police arrived, they found him in a very frightened state. The appellant was convicted of unlawful damage to the house contrary to s 1(1) of the Criminal Damage Act 1971. At the prosecutor's request, the magistrates made an award of £25 to compensate for the broken window, and of their own motion a further £25 to compensate the victim for his frightening experience. As was noted earlier, the Divisional Court held that a compensation order was appropriate for personal injury caused by an offence against property, and further held that 'personal injury' could include the sense of distress and anxiety that could follow such an offence, provided that there was a 'sufficient nexus' between the offence and that injury. Thus, if a householder were to sustain the mental harm suffered by the plaintiff in *Attia v British Gas plc*,[14] the

---

11 *R v Miller* [1954] 2 QB 282, [1954] 2 All ER 529.
12 (1983) 76 Cr App Rep 234. *Wilkinson v Downton* [1897] 2 QB 57 and, eg, an offender who was ordered to pay compensation who admitted putting pins into baby food in order to frighten its mother, Times, 25 June 1989.
13 Op cit.
14 [1988] QB 304, [1987] 3 All ER 455, CA. An order could also be made in favour of a witness to an offence against property who suffers distress amounting to a personal injury, *R v Vaughan* [1990] Crim LR 443, CA.

fire being intentionally or recklessly caused and giving rising to a conviction for arson, a compensation order could be made.

Although convictions for property offences are comparatively few in proportion to the number known to the police, the possibility that a compensation order can be made for personal injury caused by the shock the victim suffers when he returns to find that his home has been burgled or criminally damaged is of importance given that such injury would not be a qualifying injury within the terms of the Criminal Injuries Compensation Scheme.[15]

(1) Personal injury caused by road traffic offences

Injuries arising from road traffic offences were, before the 1988 amendments, specifically excluded by s 35(3) of the 1973 Act:

> 'and no such order shall be made in respect of injury . . . due to an accident arising out of the presence of a motor vehicle on the road . . .';

and as that subsection also precluded the making of an order 'in respect of loss suffered by the dependants of a person in consequence of death', neither were fatal accidents caused by road traffic offences compensable. As with the Criminal Injuries Compensation Scheme, the factor that principally weighed with the Advisory Council when recommending 'that traffic offences should be excluded from any general restatement of powers to order compensation in criminal proceedings',[16] was that compensation would be provided by the driver's insurance or by the Motor Insurers' Bureau in the event he was uninsured or untraced.

There was, however, one exception to the general exclusion of injuries arising from road accidents, in that 'damage' could be the subject of a compensation order where it resulted from an offence under the Theft Act 1968. This created an anomaly in *Quigley v Stokes*[17] where a joy-rider was involved in a collision. The owner of the car he had taken and driven away could have

---

15 Supra, pp 109-110. The desirability of compensation orders being used to appease the shock of burglary was specifically raised in the debates on the amendments to the 1973 Act introduced in the Criminal Justice Act 1982, 16 HC Official Report (6th series) col 336 (20 January 1982).

16 (1970) para 63. Supra, pp 143-147.

17 [1977] 2 All ER 317, [1977] 1 WLR 434.

an order made in his favour, but not the owner of the car into which he collided, as that damage was caused only by an offence of careless driving. The Hodgson Committee was critical of this outcome,[18] which is modified by s 104(1) of the 1988 Act. A compensation order in respect of 'a death due to an accident arising out of the presence of a motor vehicle on the road' still cannot be made, but a court is competent to make an order in respect of personal injury in the limited circumstances described by the new s 35(3):

> 'A compensation order may only be made in respect of injury, loss or damage (other than loss suffered by a person's dependants in consequence of his death) which was due to an accident arising out of the presence of a motor vehicle on a road, if—
>   (a) . . .
>   (b) it is in respect of injury . . . as respects which
>   (i) the offender is uninsured in relation to the use of the vehicle; and
>   (ii) compensation is not payable under any arrangement to which the Secretary of State is a party;
> and, where a compensation order is made in respect of injury . . . due to such an accident, the amount to be paid may include an amount representing the whole or part of any loss of or reduction in preferential rates of insurance attributable to the accident.'

The arrangement to which s 35(3)(b)(ii) refers is the agreements between the Secretary of State and the Motor Insurers' Bureau: no order can be made if the injury is compensable under either of these, for example, where the driver's identity is known, but he is uninsured. The MIB agreements exclude, however, accidents occurring off public roads, and assuming that a conviction against the driver could be secured (which does not have to be a conviction under the Road Traffic Act 1988), an order against an uninsured offender in respect of the personal injury that he caused would be competent. For the purpose of s 35(3)(b)(i), s 35(3A) provides that a vehicle the use of which is exempted from insurance by s 144 of the Road Traffic Act 1988 is not uninsured; thus an injury due to an accident arising out of the presence of a police car on a road cannot be made the object of a compensation order, even where, as is the case, it is not compensable under the MIB.[19]

Where the motor vehicle was deliberately used as a weapon to injure the victim, the conviction not being under the Road

18 (1984) 56.
19 Motor Insurers' Bureau, *Compensation of Victims of Uninsured Drivers* (21 December 1988) para 6(b).

Traffic Act 1988 but, for example, under s 18 of the Offences against the Person Act 1861, the position may be different. In *Gardner v Moore*,[20] the House of Lords held that compensation is payable by the MIB where the victim is deliberately run down by a driver whose identity is known but who is uninsured. This would appear to bring the victim within the exclusionary rule in s 35(3)(b)(ii), but the question which remains is whether the word 'accident' in the phrase, 'due to an accident arising out of the presence of a motor vehicle on a road', is confined to injuries that are colloquially 'accidentally' caused, that is, caused neither deliberately nor recklessly (nor, possibly, negligently). It does not seem appropriate to describe as an accident, the injury caused to the occupants of another car with which the offender deliberately collided; accordingly, a compensation order ought not to be precluded by this paragraph.[1]

Finally, it should be noted that where a compensation order is made in respect of a personal injury due to a road traffic accident, the order may seek to compensate the victim for loss or reduction of preferential rates of insurance attributable to the accident, that is, for the loss of his no claims bonus.

(2) Causation

Assuming that the victim's injury does constitute a 'personal injury' within s 35(1) and is not otherwise excluded,[2] the question is whether that injury was one 'resulting from that offence or any other offence which is taken into consideration by the court in determining sentence.' This causal question is one of fact and, it was held by the Court of Appeal in *R v Thomson Holidays Ltd*[3] one which is to be decided without reference to criteria applicable in civil law:

---

20 [1984] AC 548, [1984] 1 All ER 1100.
 1 If the driver is untraced, compensation will be payable under the Scheme, supra, p 144.
 2 In *Hammertons Cars Ltd v London Borough of Redbridge* [1974] 2 All ER 216, [1974] 1 WLR 484 it was held that the costs incurred by a victim in bringing a civil action against the defendant which were not ordered by the court to be paid by him could not be made the object of a compensation order following a conviction for an offence arising out of the same set of facts. Lord Widgery CJ said that it was 'abundantly clear' that the two sets of proceedings should be treated as being quite independent of one another, and that it would be 'ludicrous' if a plaintiff/victim were able in effect to reverse in a magistrates' court a High Court judge's decision not to order costs, ibid, 219.
 3 [1974] QB 592, [1974] 1 All ER 823.

'Parliament, we are sure, never intended to introduce into the criminal law the concepts of causation which apply to the assessment of damages under the law of contract and tort. Section 1(1) of [the Criminal Justice Act 1972] is intended to be applied by both justices and judges sitting in the Crown Court and the reference to offences taken "into consideration" shows that the court making a compensation order may not be apprised of the detailed facts of such offences. It must do what it can to make a just order on such information as it has. Whenever the making of an order for compensation is appropriate the court must ask itself whether the loss or damage [or personal injury] *can fairly be said* to have resulted to anyone from the offence . . .'[4]

This dictum has been cited with approval on a number of occasions, each of which has emphasised that what is required is a common sense approach to the question whether the victim's injury (or loss or damage) resulted from the offence.[5] Where, as in *Bond v Chief Constable of Kent*,[6] the offender's behaviour 'was the only cause of the occupier's terror' there will be a sufficient causal connection, but this connection will not be broken merely because there were other contributory causes: 'the question is not whether the loss results solely from the offence, but whether it can fairly be said to result from the offence'.[7] Thus, even where the facts of a case generate some issue as to causation, such as in *R v Smith*[8] (unskilful medical intervention in the victim's injured condition by a third party), *R v Blaue*[9]

4 Ibid, 378 (original emphasis).
5 In view of the accumulated dicta approving Lawton LJ's remarks on the test of causation for the purposes of s 35(1), Lloyd J's observation in *R v Schofield* [1978] 2 All ER 705 at 706 (in which these remarks were not referred to) that a compensation order may be made 'provided the loss . . . is not otherwise too remote in law', should not, it seems, be taken to require the importation of tests appropriate in contract or tort. In *Bond v Chief Constable of Kent*, op cit, McCullough J expressly approved Lawton LJ's remarks without referring to Lloyd J's observation: 'in assessing whether compensation should be awarded under s 35 of the Powers of Criminal Courts Act 1973 the court should approach the matter in a broad common sense way and should not allow itself to become enmeshed in the refined questions of causation that can sometimes arise in claims for damages under the law of contract or tort. The court simply has to ask whether the loss or damage can fairly be said to have resulted from the offence', ibid, 459. See also *Rowlston v Kenny* (1982) 4 Cr App Rep (S) 85, which also concerned causation in s 35(1), where his Lordship again expressly approved Lawton LJ's remarks, and Pain J in *R v Howell* (1978) 66 Cr App Rep 179, CA.
6 Op cit.
7 McCullough J in *Rowlston v Kenny*, op cit, 88.
8 [1959] 2 QB 35, [1959] 2 All ER 193.
9 [1975] 3 All ER 446, [1975] 1 WLR 1411.

(deliberate rejection of medical treatment by the victim for religious reasons) or *R v Roberts*[10] and *R v Lewis*[11] (victim sustaining injury by jumping out of a moving car or a building in response to a threat by the offender), a common sense approach suggests that each one would fall under s 35(1).

It is of interest to compare this approach to multiple causes with that taken by the Civil Division of the Court of Appeal to para 4 of the Scheme in *R v Criminal Injuries Compensation Board, ex p Ince*.[12] The court held that a personal injury was 'directly attributable' to a crime of violence or an act of law enforcement if either of these was a substantial cause of the injury; it did not need to be the sole cause. The court further held that the word 'substantial' be used in the sense 'that the relationship between the particular cause and the personal injury [was] such that a reasonable person, applying his common sense, would fairly and seriously regard it as being a cause.'[13] By contrast, the question of causation for the purposes of s 35(1) is satisfied by the application of a test which requires only that the injury 'can fairly be said' to have resulted from the offence.

In many personal injury cases, for example, convictions under ss 18, 20 or 47 of the Offences against the Person Act 1861, where the external elements of the offence expressly contemplate injury being caused by the offender to the victim, there will be little difficulty in concluding that the injury did result from the offence. The matter may be different, however, where on a charge that does so contemplate personal injury, the conviction is for a lesser offence that does not. Suppose a conviction for common assault is returned on a charge under s 47.[14] Where the assault does not involve a battery and there is no evidence of shock sufficient to constitute a 'personal injury' within s 35(1), a compensation order would clearly be improper. But what if there is some evidence of personal injury? In *R v Davies*[15] the offender was convicted of common assault on a charge of assault occasioning actual bodily harm arising from a fight at a party at which he and the victim had been present, as a result of which the victim received a black eye and a split lip. The court ordered the offender to pay £200 compensation to the victim. On appeal, it was argued that the jury's verdict was inconsistent with the assumption made

10 (1971) 56 Cr App Rep 95, CA.
11 [1970] Crim LR 647, CA.
12 [1973] 3 All ER 808, [1973] 1 WLR 1334.
13 Megaw LJ, ibid, 815.
14 If a count for common assault has been added; *R v Mearns* (1990) 154 JP 447, CA.
15 [1982] Crim LR 243.

by the compensation order, namely that it was the offender who had caused the victim's injuries. The appeal was dismissed on the grounds that the jury had taken a merciful view of the seriousness of the offence and that on the facts that the victim's injuries were caused by the offender and that there was no suggestion that anyone else had punched him in the face.

Two objections may be made to this decision. The first concerns a standard principle of sentencing practice: an offender should be sentenced on the basis of those offences for which he was convicted, even though the sentencer considers him lucky to have escaped conviction for a more serious offence. The second concerns the interpretation of s 35(1). This provides that a court may make a compensation order for any personal injury resulting 'from that offence', that is, the offence for which the offender is convicted. Davies was convicted of common assault. Since 'the only difference in law between an allegation of assault occasioning actual bodily harm and one of common assault is the element of actual bodily injury'[16] (for which even a slight injury will be sufficient), the jury's verdict must have meant that they were *not* satisfied beyond a reasonable doubt that the offender was responsible for the victim's injuries. There was, accordingly, no basis for saying that the victim had suffered personal injury 'resulting from' the offence for which the offender was convicted. With the lower burden of proof in civil proceedings, a different view of the relationship between the offender's behaviour and the victim's injury might be reached in a civil action; in any event, given the doubt as to the cause of the victim's injuries, it might have been better to let the victim pursue his civil remedy, if any, as has frequently been urged by the Court of Appeal in cases where liability is controversial.

The point in *Davies* is that the jury's verdict appears inconsistent with the minimum causal requirement (even though it is not trammelled by the rules of causation in contract or tort) that the victim's injury result from the offence for which the offender is *convicted* or which is taken into consideration. Provided the conviction does not, expressly or by implication, deny that causal connection, this aspect of s 35(1) would appear to be satisfied. Thus an injury may 'fairly be said to have resulted' from the offender's behaviour notwithstanding that the offence expressly contemplates some personal injury other than the one actually suffered by the victim, provided the injury is consistent with it. An offender who shoots to cause grievous bodily harm

16 Id, commentary.

but misses and is convicted of an attempt may be ordered to pay compensation for the shock suffered by the victim in consequence as much as if he had realised his intention.[17]

D. PERSONS ELIGIBLE FOR COMPENSATION

(1) Non-fatal offences

When this legislation was enacted in 1972, it was clearly contemplated that the beneficiaries of compensation orders would normally be those victims directly injured as a result of crimes against the person, and whose injuries constitute the external elements of the offences for which their offenders were convicted, or which were taken into consideration. What was contemplated appears to have been realised in practice; in all the reported cases on compensation orders in respect of personal injuries it is the victim so injured by the offender in whose favour the order has been made. The statute does not however require so restrictive an interpretation of the class of compensable persons: it makes no reference to any particular victim but instead gives a criminal court a general power to award compensation for 'any personal injury . . . resulting from that offence' or from one taken into consideration.

Considering the application of s 35(1) following a conviction under s 14 of the Trade Descriptions Act 1968 Lawton LJ said in *Thomson Holidays Ltd*:

> 'whenever the making of an order for compensation is appropriate the court must ask itself whether loss or damage can fairly be said to have resulted to *anyone* from the offence for which the accused has been convicted or has been [sic] taken into consideration.'[18]

Although his Lordship was concerned with 'loss or damage', this dictum surely applies equally to 'personal injury', so that a court must, when it is apt to make an order, ask itself whether personal injury can fairly be said to have resulted, not just to the person whose injuries constitute the external elements of the offence, but to anyone else as a result of that offence. This raises the possibility that witnesses to 'personal injury, loss or damage' suffered by another who themselves suffer distress or shock

---

17 *R v Gleaves* [1977] Crim LR 624.
18 Op cit, 378 (original emphasis).

amounting to a personal injury, may properly have compensation orders made in their favour, assuming a sufficient causal link between the offence and their injury. This seems unobjectionable in the case of a person who witnesses the commission of the offence itself, and whether the other person is related to the witness or not. As the criminal liability upon which the offender's obligation to pay compensation is founded need not be confined to offences against the person, an order may also be apt where personal injury (in the form of shock) 'can fairly be said' to have resulted to anyone witnessing an offence against another's property. Although there was no evidence of distress amounting to personal injury in *R v Vaughan*,[19] the Court of Appeal viewed with equanimity the possibility of an order being made in favour of witnesses to a series of offences of criminal damage against another's property.

The matter is less clear in the case of a witness to the aftermath of an offence. Given the reluctance of the criminal courts to make compensation orders in cases where liability (and quantum) may be controversial, it is highly unlikely that they will go beyond 'the closest of family ties' whose claims are recognised by existing law.[20] The ordinary bystander who suffers harm to his mental condition as the result of coming upon the aftermath of an offence committed against another, will probably not benefit in practice from the theoretical scope of s 35(1). In this respect the Scheme is a more likely source of compensation.

Where the victim whose injuries constitute the external elements of the offence is a child, a compensation order may, it seems, be made on application by the parents or prosecutor, by analogy with, though not in so formal a manner, as an action in tort. For example, a compensation order could be made against an offender who abducts and sexually assaults a child and,[1] in theory, also to compensate the parents for their distress and anxiety at the commission of these offences. Similarly, in theory, a criminal injury to a child in the womb who is born with disabilities attributable to that crime may be eligible independently of any compensation order made in favour of the mother; but here again the complex questions of liability and quantum would almost certainly preclude such a course in practice.

---

19 [1990] Crim LR 443.
20 Per Lord Wilberforce, *McLoughlin v O'Brian* [1983] 1 AC 410 at 422, HL.
1 Eg an order made against a child's nanny who was convicted of offences against the young girl for whom she was responsible, Times, 9 February 1990.

(2) Fatal offences

When the power to order compensation was introduced in the Criminal Justice Act 1972, compensation for the death of a victim was explicitly excluded; s 35(3) of the Powers of Criminal Courts Act 1973 providing that:

'No compensation order shall be made in respect of loss suffered by the dependants of a person in consequence of death'.

Justifying this limitation on the class of compensable persons the Advisory Council on the Penal System said:

'At common law no civil claim arises out of causing death because the victim is not available, and liability in fatal cases is the artificial creation of statute based on loss to the deceased's dependants. We think that claims of this kind are quite unsuitable for consideration by a criminal court'.[2]

Thus it was the practical and procedural objections to criminal courts making compensation orders in favour of the victim's dependants in cases of unlawful homicide that were compelling. In the first place, while there is no statutory obstacle to a compensation order being made following a conviction for murder or manslaughter, the Court of Appeal has said on a number of occasions that such orders should not routinely accompany a custodial sentence.[3] Secondly, even where presided over by High Court judges, criminal courts are not well suited procedurally to the determination of what constitutes the loss of dependency, which is central to a fatal accident action.

However, following a recommendation of the Hodgson Committee,[4] the Criminal Justice Act 1988 modified the 1973 Act in two respects. While it remains the case that there can be no order for loss of support, s 35(1) was amended to permit the court to make an order for bereavement, and to make payments in respect of funeral expenses. In these matters the powers of a criminal court resemble the terms of the Scheme.[5] By s 35(3C), an order in respect of bereavement may only be made for the benefit of those persons so entitled under s 1A of the Fatal

---

2 (1970) para 51. HC Official Report (5th series) Standing Committee G, op cit, cols 72-76.
3 Infra, pp 282-285.
4 (1984) 53.
5 Supra, pp 151-153.

Accidents Act 1976. Unlike the 1976 Act, and the Scheme, however, the order is not fixed but may be made for any sum not exceeding the amount for the time being specified in s 1A(3) of that Act, currently £3,500. This may suggest that the court is to attempt to quantify the eligible dependant's loss, but is more likely to have been intended to permit the court to make such order as is compatible with the offender's means where these are insufficient to satisfy the specified sum. Though perhaps welcome in theory, it seems unlikely that this power will be much used in practice,[6] and even where used, the amounts ordered may be thought derisory.[7] This will become more acute should the specified sum be significantly increased, for example to £7,500.

The person in whose favour an order in respect of funeral expenses may be made is not restricted to dependants, but may be made for the benefit of anyone who incurred them.

Finally we may consider the position where a victim suffers a criminal injury and later dies from other causes. There is some authority to suggest that if a compensation order has already been made prior to the victim's death, any payments made to the enforcing court but not yet transmitted to the victim should be paid over to the benefit of his estate.[8] However, not being a cause of action vested in a person on his death a compensation order is probably not enforceable in respect of payments due after the victim has died.

E. COMPENSATION FROM FORFEITED PROPERTY

By s 43 of the Powers of Criminal Courts Act 1973, a court may, upon conviction, order that the offender be deprived of any

---

6 In England and Wales in 1988 there were 306 convictions for offences of homicide, *Criminal Statistics England and Wales 1988* (1989, Cm 847) table 4.7(a).

7 Of the 9,220 offenders ordered to pay compensation on conviction before the Crown Court, only 771 orders exceeded £1,000, *Criminal Statistics: England and Wales 1988 Supplementary Tables 1988 vol 4*, table S4.9(B). See further Wasik (1984) p 714.

8 Under the equivalent Scottish legislation it has been held that a compensation order in favour of an insurance company made against the offender convicted of unlawfully damaging a stolen car could not be enforced following the death of its owner, *Tudhope v Furphy* 1984 SLT (Sh Ct) 33. Correspondence in the *Justice of the Peace* advised that moneys received in compliance with a compensation order payable in respect of an assault occasioning actual bodily harm should be paid to the victim's estate following his death from other causes, (1983) 147 JP 656.

property used or intended for use in connection with the commission of a crime. Section 43A, which is added by s 107(1) of the Criminal Justice Act 1988, gives the court a new power to order that compensation be paid from the proceeds which arise from the disposal of the property to any person who has suffered personal injury, loss or damage as a result of the offence for which the offender was convicted, or of one taken into consideration in determining sentence.[9] The court is required to specify the amount payable out of the proceeds of the forfeited property. By s 43A(2), such an order may only be made if the court 'is satisfied that but for the inadequacy of the means of the offender it would have made a compensation order under which the offender would have been required to pay compensation of an amount not less than the specified amount.' Thus when a court is disposed to make an order under s 43A, it must consider both whether the law governing compensation orders would have permitted it to make an order under s 35(1) and whether, being so permitted, it would have made one but for the inadequacy of the offender's means; if it would have made one but for the prohibitory advice of the Court of Appeal concerning, for example, the combination of a compensation order and the other sentence to be imposed in the case, then it may not make an order under s 43A. Neither may the court make such an order which exceeds what it would have ordered under s 35(1); a court cannot make an order for £150 if its s 35(1) order would have been for £50, that being the full value of the injury, simply because £150 happens to be the proceeds recovered from the sale of the property forfeited by the offender. It may however make a s 43A order in that case for £50.

The person to whom such payment may be made is, like s 35(1), anyone who has suffered personal injury; this does not have to be the victim of an assault, but may include a witness to the offence. 'Personal injury' must have the same connotation as described in section B above, and the causal test must be the same. Also like compensation orders, no application is required on behalf of a person who has so suffered, but the court may make an order under s 43A of its own motion.

There are two conditions under which a s 43A order has no effect: if the period specified in s 43(4)(a) has not yet ended, or if a successful application under s 1(1) of the Police (Property) Act 1897 has been made.

---

9 See D Thomas 'The Criminal Justice Act 1988: the sentencing provisions' [1989] Crim LR 43-55, 49-51.

Chapter Nine

Determining the Amount
of Compensation

Assuming that the victim's injury is one which falls within the
terms of s 35(1), and that the sentencer considers it appropriate
to make a compensation order against the offender, it is then
necessary to determine in what amount that order should be fixed.
This determination comprises three principal elements: a
financial evaluation of the victim's injury; an evaluation of what
it would be proper, given his means, to require the offender
to pay; and thirdly a consideration of the relevance to the order
of any subsequent award of damages or of any other benefit the
victim receives in respect of his injury.

A. THE FINANCIAL EVALUATION OF THE VICTIM'S INJURY

(1) Establishing the victim's injury

Before a compensation order can be made, the fact of the victim's
injury and the extent of any medical or financial consequences
will need to be established to the satisfaction of the sentencer.
Where it is alleged that the victim's injury was the result of
the offence for which the offender is convicted, some evidence
of it will undoubtedly have been established during the trial;
although the comprehensiveness of this account, at least so far
as the full consequences to the victim are concerned, will vary,
inter alia according to the nature of the offence.[1] If, for example,
the offender is tried for an offence against the person, it is likely
that evidence of the victim's injury will be established in more
detail than if the injury resulted from an offence against property.
Where detailed evidence of the victim's injury is not adduced

1 A Ashworth *Sentencing and Penal Policy* (1983, Weidenfeld and Nicolson)
  p 93.

during the trial, the offender pleads guilty or it is alleged that the victim's injury resulted from the commission of an offence to be taken into consideration in determining sentence, the facts will need to be established at the sentencing stage. This raises a number of questions. One of the more important of these, which is dealt with later,[2] is *who* is responsible for making an application for a compensation order? A second, equally important question, is what procedures and what standards should apply to the evidence presented in support of it?

Where, for example, there is a guilty plea, a court will usually accept (assuming there to be no objection by the offender) the statement of facts presented by the prosecution; but the court has a duty to resolve any conflict that does appear in the factual accounts given by the prosecution and the defence. In such a case a court would normally invite submissions on disputed points of fact as a first step to reaching its own view of them. Similarly where offences are taken into consideration, the sentencer may ask, if a question of compensation for a resulting injury were to arise, for some elaboration of the factual basis of the injury and its cause. The evidence adduced in these cases, or in any other where the court wishes to have further details of the victim's injury, should be first-hand rather than hearsay.[3]

Beyond these evidentiary considerations, questions may also arise as to the proper conclusions that may be drawn as to the causes of the injury, its financial implications for the victim or as to the long term medical prognosis. Criminal courts, as the Advisory Council recognised, are not well equipped to determine questions of this kind:

> 'The courts cannot go into much detail or adjourn for lengthy enquiries; they do not have the expertise needed for detailed consideration of causation, contributory negligence, provocation and medical evidence . . .'[4]

Taken together, these considerations led the Advisory Council to recommend that compensation orders be made 'only in straightforward cases':

> 'The courts should, we think, consider ordering compensation in respect of the direct consequences of an offence resulting in an appreciable loss to the victim, save where:

---

2 Infra, pp 257–262.

3 M Wasik 'Rules of evidence in the sentencing process' [1985] Current Legal Problems 187-209.

4 Advisory Council on the Penal System *Reparation by the Offender* (1970, Home Office) para 27.

. . .

(ii) a need to resolve difficult issues of liability or quantum make the civil courts a more appropriate forum for the ordering of compensation.'[5]

The Council at once tempered this caution with the observation that it did not wish 'to exclude absolutely the ordering of compensation where the assessment of loss is difficult', and instanced a case in which the victim clearly had a civil claim and the offender has assets which might otherwise be dissipated before the claim could be heard: 'a criminal court should, we think, be able to make a compensation order without attempting to quantify the loss.'[6] The history of compensation orders during the 1970s suggests, however, that the courts were more impressed by the desirability of making orders only in 'simple, straightforward cases',[7] than by the Advisory Council's hope that, by showing 'a greater readiness'[8] to invoke their powers, they might help to refine the principles suggested in its Report. Indeed, some critics have taken the view that the courts have been over-cautious as to these issues of proof and quantum and that their decisions, in particular *R v Vivian*,[9] contributed to a low incidence of compensation orders in personal injury offences.[10] In the absence of detailed comparison of the evidence in a representative sample of cases, such criticism is difficult to evaluate; there are also, of course, other considerations of sentencing policy that might weigh against the making of an order notwithstanding a straightforward case and an offender with means. We shall consider later the conclusions which the Home Office has reached based on its research into the use of compensation orders;[11] for the moment we consider the development of the law in this area.

The requirement that the full extent of the victim's injury should be well established before the court could consider making a compensation order has not been directly laid down in any reported judgment, but may be inferred from the many dicta laying down this requirement in the case of property loss or damage. For example, in *R v Kneeshaw*, Lord Widgery CJ said:

5 Ibid, paras 81 and 137.
6 Ibid, para 138. Also paras 49-50.
7 Lord Widgery CJ, *R v Kneeshaw* [1975] QB 57 at 60, CA.
8 Advisory Council on the Penal System (1970) para 139.
9 [1979] 1 All ER 48, [1979] 1 WLR 291, CA.
10 Infra, pp 322-324.
11 Infra, pp 320-322.

'It has been stressed in this court more than once recently that the machinery of a compensation order under the 1972 Act is intended for clear and simple cases. It must always be remembered that the civil rights of the victim remain. In a great majority of cases the appropriate court to deal with the issues raised by matters of this kind is in the appropriate civil proceedings. A compensation order made in the court of trial can be extremely beneficial as long as it is confined to simple, straightforward cases and generally cases where no great amount is at stake.'[12]

Where the offender has disputed the facts alleged to have caused the injury and no application for an order has been made, then a court should not make an order; and even where, his Lordship continued, the victim did make an application and could adduce evidence in support of it, the court:

'should hesitate to embark on any complicated investigation of this kind even at the suit of an applicant making a positive application.'[13]

The impact of these and similar observations in other cases concerning property offences, notably *R v Inwood*[14] and *R v Miller*,[15] appears, as suggested, to have limited the making of compensation orders for personal injury to those cases in which the injury was relatively slight and had no long term financial or medical implications for the victim. Injuries comprising bruises, cuts, fractures or broken teeth, in which the pain and suffering lasted not much more than six weeks appear to have been typical of the few compensation orders made for personal injury each year during the 1970s, and continue to comprise the typical case for compensation.[16] There are, as we shall see, other

---

12 Op cit at 60.
13 Id. As R Brazier 'Appellate attitudes towards compensation orders' [1977] Crim LR 710-719 points out, Lord Widgery CJ's references to an application by the victim as a precondition to the making of a compensation order are not especially felicitous since s 35(1) 'makes it plain that a court may make a compensation order "on application or otherwise"'.
14 (1974) 60 Cr App Rep 70, CA.
15 (1976) 68 Cr App Rep 56, CA; *R v Daly* [1974] 1 All ER 290, [1974] 1 WLR 133, CA.
16 Compensation orders were made in only 9% of the 368 convictions for wounding or assault in magistrates' courts in Softley's 1974 study. The injuries themselves typically comprised fractured or broken bones (19%), gashes or cuts but with no fractures (50%) and bruises and abrasions (40%), P Softley *Compensation Orders in Magistrates' Courts* (1978, Home Office Research Study 43) pp 7 and 10. Compare T Newburn *The Use and Enforcement of Compensation Orders in Magistrates' Courts* (1988, Home Office Research

reasons that might explain the very low number of orders following convictions for wounding or aggravated assault, most notably the absence until recently of extensive guidelines to assist magistrates to make a proper assessment of the victim's injury, but there seems little doubt that the insistence on clarity and simplicity has exercised a depressive influence on magistrates' readiness to make compensation orders in personal injury cases.

The low number of compensation orders being made became a matter of concern and was, in the opinion of some commentators,[17] aggravated by the Court of Appeal's decision in *Vivian*, where Talbot J said:

> 'no order for compensation should be made unless the sum claimed by way of compensation is either agreed or has been proved . . . in the absence of agreement or evidence as to the correct amount which could be claimed . . . no order should be made.'[18]

An editorial in the Justice of the Peace in 1980[19] commented that the effect of this observation, coupled with the accumulated dicta of the earlier cases, had been to defeat the purpose of s 35, since there was no clear mechanism for introducing in evidence at the sentencing stage, an agreed or proved statement of the victim's injury. In practice the police provided such evidence in cases they considered apt, and since 1988 have been encouraged to adopt a procedure whereby the Crown Prosecution Service will be given details of the victim's injury (or loss or damage) prior to the trial,[20] but the section imposes no legal duty on them (or anyone else) to do so.

While it was undoubtedly the case that compensation orders did not figure prominently in sentencing offenders convicted of offences against the person, this editorial comment may nevertheless be regarded as exaggerating the theoretical requirements for establishing the victim's injury, even if, in practice, magistrates did consider that *Vivian* imposed them. Talbot J spoke of the absence of 'evidence as to the correct amount' as an occasion on which a compensation order should not be

---

Study 102) pp 21-22. The generally minor and short-lived impact of injuries that figure in prosecutions before magistrates is reflected in the Home Office's guidelines for compensation for pain and suffering, infra, pp 227-228.

17 N Yell 'Compensation orders since *Vivian*' (1980) 130 New LJ 1109-1111.

18 [1979] 1 All ER 48 at 50, citing dicta of Scarman LJ in *Inwood*, op cit, and of James LJ in *Miller*, op cit.

19 (1980) 144 Justice of the Peace 409 at 416.

20 Home Office circular No 20/1988, *Victims of Crime*. Infra, pp 261-262.

made. So far as the requirement of evidence is concerned, this can hardly be said to impose either an unnecessary or an undesirable condition. As Kilner Brown J said in *R v Amey*:

'As orders for compensation, although a quick way of dealing with what is in essence a civil claim, are nevertheless part of the criminal process and may be supported by a term of imprisonment in default, care must be taken to ensure that the evidence is sufficient before making an order. Proof means proof by evidence and not by inference or guesswork.'[1]

The Home Office was, however, sufficiently concerned by the critical response to *Vivian* that it took the opportunity presented by the Criminal Justice Act 1982 to

'make it clear that the courts can order the compensation they think appropriate in a particular case, without the precise value of the victim's loss necessarily having been agreed or proved. That will rectify the results of certain court cases, which have had restrictive effect on the use of the powers of the courts to make compensation orders.'[2]

The amendment, which took effect as s 35(1A) of the Powers of Criminal Courts Act 1973, provides:

'Compensation under subsection (1) above shall be of such amount as the court considers appropriate, having regard to any evidence and to any representations that are made by or on behalf of the accused or the prosecutor.'

Estimates of the impact of this provision upon magistrates' practice would be varied. The Home Secretary evidently took the view that it would be significant, as it would no longer be necessary 'to have complete agreement on the amount claimed by way of compensation'.[3] Having heard the prosecution and defence submissions, 'a court should usually be able to offer an amount of compensation it considers reasonable'.[4] Others

---

1 [1983] 1 WLR 345 at 347, CA.
2 W Whitelaw MP, 16 HC Official Report (6th series) col 302 (20 January 1982).
3 Remarks extracted from the Home Secretary's address, 'Priority for victims' compensation' given to the annual meeting of the NAVSS, 23 March 1982, noted (1982) 132 New LJ 329-330. The section was characterised by the Home Office as having 'strengthened and clarified' the law, Home Office *Compensation and Support for Victims of Crime* (1985, Cmnd 9457) para 17.
4 (1982) 132 New LJ 329-330.

suggested that *Vivian* had been overruled,[5] but the preferable view is more cautious than this.[6]

What s 35(1A) did was to 'ease slightly the requirement'[7] that there must be evidence or agreement as to the 'correct' amount. What the amendment says, is that the *amount* of the order shall be 'as the court considers appropriate'. This by no means eliminates any need for the victim's injury and its impact to be established to the sentencer's satisfaction; rather it expressly gives what had earlier (arguably) been implied, namely a discretion to fix the quantum in the light of the evidence. This is the position adopted in *R v Swann*.[8] Apparently the first reported case to deal specifically with the impact of the amendments introduced by s 67 of the 1982 Act, the Court of Appeal's judgment was that s 35(1A) reduces only slightly the burden on the sentencer laid down in *Vivian* and *Amey*,[9] to establish the extent of the victim's injury on the basis of sufficient evidence. A trial judge or a magistrate can use his intelligence and his local or specific knowledge to supplement the evidence, but there must be evidence of the injury and its impact on the victim. Section 35(1A) may ameliorate the strict requirements of these earlier cases in so far as a compensation order can now be made though the 'correct amount' is neither agreed or proved, if the evidence will properly support an 'appropriate' amount; but there must, the court emphasised, be such evidence. Where liability to pay, or the appropriateness of the amount is in issue, the matter cannot be determined, as Neill J put it in *R v Horsham Justices, ex p Richards*, 'merely by representations'. His Lordship continued:

'. . . the court has no jurisdiction to make a compensation order without receiving any evidence where there are real issues raised whether the claimants have suffered any, and if so what, loss. The new subsection seems to contemplate that the court can make assessments and approximations where the evidence is scanty or incomplete. It can then make an order which is 'appropriate'. But here the applicant [for judicial review] was challenging the basis upon which any compensation could be paid . . . In these

---

5 C Mosier 'Compensation for victims — custodial for the offender' (1982) 146 Justice of the Peace 675-676, and W West 'Compensation orders' (1983) 147 Justice of the Peace 344.

6 D Thomas *Current Law Statutes Annotated* Criminal Justice Act 1982, and T Wilkinson 'Magistrates' courts — compensation orders' (1984) Law Soc Gaz 485-486.

7 *R v Swann* (1984) 6 Cr App Rep (S) 22; *R v Danvers* [1984] Crim LR 182.

8 Op cit.

9 Op cit.

circumstances it seems to me that justice required that the applicant should have a proper opportunity to test the grounds on which the order was to be made against him. In my view it is not enough to say that he could have given evidence himself. In such a case as the present, where there were plain issues as to liability, it was for the prosecution to place evidence before the court.'[10]

Although no reference was made to s 35(1A), *R v Welch*[11] illustrates this position. The offender was convicted of assault occasioning actual bodily harm and a compensation order of £400 was made against him. While it was apparently not exhaustive, there was some evidence of the facial injuries the offender caused to the victim. Dismissing the appeal, the court held that there was enough evidence about the assault and its consequences to permit an order for an 'appropriate' amount. As to that, £400 was thought not to be extravagant. The quantity and quality of the evidence which a sentencer considers sufficient to make a compensation order will of course vary according to a number of facts: the nature and extent of the injury, its long term effects, if any, and the behaviour of the offender[12] and of the victim. Where the injury is slight and the facts evidencing it uncontroversial, some remarks of Griffiths LJ in *Bond v Chief Constable of Kent*[13] about *Vivian* suggest that the burden of proof required to satisfy the sentencer can be readily discharged. His Lordship said:

'That case is clearly limited to what I will call "quantifiable physical damage". It has no application to small sums of money awarded for personal injury or for the results of assaults or behaviour with which we are concerned in this case.'[14]

10 [1985] 2 All ER 1114 at 1120. These points were reiterated by the Divisional Court in *R v Chorley Justices, ex p Jones* (1990) 154 JP 420.
11 [1984] Crim LR 242, CA.
12 See *R v Smith* (1987) Independent, 27 October where the offender was convicted under s 20 of the Offences against the Person Act 1861 when he shot the victim who had on a previous occasion smashed his shop window and who had been a party to further criminal damage of the shop just prior to the shooting. The offender was ordered to pay £10 compensation to his victim, who had been given a conditional discharge for the first offence of criminal damage.
13 [1983] 1 All ER 456, [1983] 1 WLR 40.
14 Ibid, 43. A proposal made in (1980) 144 Justice of the Peace 409 at 416 to the effect that it is open to the court to invite the offender to suggest a figure for compensation which can be used as the basis of an order was approved by Lawson J in *R v Cornwell* (1979) 1 Cr App Rep (S) 19, CA where there was 'clear and undeniable liability' on the part of the offender.

In more complicated cases the burden will be commensurately more onerous.

(2) Assessing the quantum of compensation

Like the assessment of damages in a civil action or of compensation under the Scheme, the financial evaluation by a criminal court of a victim's injury in respect of which it is considering making a compensation order comprises two elements: one sum to reflect general damages, and the second to reflect special damages.

(a) GENERAL DAMAGES

Two aspects of the process of assessing general damages have in the past been held to discourage the routine making of compensation orders in cases of personal injury. The first has been the lack of training or preparedness on the part of magistrates to place a monetary value on the self-reported experiences of the victim. Newburn's survey confirms the view that for many magistrates and their clerks, this process has been an unwelcome burden.[15] The second has been the perceived inadequacy of the guideline figures which the Magistrates' Association periodically published to reflect the pain and suffering, and inconvenience, of commonly occurring injuries. Like the CICB's compensation exercises,[16] the Association emphasised that these figures were intended only as starting points, but they were often criticised for being substantially out of line with the damages that would have been awarded for the given injuries in civil proceedings. Commenting on these figures in its 1985 Report, the Home Affairs Committee suggested that the reason was that they had already been adjusted downwards in an attempt to reflect the low levels of compensation that offenders in general could afford to pay:

> 'The typical sums awarded by the courts in compensation seem to bear out the contention that the guidelines observed by magistrates' courts result in payments at a lower level than would have been approved by the CICB in similar circumstances. While this is an understandable consequence of the requirement that courts must take account of the defendant's means, we do not think it desirable that

15 Newburn (1988) ch 5.
16 Supra, pp 169–170.

two different standards of financial compensation should apply depending on the victim's choice (or lack of it) of remedy.'[17]

The Committee recommended that the CICB prepare a new set of guidelines as part of its own compensation exercises, indicating the common law figure that would be appropriate for the personal injuries most commonly appearing before magistrates. This was published in 1988.[18] The figures are based on the likely course of an injury of the specified kind being sustained by a person of between 20 and 35 years of age, of average health and with no particular susceptibilities. Like the earlier advice, the circular recommends that the age and the sex of the victim be treated as factors that may materially affect the assessment. Particular mention is made of the impact of scarring upon the victim; a scar which can be seen when the victim is fully clothed, especially if it is on the face, should normally be treated as more serious that one concealed by clothing.

TYPE OF INJURY		SUGGESTED AWARD
Less serious injury		
graze	depending on size	up to £50
bruise	depending on size	up to £75
black eye		£100

---

17 House of Commons, Home Affairs Committee *Compensation and Support for Victims of Crime* (1984–85, HC 43) para 51. A further criticism levelled by the then Chairman of the Board, Sir Michael Ogden, was that even with these depressed guideline figures, magistrates were failing to order compensation in cases clearly falling within them, 'Compensation orders in cases of violence' [1985] Crim LR 500-501, and 'The work of the Criminal Injuries Compensation Board' (1984–85) 52 Medico-Legal J 227-241 where the Chairman described the Association's guidelines as 'ludicrously low'. See also (1981) 145 Justice of the Peace 180. Though they routinely exercise a civil jurisdiction, sheriffs applying the equivalent Scottish law have equally been concerned about the process of assessing compensation, G Maher and C Docherty *Compensation Orders in the Scottish Criminal Courts* (1988, Scottish Office) pp 36-37, 57-60.

18 Home Office circular No 85/1988, *Guidelines on Compensation in the Criminal Courts*, annex. The guideline figures are reproduced in the Magistrates' Association's sentencing guidelines, (1989) 139 New LJ 1291. In *R v Broughton* (1986) 8 Cr App Rep (S) 379 the Court of Appeal expressly approved the circuit judge's adoption of the earlier figures prepared on the basis of the CICB's guidelines.

cut (without permanent scarring)	depending on size and whether stitched	£75–£200
sprain	depending on loss of mobility	£100–£400
loss of a tooth (not a front tooth)	depending on position of tooth and age of victim	£250–£500
minor injury	causing reasonable absence from work of about three weeks	£550

More serious injury

loss of a front tooth		£1,000
facial scar	however small — resulting in permanent disfigurement	£550 +
facial scar	a vicious slash wound leaving scar from ear to corner of the mouth or under the chin	£5,000–£8,000 +
jaw	fractured (wired)	£1,750
nasal	undisplaced fracture of the nasal bone	£550
nasal	displaced fracture of the bone requiring manipulation under general anaesthetic	£850
nasal	not causing fracture but displaced septum requiring a sub-mucous resection	£1,500
wrist	simple fracture with complete recovery in a few weeks	£1,750–£2,500

The Committee further recommended that these figures should be updated every two years; the CICB's 25th Report indicates that its 1989-90 Report will contain a consolidated list of guidelines both for magistrates and for its own purposes.[19]

It is too early to say whether their publication has had any appreciable effect upon magistrates' willingness to order offenders to pay compensation, but Vennard's research carried out in the late 1970s suggests that an increase should occur.[20] The research design distinguished the use of compensation orders over two periods of time in two sets of courts: 'guideline courts' which were, at the end of the first period of time, given an earlier version of the Magistrates' Association guidelines, and 'other courts', which were not. The results were quite dramatic, showing that 'the use of the guidelines was associated with a marked increase in awards'.[1] As between the two periods of time, orders made in the guideline courts increased from 2% to 24% of cases, while the control group showed an increase from 4.9% to 8.7%. This much smaller increase was attributed to the 'widening concern that the criminal justice system should become more responsible to the interests of victims of crime, coupled with magistrates' increasing familiarity with their extended powers of compensation.'[2]

Any increase in the making of orders in personal injury cases that follows the publication of these guidelines may similarly be attributable to a continuation of this concern, but is also likely to be caused by two other new conditions. One was the publication in April 1988 of the Home Office recommendation that the police should routinely complete a 'Compensation Schedule' to be passed on to the CPS,[3] but more important was the coming into force of the statutory duty introduced by s 104 of the Criminal Justice Act 1988 that a court must give reasons if it does not make a compensation order in a case in which it is empowered to do so. The publication of the guidelines means that it is no longer possible for magistrates to decline to make an order because they have no guidance as to the level of compensation appropriate to the injury.

Concerning the matter of their lack of expertise in the assessment of the victim's injury in other cases, the Home Affairs Committee recommended that magistrates 'should be given discretion to refer to the Board for assessment cases of unusual

19 CICB 25th Report (1989, Cm 900) para 23.1(a).
20 J Vennard 'Magistrates' assessment of compensation for injury' [1979] Crim LR 510-523.
1 Id, p 513.
2 Id.
3 Home Office circular No 20/1988.

complexity even where the sum involved is less than the Scheme's lower limit.[4] It is not surprising that for the Board this was an unattractive option, and the Home Office reply too dwelt on the inevitable cost of referrals (and upon the delay in the conclusion of criminal trials).[5] As one of the primary reasons for the lower limit is to relieve the CICB of the work involved in assessing compensation in cases of minor injury, the likelihood of such referrals being authorised is, given the Board's present backlog, highly unlikely.[6] With the new guidelines and the other incentives to the consideration of compensation orders, magistrates and their clerks should in any event become more practised; cases that are complex should, as the courts have repeatedly said, be left to civil proceedings.

(b) SPECIAL DAMAGES

To the figure calculated for general damages should be added sums known to have been lost, and expenses incurred. Earlier guidelines instance the following as items proper for compensation: loss of earnings; expenses incurred in engaging a deputy or someone to care for the house and/or children; the cost of dental treatment and, exceptionally, of medical treatment; actual expenses incurred travelling to hospital and the cost of replacing or repairing broken spectacles or damaged clothing.[7] These reflect for the most part, items compensable both in civil proceedings and under the Scheme.[8] In each case, the sentencer will require evidence of the loss and may ask for receipts, payslips, bills and other documentary evidence of payments made or owed by the victim as a result of his injury. If the Compensation Schedule does its job, the full details of the injuries, time off work, loss of wages, period of incapacity, and incidental expenses should be readily available to the court; if not, the court may only be able to make an order for such appropriate amount as is evidenced, though this may ultimately fall short of the victim's full losses.

The discussion so far has concentrated upon the assessment of compensation in magistrates' courts. The Crown Courts have

4 House of Commons (1984–85) para 52.
5 Home Office (1985) para 17.
6 House of Commons, Home Affairs Committee *Compensating Victims Quickly: the Administration of the Criminal Injuries Compensation Board* (1989–90, HC 92).
7 'Compensation for injury' (1980) 144 Justice of the Peace 698.
8 Supra, pp 162–168.

produced no guidelines similar to those in use by magistrates, nor has the assessment of compensation by Crown Court judges been the object of criticism. This may be because so few compensation orders are made following conviction on indictment,[9] or because those orders that have been made have not been researched or are beyond reproach. So far as the issue of the assessment of compensation by Crown Court judges is concerned, the principles that are applicable to magistrates are likewise applicable at that level.

(3) Financial limits on quantum

Section 40 of the Magistrates' Courts Act 1980 provides:

> 'The compensation to be paid under a compensation order made by a magistrates' court in respect of any offence of which the court has convicted the offender shall not exceed £2,000; and the compensation or total compensation to be paid under a compensation order or compensation orders made by a magistrates' court in respect of any offence or offences taken into consideration in determining sentence shall not exceed the difference (if any) between the amount or total amount which under the preceding provisions of this subsection is the maximum for the offence or offences of which the offender has been convicted and the amount or total amounts (if any) which are in fact ordered to be paid in respect of that offence or those offences.'

The upper limit of £2,000 per offence was introduced from 1 May 1984.[10] The effect of the rest of the subsection is to limit a magistrate's power to order compensation for offences taken into consideration to no more than the difference between the theoretical maximum compensation for the number of convictions and the actual amount ordered in respect of them. Thomas explains the effect as being:

> 'a formula £(2,000) × A–B where A is the number of offences of which the offender has been convicted (irrespective of whether compensation

---

9 In 1988, approximately 3,200 orders were made by the Crown Court following convictions for violence against the person, sexual offences, and robbery, *Criminal Statistics England and Wales 1988* table 7.24.

10 Originally £400, increased to £1,000 by the Criminal Law Act 1977, and to £2,000 by the Criminal Penalties etc (Increase) Order 1984 (SI 1984/447) art 2(1) Sch 1.

orders were made in respect of them) and B is the total amount ordered to be paid as compensation in respect of any of those offences.'[11]

Suppose an offender is convicted of one offence of criminal damage and asks for ten others to be taken into consideration. The magistrate proposes to make compensation orders in respect of these ten offences in the sum of £100 each. He further proposes to make an order for £800 in respect of the offence for which the offender is convicted. This is permissible, since the aggregate of the compensation orders for the offences taken into consideration (£1,000) does not exceed the difference (£1,200) between the maximum that can be awarded for the offence for which the offender has been convicted (£2,000) and the amount that has actually been awarded for that offence (£800). The position would be different, however, if the magistrate proposed to award £200 compensation for each of the offences taken into consideration, or made an award of £1,200 for the offence for which the offender was convicted.

As the number of TIC offences will almost always exceed the number for which the offender is convicted, the effect of this section will be to place a ceiling, in most cases below £2,000, on the total amount that can be ordered for the TIC offences. However, it is possible, though unlikely, for an order to be made for a TIC offence which exceeds the statutory maximum of £2,000 for any one convicted offence. Suppose the offender is convicted of three offences and has one TIC offence. An order is made for £500 in respect of one of the convicted offences, but not in respect of the other two. In theory the maximum now available for the TIC offence is (£6,000–£500) £5,500.

B. THE EVALUATION OF WHAT THE OFFENDER CAN PAY

One of the most important distinguishing features of compensation orders is the relevance of the offender's means to the decision both to make an order, and for how much. This consideration is, of course, wholly absent from an action for damages for personal injury where, if the plaintiff is entitled to succeed, the financial status of the defendant is, so far as the formal judgment goes, neither here nor there.

The statutory obligation on a criminal court to consider the

---

11 D Thomas *Current Sentencing Practice* (1982, Sweet & Maxwell) para J2.1(b).

offender's means has two main implications for the theory and practice of compensation orders. Firstly, the reason why the offender's means is a relevant consideration is that from a sentencing perspective, a financially onerous compensation order is likely to conduce to further offending to meet its obligations, or will in some other way be incompatible with the sentencing objectives appropriate in that offender's case. The persistent and underlying conflict between the interests of the victim and of the offender is well illustrated by the many reported cases on the question, what criteria are appropriate when determining the contribution the offender ought to make to that quantum of compensation which would represent the total recompense that the law would allow in civil proceedings? (In this chapter and those following, I call this quantum the 'ideal assessment'.) Secondly, the fact that offenders do not always have sufficient means to comply with an order reflecting an ideal assessment of the victim's injuries underlines the inherently limited potential of compensation orders to effect full compensation to all victims of personal injury whose offenders are convicted. This does not mean that compensation orders will not be able to achieve this goal (assuming it to be a proper goal of a criminal court) in some cases, but these will remain, notwithstanding other changes introduced in 1982 and 1988, a minority. This suggests that it is wrong to look to compensation orders as the principal method by which victims can obtain full compensation where their offenders are convicted,[12] since, apart from all those offences causing personal injury that do not result in a conviction, some form of compensation supplement will be required even where there are convictions.

(1) The duty to consider the offender's means

Section 35(4) of the 1973 Act provides that:

'In determining whether to make a compensation order against any person, and in determining the amount to be paid by any person under such an order, the court shall have regard to his means so far as they appear or are known to the court'.[13]

---

12 As Ogden (1984–85) implies.
13 This phraseology was deliberately chosen for its repetition of the statutory duty imposed on magistrates by s 35 of the Magistrates' Courts Act 1980 when they are contemplating fining the offender, HC Official Report (5th series) Standing Committee G cols 76-89 (7 December 1971).

When an order is made under s 171 of the Criminal Justice Act 1988, this duty will be contained in s 35(4)(a) of the 1973 Act.

The inability of the offender to pay compensation was one of the reasons frequently given to the Advisory Council on the Penal System for the very low incidence of compensation orders made under s 11(2) of the Criminal Justice Act 1948,[14] and it remains a significant obstacle to the exercise of the powers conferred on criminal courts under s 35(1). For example, in *R v Webb*,[15] where the victim was 'glassed', Cantley J held that it was wholly unrealistic to make a compensation order against an offender convicted of unlawful wounding whose own income was £10 per week and whose family's income totalled £50 per week; still less, as was the case, to make an order of £200. Section 35(4) formally recognised, for the first time, the relevance of the offender's means, but as Scarman LJ observed in *Inwood*, it is unspecific as to the criteria to be applied by the court when it seeks to comply with its statutory duty:

'Compensation orders should certainly not be used . . . when there is a real doubt as to whether the convicted man can find the compensation. It is true the section leaves a considerable area of judgment to the court. The statute requires only that the courts shall have regard to the means of the convicted man, so far as they appear or are known to the court. In a number of recent cases before this court, however, it has been made clear that the courts must follow a common sense course, bearing in mind the factors to which I have referred'.[16]

The factors to which his Lordship referred included the possibility of the victim taking civil proceedings and the desirability of the obligation to compensate being uncontroversial. To these his Lordship added the undesirability of compensation orders being counter-productive to the sentencing goals apt in the offender's case; most commonly to discourage recidivism. This point has been made in general terms on a number of occasions. In *R v Oddy*, for example, Lawton LJ said:

'The means of the accused are relevant for a number of reasons. The courts have got to be realistic. It is no good courts making

14 (1970) para 28.
15 (1979) 1 Cr App Rep (S) 16, CA.
16 (1974) 60 Cr App Rep 70 at 73, CA.

compensation orders which can never be discharged by an accused person, and equally it is no good making compensation orders which, to use Counsel's phrase, are likely to be counter-productive in the sense that they may result in the accused committing further offences to discharge the order'.[17]

His Lordship's emphasis upon the importance of a compensation order not becoming counter-productive was approved in *Miller*,[18] and Scarman LJ's remarks to the same effect have likewise more recently been held to be 'as relevant today as they were when uttered'.[19] Beyond their application to the exercise of a sentencer's discretion under s 35(1), these remarks have been more specifically applied to the matter of payment of compensation by instalment.

The desirability of compensation orders not inducing 'the payer to go back to crime'[20] may, however, be tempered by a robust view of what an offender can reasonably be expected to do to compensate his victim. Merely to base an appeal against the making of a compensation order on the ground that the offender might commit further offences in order to comply with it need not be persuasive if the sum is not large and the offender is able bodied and fit for work.[1] The demands of such penal models as just deserts or modern retributivism may suggest that a compensation order is apt notwithstanding that the offender may experience difficulty complying with it:

'There are good moral reasons for making compensation orders which will in measure hurt the defendant's pocket and act to remind him of what he has done'.[2]

---

17 [1974] 2 All ER 666 at 669, CA.
18 'The compensation order must not be oppressive. The court has to bear in mind that a prisoner who has just been discharged from jail is very often short of money. He must not be tempted to commit further offences to provide cash in order to bring his compensation order up to date. That matter is dealt with in the decision of *Oddy*', per Pain J (1976) 68 Cr App Rep 56 at 58.
19 McCowan J, *R v Parker* (1981) 3 Cr App Rep (S) 278 at 281. The point is reiterated by the Court of Appeal in *R v Panayioutou* [1990] Crim LR 349, CA.
20 Lord Widgery CJ, *R v O'Donoghue* (1974) 66 Cr App Rep 116 at 118, CA.
1 *R v McKinley* [1975] Crim LR 294, CA. Cf *R v McIntosh* [1973] Crim LR 378, CA where a compensation order was quashed because the offender had a wooden leg which had made it difficult for him to obtain employment.
2 Lord Widgery CJ, *R v Bradburn* (1973) 57 Cr App Rep 948 at 953.

Nevertheless, Lord Widgery CJ continued:

> '. . . the court must try to steer a common sense path through these various considerations and come up with a solution which satisfies them'.[3]

The question, then, in all cases where the offender does not obviously possess present and sufficient resources to comply with a compensation order for the full amount representing the victim's injury and consequent losses, is, what constitutes, in Lawton LJ's words a 'common sense and realistic' assessment under s 35(4) of the offender's means?[4]

(a)   THE OFFENDER'S SOURCES OF INCOME

Firstly, it is clear that present inability to pay is not conclusive against the making of a compensation order. An offender who is without capital or income is not necessarily a person without 'means' for the purpose of s 35(4). If he enjoys good health and has a reasonable prospect of employment, an offender can be required to pay compensation, although in such a case the amount should be limited to what he can be expected to pay over a period of time which is not excessive.[5] Thus Newburn found that unemployment was not a major factor in determining whether compensation was ordered, but was important in determining the amount of the order, with a greater proportion of unemployed offenders paying less than £50 in total.[6] Where the offender is unemployed, the cases indicate clearly that care must be exercised both in determining the nature of his prospects of employment, given his own levels of skill or training, and in assessing how much of any wages received can reasonably be earmarked for the purpose of complying with the order. In particular, if the offender has dependants, the proportion available for compensation may be very small. On the other hand, if the offender has no prospects of employment or, if employed, his earnings

---

3 Id. See also *Miller* op cit, and *R v Holmes* (1982) 146 JP Jo 388, CA where the court held, following *Bradburn*, that there were good moral reasons for making a compensation order as a realistic reminder to the offender of what he had done.

4 *Oddy*, op cit, 670.

5 *R v Scott* (1986) 83 Cr App Rep 221 at 223, CA. In *Parker* op cit, *Oddy* op cit, and *O'Donoghue*, op cit, compensation orders were quashed because the offender had no prospect of employment or his employment would be so poorly paid that it would take years to pay off an order.

6 (1988) pp 17–18.

are so low that he has virtually no income in hand after deductions for rent, community charge, utilities and such other expenses, a compensation order should not be made.

Neither is there any objection in principle to an offender in receipt of state benefits being ordered to pay compensation. In 1988 the Home Office considered that £5 a week was about the maximum weekly contribution that an offender on income support could reasonably be expected to pay,[7] which suggests that compensation orders are, at least in these cases, unlikely to satisfy an ideal assessment of the victim's injury. In fact, though insufficiency of means was the most common reason given by magistrates in Newburn's study for refusing to make an order,[8] in 70% of cases in which compensation was payable by instalment, the weekly sum was less than £6, and fewer than 10% of offenders were ordered to pay more than £10 a week.[9]

Apart from employment, an offender may claim to have other sources of income, but the courts have insisted that vague assertions about the possibilities of unliquidated sums being made available to the offender which can be used to comply with a compensation order are not to be taken seriously. So, an order should not be made, for example, on the basis only of assurances that family or friends will contribute to it,[10] that the family will ensure that the offender pays,[11] or that the offender has a suitcase containing an unspecified sum of cash in a left-luggage locker in Paris.[12] Neither is the expectation of a judgment for damages in a personal injury action,[13] or of an award by the Criminal Injuries Compensation Board sufficient. In *R v*

7 Op cit, circular No 85/1988 para 8.
8 (1988) p 36.
9 Ibid, p 24. For an offender receiving income support, £3 a week is not inappropriate.
10 *Inwood*, op cit (order quashed where the offender had no present means and no more than a hope that a relative would supply the £12,000 ordered to be paid).
11 *O'Donoghue*, op cit.
12 *R v Johnstone* (1982) 4 Cr App Rep (S) 141, CA. Thomas (1982) para J2.3, and Yell (1980). In considering any capital the offender may have, a compensation order should not be based on the assumption that he will sell the matrimonial home, *R v Harrison* (1980) 2 Cr App Rep (S) 313; *R v Blackmore* (1984) 6 Cr App Rep (S) 244; *R v Butt* (1986) 8 Cr App Rep (S) 216, CA, and *R v Hackett* (1988) 10 Cr App Rep(S) 388, CA. Though not explicit, these cases presumably proceed from the basis that a sale would leave the family homeless.
13 *R v Backhouse* [1974] Crim LR 485, CA. Nor should an order be made on the basis that it will take effect only if the offender comes into funds, *R v Diggles* (1988) 10 Cr App Rep (S) 279, CA.

Fleming[14] the offender pleaded guilty to burglary. He was unemployed, but on the basis of his application pending before the Board for an assault in which he had been the victim, the Recorder made a compensation order against him, to be paid out of the award, if any. Given the Board's attitude to victims who are, or have been, themselves offenders,[15] this was an optimistic expectation on the Recorder's (and the offender's) part. The application was rejected. On appeal the compensation order was quashed, the court holding that the Recorder had no power to make a conditional order, and that orders should not in any event be made in anticipation of unliquidated sums which might or might not be recovered by the offender/victim.

Where, however, the offender has an asset (such as a car) whose value can be clearly ascertained by the court, there is no objection to its making an order on the assumption that it will have to be sold. This is so even if the asset was not used in the commission of the offence for which he was convicted.[16] The proceeds of the offence may of course be available for compensation,[17] either directly or by virtue of s 43A of the Powers of Criminal Courts Act.[18] In common with fines, moneys found on the offender when arrested or taken into custody may, by s 80(2) of the Magistrates' Courts Act 1980 be ordered to be applied to a compensation order.

(b) PAYMENT BY INSTALMENTS

One way of suiting the offender's means to the ideal assessment of the victim's injury is to order him to pay in instalments. This power exists by virtue of s 34 of the Powers of Criminal Courts Act 1973 in the case of the Crown Court, and s 75 of the Magistrates' Courts Act 1980 in the case of magistrates' courts. Like the question, *how much* should the offender be required to pay, the question over *how long* a period should he be required to pay is relative to his particular circumstances. The general answer to this second question is that the time should not be excessive, but the Court of Appeal has in recent years entertained varying notions of what constitutes excess.

In general terms, this constraint may clearly have a significant impact on a victim's expectation of receiving full compensation

---

14 (1983) 147 JP Jo 363, CA.
15 Supra, pp 91–96.
16 *R v Martin* [1990] Crim LR 132, CA.
17 *R v Workman* (1979) 1 Cr App Rep (S) 335, CA, and *R v Chambers* (1981) 3 Cr App Rep (S) 318.
18 Supra, pp 216–217.

for his injuries. Suppose a victim suffers a broken nose in an unprovoked assault by the offender. If an undisplaced fracture, this injury would attract an award of £550 under the Home Office's 1988 guidelines. From the victim's standpoint a lump sum payment of the full amount would probably represent the ideal outcome (at least in terms of compensation and assuming no other injurious consequences), but the offender may have insufficient present means to comply with such an order. On the other hand, if the court can predict that he will have sufficient means over a period of around two years, an order requiring payment of, say, £5 a week for 110 weeks would both satisfy the requirement that compensation orders be made having regard to the offender's means and ultimately yield full compensation to the victim. The outcome for the victim will clearly be less satisfactory where the court concludes that the offender could only afford, say, £3 a week from his predicted resources, or if the injury were more serious. If there were no limitation on the period of time over which instalments could be required, the victim would eventually (but leaving aside inflation) receive full compensation; as the law now is, a period in excess of three years would have to be clearly justifiable.

Until *R v Olliver*,[19] the Court of Appeal had settled, albeit not for very long, on a limit of one year for payment by instalments. This limit was itself reached after a number of appeals against compensation orders contemplating much longer periods of time. In *Bradburn*[20] a period of four years was held to be excessive and in *R v Daly*, where an order requiring payment over six years was quashed, Lord Widgery CJ said:

'the court has said on more than one occasion that it is not appropriate to use this machinery or to claim that regard has been had to the means of the defendant if the outcome of the order will involve his being committed to this kind of payment for as long as that'.[1]

While these observations were repeatedly affirmed by the Court of Appeal during the 1970s and early 1980s,[2] sentencers had nevertheless imposed compensation orders contemplating

---

19 (1989) 11 Cr App Rep (S) 10.
20 Op cit.
1 [1974] 1 WLR 133 at 134.
2 *Miller*, op cit, *Workman*, op cit, *R v Blake* (1980) 144 JP Jo 267, CA, and *R v Hunt* [1983] Crim LR 270, CA.

lengthy periods of payment, in one case as much as 40 years.[3] Quashing these and, in some instances, reducing the period of payment, the Court of Appeal settled for a while on two years as the permissible maximum for payment by instalments,[4] but in *R v Holden*[5] suggested that 12 months (as in the case of payment of a fine) should be the normal maximum. This appeared to be well settled, the Court of Appeal observing in *R v Hobbs*,[6] that it had said over and over again, that instalments must not be ordered to be paid over more than a year, a limit which coincided with the Home Office's guidelines.[7] However, in *Olliver*, the court shifted its position once more, holding that two years would seldom be too long, and that payment over three years could, given appropriate circumstances, be unassailable. This case involved both fines and compensation orders payable over periods of 30 weeks. The court held that on a true reading of its earlier decisions, there was nothing wrong in principle with the period of payment being longer that 12 months, provided that this did not impose an undue burden or involve too severe a punishment. In the context of efforts to find alternatives to custody, a compensation order payable over two or three years that is within the offender's capacity to pay, and in respect of which default is unlikely, is quite proper. Though within the spirit of the earlier dicta, this more recent pronouncement, itself since extended to include a four year term,[8] is likely to engender further confusion.

(c) CONFIRMING EVIDENCE OF THE OFFENDER'S MEANS

Section 35(4) requires the court to have regard to the offender's means 'so far as they appear or are known to the court'. The question arises, with what degree of specificity should the court be able to assess the offender's means, and how are they to be proved? In *R v Howell*,[9] Pain J held that a court does not require

---

3 *R v McCullough* (1982) 4 Cr App Rep (S) 98, CA, and *R v Makin* (1982) 4 Cr App Rep (S) 180 where instalments payable over 7½ years were held to be 'wildly excessive'.
4 A period of two years was approved in *McKinley*, op cit, and was substituted for the 7½ year period in *Makin*, op cit. In *R v Brown* (1984) Times, 16 October, CA instalments payable over 2½ years was held to be too long a period.
5 (1985) 7 Cr App Rep (S) 7.
6 (1987) Independent, 29 June, CA. *Broughton*, op cit, and *R v Hills* (1986) 8 Cr App Rep (S) 199, CA.
7 Op cit, circular No 85/1988.
8 *R v Bagga* [1990] Crim LR 128, CA.
9 (1978) 66 Cr App Rep 179, CA.

a specific calculation of the offender's means; a 'broad picture' will suffice. If it is clear that he has means (and often the offender will volunteer this information in the hope of a lighter sentence), the court does not need to itemise his income and expenditure before making an order. The same view was taken in *R v Bolden*[10] where the offender, while neither confirming nor denying the fact, was clearly in funds. The Court of Appeal held that the court had no duty to verify the offender's means if it was satisfied that he had sufficient to pay the order. Other recent decisions suggest a more rigorous approach, requiring a 'most careful inquiry' into the capacity of the offender to pay.[11] To what extent does this assume any duty on the prosecution or the defence to confirm that the offender does indeed have the means to comply?

This raises issues similar to, and derives its difficulties from, those same institutional ambiguities that are associated with the question of proving the victim's injury. The problem of imperfect information has arisen in the past in part because there has been no institutional responsibility for supplying and authenticating evidence about the victim's injury. So it is also with evidence of the offender's means: he cannot be compelled to testify as to this issue, nor it seems, is it the prosecution's task to investigate the matter if it is not raised by them. This arguably unsatisfactory position was confirmed by the judgment of Pain J in *R v Johnstone*.[12] There it was argued on appeal against a compensation order in the sum of £12,000, that as the prosecution had not proved the existence of means sufficient to comply with such an order, it was bad. While reducing the sum to £500 (there being some evidence of means), Pain J held that, although s 35(4) requires the court to have regard to the offender's means, this did not impose on the prosecution a duty to conduct an inquiry into the existence or adequacy of the offender's means, as this was a matter within the offender's own knowledge. In this respect the matter is similar to the courts' approach to the question of the offender's ability to pay a fine. However, if the prosecution wishes to advance the proposition that the offender should be ordered to pay compensation, then it is, the Court of Appeal held in *R v Hobbs*,[13] under a duty to ensure that any information about the offender's financial position is accurate.

10 (1987) 9 Cr App Rep (S) 83.
11 Watkins LJ, *R v Scott* (1986) 83 Cr App Rep 221 at 223; *R v Phillips* (1988) 10 Cr App Rep (S) 419, CA.
12 (1982) 4 Cr App Rep (S) 141, CA.
13 (1987) Independent, 29 June, CA.

This duty extends to cases where the offender puts before the court proposals for compensation; both *R v Bond*[14] and *R v Slack*[15] holding that before any plea in mitigation, in particular where a custodial sentence may normally be expected, the defence should seek to verify the offender's means. This exception to the general rule that counsel is not expected to vouch for the truth of mitigating factors goes only so far as the offender's present circumstances; if the offender was unambiguous in his wish to compensate, and then had the means to comply, he cannot subsequently expect the court to quash the order if his expectations are unrealised, at least where they were fully thought out. The problem here is that if the offender presents an over-optimistic picture of his capacity to pay, as a result of which the primary sentence is adjusted, there may be nothing which the court can do to readjust it if the offender successfully appeals the order on the ground that it is unrealistic.[16]

But suppose the offender genuinely is in funds, but being confident of a custodial sentence, is not forthcoming on this matter, as he does not want to have to pay compensation as well: should the court decline to make an order at all notwithstanding the evidence it has, or make an order and let the offender contest it on appeal? *Bolden* and *Phillips* suggest that if the evidence as to his means is unclear and the offender is not prepared to speak on the matter then the sentencer should refrain from making an order. If, however, the court has no real doubt of the offender's ability to pay, and takes the view that he is merely endeavouring to mislead, then the trial judge may properly indicate that he is minded to make an order, and invite the offender to contest the matter. If he does not, then he cannot complain if a monetary order is made against him. In effect, it is for the offender to show that he cannot comply with an order when he apparently has funds available for that purpose.

(2) Assessing the sufficiency of the offender's means

Assuming the offender has some means, the question arises whether they will be sufficient to comply with the order. Sufficiency is, as has been implied in the discussion so far, a complex notion. It is important to distinguish the manner in

14 (1986) 8 Cr App Rep (S) 11, CA.
15 (1987) 9 Cr App Rep (S) 65, CA. See also *R v Roberts* (1987) 9 Cr App Rep (S) 275, CA.
16 *R v Huish* (1985) 7 Cr App Rep (S) 272, CA.

which content is given to it, since the reasons that can be and are given for not making an order on the ground of insufficiency in some cases confuse two separate meanings. These different meanings of insufficiency also have significance for sentencing practice.

(a) THE RELATIONSHIP BETWEEN THE OFFENDER'S MEANS AND
THE VICTIM'S INJURY

Firstly, sufficiency involves a judgment about the relationship between the offender's means and the ideal assessment of the victim's injury. An offender's means may be sufficient in the sense that he can pay, either as a lump sum or in instalments, a sum that amounts to the ideal assessment of the victim's injury. There may be few and possibly no instances in which an offender would be wealthy enough to pay the kind of sums which figure as the highest award in each year's CICB Report,[17] but for many less serious injuries, the possibility must exist. The sufficiency of the offender's means is thus not an absolute matter, but one that is relative to the injury he caused to the victim. If the injury is slight, attracting a sum for example only of £50-100 (the average figure payable under orders made on summary conviction for indictable offences against the person in 1988 was £87[18]), it is quite in order to require the offender to pay £2 or £3 a week notwithstanding he has little disposable income.

Insufficiency exists in this first sense when the offender does not have the means to pay even in instalments that are not excessively protracted, a sum commensurate with the ideal assessment of the victim's injury. The question that arises in these cases is, at what point in the possible discrepancies between the offender's means and the ideal assessment of the victim's injury does the insufficiency become so great that a court should refrain from ordering any compensation at all? Should the offender be required to pay even a little of the amount that would fully compensate the victim, or would very small amounts tend, as Thomas and others have argued,[19] to diminish the gravity of the offence?:

17 CICB (1989) para 9.1, total award of £307,381.
18 *Criminal Statistics: England and Wales 1988*, op cit, table 7.24.
19 See Thomas' views on *R v Daly* [1974] 1 All ER 290, [1974] 1 WLR 133, CA, included in his commentaries on *R v Kneeshaw* and *R v Keep* [1974] Crim LR 263, CA, on *R v Wylie* [1974] Crim LR 608, CA, and in *Current Sentencing Practice* (1982) para J2.3(f).

'The unpalatable fact is that in some cases the amount which the offender could reasonably be expected to pay must often be derisory in comparison with the extent of the victim's loss, and in these circumstances there would be a strong incentive for the criminal courts to refrain from ordering any compensation'.[20]

Two specimen awards noted in the Board's Twentieth Report illustrate the dilemma. In the first a 71 year old widower, blind in one eye, reproved without using or threatening violence, a young child who had ridden his tricycle into his back. The child's father approached the victim and, after a verbal assault, struck him in the face with a billiard cue. The victim lost the sight of his good eye and became wholly blind. The father was convicted of causing grievous bodily harm. No compensation order was made, although he was, inter alia, fined £200.[1] The relevance of the fine is that, like a compensation order, it is fixed by taking into consideration among other things the means of the person on whom the fine is imposed, and, as Ashworth comments, 'is generally understood to mean that courts should reduce the level of a fine where it appears that the offender's income is so low that a fine of the "normal" amount would cause hardship to him'.[2] Assuming the £200 fine to be the Crown Court's assessment of what the offender could properly be expected to pay, this suggests that the figure which would have been chosen had a compensation order been made would have been much the same. The Board's award to the victim was £55,000 for general damages and future expenses. Should a compensation order, even for £200, be made against the offender in such a case?

In the second case the offender was charged under s 24 of the Offences against the Person Act 1861 when it was discovered that he had been systematically poisoning his flatmate. The victim's injuries were assessed at £1,380 from which £350 was deducted, having been paid by the offender in compliance with a compensation order made against him on conviction.[3] In the absence of full details about the offender's means in each case, comment is speculative; but the two cases illustrate some recurring and problematic issues about the making of compensation orders.

There are two main arguments in support of compensation

---

20 Advisory Council on the Penal System (1970) para 28.
1 CICB 20th Report (1984, Cmnd 9399) para 36.
2 Ashworth (1983) p 286.
3 CICB (1984) para 38.

orders being a sentencing alternative. One is that the making of the order will have a beneficial impact *on the offender*: it will bring home to him the injury and distress that he has caused to another human being and will, it is surmised, discourage further offending. On this basis, a compensation order is surely apt every time an offender causes injury and has means, since like unit fines, the order has an impact on the offender in proportion to his means. But this apparently simple proposition masks some troubling issues within sentencing theory and practice. Where the offender is poor *in relation to the injury* (as in the first case mentioned above) there will inevitably be pressure to impose an additional or alternative sentence to reflect the seriousness of the injury caused, in that case total blindness. The matter is much as Ashworth has described in relation to the tendencies among sentencers to impose, for example, a suspended sentence on a poor offender where a wealthy offender would only be fined:

'The reason why sentencers feel themselves driven to use these expedients is not far to seek: they believe that it would be inappropriate to impose upon the poorer offender a fine small enough to reflect his lack of means, this belief being closely linked to the seriousness of the case, and the belief derives ultimately from a crude conception of sentencing which ties the penalty to the gravity of the crime itself.'[4]

Ashworth criticises this belief for its ignorance of such other relevant factors as the desirability of sentences having an equal impact on the individual offender and of each offender being sentenced, so far as this crime is commensurate with anyone else's, in a commensurate way. This criticism seems to apply now with equal force to the making of compensation orders, though unlike fines, these orders have only been available as an independent sentencing alternative since 1982, and there is virtually no guidance as to the principles that should apply to their use qua sentences.[5] Nor do the sentencing difficulties end where the offender does have sufficient income in relation to the victim's injury; here again, as with fines, the question arises, should the wealthy offender be sentenced *in addition* to the monetary order, lest it be thought that he is buying his way out of his offence? We return to this point later.[6]

Thus, so far as the first objective of compensation orders is concerned, simply requiring the relatively poor offender to pay

4 (1983) p 287.
5 *Infra*, pp 279–282.
6 *Infra*, pp 292–293.

something (as in the second example mentioned earlier), or even requiring the wealthy offender to pay an amount equal to the ideal assessment of the victim's injury, does not exhaust the sentencer's decision: should I impose some further sentence to reflect the gravity of the injury or to deflect public criticism that there is one law for the rich and another for the poor?

Unlike the first objective, the second, which is intended to have a beneficial impact *on the victim*, is statutorily qualified: it is to compensate the victim for his injury, but only so far as can be expected in view of the offender's means. Where the offender has sufficient means to compensate the victim fully, an order to that effect should, it seems, be routinely made in the absence of prior sentencing objectives. Where the offender's means preclude such a course, it seems that he should, other things being equal, contribute what he can. What Thomas has argued, in effect, is that a further criterion should be applied: where that contribution is so out of proportion to the injury caused as to minimise or trivialise it, no order should be made. So an order is proper in the second example mentioned earlier, since the poisoner was in a position to contribute about a quarter of the ideal assessment of the victim's injury, but not so in the first, where it would be less than 1%.

But we might ask whether even so small a sum would indeed be regarded as derisory by the victim, or by anyone else. Surely the fact of a very substantial discrepancy, far from devaluing the victim's injury, merely underlines its impact upon him. So far as the offender's contribution goes, it would remain that: a token payment perhaps, but *some* recognition of the injury done to the victim. Since the issue is not whether the offender *can* pay, but whether he *should* pay a small sum in compensation, it seems right that it is the victim who should be the judge of what is derisory. This is, in some measure, contemplated by the frequent justification for appellate intervention: the victim is free to pursue his civil remedy. In reality the impracticability of this course of action will preclude the option; which is all the more reason for a sentencer not rejecting out of hand as derisory, compensation which the victim might be well pleased to receive, and the offender able and willing to make, if they are both given the chance.

A second objection that has been made to small compensation orders is that they might dissuade the victim from applying to the Board, since he might conclude that his injuries do not satisfy the minimum loss requirement. But here too, there seems little danger of such misconstruction where the discrepancy is large;

it is where the offender's means are only just short of being sufficient to meet an ideal assessment that this danger arises. In any event, if the *Victim's Charter*[7] delivers on its promise to advise victims as a matter of course of their right to apply to the Board, failure to apply because an offender's small contribution is perceived to be more or less equal to what the victim could expect from a personal injury assessment under the Scheme should be prevented.

(b) THE RELATIONSHIP BETWEEN THE OFFENDER'S MEANS AND HIS ABILITY TO PAY

Sufficiency may, secondly, involve a judgment about the relationship between the offender's means and the likelihood of his being able to comply with an order, irrespective of its commensurability with an ideal assessment of the victim's injury. Here the issue is not whether he *should* pay at all, but whether he *can* pay. Frequently (and in many of the cases that have come on appeal) an offender will have insufficient means in both senses, and so it is considered right that no order be made, or that it be substantially reduced; but where only one sense is apt on the facts of the case, it is important that the right reasons for not making an order or for appellate intervention are relied upon.

Whereas good reasons for not making a compensation order because of the insufficiency in the first sense of the offender's means must rely on the court's perception of the relationship between those means and the ideal assessment of the victim's injury, good reasons for not making a compensation order because of the insufficiency in the second sense of the offender's means must rely on the court's perception of the relationship between those means and the likelihood of his being able to comply without simultaneously frustrating any individualised or general sentencing objectives. This is what the courts mean when they have said that compensation orders should not be oppressive or worse, conducive to recidivism:

'The crux of the matter is, of course, that while reparation remains an integral part of sentencing the criminal courts must have regard to the other objectives of sentencing, and the needs of prevention of crime and the treatment of the offender may often have to be the dominant consideration'.[8]

7 Published by the Home Office, February 1990.
8 Advisory Council on the Penal System (1970) para 28.

Accordingly, it is not appropriate in this case to justify withholding an order on the ground that the victim can pursue his civil remedy, since, if he were to do so (though this is admittedly unlikely), a civil judgment in damages (assessed without regard to the offender's means and payable by him in a lump sum) would surely produce exactly that set of circumstances eschewed by the criminal courts in the interests of achieving the sentencing goals apt in this offender's case.

C. FINANCIAL RECOVERY BY THE VICTIM OTHERWISE THAN UNDER A COMPENSATION ORDER

It is always possible that the victim may recover some or all of the financial loss resulting from his injury, or obtain compensation for the injury itself, otherwise than by virtue of a criminal court making a compensation order against the offender. The sources of such recovery include personal accident insurance, occupational sick pay, the CICB, damages payments by the offender and DSS benefits. What effect, if any, does the receipt of moneys from these various sources have upon the assessment of a compensation order, and what is the effect of a compensation order on a subsequent award of damages? In some instances there is a statutory answer to these questions; in others, answers are at best dependent upon analogies drawn from the law governing personal injury actions. It is convenient to distinguish initially between payments received from the offender otherwise than under a compensation order, and payments received from other sources.

(1) Other payments by the offender

Apart from making an order under s 35(1), a criminal court may accept and formalise the offender's offer to compensate his victim as a condition to be considered in the deferment of sentence under s 1(1) of the Powers of Criminal Courts Act 1973. This provides that a Crown Court or magistrates' court may defer passing sentence for up to six months:

'for the purpose of enabling the court to have regard, in determining his sentence, to his conduct after conviction (including, where appropriate, the making by him of reparation for his offence)'.

Though not defined in the interpretation section, 'reparation' is surely broad enough to include compensation by an offender to a victim injured by his offence. Where such reparation is made and is subsequently considered by the court to be appropriate in respect of the victim's injury, an order should not be an option open to the court. There is no direct authority on this point, but the statutory provisions which permit modification of a compensation order where damages have been recovered from the offender imply that it would be wrong to permit the victim double recovery from the offender for the same assessment of his injury. The matter is arguably different where, in the time that has elapsed between the act of deferring sentence and its subsequent determination, the effects of the injury have worsened; but as this would involve a criminal court in a consideration of the change and of the consequences of the assessment of pecuniary and/or non-pecuniary loss, it is very unlikely that a compensation order would be made in such circumstances, the victim being left to pursue his civil remedy.

Actions in tort for personal injury that also constitute crimes are rare events. Despite their low incidence, they raise two important questions about the relationship between civil and criminal proceedings. Firstly, to what extent, if at all, should the fact of criminal proceedings pre-empt any civil action by the victim? Secondly, if victims are permitted to retain their right to sue, what effect should a compensation order have upon the judgment of the civil court, and vice-versa?

(a) CRIMINAL AND CIVIL PROCEEDINGS

As to the first question, the Advisory Council took the view that, subject to one exception:

> 'neither the institution of criminal proceedings, nor the satisfaction of any penalty imposed or compensation ordered, should exclude any civil remedies which the victim may have'.[9]

Indeed, with the exception of s 45 of the Offences against the Person Act 1861, it would constitute a very substantial change in the rights of the individual to seek redress for grievances, that he should be formally precluded from bringing a civil action against an offender who has wounded or caused him grievous bodily harm, but who has been acquitted in criminal proceedings.

9 Ibid, para 38.

There are many reasons why an offender may properly be found not guilty which are in no way inconsistent, either on technical legal grounds or for broader reasons of justice, with a finding of liability by a civil court.

Before the enactment of s 39 of the Criminal Justice Act 1988, ss 42–45 of the Offences against the Person Act 1861 provided that where an offender was summarily prosecuted by, or on behalf of, the victim of an offence under s 42 (common assault) or 43 (assault or battery on a female, or on a boy under 14) and, after a hearing on the merits, the case was either dismissed or the assault was considered justified or so trifling as not to merit punishment, the magistrate was required by s 44 to issue a certificate which by s 45 constituted a complete bar on any further proceedings against him, whether civil or criminal, for the same cause. The justification for these provisions was that in these cases of minor quarrels responsibility for the victim's injuries is probably equally shared and so the 'victim' should not be permitted a second action against the 'offender'. Their practical effect was that the police would seldom bring prosecutions under s 42 or 43 'on behalf of the party aggrieved', leaving the victim to initiate proceedings should he so wish. The Advisory Council was uncertain whether to recommend repeal or retention of these provisions. It recognised the value both of a safeguard against the vindictive pursuit of an offender in criminal and civil proceedings by the victim of a trivial assault and of the desirability of permitting a victim to seek a remedy for what might, to him, be an injury having significant impact but which could not be proved against the offender in criminal proceedings beyond a reasonable doubt. However, as the Criminal Law Revision Committee was simultaneously considering reforms to the law governing offences against the person, the Advisory Council felt able to avoid having to resolve its uncertainty, leaving the issue for the Committee to decide.[10] Considering that it was 'fairer for victims of assault to be in the same position as other victims of offences against the person',[11] the CLRC recommended that these provisions be repealed as part of its broader reforms for the law of assault. In the event, ss 42-43 were repealed by the 1988 Act, but ss 44 and 45 continue to apply to the summary offences of assault and battery.

---

10 Ibid, paras 41-43.
11 Criminal Law Revision Committee *Offences Against the Person* (1980, Cmnd 7844) para 164.

(b) COMPENSATION ORDERS AND CIVIL DAMAGES

As to the second question, the Advisory Committee took the view that, in general, a victim should not be able to recover, in the two sets of proceedings, more than the amount of his loss.[12] It is indeed difficult to imagine any set of circumstances in which it would be right for an offender to be required to pay compensation to his victim in excess of the ideal assessment of the injury he has caused.[13] Assuming then, that the objective is to ensure that the victim receives compensation for no more than an ideal assessment of his injury, and that in almost all cases, criminal proceedings will precede civil action, there are two main factors that are relevant to the answer to the question, what effect should a compensation order have upon the judgment of a civil court, and vice-versa? These factors are, firstly, whether in the judgment of the civil court, the damages ordered to be paid exceed or are less than the sum specified in the compensation order; and secondly, whether the order has been fully complied with or not. The powers and duties of civil and criminal courts with respect to this question are contained in ss 37 and 38 of the Powers of Criminal Courts Act 1973, as amended by the Criminal Justice Act 1988. Section 37 provides:

'At any time before the person against whom a compensation order has been made has paid into court the whole of the compensation which the order requires him to pay, but at a time when (disregarding any power of a court to grant leave to appeal out of time) there is no further possibility of an appeal on which the order could be varied or set aside, the magistrates' court for the time being having functions in relation to the enforcement of the order may, on the application of the person against whom it was made, discharge the order, or reduce the amount which remains to be paid, if it appears to the court —

(a) that the injury, loss or damage in respect of which the order was made has been held in civil proceedings to be less than it was taken to be for the purposes of the order'.

Section 38 provides:

'(1) This section shall have effect where a compensation order has been made in favour of any person in respect of any injury, loss

---

12 (1970) para 38.
13 This does not take into account punitive damages, but they are not awarded to compensate the victim/plaintiff.

or damage and a claim by him in civil proceedings for damages in respect thereof subsequently falls to be determined.

(2) The damages in the civil proceedings shall be assessed without regard to the order; but the plaintiff may only recover an amount equal to the aggregate of the following —
　　(a) any amount by which they exceed the compensation; and
　　(b) a sum equal to any portion of the compensation which he fails to recover,
and may not enforce the judgment, so far as it relates to a sum such as is mentioned in paragraph (b) above, without the leave of the court.'

The general effect of these two sections is to require a civil court to assess the damages payable to the victim without regard to the amount specified in the compensation order already made against the offender, to give formal recognition to any amounts paid by the offender in compliance with the order, and to give the enforcing magistrates' court the power to reduce or discharge the order where the civil court makes a more modest assessment of the victim's loss than did the sentencer.[14] Since s 38 was amended by the Criminal Justice Act 1988, the Social Security Act 1989 has provided that compensation orders are, so far as a 'compensator' as defined by s 22(1) is concerned, 'exempt payments' within s 22(4), which thus do not fall to be deducted from any judgment or settlement before payment of it. Accordingly, a civil court must approach the assessment of damages as is required by s 38. The particular effect of that and s 37 is best explained by distinguishing the four situations that can arise from a combination of the two factors mentioned above.

(i)　Compensation order made and fully paid; damages for a greater sum

Perhaps the simplest case is one where a compensation order for an amount less than an ideal assessment of the victim's injury is made payable as a lump sum or in instalments over a short period of time and which, by the time of the civil judgment for the ideal assessment, has been fully paid by the offender.

14 In *Berry v Cooper* (1983) Times, 30 March a civil action for damages for mental anguish was brought against the two offenders who were convicted of the burglary of the plaintiff's house. They had been ordered to pay compensation by the criminal court, which the lower court had, contrary to the requirements of s 38, ignored when determining the damages payable. The appeal against the civil judgment was allowed.

Section 38(2) requires the civil court to assess the damages payable without regard to the order, but goes on to provide that the plaintiff may only recover in those proceedings 'the amount by which they exceed the compensation order'. If the damages are assessed at £1,000, but the offender has already fully paid the compensation order made against him in the sum of £400, the plaintiff may only recover £600 in the civil proceedings. In this way the offender's 'contribution' to the civil judgment is recognised, and the victim is prevented from recovering twice for (some of) the same injury.

(ii) Compensation order made but not fully paid; damages for a greater sum

Here again, the civil court must assess the damages payable without regard to the compensation order, but there is a restriction on the plaintiff's power to enforce the payment of any amount which he fails to recover via the order. Under the repealed s 38, there were different and somewhat complex provisions whose effect depended on whether the offender had made any payment in compliance with the order before the civil action was heard, or none at all. Now s 38(2) simply provides that the plaintiff may only recover an amount equal to the aggregate of the excess of the damages over the order and of a sum equal to any portion of the compensation order which he fails to recover. If the damages are assessed at £1,000, and the offender has already paid £300 of a compensation order made against him in the sum of £400, the plaintiff may only recover £700 from the civil proceedings. However, he may not enforce the £100 without the leave of the court. The purpose of s 38 in this case is therefore both to recognise any contribution the offender has made or may make under a compensation order to the satisfaction of the damages awarded in the subsequent civil judgment, and to ensure that the enforcement of any remaining liability acknowledges the offender/defendant's liability under the two processes.

(iii) Compensation made but not fully paid; damages for a lesser sum

Suppose the sentencer makes an order for £300 to be paid in weekly instalments of £10; but in the subsequent civil proceedings ten weeks later the civil court, addressing evidence as to the contributory negligence of the victim, assesses the damages at £200. As in the other two cases just discussed, the court will have made that assessment without regard to the order, but as the compensation order exceeds the civil judgment, the plaintiff is precluded by s 38 from enforcing the judgment. This will leave the offender/defendant liable to pay the remaining £200 in compliance with the order, being £100 more than the damages award. It is then for him to apply to the magistrates' court enforcing the order to exercise its discretion under s 37. The court has power to discharge the order, which would be appropriate where the compensation so far paid under the order equals the sum awarded by way of damages, or to reduce the amount to be paid, which would be appropriate in the example given above, where £100 of the £300 order has been paid, reducing the remaining payment to £100.

(iv) Compensation order made and fully paid; damages for a lesser sum

Unlike the three preceding cases, there is no provision in the Act permitting the recognition of the offender's *excessive* payment to the victim. Section 38(2) ensures that the victim cannot recover twice for the same injury, but it does not do anything to prevent the victim from retaining the £300 fully paid under a compensation order, in respect of an injury the civil court values at £200. Nor has the enforcing magistrates' court any jurisdiction under s 37. It specifically confers the discretion to vary the order only 'at any time before the person against whom a compensation order has been made has paid into court the whole of the compensation which the order requires him to pay'. The Advisory Council considered that in these circumstances, if the offender has already paid the compensation order 'it would seem impracticable to disturb the situation',[15] but it might also be surmised that the inclusion of provisions permitting the offender to sue the victim to recover the discrepancy between the order and the civil judgment would be unpopular.[16] No doubt the possibility of such discrepancies (or indeed of civil action more generally being pursued following the making of a compensation order upon conviction) will be rare; but these provisions in ss 37 and 38 have important implications at least for the theory of compensation as a sentencing alternative. In short: if the only sentence a criminal court were to impose were a compensation order for an amount which was subsequently shown to be

---

15 (1970) para 40.
16 Atiyah (1979) and Thomas (1989).

equivalent to the assessment of the victim's injuries by a civil court, whose award of damages would in turn, by virtue of s 38 be unenforceable by him, then, apart from the technical recording of the conviction, there would in substance be nothing to distinguish the public from the private aspect of the injury caused. The criminal court is, in such a case, an efficient surrogate for a civil action; but if this is so, how can a compensation order be regarded as a sentencing alternative? One might, since their impact is the same, as well regard an order for damages as a sentence.

(2) Payment from other sources

There are various sources other than the offender from which the victim may receive compensation or reimbursement for losses that result from his injuries. In some cases the position concerning the relationship between a compensation order and these various sources is clear; in others, less so. The CICB is one obvious source of compensation. The Scheme requires the Board to reduce any award it might make by the full value of any entitlement to compensation payable by order of a criminal court (or in a civil action), and imposes on the victim an obligation to repay the Board should he subsequently become so entitled. The object of this paragraph is not to prevent double recovery from the same source, but to relieve the taxpayer where the victim can obtain compensation from the offender and indirectly therefore to prevent double recovery; the mechanics of collection were explained in chapter 7.[17]

It is unusual for individuals to hold private insurance policies covering them in the event of personal accident.[18] Where they do, the analogies with a personal injury action for damages suggests that a criminal court ought not to take account of any moneys received under a policy wholly private in nature. Accordingly, it would be improper for a sentencer to refuse to make a compensation order because the victim has received, or may receive, compensation from this source. Insurance companies, on the other hand, will undoubtedly take account of any moneys payable to the victim by court order. It is their universal practice to require the insured to pay over all sums received as a consequence of legal proceedings, a practice more

17 Supra, pp 189–190.
18 D Harris et al *Compensation and Support for Illness and Injury* (1984, Oxford UP) ch 8.

commonly encountered in connection with property loss and damage than with personal injury.

There is no direct authority on the question whether, and by how much, DSS benefits are deductible from a compensation order. The Scheme requires full deduction of all such benefits without limitation of time, but this is intended to prevent double recovery from the same source, the taxpayer. The closer analogy that exists between a compensation order and an award of damages suggests that the statutory rules applicable to personal injury actions are appropriate where the victim's injuries have caused him loss of earnings and he has received state benefits in respect of that loss. Prior to the coming into force of s 22 of the Social Security Act 1989, this would have required the application of the complex body of law which that provision seeks to obviate,[19] but it is unclear what impact s 22 has upon the making of a compensation order. The 'Compensation Schedule' asks for details of loss of earnings, and of 'any income that you may have received as a result of the offence, for example DSS benefits.' As s 35(1) speaks of compensation for 'any personal injury, loss or damage', it may be thought appropriate that the victim should be compensated only for his net loss, but s 22 and Sch 4 to the 1989 Act contain detailed administrative arrangements for the notification and deduction of specified sums, none of which applies to a criminal court making a compensation order.

The position with regard to general damages is perhaps clearer. Given the purpose of the cash benefits payable by the DSS, there can be little objection to the offender being required to pay compensation on the basis of the 1988 guidelines, notwithstanding that the victim has suffered no financial loss from his injury because it has all been met by state benefits. The same is arguably the case where the victim receives sick pay under a scheme associated with his employment. Wages or sick pay paid by an employer as a matter of contractual obligation reduce the victim's loss and are deductible under the principles developed in *Parry v Cleaver*.[20] Accordingly, it would seem right that where a sentencer is contemplating making a compensation order in favour of a victim whose injuries resulted in time off work, it is proper to make an award for the 'personal injury' but not for the 'loss' that results from it if that loss is in fact covered by occupational sick pay arrangements.

19 Supra, pp 182–183.
20 [1970] AC 1, [1969] 1 All ER 555, HL.

Chapter Ten

Compensation Orders: Procedure

A. APPLICATIONS FOR COMPENSATION

In its review of the pre-1972 statutory arrangements providing
compensation for the victim, the Advisory Council on the Penal
System identified as undesirable their inclusion of a requirement
that the victim should have to make an application. While
recognising that it would in many cases be difficult to arrive
at a satisfactory assessment of the victim's loss if he were not
present or represented at the trial, the Advisory Council
nevertheless felt that this requirement was unrealistic.[1] The basis
of this judgment was that criminal courts ought not to be expected
to conduct enquiries into conflicting submissions as to liability
and quantum:

> 'We recognise that the victim may have a grievance if there is no
> means of making his wishes known to the court, but we do not
> think it realistic to require that the ordering of compensation should
> be dependent on the presence of the victim or his representative in
> court, or upon his written application. It is true that an appeal lies
> against a compensation order and that the appeal court would have
> to consider argument by the appellant that the compensation order
> was excessive or unjustified, but the criminal courts cannot be
> expected to hold the scales between the victim and the defendant
> in a matter of this kind. Arguments during a criminal trial about
> the desirability of awarding compensation, and the amount, would
> distract the courts from their primary function and seriously hamper
> their work. In criminal proceedings the parties are the prosecutor
> and the accused person, and save in cases where liability and quantum
> are clear the courts would be well advised not to order compensation.
> It may be that some victims tend to inflate their assessment of loss
> or damage when reporting to the police but in practice the courts

1 Advisory Council on the Penal System *Reparation by the Offender* (1970, Home
  Office) para 76.

will have to accept this assessment, unless there is any good ground for disputing it. As indicated in para 73(a), we do not see this as a fatal objection; in many cases, compensation ordered by the criminal courts will have to be accepted as no more than a partial offset of the victim's loss, and inquisitorial examination of the exact extent of that loss would be pointless and impracticable.'[2]

This may have been a valid objection to an inquisitorial examination of the offender's and victim's accounts of the criminal injury and its consequences, but it did not meet the problem that the Advisory Council earlier identified which arose following the introduction in 1972 of the new powers to order compensation, namely, whose was the responsibility for adducing evidence of the victim's injury? The irony of the Advisory Council's recommendation, which was implemented in the Criminal Justice Act 1972, was that by removing one apparent obstacle to victims obtaining compensation, it created the conditions for the emergence of another. The following paragraphs consider the nature and impact of these conditions, which the Home Office believes will no longer prevail following the coming into force of the statutory obligation on a court to give reasons why it has not made an order in a case in which it has power to do so, and the publication of its 'Compensation Schedule' which all police forces are meant to use to pass information concerning the victim's injury, loss or damage on to the Crown Prosecution Service.[3]

Compensation is payable under s 35(1) 'on application or otherwise'. Since the victim has no right of audience, the question of compensation can only be raised by the prosecution or the defence as the parties to the proceedings, or of the court's own motion. Research shows that one of the most significant variables has been whether a specific request for compensation was made. Newburn found that 'the chance of an eligible victim being awarded compensation from a magistrates' court is four times greater if a request for compensation is made,'[4] a dependence of which the Home Affairs Committee was critical.[5]

---

2 Ibid, para 78.
3 See the Minister's remarks made in connection with the equivalent clause in the Criminal Justice Bill 1986, 106 HC Official Report (6th series) col 470 (27 November 1986).
4 T Newburn *The Use and Enforcement of Compensation Orders in Magistrates' Courts* (1988, Home Office Research Study 102) p 25.
5 House of Commons *Compensation and Support for Victims of Crime* (1984–85, HC 43) para 46.

The relationship between requests and orders is not, however, a simple one. In the assault cases in Newburn's sample, 62.5% of requests resulted in compensation being ordered, whereas the success rate for criminal damage (93%) and theft (84%) was considerably higher. The discrepancy is probably attributable to such other factors as the greater uncertainty that accompanies the fixing of quantum in personal injury cases by comparison with offences against property. Neither did failure to request show a simple relationship. In 44% of the assault cases in which no request was made compensation was nevertheless awarded; the percentages for theft (3%) and criminal damage (21%) were substantially lower.[6] Newburn was unable to identify any single factor that would explain these different responses.

Apart from a specific request for compensation, a further significant variable has been whether compensation was mentioned at some point during the sentencing stage. Shapland's research demonstrates the importance of the prosecution's contribution in this respect:

'... one of the most important predictors of the making of a compensation order was whether the prosecution mentioned the word "compensation" during the court appearance. Such a reference might have been made in any context. Some mentions were a specific application for compensation, but others involved merely reminding the sentencer of his powers or even citing the making of a compensation order in the sentence for a previous conviction.'[7]

Where compensation was neither requested nor mentioned, Newburn's research confirms that the likelihood of an order being made has depended, inter alia, on how the court perceives the requirements of s 35(1) and its role vis-à-vis the victim.[8] Some magistrates have taken the view that a formal request is necessary before an order could be made (this is clearly wrong in law), while others have felt that it was for the other actors in the system, notably the police, to trigger the issue of compensation. For this second group, the fact that victims were not routinely requesting

---

6 (1988) p 25.
7 J Shapland et al *Victims in the Criminal Justice System* (1985, Gower) p 137. The police list compensation orders on criminal records as they do fines, W West 'Compensation orders' (1983) 147 Justice of the Peace 344.
8 (1988) pp 31-2.

compensation indicated that any fault lay with the police who were not informing them of the possibility.[9]

Such observations underline the problems of disseminating information about opportunities for compensation, and of validating the information that the victim wishes to be presented to the court. During the 1970s and early 1980s the police developed administrative routines for checking whether the victim wished to receive compensation and, if so, for verifying his claim, but Shapland's research also showed that they were on occasion reluctant to take the initiative, and that their procedures were not always thorough.[10] Shapland and Cohen found that while 91% of their police sample said that they used a form on which to record the victim's losses for court use, these forms were, on later inquiry found to be out of date, or simply not available to the victim at the time of reporting the offence.[11] There has also been some doubt about the efficacy of these forms to elicit information about injuries received, where the questions they ask appear to focus principally on property loss and property damage. Newburn reviewed some forms in use by the police in his sample and concluded that, by virtue of their phraseology (referring only to compensation for loss or damage), they were likely to exclude from the thoughts of those police officers attending the scene of the crime any question of compensation for personal injury. This conclusion was confirmed by a police respondent.[12] Similar problems were found in connection with the forms issued by procurators fiscal for use in sheriff courts.[13]

A reason commonly offered by the police in response to criticism that they were not informing victims of the possibilities of compensation, or of helping them to obtain it, has been the pressure of other responsibilities.[14] This also figured in the responses of prosecuting solicitors interviewed by Shapland, who explained their reluctance to assist the victim on the ground that the question of victim compensation was not 'their job', but that of the magistrates (or more specifically the clerk).[15] The

9 Ibid p 32. See also T Newburn *Compensation for Injury in the Magistrates' Courts* (1987, Home Office Research Bulletin No 23).

10 (1985) pp 140-143.

11 J Shapland and D Cohen 'Facilities for victims: the role of the police and the courts' [1987] Crim LR 28-38.

12 Newburn (1988) p 32.

13 G Maher and C Docherty *Compensation in the Scottish Criminal Courts* (1988, Scottish Office) pp 49-57.

14 Newburn (1988) p 33.

15 Shapland et al (1985) pp 142-143.

matter has been unsatisfactory too because practice varied between different prosecuting authorities. Some, as already indicated, indicated that they regarded the issue as being one for the bench; others referred to the existence of standing instructions which they had introduced to the effect that they were to draw magistrates' attention to their powers under s 35.[16]

These problems arose in large measure because the change in 1973 which sought to relieve the victim of the obligation to attend the trial in order to make a claim for compensation (which in effect meant that the prosecution would, in the limited cases in which this was a possibility, ensure the victim's presence), did not transfer this obligation to anyone else. Although concern had been expressed for some time about this state of affairs, there was no agreement on who was to assume responsibility for raising the question of compensation. Not unnaturally, each one of those groups which was nominated for the task resisted on the ground that it was someone else's. In his evidence to the Home Affairs Committee in 1984, the Home Secretary indicated that he was thinking of placing courts under a statutory obligation to give reasons why compensation had not been ordered in any case where it was possible.[17] Though there were objections from magistrates and justices' clerks, the proposal took effect as an amendment to s 35 introduced by s 104 of the Criminal Justice Act 1988: 'to give reasons, on passing sentence, if [the court] does not make an order in a case where it is empowered to do so.' We consider later in this chapter what may count as an acceptable reason.

In a further response to the Home Affairs Committee's report,[18] the Home Office reconsidered how information about compensation could be delivered to victims, and how information about their injury, loss or damage could be delivered to the court. Its recommendations are contained in a circular distributed to Chief Officers of Police, the DPP, and to the justices' and to Crown Court clerks in April 1988.[19] The circular recommends that police forces should routinely give victims who have suffered personal injury, loss or damage, copies of a leaflet accompanying the circular which outlines the possibility of compensation being ordered by the court or being awarded following a claim to the

16 403 HL Official Report (5th series) cols 2-4 (20 November 1979), and (1980) 144 JP 409, 416.
17 House of Commons (1984-85) para 46.
18 Home Office *Compensation and Support for Victims of Crime* (1985, Cmnd 9457) para 12.
19 Home Office Circular No 20/1988 *Victims of Crime*.

CICB. The circular secondly recommends that police forces record details of loss of earnings, bills for repair or replacement of property, medical expenses and the like, which can be passed on to the Crown Prosecution Service in the event that criminal proceedings are pursued. Whether the specimen form, which the circular indicates is to be treated as a minimum standard for police forces, achieves the desired result has yet to be determined, though one implication of Vennard's research on the impact of compensation guidelines in magistrates' courts suggests that it will lead to an increase in making of orders, if for no other reason than that it is the 'official' form.[20]

B.　THE FORM OF THE ORDER

One of the principles enumerated by Pain J in *R v Miller*[1] was that a compensation order must be precise in its terms. Precision is required as to five matters:

(1)　the offence in respect of which the offender has been convicted or which he has asked to be taken into consideration;

(2)　the date by which payment is to be made or, if by instalments, to commence;

(3)　the amount to be paid, or if by instalments, the amount of each instalment;

(4)　where there is more than one victim, the amount payable to each victim; and

(5)　where there is more than one offender, the amount payable by each offender.

These requirements were discussed by Scarman LJ in *R v Inwood*:

'A compensation order must be related to a particular sum of money owing to a particular person, firm or other body. It is, so far as it goes, a substitute for a sum of money ordered by a court to be paid by a defendant to a plaintiff. In fact it is only fair to say that the sentencing judge in this case acted correctly in obtaining a statement of account and in relating the compensation order to the specific amounts particularised in that statement of account. It may be that in cases of this sort, where there is a large number of offences, there ought to be not one compensation order, but a separate compensation order for each sum of money in respect of each offence.

Strictly, there should be in this case a great number of compensation orders, each related to a specific offence. In our judgment judges who are considering making compensation orders must be very clear that what they are doing is within the policy of the law as now stated in the Act of 1973; and very clear as to the relationship between the compensation order, the offence and the victim to whom it relates. A single compensation order when there are different offences and different victims contravenes good practice, and is, perhaps, even a nullity.'[2]

A compensation order can only be made for a precise amount representing the victim's special and general damages arising from an injury caused by an offence for which the offender is convicted or which he asks to be taken into consideration. An order is not apt as a means of penalising the offender in the absence of any injury, etc to the victim,[3] or in an amount exceeding the ideal assessment of the victim's injury.[4] Conversely, an order is quite appropriate if the victim is injured, notwithstanding that the offender made no profit from the offence.[5] Where it is proposed that the compensation be paid in instalments, the amount of each instalment must be specified when the order is made; the court cannot, perhaps in the expectation that the offender will default, leave the amounts to be paid to the enforcing magistrates' court to determine following a means inquiry.[6]

An omnibus order is proper if there is only one victim and one offender; otherwise it is, as Lawton LJ said in *R v Oddy*,[7] 'a grave defect' to make an order for a global sum not related to any specific offence or any specific loser. Apart from legal grounds (those referred to by Scarman LJ in *Inwood*,[8]) Lawton LJ thought such an order defective 'because if any loser does seek to proceed by way of civil action how is he to know what he is going to get out of the compensation order?'[9] The proper procedure is that indicated in the commentary to *R v Reardon*.[10] The sentencer should fix a specific amount in relation to the offence and the victim concerned, having regard to the injury sustained. He should then consider the offender's means and

2 (1974) 60 Cr App Rep 70 at 74, CA.
3 *R v Vaughan* [1990] Crim LR 443, CA.
4 *R v Maynard* [1983] Crim LR 821, CA.
5 *R v Ford* [1977] Crim LR 114, CA.
6 *R v Bagga* [1990] Crim LR 128, CA.
7 [1974] 2 All ER 666 at 671, CA; *R v Warton* [1976] Crim LR 520, CA.
8 Op cit.
9 [1974] 2 All ER 666 at 671.
10 [1981] Crim LR 187, CA.

decide whether it is realistic to expect him to pay the whole amount or part of it, and if it is, by what method and over how long a period.

Where there are two or more victims it is usual to apportion the total that the offender can afford on a pro rata basis. So if five victims injured by one offender have claims totalling £500, comprising one at £200, two at £100 and two at £50, they will receive, if the offender's means are sufficient to pay only £200 in all, £80, £40 and £20 each respectively. On rare occasions however, the court may select from among the victims otherwise than on a pro rata basis, so that some victims will receive a reduced amount and others none at all. One of these occasions is where the victim is favourably placed to sue the offender. This was so in *R v Amey*,[11] where one of eight claimants against the offender whose claim comprised 3/5 of the total sought, was a bank. Quashing the order in favour of the bank, Kilner Brown J said:

> 'If ever there was an instance of the rare occasion when the claimants should have been selected and no order on a pro rata basis have been made, this was it. It would be a great hardship on the eight individuals to receive ony two-fifths of their proved claim and to be forced to resort to civil process for the balance. On the other hand the bank would be far better placed to seek and obtain judgment in the county court for the amount they were entitled to. It would not be a futile exercise and the judgment debt could probably be met in full over a period of years. By excluding the bank from the order for compensation, it does not mean they are excluded from a proper claim; they are being denied the quick opportunity of getting their money, and that is all.'[12]

Commenting on this decision, West foresaw some difficulties in practice for magistrates.[13] While it may seem right that institutions such as banks should be left (since they can well afford it) to pursue the offender in civil law, the question arises whether the principle of pro rata apportionment should be departed from in other cases where one of a number of victims claiming against the offender may likewise be judged able to afford such action. If so, magistrates will have the difficult task of assessing degrees of hardship on victims not compensated by

11 [1983] 1 All ER 865, [1983] 1 WLR 345, CA.
12 Ibid, 349.
13 (1983) 16% of Newburn's sample involved more than one victim, Newburn (1988) p 29.

their order. Another awkward question of degree is how much greater does one claim have to be over the others to justify departure from a pro rata basis? In *Amey*, the bank's claim was substantial in comparison with the others; but in other cases the discrepancy may obviously be far less, or there may be other configurations (one victim claiming half the total, the other half more or less equally distributed between the other victims; one victim claiming half the total, the other half unequally distributed; and so on), upon which there is no appellate guidance.

Where there are two or more offenders equally responsible for causing the victim's injury, each of whom has sufficient means, it is usual to require equal contributions. Unequal contributions may be required to reflect unequal responsibility as was the case in *R v James*,[14] where the order was made in the proportion of two to one. In these cases orders should be made severally, and not, although this is permitted by s 35, jointly and severally. In *R v Grundy*[15] the Court of Appeal agreed that payment of compensation could be made on a joint and several basis, but the Lord Chief Justice was emphatic that, at least so soon after the enactment of these provisions, such an order should not be considered. The reasons were largely of an administrative nature:

'However the matter does not rest there because in a discretionary remedy of this kind one must have some regard to the practicability of making it work. This court is concerned, to say the least of it, at the practical and administrative complications which might arise if an undue number of these joint and several orders came into circulation. The complication which we see is this. There may well be two justices' clerks looking after the two accounts, as it were, and receiving the inevitable instalments which a small order of this kind involves. If the order is to be on a joint and several basis, the two justices' clerks would have to be in constant liaison in order to make sure that their combined efforts did not produce from the two offenders a sum greater than that which they are jointly and severally responsible to pay. It is quite obvious that the danger would arise of each paying his instalments to a different office and in the result the two offices together collecting more than the total sum which is involved. At a time when the workings of the 1972 Act are still not fully explored we think it would be wrong to encourage

14 [1983] 1 All ER 865, [1983] 1 WLR 345, CA. Though heard with *Amey*, *R v James* 'did not call for report', at p 346.
15 [1974] 1 All ER 292, [1974] 1 WLR 139, CA.

courts to make joint and several orders with the potential practical disadvantages to which I have briefly referred.'[16]

As there appear to have been no efforts to deal with the administrative routines that would be required by such an order, this advice still holds good.[17]

It is also permissible to order the one of a number of offenders who has means, the others having none, to make compensation, though they were all equally responsible for the injury. In *R v Beddow*[18] it was held that though it would be normal practice to divide liability for the order equally among the offenders, it was not objectionable on the ground of disparity of sentence that the one with means should bear the whole burden. Whether it would be objectionable if the offender with means were *only* to be ordered to pay compensation, the others receiving other non-custodial sentences, is an open question.

C. ENFORCEMENT

Once made, there remains the matter of enforcing the order. Although Roskill LJ once described the relevant provisions as a 'statutory jungle',[19] compensation orders are enforced in substantially the same manner as fines.

A compensation order made by the Crown Court is enforceable as a sum adjudged to be paid on conviction by a magistrates' court.[20] By ss 31 and 34 of the Powers of Criminal Courts Act 1973, the Crown Court may allow time for payment or order payment by instalments. Unlike a fine, the Crown Court cannot, when making a compensation order, fix a term of imprisonment in the event of default, unless it considers that the maximum period of imprisonment that can be ordered by a magistrates' court in respect of the amount ordered, is itself insufficient. Section 41(8) of the Administration of Justice Act 1970 which

---

16 Ibid, 294.
17 *R v Grundy* continues to be cited in the textbooks as authority for this proposition. 14.5% of Newburn's sample involved more than one defendant, Newburn (1988) p 18.
18 (1987) 9 Cr App Rep (S) 235, CA, and *Bagga*, op cit.
19 *R v Bunce* (1977) 66 Cr App Rep 109 at 113. S Wilton 'Blood from a stone' (1988) 138 New LJ 107-109, 128-130, and 165-167.
20 Administration of Justice Act 1970, s 41(1) and Part 1 of Sch 1 as amended by para 40 of Sch 5 to the Powers of Criminal Courts Act 1973 and by s 106 of the Criminal Justice Act 1988.

gives the Crown Court this power, then provides that para 4 of Sch 4 to the Magistrates' Courts Act 1980 (which specifies the limits on imprisonment for default in accordance with the amount of the fine) shall apply with any modification for part payment of the order, and that the period so specified by the Crown Court is to be treated as the maximum for which the defaulter may be imprisoned under s 76 of the 1980 Act. To these powers s 106 of the Criminal Justice Act 1988 added an amendment (s 41(8A)) to the effect that the Crown Court shall not impose a period of imprisonment longer than it could have done had it imposed a fine in the same amount as the compensation order. This has no effect so long as the period of imprisonment for default of payment of a fine which the Crown Court can impose is no greater than the period for default of a compensation order which magistrates can impose. However, s 60 of the Criminal Justice Act 1988 alters the two existing tables setting out the periods of imprisonment for default, decreasing the periods of imprisonment in respect of sums not exceeding £10,000, and increasing the periods in respect of sums in excess of that figure. Under this section, the Crown Court may order a term of imprisonment on the higher scale which is beyond the scale applicable in a magistrates' court. However, as compensation orders for sums in excess of £10,000 are likely to be very rare,[1] it is equally likely that these provisions will seldom be invoked, the normal term for default not exceeding the maximum prescribed by the lower table, six months.[2]

Like the Crown Court, a magistrates' court may, by s 75 of the Magistrates' Courts Act 1980, permit the offender time to pay or to pay by instalments. The maximum periods for which a magistrates' court can imprison a defaulter (or which the Crown Court can specify under s 41(8) of the Administration of Justice Act 1980 in the event of default on an order made by it) are the same as those applicable to fines; they increase with the amount ordered to be paid. However, in the case of amounts not exceeding £10,000, s 60 of the Criminal Justice Act 1988 has substantially reduced the periods of imprisonment for default, from five days for sums not exceeding £50 to six months for

---

1 In 1988 3,026 offenders were ordered to pay compensation by the Crown Court upon conviction of an offence against the person; in 29 cases only the order exceeded £1,000. *Criminal Statistics England and Wales Supplementary Tables 1988 vol 4* table S4.11(A).
2 D Thomas 'The Criminal Justice Act 1988: the sentencing provisions' [1989] Crim LR 43-55, 49.

sums between £5,000 and £9,999, terms that can be halved with remission. Thomas has asked why, if the Home Office is keen to encourage courts to order compensation, the sanction for default should be reduced. He argues that for some, a prison term (with remission) may well make better financial sense than compliance with the order.[3]

Payment is made to the magistrates' court for the time being having functions by virtue of s 41(1) of the Administration of Justice Act 1970, and if both a compensation order and a fine were ordered, the payments are allocated first to the compensation order until it is satisfied. One of the problems with their enforcement which Newburn's research uncovered was that a number of victims were neither informed prior to the receipt of (the first, if by instalment) payment, nor were told whether the amount represented an ideal assessment of their injuries or had been reduced on account of the offender's means. Similarly, a major source of dissatisfaction was the lack of any communication from the court in response to their inquiries when instalments lapsed.[4]

Enforcement is also a problem for the court. For the justices' clerks the handling of even the compliant offender's instalments represents a continuing burden of checking and cross-checking what are typically small sums (£5 a week or less) against the amount owed and the amount paid, a task which becomes increasingly burdensome when payments are irregular in time or amount. At that point the clerks find themselves both chasing the offender and being themselves chased by the victim.[5] In the event of default, the court has a number of options open to it. Newburn's enforcement study came to a very similar conclusion to that reached by Softley in 1978.[6] Then, 75% of orders had been paid in full within 18 months, while in the later survey, this had risen to 80%. One third of Newburn's sample resulted in enforcement action, following a 'fairly regular pattern of arrears letter, summons, means enquiry (at least once), before either a distress or, more usually, a commitment warrant was

---

3 Ibid, p 44.
4 (1988) pp 37-38. See also the position in Scotland, Maher and Docherty (1988) pp 63-71.
5 Newburn (1988) pp 46-47.
6 P Softley *Compensation Orders in Magistrates' Courts* (1978, Home Office Research Study 43).

issued, and if necessary executed.'[7] Thus the large provincial court began using enforcement measures when the payments were two weeks in arrears, issuing reminders to the offender. If payment was not resumed within four weeks of the arrears letter, he would be summonsed to attend court, usually for a means inquiry. This in turn might be adjourned to allow payment under revised conditions (often involving variation of the quantity and duration of instalments); sometimes Money Payment Supervision orders were used, sometimes attachment of earnings. In the event that these measures did not prompt a resumption of payments, the supervisor would initiate the process from the beginning, or issue a committal warning; finally a commitment warrant was used in recalcitrant cases.

A warrant of commitment may be issued where it appears on the return of a warrant of distress that the property of the defaulter is insufficient to satisfy the sum due and the charges of levying the sum. Distress warrants were the preferred method for the London court in Newburn's sample. Though attractive because they are self-financing, distress warrants are regarded by some magistrates as harsh, and are as unpopular with the bailiffs and the police who have to enforce them as they are with those subject to them. Resort to imprisonment for default is infrequent, only 45 of the 550 cases in Newburn's sample ending in custody.[8]

D. COMMITTAL AND APPEALS

(1) Committal to the Crown Court for sentence

By s 38 of the Magistrates' Courts Act 1980, a magistrates' court may commit an offender to the Crown Court for sentence where it considers that 'greater punishment should be inflicted for the offence' than it has power to impose. It is not clear whether a magistrates' court can commit an offender against whom it would like to make a compensation order, where the ideal

---

7 Wilton (1988) describes the activities of the fine default court. Enforcement becomes more difficult as the amount due increases, 395 HL Official Report (5th series) col 299 (10 July 1978) and where the court has to deal with many orders paid in small instalments. A compensation order may also be enforced by garnishee order, *Gooch v Ewing* [1986] QB 791, [1985] 3 All ER 654.

8 Newburn (1988) p 43. There were also some offenders already in custody as a result of other charges or for defaulting on other payments; consequently compensation was not paid in these cases. See also Wilton (1988) p 129.

assessment of the victim's injury (assuming the offender has sufficient means) exceeds the £2,000 maximum currently applicable under s 40 of the 1980 Act. Prior to the commencement of s 67 of the Criminal Justice Act 1982, compensation was an ancillary order, so this question could not have arisen as a single ground on which committal could be ordered (nor do any of the reported cases indicate that this question was raised in connection with any committal); now that it may be the only sentence, the question assumes importance.

It is, on the other hand, clear that where a magistrates' court does commit an offender to the Crown Court for sentence, it should not at the same time impose a compensation order. This was established in *R v Brogan* where Scarman LJ said:

'I now pass to the disturbing feature of the case and one which is of some importance in the administration of the law. This woman, as I have already mentioned, was committed for sentence under s 29 of the Magistrates' Courts Act 1952; at the same time the magistrate imposed a compensation order. Whatever their legal powers are — as to that I shall have a few words to say later — it is undesirable that magistrates who are committing for sentence under s 29 should themselves impose a compensation order. A compensation order can be made only in the circumstances which are set out in ss 35-38 of the Powers of Criminal Courts Act 1973, and one of the matters that has to be considered by the court in making a compensation order is the means of the offender so far as known to the court. It is not desirable for a compensation order to be made except at the time of sentence, ie final disposal of the offender. There is an important relationship between the sentence of the court and the desirability or otherwise of making a compensation order. It is also very important that, if a sentence is to be reviewed, the reviewing court should be able to look also at the compensation order.

Look now what has happened in this case. We are unable to review the compensation order because it was made by the magistrate. The Crown Court when imposing sentence was itself unable to deal with the compensation order. The result is that, that which should be regarded as a whole, the sentence and the ancillary orders linked with it, has been split into separate parts: and not all those parts can be reviewed as a whole by the Court of Appeal.

A compensation order is not part of the sentence of the court strictly speaking; it is an order analogous to an order for restitution of property and, when made by the Crown Court, the Court of Appeal can annul or vary the orders pursuant to s 30 of the Criminal Appeal Act 1968, and s 36(1) of the Powers of Criminal Courts Act 1973. The fact that care has been taken by the legislature to ensure that the Court of Appeal, when dealing with sentence, can also review a compensation order indicates that Parliament was concerned to avoid the mischief of a compensation order being incapable of review when sentence is under appeal in this court.

Though we have heard no argument, we think it clear that magistrates who commit an offender under s 29 of the Magistrates' Courts Act 1952 have no power to impose any order subsequent to conviction. The section provides that, where on summary trial a person is convicted of an offence, if on obtaining certain information the court is of the opinion that there is a case for greater punishment than the court itself has power to inflict, 'the court may, instead of dealing with him in any other manner, commit him in custody to [the Crown Court] for sentence . . .'9

Leaving aside the reference to compensation orders being ancillary to the sentence, the principle must equally apply now that they are independent.

(2) Appeals

(a) BY THE OFFENDER

The offender against whom a compensation order has been made by magistrates or by the Crown Court may appeal against either that decision, some other aspect of the sentence of the court, or the conviction itself if he pleaded not guilty. Prior to the amendments made by s 105 of the Criminal Justice Act 1988 to s 36 of the Powers of Criminal Courts Act 1973, an appeal by the offender had the effect of suspending his obligation to make payment to the enforcing magistrates' court. This was thought to be open to abuse.[10] The amendments permit the continued enforcement of the payments, while suspending the victim's right to them. Section 36(1) provides that this suspension shall continue until, disregarding any power of a court to grant leave to appeal out of time, 'there is no further possibility of an appeal on which the order could be varied or set aside.'

These provisions assume that the offender has been 'convicted' within the limited definition given in the Powers of Criminal Courts Act 1973. By s 13(1), a conviction which results in the offender being placed on probation, or absolutely or conditionally discharged, is deemed not to be a conviction for any purpose other than the proceedings in which the order was made. In

---

9 [1975] 1 All ER 879 at 880-881, CA.
10 See the comments on the equivalent clause in the Criminal Justice Bill 1986, 113 HC Official Report (6th series) cols 919-920 (31 March 1987).

R v Robinson[11] the offender was convicted of common assault and conditionally discharged with a compensation order being imposed. The offender sought to appeal against the compensation order, which raised the preliminary question (since the compensation order itself was only ancillary to the conditional discharge), whether the Court of Appeal had jurisdiction to hear the appeal. The court was referred to *R v Tucker*,[12] where it was held that there could be no appeal against a probation order, the offender not being 'convicted' for any purpose other than that order. Accepting the correctness of that decision, and in the absence of full argument on the question, Neill J heard the appeal, while also commenting on the lack of clarity in the court's jurisdiction.

By s 36(3) of the 1973 Act (as amended), the Court of Appeal may annul or vary any compensation order made by the court of trial, although the conviction is not quashed, and can therefore increase the amount ordered by a Crown Court judge to be paid to the victim. On appeal from a magistrates' court the Crown Court can likewise impose a more severe sentence, provided that it is one within the magistrates' powers. The House of Lords may, in restoring a conviction, 'make any compensation order which the court of trial could have made.'[13]

In the case of a compensation order being made against the offender in respect of an offence taken into consideration, s 36(5) of the Powers of Criminal Courts Act 1973, re-enacting s 35(3), provides:

> '(a) the order shall cease to have effect if he successfully appeals against his conviction of the offence or, if more than one, all the offences, of which he was convicted in the proceedings in which the order was made;
> (b) he may appeal against the order as if it were part of the sentence imposed in respect of the offence or, if more than one, any of the offences, of which he was so convicted.'

(b)   BY A PERSON AGGRIEVED

Prior to the enactment of the Criminal Justice Act 1988, a victim in whose favour an order was not made despite an offender willing and able to make compensation and clear and undisputed

---

11 (1979) 1 Cr App Rep (S) 282, CA.
12 [1974] 2 All ER 639, [1974] 1 WLR 615, CA.
13 Powers of Criminal Courts Act 1973, s 36(4), added by the Criminal Justice Act 1988, s 105.

evidence of injury, could well have been 'a person aggrieved' by the court's 'order, determination or other proceeding', but would have been unable to pursue the matter via s 111 of the Magistrates' Courts Act 1980 since the magistrates' failure to make an order would not have been wrong in law.[14] That position has now changed. By s 104 the court has a duty to give reasons if it makes no order in a case in which it is empowered to do so, and this must surely be enforceable under s 111.[15] Accordingly, the reasons the magistrates give will assume considerable importance, since reliance on bad reasons will amount to a failure to comply with this duty.

Assuming a proper consideration of the relevant circumstances, the following are suggested as being good reasons: that the victim does not wish for compensation;[16] that an order might aggravate an existing unhappy relationship between the victim and the offender;[17] that the victim was injured by an offender with whom he had a close relationship;[18] that on a charge involving an offence against the person, an issue of self-defence was left to the jury, or following a guilty plea, the defendant argued in mitigation that he was provoked or challenged the summary given by the prosecution of the respective roles in the incident of himself and the victim;[19] that the offender has no clearly identifiable means to pay the order, even in instalments over a period which is not excessive;[20] that as between a number of victims, this victim

---

14 N Walker *Sentencing: Theory and Practice* (1985, Butterworths) para 1.13.
15 Only in the case of the magistrates' court; the Crown Court is not subject to the supervisory jurisdiction of the High Court.
16 The Home Office circular, *Victims of Crime*, No 20/1988 para 5(a)(iv) recommends that 'officers preparing case summaries for the Crown Prosecution Service should indicate whether the victim wishes to receive compensation from the offender'.
17 *R v Jordan* (1981) 145 JP Jo 88, CA.
18 Newburn (1988) pp 19-20.
19 Even where a jury or magistrates reject evidence of self-defence, their decision is consistent with the belief that the victim might himself have been acting unlawfully, so that if he were to bring a civil action he might be defeated by the application of the maxim *ex turpi causa non oritur actio*; supra, pp 87–90. In the case of provocation, which is no formal defence to a prosecution for an offence against the person, the same maxim may apply, or, in terms of tort law, the victim's behaviour may have been contributorily negligent. Similarly in a case where, on a guilty plea, the defendant challenges the prosecution's account of the incident, the court would be justified in letting the victim and offender settle the matter in a civil action where evidence can be properly adduced and the factual disagreement resolved.
20 *Miller*, op cit, and *R v Olliver* (1989) 11 Crim App Rep (S) 10, CA.

is better placed to pursue a civil action;[1] that a custodial sentence is to be imposed at whose nominal termination there is no evidence that the offender will have the means to pay;[2] and that the offender should not be permitted to buy his way out of what would otherwise be the appropriate sentence for his offence.[3]

On the other hand, it would be bad to decline to make an order merely because an exact assessment of the victim's injury, loss or damage cannot be made if there is evidence upon which an assessment can be made in an appropriate amount;[4] because the court cannot fix upon a sum for pain and suffering in a case where there is agreed evidence on the nature and impact of the injury;[5] because the offender is presently unemployed though otherwise fit for work;[6] or because the court wishes to impose a fine or a confiscation order and the offender has insufficient means to pay both the compensation and the other monetary order.[7] There are also some reasons whose judicial acceptability are open to question, namely where the court considers the disparity between the ideal assessment of the victim's injury and what the offender could be expected to pay is so great that even over a period of two or three years the sum would be derisory,[8] and where the victim is known to the court.

These instances are based on existing law and practice, but no doubt do not exhaust the range of good and bad reasons for refusing to make an order. It is important to stress that the duty is to give reasons where *no* order is made; if an order is made though for less than the ideal assessment of the victim's injury, the court is not obliged to give reasons. The judicial acceptability of the reasons that are given will depend in practice on how magistrates, and to a lesser extent, Crown Courts, set

---

1 *Amey*, op cit.
2 *R v Chambers* (1981) 3 Cr App Rep (S) 318 and *R v Dorton* (1987) 9 Cr App Rep (S) 514, CA.
3 *R v Copley* (1979) 1 Cr App Rep (S) 55, CA; *R v Barney* [1990] Crim LR 209, CA.
4 As s 35(1A) of the Act requires.
5 All courts have been sent the Home Office circular, *Guidelines on Compensation in the Criminal Courts*, No 25/1988 which contains suggested awards for commonly occurring injuries.
6 *R v McKinley* [1975] Crim LR 294, CA and *R v McIntosh* [1973] Crim LR 378, CA.
7 Section 35(4A) of the Powers of Criminal Courts Act 1973 and s 72(7) of the Criminal Justice Act 1988, infra, pp 289-291.
8 See the commentary on *R v Keep* [1974] Crim LR 264, CA and *R v Wylie* [1975] Crim LR 608, CA.

about the administrative aspects of this new duty. Assuming the Home Office's advice on the use of its Compensation Schedule is followed, the CPS will have the information concerning the victim's injury and any pecuniary loss, and can raise the matter at the sentencing stage. In cases where the CPS is not prosecuting, it will presumably be the clerk's responsibility to draw attention to the possibility of compensation; in any event, it would probably be good practice for justices' clerks to devise procedures whereby magistrates' attention is routinely drawn to their powers under s 35. This no doubt will be an onerous task, for these powers apply not merely to the obvious cases of theft, criminal damage and offences against the person, but, as we saw in chapter 8, to any offence, including regulatory offences, from which personal injury, loss or damage result.

E. REVIEW

Appeal against the making or quantum of a compensation order is possible so long as the time for appeal has not elapsed (disregarding any power to grant leave to appeal out of time). Section 37 permits the magistrates' court enforcing the order to review it at any time thereafter, so long as the order has not yet been fully complied with. The order may, on the application of the offender, be discharged or reduced if any one of four conditions is satisfied. We dealt with one of these in the preceding chapter, namely where the injury in respect of which the order was made has been held in civil proceedings to be less than it was taken to be for the purposes of the order.[9] Two of the three other conditions are of principal relevance to orders compensating for the loss of property; s 37(a) is explicitly in those terms, while s 37(b) concerns the making of a compensation order together with a confiscation order under Part VI of the 1988 Act. Section 37(d) is of importance where the compensation order was made, for example, in the expectation of future earnings which are not in the event realised. This permits the reduction or discharge where

> 'the person against whom the order was made has suffered a substantial reduction in his means which was unexpected at the time when the compensation order was made, and that his means seem unlikely to increase for a substantial period'.

9 Supra, pp 253-254.

If the compensation order was made by a Crown Court, the enforcing magistrates' court may not exercise any power conferred by s 37 unless it has first obtained the consent of the Crown Court.

Chapter Eleven

Compensation Orders as Sentences

Compensation orders benefit the victim of crime, but they also constitute a sentence of the court and as such must attract some consideration based on current sentencing theory and practice. From this perspective, undoubtedly the single most significant development was the amendment introduced in the Criminal Justice Act 1982 which permits a court to impose a compensation order instead of and not, as was formerly the case, only in addition to dealing with the offender in any other way. This change was criticised at the time, not least because little thought appears to have been given to such questions as what criteria are apt when considering whether to impose a compensation order as the only sentence, and what its relationship to other sentences ought to be. As with the enactment of other penal reforms, it is arguable that the ideological and political appeal of compensation orders displaced any detailed consideration of these questions;[1] though the Advisory Council was emphatic in its view that offenders ought to be required to compensate their victims, it gave little guidance as to how compensation would fit alongside the traditional sentencing options.[2]

Further, this radical shift in the status of compensation orders from the merely ancillary to the independent may be thought to aggravate the principal difficulties that already accompany their underlying problems within penal theory. Compensation orders may be seen as having a variety of beneficial impacts upon the offender: retributive (by depriving him of his assets so as to pay for the harm done, in particular orders under s 43A); reparative (by requiring him to compensate the victim for the injuries he has caused) and rehabilitative (by drawing his

1 R Hood 'Criminology and penal change' in R Hood ed *Crime, Criminology and Public Policy* (1974, Heinemann) pp 375-419, esp 381-390.
2 M Wasik 'The place of compensation in the penal system' [1978] Crim LR 599-611.

attention to the pain and misery he has caused to another human being, and so to change for the better his attitudes towards himself and to others). As we have seen, the practical realisation of any or all of these objectives is seriously constrained by the obligation to take account of the offender's means, and is especially problematic where the offender is either poor or very rich.[3]

Prior to the changes introduced by the Criminal Justice Act 1972, a compensation order for personal injury could only be made by a court when making a probation order, or when discharging the offender absolutely or conditionally. After 1972, the only formal restriction was that a compensation order could not be made where a Crown Court had made a criminal bankruptcy order against the offender.[4] Apart from that, an order could in theory be made by the court in addition to dealing with him in any other way, although in practice its use ancillary to a custodial sentence has been limited. The restriction on contemporaneous criminal bankruptcy orders survived the change introduced by the Criminal Justice Act 1982 that has already been remarked upon: a criminal court may make a compensation order against the offender 'instead of or in addition to dealing with him in any other way'. The 1982 Act introduced another important change, requiring the court to give preference to the compensation order where it considers both the order and a fine to be appropriate sentences, but the offender lacks the means to comply with both. Criminal bankruptcy orders were abolished by the Criminal Justice Act 1988, and confiscation orders, which were established in their place, are subject to the same statutory subordination vis-à-vis a compensation order as are fines. Since the order can still be made in addition to other sentences, the authorities interpreting and applying the pre-1982 version of s 35 remain persuasive indicators of when an order is an appropriate sentence in conjunction with another, whether custodial or non-custodial.

In this chapter we consider firstly the use of compensation orders as the sole sentence of the court, and secondly their use ancillary to another option; this section also reviews some difficulties that can arise when seeking justice between offenders. The final section recapitulates the detailed guidance that the Court of Appeal has given on the factors to be taken into account when ordering compensation.

---

3 Supra pp 243–247.
4 Powers of Criminal Courts Act 1973 s 39. Hodgson J, *R v Garner* [1986] 1 All ER 78, [1986] 1 WLR 73, CA.

A. COMPENSATION ORDERS AS INDEPENDENT SENTENCES

The question which arises here is where in the range of other (mainly non-custodial) sentences do compensation orders fit for the purpose of selection as the *only* sentence, as distinct from those cases where it is made in conjunction with another sentence. That this is not easily answered is due largely to two factors. The first is that compensation orders only became available as autonomous sentences in 1982, and at the time of writing no case has come on appeal which raises this question. The second is that there is very little general appellate guidance on the use of non-custodial sentences.[5] If compensation orders are to be routinely imposed independent of any other sentence, some effort will have to be made to rank them within the hierarchy of sentences, and in particular within non-custodial sentences, even if Newburn's research suggests their routine use is unlikely.[6]

It is possible, for example, to adapt the framework that Ashworth derives from *R v O'Keefe*[7] and *R v Clarke*,[8] and suggest that sentencers should go through the following process of elimination:

i. is an absolute discharge appropriate;
ii. is a conditional discharge appropriate;
iii. is a compensation order appropriate;
iv. is a fine appropriate;
v. is a confiscation order appropriate (if both a fine or a confiscation order and a compensation order are appropriate but the offender is of limited means, the compensation order must be preferred);
vi. is a short community service order appropriate?[9]

A number of objections can readily be made to an approach of this kind. Firstly, we may share Ashworth's scepticism about the value of such frameworks: they assume 'a particular ranking

5 In 1989 the Magistrates' Association published guidelines on the use of fines in relation to the 25 most common offences, (1989) 139 New LJ 354.
6 T Newburn *The Use and Enforcement of Compensation Orders in Magistrates' Courts* (1988, Home Office Research Study 102) ch 8.
7 [1969] 2 QB 29, [1969] 1 All ER 426, CA.
8 [1982] 3 All ER 232, [1982] 1 WLR 1090, CA.
9 A Ashworth *Sentencing and Penal Policy* (1983, Weidenfeld and Nicolson) pp 34-55. See also T Wilkinson 'Magistrates' courts — compensation orders' (1984) Law Soc Gaz, 22 February 1984, 485-486.

of non-custodial measures which has not been authoritatively established',[10] and as such say nothing about the criteria or the appropriateness of any choice, or, with the exception of compensation orders and fines or confiscation orders, of what priority should attach to any of them. Compensation orders are to be preferred in these two instances, but the remainder of this admittedly speculative ranking does not answer the question, when is a compensation order alone, the apt sentence? In the absence of judicial guidance, it is necessary to consider the question as a matter of sentencing principle.

The central issue is whether, notwithstanding its statutory independence, a compensation order can indeed be regarded as a credible sentence *sui generis*.[11] As well as serving a compensatory function, compensation orders can be intended to bear a penal emphasis, as *R v Bradburn*[12] and more recent comments by the Home Office indicate: 'it is right that [a compensation order] should hurt and it should be a penalty that brings home to [the offender] the wrong that he has done to his victim.'[13] But how can a single monetary order serve both the function of compensation and of punishment if it does no more than compensate the victim? If the victim's injury is valued at £500, which the offender can pay, how can that order be said to hurt him any more than an award of damages? The court cannot increase the compensation order above the ideal assessment of the injury, and can only hurt the offender by the imposition of a further sentence; but that subverts the integrity of the compensation order as the sole sentence. Where the offender has sufficient means to meet the ideal assessment of the victim's injury and a compensation order is the sole sentence, it may thus be objected that no formal sanction has been imposed on him to reflect the public aspect of his offence,[14] since the order is in effect functioning as a surrogate for the victim's civil action. The result is the same, and arguably equally objectionable, should the court make an order for the ideal assessment of the victim's injury, in respect of which the victim subsequently recovers the same or an increased sum in civil proceedings. As we saw in

---

10 (1983) p 46.
11 Ibid, p 315, observing that compensation 'raises issues which are separate from sentencing'.
12 (1973) 57 Cr App Rep 948, CA.
13 Attributed to the Home Secretary in an editorial (1982) 132 New LJ 329.
14 A Ashworth, 'Punishment and compensation: victims, offenders and the state' (1986) 6 Oxford J Legal Studies 86-122.

chapter 9, the victim/plaintiff is precluded by s 38 of the Powers of Criminal Courts Act 1973 from enforcing so much of the civil judgment as is accounted for in the order; thus here too the offender's public wrong has been rectified by the private cost set upon it. The complete aetiolation of the criminal sanction in these cases is prevented only by the ceremonial attached to the criminal trial, and by the stigma of conviction.

If compensation as the sole sentence can, even where he has sufficient means, only with difficulty serve both to punish the offender and compensate the victim, the realisation of this twin objective is yet more remote where the offender has insufficient means. The amount ordered to be paid can, like a fine, be punitive in relation to the offender's circumstances, but equally may come nowhere close to the ideal assessment of the victim's injury. Thus in this case, a compensation order is functionally equivalent to a fine, save that the moneys are being transmitted to the victim rather than to the Lord Chancellor.

It is considerations such as these that explain the very limited use magistrates make of compensation orders as the sole sentence. Between 1985 and 1987 the total number of such orders did not exceed 3,700 in any one year; in 1988 about 4,500 such orders were made.[15] In Newburn's sample of magistrates' courts, the frequency of sole use did not exceed 5% of cases in which compensation was ordered;[16] this compares well with the data from the *Criminal Statistics* for 1984, which also showed that during 1984 only 20 of 651 magistrates' courts in England and Wales made a compensation order as the sole sentence on more than ten occasions. He concluded:

'In most cases, when it is used, compensation is still generally imposed in conjunction with another penalty (usually a fine) and only rarely is it used on its own. Only in the larger courts does the number of compensation orders used in this fashion appear to reach double figures annually, the vast majority of magistrates' courts registering fewer than ten compensation orders on their own in a year.'[17]

Newburn's research clearly shows that many magistrates have a deep-seated sense of unease about the use of compensation orders in preference to the more familiar non-custodial measures. This

---

15 Home Office *Criminal Statistics England and Wales 1988* (1989, Cm 847) para 7.38.
16 (1988) p 11.
17 Ibid, p 10.

sense of unease stems from their strongly-held belief that compensation and punishment are not interchangeable responses to victimisation, and cannot be realised in a single order. Newburn quotes a number of magistrates' reservations about the use of compensation orders, of which the following is typical: 'There needs to be another penalty on top of compensation to punish the offender for the act itself.'[18] They consistently expressed the view that, even if it were only a nominal fine, some response by the court to the offence other than the making of a compensation order, was both normal and desirable.[19]

B.   COMPENSATION ORDERS AS ANCILLARY SENTENCES

(1)   Compensation orders and custodial sentences

The basic position approved by the Court of Appeal is that while the fact that the offender has received an immediate, and possibly substantial, custodial sentence is no ground for not ordering compensation if he clearly has the means to pay, an order should not be made if its effect would be to subject him, on his release from custody, to a financial burden which he would not be able to meet from his available resources and which might encourage him to commit further offences to obtain the means to meet the requirements of the order.[20] The longer the postponement of the initial payment of compensation, the more certain the court needs to be about the chances of the offender being able to comply.[1] These considerations apply equally to sentences to

---

18 Ibid, p 12.
19 Magistrates' reluctance to make compensation orders as a sole sentence stands in stark contrast to their equally firmly held view that offenders ought to compensate their victims so as to re-establish justice between them. Similar inconsistencies are evident in the attitudes of sheriffs to the equivalent Scottish law, G Maher and C Docherty, *Compensation Orders in Scottish Criminal Courts* (1988, Scottish Office) pp 31-32.
20 *R v Panayioutou* [1990] Crim LR 349, CA and *R v Martin* [1990] Crim LR 132, CA. See also *R v Wylie* [1975] RTR 94, CA; *R v McKinley* [1975] Crim LR 294, CA; *R v Copley* (1979) 1 Cr App Rep (S) 55, CA; *R v Townsend* (1980) 2 Cr App Rep (S) 328, CA; *R v Morgan* (1982) 4 Cr App Rep (S) 358, CA; *R v Coughlin* (1984) 6 Cr App Rep (S) 102, CA; *R v Huish* (1985) 7 Cr App Rep (S) 272, CA and *R v Ramsey* (1987) 9 Cr App Rep (S) 251, CA.
 1 *R v Whenman* [1977] Crim LR 430, CA, and *Huish*, op cit.

periods of detention in a young offender institution as they do to sentences of imprisonment.[2]

The reason for this caution is not far to seek: offenders who are released from custodial sentences typically experience problems finding employment. With the obligation to comply backed by imprisonment for default, the temptation to re-offend in order to acquire funds would be quite real. Scarman LJ put the matter thus in *R v Inwood*:

'There is a further matter to which this court desires to draw attention. Compensation orders, which may appear at the trial to the convicted man to be a life line, can, however, become a millstone round his neck, when he is released from prison. They can be counter-productive, and force him back into crime to find the money.

Looking at the present case, the prospect now of the Belgian lady finding £12,000 odd to pay the victims of her criminal relative, he being in prison for the period of four years, is slender. It would be very surprising if the money were found. If it is not found, then it is this appellant, who will be in his late fifties and approaching his sixtieth birthday when he is released from prison, who will be under an obligation to pay over £12,000 in compensation. The risk that he may resort to the sort of criminal activity, at which he found it to be so easy to be successful for a period of five years, is one which the courts have to consider. In our judgment, this appellant has no means with which he can meet the compensation order. Accordingly, in our judgment, the order should not have been made and must now be quashed.'[3]

Here we see the recurring conflict between the interests of the victim and those of the offender: to make an order to compensate the victim will impede the sentencing objectives apt in this offender's case; accordingly it should not be made. This conflict was well illustrated by the controversy generated by advice formerly given by the Home Office to magistrates concerning the enforcement of compensation orders against certain young offenders. This advice was that such an order should not be enforced where it remained outstanding against a young offender upon his release from a period of borstal training or of detention in a detention centre. The object was to give the offender a fresh

---

2 *Bradburn*, op cit; *R v Wilkinson* [1980] 1 All ER 597, [1980] 1 WLR 396, and *R v Parker* (1981) 3 Cr App Rep (S) 278, CA. Neither should a compensation order necessarily be regarded as an additional punishment where a custodial sentence has been imposed, as it may be less onerous for the offender to comply with it rather than being sued, *R v Dorton* (1987) 9 Cr App Rep (S) 514, CA.

3 (1974) 60 Cr App Rep 70 at 73, CA. Also *Wilkinson*, op cit.

start; the uncompleted compensation order represented an obstacle to his rehabilitation. This advice was revised following representations, so as to place the emphasis upon the satisfaction of the victim's interests.[4] However, it should also be emphasised that this revision does not resolve the underlying conflict of interest; it simply gives priority to one side for the time being.

The various implications for the offender of the combination of a compensation order and a custodial sentence were considered at some length by the Advisory Council on the Penal System. The reasons that it gave for its recommendation that a compensation order should not normally be made where a custodial sentence is imposed are worth repeating in full:

'The enforcement of monetary payments after a custodial sentence raises special problems; the courts could not know the details of the offender's prospective circumstances on discharge, and enforcement might well prejudice his rehabilitation and resettlement. An offender subject to a compensation order designed to be enforced after his release might well be subject also to statutory after-care, and in these circumstances the task of the probation officer would be a difficult one. It is true that under s 11(2) of the Criminal Justice Act 1948 an order for compensation may be combined with a probation order, but the two situations are hardly comparable; a prisoner is very likely to resent having to meet an order for compensation on discharge, perhaps long after the offence was committed, and the probation officer's efforts at rehabilitation through after-care are bound to be affected. The offender might, moreover, have to face the competing demands of the victim and of his own family, and might resort to further crime to find the money. And the deferment of compliance with a compensation order for a substantial period might well cause administrative difficulties; it might, for example, no longer be possible to trace the victim. All these considerations may be thought to rule out the making of compensation orders with a view to their enforcement after a prisoner's release, save perhaps in cases in which the court thinks it necessary to mark the gravity of the offence by imposing a short custodial sentence in addition to an order for compensation.'[5]

In practice, compensation orders for personal injury made in conjunction with a custodial sentence appear to be rare. Home Office research conducted during the mid-1970s indicated 'that

4 971 HC Official Report (5th series) cols 17-18 (23 July 1979), 978 HC Official Report (5th series) col 418 (11 February 1980), and Home Office circular No 22/1983 para 20.

5 Advisory Council on the Penal System *Reparation by the Offender* (1970, Home Office) para 121.

both Crown Courts and magistrates' courts are reluctant to combine compensation orders with custodial sentences', at least following convictions for property offences.[6] This reluctance has also been a matter of comment in the Criminal Statistics. In 1982 it was observed that 'the proportionate use of compensation orders was much lower at the Crown Court (7% in 1982) than at magistrates' courts (15% in 1982), particularly for those types of offences for which custodial sentences were given more often by the Crown Court, because compensation is not often ordered in association with this type of sentence.'[7] Newburn's research, conducted in the mid-1980s, showed that of 848 cases in which compensation orders were made by magistrates in combination with one or more penalty, in only eight instances were these combined with a custodial sentence taking immediate effect; a further 36 orders were made in conjunction with a suspended sentence.[8] The figures upon which he relied do not indicate the distribution of compensation orders and custodial offences in the particular case of offences against the person, but it is clearly very low, which suggests that the Advisory Council's views, as adopted by the Court of Appeal, are largely followed in practice.

(2) Compensation orders and non-custodial sentences

Some of the considerations mentioned by the Advisory Council concerning the general inadvisability of combining compensation orders with custodial sentences are relevant also to their combination with non-custodial sentences. The most obvious of these is whether the offender is likely to obtain or retain any regular employment during the currency of a deferred, suspended or partly suspended sentence, while on probation or under supervision, or otherwise complying with the terms of the court's sentence. Particular difficulties might be expected where the court imposes monetary orders other than the compensation order, but the potential for conflict is in theory dealt with, in the case of fines and confiscation orders, by a statutory preference for compensation, and in the case of costs, by arrangements in practice agreed by the Lord Chancellor's Department. These preferences are examined in more detail below.

6 P Softley and R Tarling 'Compensation orders and custodial sentences' [1977] Crim LR 720-722, 721.
7 Home Office *Criminal Statistics England and Wales 1982* (1983, Cmnd 9048) para 7.39.
8 (1988) p 13.

In one respect, the combination of a compensation order and a suspended sentence raises a particularly difficult problem to which Thomas has drawn attention.[9] A compensation order imposed at the same time that a sentence of imprisonment is suspended will be made on the basis of the offender's present or future ability to pay from capital or income. It will also probably be made, other things being equal, on terms more onerous than would be the case if an immediate custodial sentence were imposed, for example, to be paid in larger instalments over a shorter period of time. If the offender commits a further offence, the court considering whether to activate the suspended sentence is faced with a dilemma. The court has no power to vary the compensation in such a case, and the existence of the order is not a ground on which the court may decide not to enforce the suspended sentence or to enforce it to a reduced degree; at the same time, the offender remains under an obligation to comply with a compensation order made on the basis of expectations now wholly unrealistic, and which will subsist during the period of imprisonment.

Brazier, who was also critical of this possibility,[10] proposed that courts should not be permitted to impose a suspended sentence in conjunction with a compensation order at all. This might be regarded as a remedy excessive for the mischief, since it remains desirable that victims be compensated as part of the sentencing process, and the exclusion of this combination of sentences is likely to create other sentencing difficulties: what does the court do, when it considers this particular combination apt in a given case? It may also be the case (there is no evidence available) that where the combination of suspended sentence and compensation order has been imposed, offenders have substantially or even wholly complied with the order to the benefit of their victims before they re-offended or the period of suspension had terminated.[11]

Thomas' suggestion was that the courts be given the power,

---

9 See his commentary on *Whenman* op cit; *R v McGee* [1978] Crim LR 370, CA; *R v Wallis* (1979) 1 Cr App Rep (S) 168, CA, and *R v Mathieson* (1987) 9 Cr App Rep (S) 54, CA.

10 R Brazier 'Appellate attitudes toward compensation orders' [1977] Crim LR 710-719, 714.

11 Home Office research conducted in the mid-1970s indicated that magistrates made orders in nearly 70% of property offences for which a suspended sentence was imposed, but there are no figures for the proportion of offences against the person, P Softley *Compensation Orders in Magistrates' Courts* (1978, Home Office Research Study 43) p 18.

when activating a suspended sentence or imposing an immediate custodial sentence (for example for breach of a community service order) on an offender against whom a compensation order is outstanding, to review the order and to set it aside or vary it as seems right in the circumstances. This was accepted by the Advisory Council in 1981,[12] and although Thomas' exact proposal has not been introduced, changes made by the Criminal Justice Act 1988 to s 37(d) of the Powers of Criminal Courts Act 1973 may operate to the same effect.[13] That section provides that upon application by the offender, the enforcing magistrates' court may discharge or reduce the order if it appears 'that the person against whom the order was made has suffered a substantial reduction in his means which was unexpected at the time when the compensation order was made, and that his means seem unlikely to increase for a considerable period.' There is no statutory guidance on what constitutes either a 'substantial' reduction, or a 'considerable' period, but it may be appropriate to compare, for the former, the amount of the order with the offender's reduced means, and for the latter, the period of time ordered for payment by instalments with the term of imprisonment. If these criteria are met, and the activation of the suspended sentence before the order has been fully met can be regarded as 'unexpected', the magistrates may discharge or reduce the order.

Home Office research published in the 1970s shows a substantial use of compensation orders in property offences in combination with absolute and conditional discharges (67%), probation orders (75%) and fines (76%).[14] In general it would be unusual to encounter any conflict in sentencing theory or practice between the making of a compensation order for personal injury and the first two of these three non-custodial sentences. It may be recalled that it was only ancillary to these two that a compensation order for personal injury could be made before 1972. Fines, on the other hand, do pose problems. Here the sentencer is trying to impose two monetary orders, one commensurate with the gravity of the offence (subject to the offender's means) and the other commensurate with the gravity of the victim's injury (again, subject to the offender's means), the satisfaction of the one posing a threat to the satisfaction

---

12 Advisory Council on the Penal System, *Sentences of Imprisonment* (1978, Home Office) para 267. See A Bottoms 'The Advisory Council and the suspended sentence' [1979] Crim LR 435-446.

13 D Thomas 'The Criminal Justice Act 1988: the sentencing provisions' [1989] Crim LR 43-55, 48.

14 Softley (1978) Table 7 p 18.

of the other. Hence Softley's remarks concerning his findings on magistrates' experience when coping with this conflict:

'The ordering of compensation for loss or damage resulting from offences for which fines are imposed presumbly gives rise to difficulties in assessing the amount to be paid, since courts would not wish the total imposition to be excessive in relation to the means of the offender. These difficulties are not essentially different from those which must frequently arise in cases where compensation is not ordered, but they are aggravated by the additional burden which the payment of compensation must place on the offender's resources. In cases where the fine and compensation together seemed excessive, it is conceivable that courts sometimes reduced the amount of fine, or had second thoughts about ordering compensation.'[15]

Newburn's research confirms Softley's conclusion that fines are the most common sentence used in conjunction with compensation orders: they were imposed in 50% of the 848 cases in the sample in which a compensation order was combined with another penalty.[16] There are also an unknown number of cases in which the two monetary orders would have been combined, but were kept formally separate. Where an offender is convicted on several charges, magistrates will, for simplicity's sake, sometimes total all the fines and the compensation payable, and then record the whole of the fine as being imposed in respect of one set of convictions, the whole of the compensation order as being imposed in respect of the other: 'in this way compensation appears to have been used as a sole penalty when it has actually been used with . . . a fine.'[17] However, there is no published statistical evidence on the use of fines and compensation orders following convictions for offences causing personal injury, so it is not possible to say what proportion of that 50% (or more) of cases where fines are imposed in combination with compensation orders, are personal injury offences.

The conflict between the two orders that is created by the insufficiency of the offender's means was statutorily resolved in favour of the compensation order by an amendment to s 35 of the Powers of Criminal Courts Act 1973.[18] This was introduced by s 67 of the Criminal Justice Act 1982, inserting s 35(4A):

15 Ibid, p 16.
16 Newburn (1988) p 13.
17 Ibid, p 10.
18 On the ways in which the offender's means may be insufficient, supra, pp 242–248.

'Where the court considers —

(a) that it would be appropriate both to impose a fine and to make a compensation order; but
(b) that the offender has insufficient means to pay both an appropriate fine and appropriate compensation, the court shall give preference to compensation (though it may impose a fine as well)'.

It is unusual for sentencing legislation to go further than to empower a court to impose sentences within limits, and it remains to be seen what impact this statutorily imposed preference will have upon the practices of magistrates and Crown Court judges.[19] One possible effect which can be inferred from Newburn's research, is that this section may have encouraged magistrates to the view that compensation orders should only be used as a sole sentence where a fine would normally be considered the appropriate penalty; but this inference may be reading too much into his observations, which are on a slightly different point.[20]

One aspect of the imposition of fines and of their relationship to the principle of compensation via the criminal courts was considered in *R v Garner.*[1] This case was principally concerned with the use of fines as a means of confiscating the proceeds of crime, and with their relationship, inter alia, to criminal bankruptcy orders under s 39(1) of the Powers of Criminal Courts Act 1973. Giving the judgment of the Court of Appeal, Hodgson J held that where such an order was made, an additional fine should only be imposed if it is clear that after payment of the fine, there will be ample funds to compensate the creditors named in the order. This case does not directly concern compensation orders, but it does underline the Court of Appeal's preference for compensation. 'To do otherwise', said Hodgson J, 'would be to give priority to the fine over compensation.'[2]

By Part VI of the Criminal Justice Act 1988, Crown Courts,

---

19 In *Wings v Ellis* [1984] 3 All ER 577 at 583, HL Lord Hailsham LC indicated his preference for the making of a compensation order over a fine following conviction under the Trade Descriptions Act 1968 for misleading statements in holiday brochures. See also *R v Thomson Holidays Ltd* [1974] QB 592, [1974] 1 All ER 823, CA.

20 (1988) p 11.

1 [1986] 1 All ER 78, [1986] 1 WLR 73, CA.

2 Ibid, p 90. Hodgson J was Chairman of the review that considered in detail how to separate offenders from the proceeds of crime, and how to direct those proceeds to compensate their victims, *The Profits of Crime and Their Recovery* (1984, Heinemann).

and in some cases, magistrates' courts, can make confiscation orders against the offender. The court may impose both monetary orders, but as with fines, there is a statutory preference for the satisfaction of the compensation order where it appears that there is an insufficiency of means to satisfy both orders in full. Section 72(7) of the 1988 Act provides that in such a case, the court 'shall direct that so much of the compensation as will not in its opinion be recoverable because of the insufficiency of his means shall be paid out of any sums recovered under the confiscation order.' Schedule 15 of the Act amends the Powers of Criminal Courts Act 1973 so that in determining whether to make a compensation order, and in what amount, the court shall have regard to its duty under s 72(7); this duty will be contained in s 35(4)(b) of the 1973 Act when a commencement order is made under s 171 of the 1988 Act. In other words, a court that is minded to make both a compensation and a confiscation order must, in addition to the universal requirement to have regard to the offender's means, have regard to the possibility that these will be insufficient to satisfy both orders in full, and, if that is so, direct that the difference between what he can afford and the amount of the compensation order be met from the sums recovered under the confiscation order.

Section 81 of the Act specifies how moneys received under a confiscation order are to be applied by the justices' clerk of the enforcing magistrates' court. Following deductions to reimburse expenses incurred in connection with the process of confiscation, the clerk shall, by s 81(7) pay any compensation directed to be paid under s 72(7). However, prior to that, a further deduction shall be made, being such proportion of the total expenses incurred in the process of confiscation as is represented by the amount of the compensation to be paid compared with the total sum confiscated. The idea is that the victim ought to make a contribution to the expenses incurred by the receiver appointed to trace and to secure the assets to be confiscated, an expertise which would normally be unavailable in the absence of costly litigation. Though this deduction is made, and the victim therefore actually receives less than the sum that was directed to be paid under s 72(7), he is treated as having received the sum as directed. This is of importance if the victim should then initiate civil proceedings against the offender.

Finally, in keeping with these statutory preferences, the Lord Chancellor's Department and the Crown Prosecution Service have agreed that where the court is minded to make an order for costs, any question of compensation should be settled first, and given priority in the event that the offender's means would be insufficient to pay both.[3]

C. COMPENSATION ORDERS AND SENTENCING THEORY

The difficulties discussed above largely stem from a lack of thought as to the place of compensation orders within the existing penal framework.[4] Adapting a hypothetical case considered by Walker,[5] suppose two offenders are jointly charged and convicted of an offence against the person, attracting a normal tariff of up to three years' imprisonment and:

V1. the victim sustained substantial loss of earnings which were fully met by occupational sick pay arrangements, and only slight pain and suffering;

V2. the victim sustained virtually no pecuniary loss, but has sustained harm to his mental condition as a result of the offence; and

O1. one offender is relatively wealthy;

O2. the other offender is relatively poor but with good employment prospects; and

P1. one offender has previous convictions for similar offences,

P2. the other offender has previous convictions for minor offences against property.

In some of these permutations it would be entirely apt to impose the tariff sentence and a compensation order (typically in the case of the persistent offender P1). In the case of the poor offender with minor convictions (O2/P2), a court might find it hard to choose in case V1 between a compensation order only and the custodial sentence. The tariff sentence will make the compensation order useless, yet it may be possible, since the award will not be great in relation to his means, for the offender fully to

---

3 Home Office Circular No 85/1988 *Guidelines on Compensation in the Criminal Courts* para 14. This arrangement answers the point raised in the commentary to *R v Hackett* (1988) 10 Cr App Rep (S) 388, CA.

4 Though the relationship between compensation and sentencing was not always uncontroversial even before 1972 when it was very much an ancillary matter, *R v Ironfield* [1971] 1 All ER 202, [1971] 1 WLR 90, CA and *R v McDevitt* (1972) 56 Cr App Rep 851, CA.

5 N Walker *Sentencing: Theory and Practice* (1985, Butterworths) para 8.37.

compensate the victim. If the court believes that compensation should take precedence over punishment, the offender is not being imprisoned because he is fortunate enough to have a good job to go to. On the other hand, if the injury is as in V2, the court may feel, as Thomas has argued,[6] that it is improper to impose a compensation order where the ideal assessment of the victim's injury would require a sum far in excess of what the offender could pay either in a lump sum or in no more than two-three years' instalments.

The problem of securing even-handed justice becomes more acute when the court has to deal with the wealthy offender (O1) in cases V1 and V2. Although it may feel that it is quite proper to impose a compensation order in either case, it may also be moved to impose an immediate custodial sentence even if the offender's prior convictions are not for similar offences lest it be thought that he is buying his way out of the penalty. This is a purpose for which, as Scarman LJ forcefully said in *Inwood*, 'compensation orders were not introduced into our law'.[7] The objection here is stronger if the offence for which the offender is convicted normally attracts a custodial sentence. The Court of Appeal has continued to emphasise that an offender who has the means to pay a substantial amount by way of compensation (or fine) should not escape a custodial sentence if this would be apt for a less wealthy offender. In *R v Copley* Lane LJ said:

'It is to be observed — if it needs observing — that it is not open to persons who participate in crime and plead guilty to try to buy their way out of prison, or to buy shorter sentences by offering money in the way of compensation.'[8]

6 Supra, pp 243–244.
7 (1974) 60 Cr App Rep 70 at 73, CA. Also *R v Morris* [1973] Crim LR 451, CA and *R v Stapleton and Lawrie* [1977] Crim LR 366, CA. It has also been argued, that rendered in purely financial terms, the offender will perceive compensation merely as an opportunity cost, which perception will in turn encourage him to devalue the victim, G Mueller 'Victims of violence: a round table' (1959) 8 J Public L 218-236.
8 Op cit, p 57. See also *R v Barney* [1990] Crim LR 209 where the Court of Appeal held that an indication by the trial judge that the offender could expect a shorter custodial sentence if he could make compensation was wrong. Willingness to make reparation may show contrition, but the making of a compensation order could never have an effect upon the length of a sentence of imprisonment, *Dorton*, op cit.

Even where this is not the normal sentence, the pressure to impose a sentence in addition to the compensation will be considerable, if the court wishes to avoid the criticism that the offender is purchasing his freedom. Yet this in turn can produce the odd result that the poor offender with good job prospects goes to prison in case V2 but not V1, while the wealthy offender goes to prison in both cases, and is also required to pay compensation.[9] It is worth repeating that the notion of a 'wealthy' offender is, like the issue of the sufficiency of his means, not an absolute one; the offender is rich or poor *in relation to the victim's injury.* Accordingly, a court may feel that it is right to impose a fine in addition to a compensation order on an offender who is wealthy in relation to an injury ideally valued at £500 (O1, who can readily pay the sum), but not an offender who is poor in relation to the injury (O2, who can pay only in instalments over, say, two years). But that same poor offender would be wealthy in relation to an injury ideally valued at £50, and so the question arises whether in that case, he ought not to be further punished. And if the offender who is wealthy in relation to the injury valued at £500 causes an injury valued at £50, then as between him and O2, it may be thought just that any additional fine should be much greater than for the relatively less wealthy offender.

Nor do these various permutations take any account of any differences in the degree of participation in the offence, or of the offenders' respective degrees of fault. Thus a third major difficulty is that compensation orders are flexible sentencing options (assuming the offender has sufficient means) in only one dimension: the seriousness of the victim's injury.[10] Assume two offenders whose attacks upon their victims present equal threats of harm, and:

O1. the offender intends to cause harm;

---

9 On the problems of adjusting fines to the very rich and the very poor, Ashworth (1984) pp 279-291. It is not a legitimate objective of a fine to seek to recoup to the public purse a quid pro quo for the fact that the victim will be seeking compensation from the CICB. So held Griffiths J in *R v Roberts* (1980) 2 Cr App Rep (S) 121, CA, reducing a fine from £1,000 to £250. The Crown Court judge 'took into account the fact that the injured man would undoubtedly have recourse to the CICB to obtain damages for the injuries he had received. Those damages of course would come out of the public purse and the judge apparently conceived it as part of his duty to try and recoup the public purse by the imposition of a fine . . .' This was an inappropriate consideration in determining the level of the fine. It would have made more sense to make a compensation order.

10 The victim's own conduct may be a consideration.

O2.   the offender is reckless as to whether harm is caused; and
V1.   the victim suffers the kind of injury that the offender's harmful actions would normally cause to a person like him; and
V2.   the victim is saved from the normal effects of that kind of injury by the speedy arrival of an ambulance.

A fine or a custodial sentence can be increased or decreased to reflect the combination of factors present, and can be varied also to take account of the offender's age, previous convictions or any other factor considered relevant by the sentencer. A compensation order, on the other hand, can reflect none of these considerations, save the severity of the harm caused. Where, as is assumed, the offender has sufficient means to meet the ideal assessment of the victim's injury in the more serious case (V1), it seems capricious to make an award for less than that assessment because the offender was only reckless as to the injury (O2). It would be similarly unjust to the victim if V1 were awarded less compensation than V2 because the offender was in his case only reckless, while in the second case the offender intended the harm. Similar considerations apply where the offender is poor in relation to the ideal assessment of the victim's injury. Suppose the offender's means were sufficient to meet the ideal assessment only of the less serious case (V1): from the victim's standpoint, it would be unjust if O2 were ordered to make less compensation than O1.

If the purpose of a compensation order is to compensate the victim for the ideal assessment of his injury, or for such proportion of it as can be met from the offender's means, it cannot be appropriate to vary the amount ordered to be paid to reflect such factors as differences in the offenders' states of mind, prior convictions, or even the cardinal or ordinal value of the offence itself.[11] These factors are entirely proper considerations when the court is imposing a fine, but if they were proper also to compensation, then the only difference between these two monetary penalties would be the destination of the revenue; that in turn would suggest some reconsideration of the place of compensation in the sentencing process.

At first sight, compensation orders appear to fit well with such sentencing notions as balancing the harm caused by the offender and of correcting injustice as between him and his victim, yet

11   A Ashworth 'Criminal Justice and Deserved Sentences' [1989] Crim LR 340-355.

considered against a statement of current sentencing theory, the limited scope of compensation orders as sentencing options becomes obvious:

> 'On the theory on modern retributivism, sentences may be seen as "cancelling out" the unfair advantage gained by the offender in committing the crime. The cancellation takes place only in a metaphorical or symbolic way, and is calculated by reference not solely to the gravity of the offence but also to the offender's culpability, his previous record, the principles of equality before the law and equality of impact, and other relevant principles. The accommodation of these other factors suggests that English sentencing has a loose connection with the notion of moral accounting: in other words, sentencing may be intended as a broader social judgment upon the offender, not dealing only with his offence and his probable relation to the sentence, but considering them in the wider context of his contribution to society.'[12]

A compensation order may cancel out the unfair treatment of the victim by the offender; but that is all. It cannot cancel out, since it does not address, the public aspect of the offender's conduct. Nor, since it is calculated primarily by reference to the *actual* harm sustained by the victim, is it sufficiently sensitive to permit individualised sentencing beyond adjustment according to the offender's means; and as we have seen, the individualisation of compensation orders is problematic not only where the offender does not have sufficient means, but also where he does.

D. GUIDELINES ON THE USE OF COMPENSATION ORDERS

Notwithstanding the difficulties in sentencing theory which can be posed by compensation orders, some quite clear and workable guidelines have been developed by the Court of Appeal for cases in which they are apt. Although superseded in one or two matters (which are omitted from the list set out below), the guidance laid down by Pain J in *Miller*[13] continues to be persuasive. Some of the points listed below recapitulate those made in earlier chapters; it is however useful to restate them in one place.

---

12 Ashworth (1983) pp 305–06.
13 (1976) 68 Cr App Rep 56 at 57-58, CA. See generally, D Thomas *Current Sentencing Practice* (Sweet & Maxwell) para J2.

1. 'A compensation order in terms of money should be made only where the legal position is quite clear.' As shown by *R v Horsham Justices, ex p Richards*,[14] clarity as to both the evidence and the evaluation of the victim's injury remains a pre-condition to the making of a compensation order despite the intended 'loosening' which was thought to have been effected by s 35(1A) of the 1973 Act of the evidential requirement set out in *R v Vivian*.[15] If there is doubt about these matters, the victim should be left to pursue his civil remedy. The civil liability of the offender is not, however, a pre-condition to an order.[16]

2. 'In making a compensation order the Court must have regard to the means of the defendant.' This simply paraphrases s 35(4).

3. 'The compensation order must be precise. It must be related to an offence in respect of which the defendant has been convicted or to an offence which he has asked to have taken into account. It must specify the amount and if there is to be payment by instalments it must specify the instalments.'[17]

4. 'The compensation order must not be oppressive. The court has to bear in mind that a prisoner who has just been discharged from jail is very often short of money. He must not be tempted to commit further offences to provide cash in order to bring his compensation order up to date.'

5. 'On the other hand there may be good moral grounds for making a compensation order including the order for payment by instalments to remind the defendant of the evil he has done . . . This, we think, may particularly apply in the case where a non-custodial penalty is imposed and the compensation which is appropriate is a sum which is not too great.'

6. 'Finally, a compensation order must be realistic. An order for payment by instalments over a long period is to be avoided.' Two to three years' instalments are quite in order, as is a longer period if the offender has funds and the likelihood of default is low; but the period must not be excessive.[18]

To these may be added some further guidelines developed since *Miller* was decided. A number of these are set out in Thomas' commentary on *R v Chambers*.[19]

7. If the case is one in which immediate imprisonment should

---

14 [1985] 2 All ER 1114, [1985] 1 WLR 986.

15 [1979] 1 All ER 48, [1979] 1 WLR 291, CA.

16 *R v Chappell* (1984) 6 Cr App Rep (S) 342, CA.

17 *R v Bagga* [1990] Crim LR 128, CA.

18 *R v Scott* (1986) 83 Cr App Rep 221, CA, and *R v Olliver* (1989) 11 Cr App Rep (S) 10, CA.

19 (1981) 3 Cr App Rep (S) 318. They are also set out in Walker (1985) para 16.45.

be imposed, the court should so sentence notwithstanding that the offender is in a position to pay compensation.[20] This also applies to a term in a young offenders' institution.

8. If the offender puts forward evidence that he will be able to pay compensation, an order may be made even if he is sentenced to imprisonment.[1]

9. If counsel is instructed by his client to offer compensation in mitigation, counsel should press him in order to make sure that he can in fact pay.[2]

10. If the court has no real doubt that the offender has sufficient means, and he does nothing to disabuse it of this view, the court may impose an order and the offender cannot thereafter complain.[3]

11. A compensation order should not be made on the assumption that the offender's family or friends will assist him to find the money, or that he merely hopes to receive an unliquidated sum from an unspecified source; nor on the assumption that the payments will be made from the sale of the matrimonial home or from an asset whose value is unknown to the court.[4]

12. A compensation order can be made although the offender has no income, if he is in possession of property to which the court can give a satisfactory evaluation, irrespective of whether it is traceable to the offence in respect of which the order is made.[5]

13. An order should not be made if it is likely to aggravate a continuing bad relationship between the victim and the offender.[6]

14. An offender should not receive a reduced sentence *merely* because he is able to pay compensation. This applies *a fortiori* where one of a number of co-defendants can offer compensation but the others cannot.[7]

---

20 *Copley*, op cit.

1 *Townsend*, op cit.

2 Supra, pp 240-242.

3 *Bolden*, op cit.

4 Supra, pp 236-238.

5 *R v Martin* [1990] Crim LR 132, CA; *R v Workman* (1979) 1 Cr App Rep (S) 335, CA. Cf orders made under s 43A, supra, pp 216-217.

6 *R v Jordan* (1981) 145 JP Jo 88, CA. A compensation order imposed on the offender for an assault on her next door neighbour with whom she thought her husband was having an affair was quashed on appeal as being likely to cause trouble in the future.

7 *R v Morris* [1973] Crim LR 451, CA, and *Stapleton and Lawrie*, op cit.

Chapter Twelve

Evaluation

In this chapter we consider how the arrangements described above may be evaluated, dealing firstly with compensation by the state and secondly with compensation by the offender. The chapter concludes with a discussion of the various proposals that have been made to establish a victim compensation fund. These proposals include the suggestion that the compensation of victims of personal crime would be better served by arrangements which, if they were not part of a wider accident compensation scheme, at the least made compensation available to all such victims above a much lower financial threshold than currently obtains under the Scheme, and irrespective of the offender's means.

A. COMPENSATION BY THE STATE

(1) Instrumental values

Instrumental values are those whose adoption by policy makers as the basis for the allocation of resources are thought to result in a desired change in relevant conditions. Two groups of such values are discernible in the literature on criminal injury compensation schemes. The first is concerned with the relief of financial hardship: a criminal injuries compensation scheme should meet those financial needs created by victimisation (medical bills, loss of earnings and incidental expenses) where they are not otherwise met by private or public funds. Such a scheme is therefore a pressing matter of social policy only in those countries which provide limited support for those in need; but as we saw in chapter 1,[1] many compensation schemes go well beyond such provision.

A second set of instrumental values derive from criminal justice

1 Supra, pp 3-8.

considerations. The citizen obviously has an important role to play in the criminal justice process. Whether as gatekeepers to the mobilisation of law enforcement agencies, or as witnesses in a subsequent trial, it is considered essential that victims of crime have positive feelings about the process and its personnel, and are prepared to co-operate with them. State compensation is thought to encourage these attitudes. Likewise, it is well established that a major reason why victims do not report their injuries is because they do not think it worthwhile to do so. As it is also the case that there are very high levels of reporting of crimes for which insurance may be payable for the loss or damage sustained, some have considered that victims' negative attitudes towards reporting might be reversed if it were a preliminary to routine compensation. A further consideration is that the provision of compensation may encourage individuals to come more readily to the aid of a police officer, or to co-operate in such as neighbourhood watch schemes where the risk of victimisation may itself be higher.

To the extent that these concerns may have been influential when the Scheme was established in 1964, they have never been articulated with the degree of precision that would make them amenable to empirical testing. Elsewhere, as reviews by Lamborn,[2] and research by Elias[3] and others[4] attests, so far from encouraging pro-criminal justice sentiments in the population, the introduction of state compensation may have exacerbated existing negative attitudes. In his extensive survey of the schemes operating in New Jersey and New York State, Elias concluded of his interviews with their claimants that:

'The present, adverse attitudes of this study's victims towards criminal justice and its officials are especially alarming since much ill-will comes from victims who had applied for compensation. These claimant victims were supposed to have been induced by victim compensation toward more positive attitudes about the system, and toward greater co-operation. What is worse, however, is that not only

2 L Lamborn 'Crime victim compensation: theory and practice in the second decade' (1976) 1 Victimology 503-516, and 'Reparations for victims of crime: developments and directions' (1979) 4 Victimology 214-228.
3 R Elias *Victims of the System* (1983, Transaction Books), 'The symbolic politics of victim compensation' (1983) 8 Victimology 213-224, and 'Alienating the victim: compensation and victim attitudes' (1984) 40 J Social Issues 103-116.
4 W Doerner et al 'An analysis of victim compensation programs as a time-series experiment' (1976) 1 Victimology 295-313, and S Silverman and W Doerner 'The effect of victim compensation programs upon conviction rates' (1979) 25 Sociological Symposium 40-60.

are claimants poorly disposed toward the court system, but they are often actually significantly *more negative* than non-claimants . . .'[5]

So far as the achievement of the first subset of goals is concerned, Lamborn's review in 1979 principally of the American arrangements was equivocal, 'neither the best of the expectations nor the worst of the doubts of the 1960s has been realised'.[6] He attributed the failure of these programmes to reach the entirety of their eligible populations to a variety of factors including ignorance of the existence of the programme, an unwillingness to be subjected to formal scrutiny, delay in processing claims, excessive bureaucracy, restricted eligibility for compensation and modest fiscal allocations. These factors were likewise identified by Elias:

> 'Almost invariably, crime victims become alienated by their victimisation and by their treatment in the criminal process. Attempting to use victim compensation to overcome that alienation apparently does not succeed for most victims. Only a fraction of all victims apply, and most who do are denied an award. Even many who actually receive an award are disenchanted, usually because the payments are inadequate or because they have to contend with a series of administrative obstacles such as delay, inconvenience, and bureaucratic indifference. In fact, there seems to be greater dissatisfaction among victims who have encountered a program than among those victims who have not. Perhaps applicants' expectations rise when they learn how to apply for compensation, only to have those hopes dashed rather consistently.'[7]

To what extent does this depressing conclusion reflect the experience of 25 years of the Criminal Injuries Compensation Scheme?

(a)   SELF-EVALUATION

The Board itself appears to be in little doubt about the significance of the Scheme. In 1980, to mark 15 years of its existence, it reflected with some satisfaction: 'We think it can be said with confidence that the Scheme is now part of the nation's legal and social system',[8] a sentiment that was echoed five years later in the Report of the Home Affairs Committee, *Compensation and Support for*

---

5 Elias *Victims of the System*, p 139.
6 Lamborn (1976) p 512.
7 Elias (1984) p 113.
8 CICB 16th Report (1980, Cmnd 8081) para 1.

Victims of Crime,[9] and in the Home Secretary's observation in 1987 that the Board had 'evolved into a new social service'.[10] The Board's perception of its own significance is marked in a number of ways. In its 1980 Report the Board commented that it suspected that 'the public does not realise how many cases are dealt with under the Scheme compared with those dealt with by the courts',[11] and proceeded to make the point that each member deals with more cases each year than all the personal injury cases determined after trial in the High Court in England and Wales. However, this level of productivity generates its own costs. These appear principally in the increasing delay which exists both for the resolution of applications and the holding of hearings, whether requested by the applicant or by a single member, and which were examined by the Home Affairs Committee in 1990.[12]

Besides the statistical significance of its decisions, the Board regards some requirements of the Scheme (particularly as to reporting the incident to the police) as contributing to good citizenship, and in this respect sees itself as reinforcing 'law and order'.[13] Its conception of law and order is a conservative one, and following some comments in earlier Reports about 'senseless' and 'mindless' violence in various contexts.[14] the Board addressed

9 House of Commons, Home Affairs Committee *Compensation and Support for Victims of Crime* (1984-85, HC 43) para 31.

10 106 HC Official Report (6th series) col 471 (27 November 1986). Commending the 1986 Bill in Committee, the Minister of State observed that the Board had 'come of age', HC Official Report (6th series) Standing Committee F col 738 (24 February 1987).

11 CICB (1980) and (1982) 132 New LJ 1134.

12 House of Commons, Home Affairs Committee *Compensating Victims Quickly: the Administration of the Criminal Injuries Compensation Scheme* (1989-90, HC 92).

13 The Board's attitude to delinquent victims is consistent with this position, supra, pp 81–82.

14 CICB 13th Report (1977, Cmnd 7022) para 23 (mass disorders), 14th Report (1978, Cmnd 7396) paras 30, 51 ('a matter of astonishment' that parents permit children to play with dangerous weapons) and 32 (mass disorders), (1980) paras 28 (bouncers) and 29-30 (football violence, both on and off the pitch), 17th Report (1981, Cmnd 8401) paras 40-41 (mass disorders), 42-43 (assaults on police transport staff) and 44 (violence in sport 'a growing cancer'), 18th Report (1982, Cmnd 8752) paras 52-53 (mass disorder), and 19th Report (1983, Cmnd 9093) paras 37 and 43. The Reports for the following two years, while noting the number of claims arising from such events as the Brixton and Toxteth riots, the miners' strike and various terrorist bombings, eschewed the judgmental character of these earlier accounts, CICB 20th Report (1984, Cmnd 9399) para 43, and 21st Report (1985, Cmnd 9684) paras 44 and 45. Cf the Board's views on 'senseless and wanton violence' associated with solvent abuse (1984) para 45.

itself in 1982 in censorious tones to what it perceived to be the 'inexplicably' lenient sentencing of some offenders.[15] Such observations are, as in this instance, on occasion accompanied by references to the impact of violence upon the elderly;[16] comparisons between 'soft' sentences and injury to the vulnerable are of course a staple ingredient of the law and order lobby. This is not to deny that these offences of violence against the elderly are objectionable, but they are statistically the least common. In these respects the Board's populist views on the nature and the incidence of crime appear ill-informed, the more so given that its parent department has, through the British Crime Survey, been responsible for the substantial improvement in research in this area. Despite the protective answer which the Minister of State gave to a parliamentary question that criticised the Board's observations on sentencing, its views have been out of line with Home Office thinking.[17]

(b) CLIENT EVALUATION

Since 1964 the Board has received 498,568 applications and awarded £431,532,702 to 323,528 applicants, rejecting 77,682 in all: a 65% success rate.[18] However, because no analysis of victims' losses and attitudes was undertaken when the Scheme was established,[19] and because neither the Home Office reviews of 1978 and 1986[20] nor the Board's annual Reports have systematically analysed a sample of applications, it has never been easy to evaluate the impact of the Scheme upon its client population, either in terms of its meeting the financial consequences of personal crime, or in terms of applicants'

---

15 CICB (1982) paras 49-51. Its earlier criticisms were rather more moderate in tone, (1977) para 14, and 15th Report (1979, Cmnd 7752) para 34.

16 CICB (1977) para 15, (1978) paras 33-34, (1979) paras 31-34, and (1982) para 50.

17 437 HL Official Report (6th series) cols 116-117 (7 December 1982).

18 CICB 25th Report (1989, Cm 900) App A.

19 An important exception, though not directly related to the British Scheme, was the victimisation survey conducted by Professor Linden of Osgoode Hall Law School, Toronto.

20 Home Office, *Review of the Criminal Injuries Compensation Scheme: Report of an Interdepartmental Working Party* (1978), *Criminal Injuries Compensation: a Statutory Scheme* (1986).

dealings with the Board. Aspects of these questions are now illuminated by the Reports of the Home Affairs Committee and by research conducted by Shapland[1] and Newburn,[2] but as a public body currently with a budget of £77m, the Board has remained remarkably under-researched. It may be that because it confers no rights enforceable at law (notwithstanding the availability of judicial review), extensive research evaluating the impact of the Scheme has not been considered either urgent or especially necessary. However, the critical reception accorded by the Home Affairs Committee in 1990 to the backlog of applications at the Board suggests that a number of matters stand in need of clarification.

(i) The eligible population

Any evaluation of the success of the Scheme in delivering compensation to victims of personal crime assumes a relatively close estimate of the client base. As we saw in chapter 2, there is a pressing need for research on the size of the eligible population.[3] As the Home Affairs Committee made quite clear, such information is important for determining future levels of funding for the Board, both for administration and for the purpose of compensation, and for determining the relative frequency, of the kind of serious injury for which the Scheme now seems to be intended.[4] As the compensation gap which has already appeared between those victims fortunate enough to come within its terms and those whose offenders have the means to pay the ideal assessment of the injury widens further, it will also become desirable to consider the wisdom of a policy that leaves uncompensated those whose injuries are worth less than the Scheme's lower limit, and whose convicted offenders (assuming a prosecution) have insufficient means to pay a

---

1 J Shapland et al *Victims in the Criminal Justice System* (1985, Gower) ch 9.
2 T Newburn *The Settlement of Claims at the Criminal Injuries Compensation Board* (1989, Home Office Research Study 112).
3 Supra, pp 29-36. There are, however, considerable methodological difficulties, in particular in devising an instrument that would catch a usable sample; only 21 victims of personal crime were uncovered in a sample of 5,036 respondents in the Compensation Survey conducted by the Centre for Socio-Legal Studies, D Harris et al *Compensation and Support for Illness and Injury* (1984, Oxford UP) ch 12.
4 House of Commons (1989-90) para 24.

compensation order. Currently we have little idea of the size of this population.

(ii) Claims consciousness

Assuming a reasonable estimate of the size of the eligible population, it is also important to research the level of claims consciousness, particularly as the Home Office has published new leaflets, including the *Victim's Charter*, explaining how compensation may be available from the Board. Who applies, with what legal advice or representation, and for what reasons? Conversely, why do those who prima facie have a compensable injury, not apply? This information is again of financial and administrative importance, but it would also help to answer the question whether the Scheme is reaching those whose pecuniary or non-pecuniary losses are not otherwise being met from private insurance or public benefit.[5]

(iii) Client satisfaction: hearings

As we saw in chapter 2, all applications have been dealt with firstly by a single member on the basis of documentary evidence alone, with an oral hearing before three other members of the Board if the applicant is dissatisfied. With the possibility of some initial decisions being taken by the Board's staff, the introduction of pre-conditions to the grant of a hearing, and the reduction in the number of Board members sitting at a hearing to two, this two-tiered structure continues under the 1990 revisions.

Difficulties arise, however, when one tries to determine whether applicants are satisfied with the outcome of their applications. The Board's Reports do not permit a comparison to be made simply between the number of cases resolved in any one year and the number of requests by applicants for hearings in that year, since the latter may well refer to an application resolved in a previous year. However, making this comparison over a series of the Board's Reports suggests that until 1982-83, about 90% of single member decisions were accepted. The 1983-84 Report notes a 43% increase in hearing requests by applicants (4,339),[6] which figure fell to 4,244 in the following year.[7] Despite this reduction to around 85% of single member decisions, these figures suggest a high level of satisfaction; in 1988-89 the figure for

5 Ibid, paras 44-46.
6 CICB (1984) para 51.
7 CICB (1985) para 9.

hearing requests was 6,037, but this increase of 32% over 1987-88 is probably attributable simply to a higher number of case resolutions.[8] In the absence of any large-scale research we may only speculate as to the reasons why those who might wish to request a hearing do not do so, assuming that the population of dissatisfied applicants is indeed greater than those who do take action.

One obvious factor is access to legal or other representation. Until the Board discontinued giving the figures, about a third of applicants were professionally advised when making an application, and a further 20% were advised by their trade union representatives.[9] There is no way of knowing from the published Reports, how many of these applicants were dissatisfied with the single member decisions and how many requested hearings, nor how these proportions might compare with unrepresented applicants. Nor can we know how many were dissatisfied but were discouraged from pursuing matters to a hearing by the unavailability of legal aid or the advice of their representatives. However, there does appear to be some correlation between legal representation and success at the hearing stage. The Board's 11th Report shows that 60% of applicants were represented at the hearing, either by a lawyer (55%) or by a trade union official (5%). Though the Board has indicated that it will assist the unrepresented applicant, their success rate (45%) compared badly with those who were represented, 71% with a lawyer, 85% with a trade union official.[10] It may well be that some groups of victims, notably the police, whose representatives are familiar with the Board's practices, do generally stand a better chance of increasing an award at a hearing, but there are no figures publicly available to confirm or deny this.

However, even these figures are by no means unambiguous. The Board's experience is that there is widespread variation in the quality of advice given by practitioners at hearings. To a considerable extent it is a matter of expertise in personal injury cases, bringing out, for example, in the case of a victim who sustained a back injury, that he has to sleep in an orthopaedic bed, or can no longer enjoy gardening or swimming, or in the case of a victim who suffered facial scarring, its impact on his

---

8 CICB (1989) para 10.2.

9 CICB (1980) para 34. Four years later the Board did not consider that there had been any significant change in this pattern of representation, (1984) para 50.

10 CICB 11th Report (1975, Cmnd 6291) para 17. Whether the applicant would, however, perceive the Board's advocate as being 'neutral' is open to question.

employment prospects. Some fail even to mention comparable cases from the Board's own Reports, whether based on its own guidelines or reported in Kemp and Kemp,[11] which suggests that some applicants who do achieve an increased award do so despite rather than because of the presence of their lawyers.

Other considerations dissuading applicants from requesting a hearing which Shapland noted in her sample were an inability to understand how the award was made up, with a consequent inability to identify the 'appealable' issue, while others felt that, given the ex gratia nature of the award, it would be wrong to complain about what they perceived to be a gift.[12] It is also the case that, being heard *de novo*, the members at the hearing may reduce or even deny altogether an award made by the single member. Factors such as these may thus deter those who would otherwise be minded to request a hearing, although it may be observed that the success rate of those applicants in Newburn's sample who did seek either an increase in the single Member's award or an award where none was originally given, was high, just over 80% and nearly 60% respectively.[13]

No doubt welcomed by the applicants, this success rate is disquieting if it is generalisable. Though based on only 23 successful hearing requests, in 18 cases a nil award was changed, from a minimum of £400-500 to, in one case, an award of over £5,000, and in the five cases in which the original sum was under review, the percentage increase ranged from 47% to 650%. As Newburn pertinently asks:

> 'What is it about the method of assessment by single Board members that allows such gross underestimations of compensation? Following on from this, how many cases are there which are underestimated or undervalued in such a way? Finally, what proportion of those applicants whose injuries are underestimated, actually request a hearing? . . . It is difficult to see how members of the public would be in a position to judge whether the sum of money they have been offered by the Board is a realistic one or not, and unless they have specialist legal advice it seems likely that the majority of applicants who request hearings will be those who contest the rejection of the application rather than the size of their award . . . Until there is more research . . . these questions will remain unanswered.'[14]

11 *The Quantum of Damages* (Sweet & Maxwell).
12 Shapland et al (1985) pp 166-167. The question arises whether this perception will change as victims are encouraged by such as the *Victim's Charter* to consider that they have a 'right' to compensation.
13 Newburn (1989) pp 22-23.
14 Ibid, p 24. The Official Solicitor has routinely requested hearings with a view to increasing quantum, and claims always to have succeeded.

(iv) Client satisfaction: resolution time

Whereas it appears that a substantial majority of applicants are satisfied (or at least not so dissatisfied as to take action) with the outcome of their applications, a major ground of discontent concerns the increasing delays that attend their resolution.[15] About 70% of applications are received within three months of the incident, but early submission (though encouraged by the participation of victim support groups) will 'not usually result in a commensurately early award; the resolution of an application normally has to await the outcome of criminal proceedings, a firm medical prognosis and, possibly, inspection of residual scarring or disfigurement.'[16]

The Board in fact faces two problems which are very closely linked. The first is delay in the resolution of applications. The length of time within which applications are resolved has deteriorated rapidly over the past two-three years. In 1988-89, 1.0% of applications were resolved within three months, 2.1% between three-six months, 4.8% between six-nine months, 19.0% between nine-twelve months and 73.1% over twelve months.[17] No more than five years ago, these figures were 5%, 27.3%, 25.2%, 17.0% and 25.5% respectively, and even in 1986-87 nearly 50% of applications were resolved within a year; as the Home Affairs Committee put it: 'In simple terms, most victims can now expect to wait at least a year until their claim is met. Fifteen years ago, around 1 in 20 had to do so.'[18] Furthermore, the category 'over 12 months' disguises the fact that a number of applications take over 18 months to resolve, which prompted Newburn to suggest that the Board should amend its classification;[19] such an obvious indicator of the increasing delay in resolving

---

15 This is by no means a new complaint, but has been frequently raised in the past, eg 985 HC Official Report (5th series) col 790 (5 June 1980), 7 HC Official Report (6th series) cols 14-15 (22 June 1981), 27 HC Official Report (6th series) cols 438-39 (15 July 1982), 31 HC Official Report (6th series) cols 283-84 (12 November 1982), and 45 HC Official Report (6th series) cols 356-58 (13 July 1983). An application for judicial review of the Board's two-year delay in resolving a claim was made in 1990, Times, 30 April 1990.

16 CICB (1977) para 6. An example of delay caused by instability in the applicant's medical condition is the application made in 1968 which could not be finalised until 1984 (a number of interim awards were made) 56 HC Official Report (6th series) col 324 (19 March 1984). See also CICB (1977) paras 32-33, (1978) para 40, (1979) paras 36-37, (1980) para 31, (1981) paras 46-47, (1982) paras 56-57, and (1983) para 39.

17 CICB (1989) para 6.1.

18 House of Commons (1989-90) para 5.

19 Newburn (1989) p 8.

applications is unlikely to prove attractive. The second is the 'appalling backlog'[20] of applications that is substantially a consequence of these delays, now amounting to over 92,000 applications, and representing two years' work for the Board without more.[1] However, the backlog is not only a consequence of delay: as the Home Affairs Committee observed, it in turn causes further delay as case workers are diverted from the task of dealing with the newly arrived applications to answer phone calls from anxious applicants.[2]

The Board is by no means sanguine about this situation, and has endeavoured to make allowances in its procedures, but the comments in its 25th Report suggest that it is resigned to there being a substantial backlog for the foreseeable future.[3] In its investigation of this issue, the Home Affairs Committee identified two varieties of delay. The first, investigative delay, is inevitable. However, even allowing for the fact that the Board must rely on the co-operation of other agencies and individuals for the verification and completion of the information supplied by the applicant,[4] the Committee was critical of the procedures adopted by the Board for monitoring progress at the investigative stage. So far as administrative delay was concerned, the Committee considered that two factors were mainly responsible: inadequate resourcing and inefficient procedures. Much of the evidence presented to the Committee concerned the allocation of responsibility for resourcing; the CICB arguing that the Home Office had consistently failed over the years to predict accurately each year's increase in applications and thus had under-funded the Board, the Home Office replying that its predictions, which had been as carefully prepared as data and its own resources allowed, had in recent years been confounded by substantial fluctuations in the application rate. Eschewing a post-mortem, the Committee agreed that the Board had probably not been

---

20 Sir Michael Ogden QC, a former Chairman of the Board, CICB 22nd Report (1986, Cm 42) para 1 and House of Commons (1984-85) para 30. One consequence of delay is that the eventual award may have to be increased to reflect the functional overlay affecting the victim, CICB (1984) para 52. See also (1977) paras 7-8 and 34, (1978) paras 7-9 and 42-43, (1979) paras 12-14 and 38, (1980) paras 14 and 32, (1981) paras 4-5 and 48-49, (1982) paras 7 and 58-61, and (1983) paras 3-5.

1 CICB (1989) para 1.3.

2 House of Commons (1989-90) para 14.

3 CICB (1989) paras 1.1-1.7.

4 The Board's routine reliance on other agencies (police, hospitals, doctors, employers and the DSS) is highlighted in CICB (1985) paras 3-5, (1986) para 1 and (1989) para 1.4.

sufficiently well funded and recommended an immediate increase of 60 staff, but also observed that notwithstanding the increases that had taken place, productivity had declined from 169.1 applications resolved per staff member in 1980-81 (155 staff) to 124.5 in 1988-89 (312 staff).[5]

The Committee identified the Board's cumbersome procedures as a major reason for this deterioration. One aspect is its record system, which a Rayner scrutiny concluded in 1982 was a shambles, and which the Committee considered had only slightly improved. To some extent this also represents a failure to resource the Board adequately with appropriate information technology, and it recommended immediate action on this matter.[6] Other facets of the Board's procedures which the Committee concluded would repay consideration concerned the obtaining of external advice on the layout of its application forms and the calculation of loss of earnings, and of better quality medical evidence.[7] Beyond these, a prime factor contributing to low productivity was the failure of the second Board office established in Glasgow to come on stream as quickly as had been expected;[8] this in turn had created poor conditions for work and low staff morale, for whom the CICB represented a career backwater.[9]

How long it will take for the measures adopted in response to the Committee's Report to effect a significant cut in the backlog and to reverse the trend to longer delay in the resolution of applications remains to be seen. These measures include procedural priority being given to applications from elderly victims,[10] but in the long term much more important are the structural changes which are intended to make yet more efficient use of the Board's members, the one group who escaped censure.[11]

(v) The role of the police

The police perform an important role in connection with the Scheme. They will frequently be the source of initial information about the Board, and will no doubt be asked by the victim for an informal assessment of his chances of a successful application. Later in the process, they will be asked to verify the details of

---

5 House of Commons (1989-90) paras 14-16.
6 Ibid, paras 27-30.
7 Ibid, paras 33-34, and 36.
8 Ibid, para 16.
9 Ibid, paras 13, and 31-32.
10 (1989) 139 New LJ 547.
11 House of Commons (1989-90) paras 8-12.

the incident reported to them, will be asked whether the applicant is known to them in any way, and may be asked to appear at a hearing. How the police routinely discharge these gatekeeping, verifying and judgmental functions is an unknown quantity, yet a critical one.

(vi)   The exercise of discretion by the Board

Further research is required on a number of aspects of the Board's implementation of the Scheme. Newburn noted a willingness on the part of the Board to interpret the lower limit somewhat generously in connection with applications by the elderly.[12] It would be instructive to ascertain whether this is a general tendency in such cases, and to compare it against other applicant groups. He also noted that it was not possible to discern in his sample any clear differentiation in the Board's treatment of applicants with prior convictions from its treatment of those without; given that in these cases the formal text of the Scheme at least permits variation (unlike the lower limit), there is a need for elucidation. There was also evidence both of discrepant assessments for similar injuries and, as noted earlier, of substantial under-assessments.

(vii)   The Board's Reports

These are the only regular source of information about the implementation of the Scheme, and could be improved. They routinely contain statistics on numbers of new applications, applications resolved, hearings, the size of awards and the cost of the Scheme. However, the Board has, over the years, discontinued some tables which the Reports once contained, of which representation and success at hearings is an example. Another is a comparison between the rate of new applications and the numbers of notifiable offences falling within the Scheme's definition of a criminal injury recorded in the *Criminal Statistics*. It is true that there will be no direct relationship between these figures, if only because they relate to different time periods, but their absence, like others discontinued in the name of cost,[13] serves to make it more difficult for the interested reader to identify, for example, any increase or decrease in the ratio of claimants to recorded offences.

Besides the tables, the Reports typically contain a selection of applications chosen to illustrate particular aspects of the

12 Newburn (1989) pp 14-15.
13 Editorial 'Criminal injuries' (1980) 130 New LJ 1163.

Scheme, for example, the definition of a crime of violence, reduction or refusal of an award because of the victim's behaviour or biography, pain and suffering assessments, and assessment in fatal cases. From the standpoint of the potential applicant, these are now better presented than in the past, typically commencing with a resume of the requirements of the Scheme and the Board's approach to them. In addition, the Board will often highlight what it perceives to be a recurring problem, for example, sporting injuries,[14] co-operation with the police,[15] offences committed by children,[16] and the problems of delay. Of course these are all important issues, but they are ones selected by the Board to present its view as to their diagnosis and resolution; there is simply no opportunity to examine the Board's records to judge whether another point of view might be a valid interpretation of events.

(2) Symbolic values

As Rock has reminded us, it would be unwise to see general shifts in social values, and more particularly in connection with the victims' movement, as being attributable to a single event,[17] but one of the most notable features of the introduction of criminal injury compensation schemes in common law jurisdictions has been that they were often the direct result of the commission of an offence of violence against a vulnerable or an altruistic victim. This was true, for example, of the earliest schemes introduced in the 1960s, in New Zealand, Ontario and New York;[18] the first full House of Lords debate for 17 years was prompted by the murder of an MP's daughter.[19] The symbolic value of criminal victimisation had long been recognised;[20] what took place during the 1960s in both Great Britain and North America was the *politicisation* of the symbol, that is, its explicit

14 CICB (1987) para 37.
15 CICB (1986) paras 25-36.
16 CICB (1978) paras 30-31, and (1979) paras 21-22.
17 P Rock *A View from the Shadows* (1986, Oxford UP) pp 79-93.
18 For New Zealand see B Cameron 'Compensation of victims of crime: the New Zealand experiment' (1963) 12 J Public Law 367-375, for Ontario and New York, H Edelhertz and G Geis *Public Compensation to Victims of Crime* (1974, Praeger) pp 21-38, and 243. See also D Chappell 'Compensating Australian victims of violent crimes' (1967) 41 Aust LJ 3-11.
19 Lord Longford, 395 HL Official Report (5th series) col 255 (18 July 1978).
20 L Henderson 'The wrongs of victims' rights' (1985-86) 37 Stanford LR 937-1021.

use for political purposes, in particular, in connection with successive governments' credibility in matters of penal policy and reform.

In contrast to the punitive values embodied in earlier regimes, the penal policies of most common law jurisdictions during the late 1950s and early 1960s were informed by a more liberal ideology that in Great Britain found expression in a variety of measures: the first steps were taken to abolish the death penalty,[1] imprisonment for offenders under 21 was effectively removed,[2] the Report of the Streatfield Committee ushered in a fresh approach to the sentencing process,[3] and the Home Office paved the way for the introduction of suspended sentences and the Parole Board in the Criminal Justice Act 1967. The demand for reform in penal policy was at once matched by an equally vigorous campaign that 'something be done' for victims of crime. Invidious comparisons were drawn between the lot of the victim of crime, and that of the offender. These comparisons formed much of the evidence that fired a vocal moral panic: victims were neglected and ignored, while offenders were excused their wrongdoing and cosseted by the state. The tenor of this campaign is well summed up in the Report of the Massachusetts Special Commission on victim compensation:

'Consider the plight of the innocent victim of a violent crime . . . After he is picked up off the pavement and delivered to the handiest hospital (where, of course, responsibility for his repair is his own), he slowly mends and resigns himself to any permanent impairment. He also resigns himself to the loss of pay he suffers during his recovery. Finally he can return to work — if the job is still there. But the state is not satisfied, there must be a trial. The victim is a key witness to a crime. He must give up more of his time, more of his pay, relive an unpleasant experience, and submit himself to questioning, the object of which can be to impugn his dignity, competence and integrity. When it is finally over, he can watch the prisoner being led away to free room, board, recreation to which he contributes through his tax payments. The prosecutor, the police and the judge give him his recompense; a few words of praise for his public spirited co-operation.

Such an individual would have earned the right to label as a callous, barbaric, foolish hypocrite anyone, including political scientists or

---

1 Murder (Abolition of the Death Penalty) Act 1965.
2 Criminal Justice Act 1961.
3 *Interdepartmental Committee on the Business of the Criminal Courts* (1961, Cmnd 1289).

journalists, who tried to convince him of the importance of individuals to the functioning of our democratic institutions.'4

Leaving aside the substantive points of difference between the United States and Great Britain in the matter of the public provision of health care and of welfare benefits, these sentiments accurately reflect the substance of the moral panic that 'something be done' for victims of crime.5 Any perceived discrepant treatment continues to be highlighted by juxtaposing paradigm victims such as the elderly or the vulnerable with paradigm offenders such as teenage delinquents. The following is a typical example:

> 'Rarely does a weekend go by . . . without news . . . of someone being mugged or someone's home being broken into, lives shattered and people left helpless after gangs of marauding youngsters have ransacked homes for little or no financial gain.'6

This moral panic has, in recent years, achieved, at least in the United States, a significant shift in criminal justice and penal policy which contemplates, in some measure, a return to more retributive values.7 While evidence of such a shift in this country is equivocal, there can be no doubt of the continued use of the

---

4 Commonwealth of Massachusetts *Report of the Special Commission on the Compensation of Victims of Violent Crimes* (1967, House no 5151) p 13. In similar vein, an article by a lawyer who had been attacked, L Spry-Leverton, Guardian, 2 May 1985.

5 Correspondence in the Times, 15 and 20 March 1976. Earlier that year a survey carried out by the Police Federation reported that 8/10 respondents accepted the view that 'too much is done for criminals and not enough for the victim', The Times, 22 January 1976. This discrepancy was a 'thumping national disgrace', Times, 3 February 1976. In 1979 Lord Longford, 401 HL Official Report (5th series), col 229, commenting on the 'massive increase in crime' between 1962 and 1978 observed that while every other associated social issue had been debated, there was a 'deafening silence' on its victims. See also the earlier debate initiated by Lord Longford, 395 HL Official Report (op cit) cols 255-307 in which he proposed a Minister for Victims, which the government regarded as 'arrant nonsense', 955 HC Official Report (5th series) col 929 (3 August 1978).

6 D Alton MP, 26 HC Official Report (6th series) col 903 (20 June 1982). Further examples can readily be found in the press, especially the tabloids. The use of paradigm victims — the elderly and women (especially widows living alone) — to highlight perceived penal injustice is so deeply rooted that any criticism that relies upon them appears entirely unreflective, eg on the restoration of the death penalty, Times, 5 and 6 July 1983, on sentences for firearms offences, Times, 19 September 1983.

7 Henderson (1985-86).

stereotypical victim of crime for the purpose of criticising the criminal justice and penal systems.

If critics of the system were quick to rely upon apparent discrepancies in the treatment of offenders and victims, neither were those responsible for formulating penal policy slow to recognise the political capital that could be made by juxtaposing neglect of the victim with care for the offender. Both the credibility of official penal policy and the acceptability of reform were regarded by the Home Office as being seriously challenged by public sensitivity to any discrepancy:

> 'The assumption that the claims of the victim are sufficiently satisfied if the offender is punished by society becomes less persuasive as society in its dealing with offenders increasingly emphasises the reformative aspects of punishment. Indeed in the public mind the interests of the offender may not infrequently seem to be placed before those of the victim. This is certainly not the correct emphasis . . .'[8]

This observation was cited approvingly a few years later in the White Paper, 'Compensation for Victims of Crimes of Violence' which included the specific proposals that became the Criminal Injuries Compensation Scheme.[9]

A key feature of the comparison between the state's treatment of victims and offenders to which attention was and continues to be drawn, is, as noted above, an apparent difference in the *direct* government funding of their respective interests. A common, but highly misleading tactic is to posit, for example, that for every £1 spent on the offender, 1p is spent on the victim.[10] To satisfy the demand that 'something be done' for victims of crime, any compensatory arrangements established had therefore to be both *visibly* and *uniquely* directed to the victim of crime. As the California legislature soon discovered, to treat victims

---

8 Home Office *Penal Practice in a Changing Society* (1959, Cmnd 645) p 7.
9 Home Office *Compensation for Victims of Crimes of Violence* (1963, Cmnd 2323) para 2.
10 D Alton MP, 26 HC Official Report, op cit, col 903. See further, 38 HC Official Report (6th series) cols 359-360 (3 March 1983). In 1985 the government acknowledged (82 HC Official Report (6th series) col 234 (4 July 1985)) that the total of the Home Office vote being expended on the CICB and the NAVSS was 3.4% of the allocated law and order budget, but also observed 'that this took no account of the "unquantifiable" time and money expended by the police and the DSS; which benefits should not be underrated', see Lord Allen, 395 HL Official Report (5th series), op cit, col 284.

of crime on the same terms as the indigent, the sick and the disabled, was not merely an insufficient gesture, but was widely regarded by the victims' lobby as adding insult to injury.[11] Likewise, Elias found that the need basis of the New York programme was viewed negatively by its clients, whereas the New Jersey programme, which entitled the victim to compensation without more, elicited a more positive response.[12] The demand that victims of crime be treated uniquely among the disadvantaged has resulted in the anomalous situation that those jurisdictions with limited welfare programmes typically administer compensation schemes which accord victims not significantly more than those benefits to which they would in this country be entitled via the NHS and the DSS, while in those countries (including Great Britain and Northern Ireland) where such benefits are already provided, victims of crime have more financial assistance than that which is available to the victims of disease or injury. The politics of victimisation require that victims of crime be treated *differently from* and *better than* other victims, and be distinguished from them by the allocation of additional financial resources.

Given this background, it is not surprising perhaps that those who supported the introduction of special arrangements for victims of personal crime found it difficult to identify a justificatory base beyond appeals to humanitarianism or the need to redress the balance in favour of the victim as part of a broader law and order package which could be initiated at little cost;[13] certainly, once a scheme had been suggested, it would not be, as Edelhertz and Geis observed in their review of the United States' schemes, 'the best kind of politics for an elected official to be seen as antagonistic to the interests of innocent victims of violent crimes.'[14] The legislative confusion that accompanied the introduction of the Scheme in 1964 was, for Chappell and Sutton, 'compelling evidence that compensation is not and never was conceived as anything more than a symbolic palliative for victims of crime.'[15] Viewed simply as an expression of populist

11 Edelhertz and Geis (1974) pp 76-92.
12 Elias *Victims of the System* ch 9.
13 R Meiners *Victim Compensation: Economic, Legal and Political Aspects* (1978, Lexington Books) ch 6. See also R Mawby and M Gill *Crime Victims* (1987, Tavistock) ch 3.
14 Edelhertz and Geis (1974) p 1.
15 D Chappell and L Sutton 'Evaluating the effectiveness of programs to compensate the victims of crime' in I Drapkin and E Viano eds *Victimology: a New Focus* (1974, Lexington Books) pp 207-220, 212.

values about crime, the question whether the Scheme serves any instrumental values thus assumes a secondary importance. It is essential that the Scheme does not deliver compensation to delinquent victims, but its success in reaching all who might constitute its client base is not central to the message.

B. COMPENSATION BY THE OFFENDER

There are many benefits claimed for the principle of compensation by the offender. Some see it primarily as a means of benefiting the victim, recouping some or all of the loss he has suffered as a result of the offence. Such benefit is usually associated with compensation for property offences, though it may equally be advocated in association with offences against the person, even if the loss here is typically less easy to determine. Others emphasise the benefits for the offender, commonly including some element of rehabilitation together with an emphasis on the harm done to his victim as a means of moral education.[16] Connected with this is the more pragmatic objective of separating the offender from the proceeds of his offences, an objective which substantially informed the recommendations of the Advisory Committee on the Penal System in 1970 and the Hodgson Committee in 1978,[17] and which finds expression, for example, in confiscation orders made under the Drug Trafficking Act 1986 and the Criminal Justice Act 1988. Compensating victims, when coupled with such as mediation or reparation schemes, is strongly favoured as a method by which suitable offenders can be diverted from an increasingly ineffective and costly penal system.[18]

16 R Barnett 'Restitution: a new paradigm of criminal justice' (1976) 87 Ethics 279-301, J Harding *Victims and Offenders: Needs and Responsibilities* (1982, Bedford Square Press), M Wasik 'The place of compensation in the penal system' [1978] Crim LR 599-611, and M Wright *Making Good* (1982, Burnett Books).

17 Advisory Council on the Penal System *Reparation by the Offender* (1970, Home Office) paras 8 and 9 and Sir D Hodgson *The Profits of Crime and their Recovery* (1984, Heinemann) chs 6, 9-13. See further M Wasik 'The Hodgson Committee Report on the Profits of Crime and their Recovery' [1984] Crim LR 708-725.

18 T Marshall *Reparation, Conciliation and Mediation* (1984, Home Office Research and Planning Unit paper 27), T Marshall and M Walpole *Bringing People Together* (1985, Home Office Research and Planning Unit paper 33), G Davies et al *A Preliminary Study of Victim Offender Mediation and Reparation Schemes in England and Wales* (1987, Home Office Research

Compensation by offenders has also been thought to benefit the criminal justice system, conducing to higher levels of reporting offences and to greater co-operation with the police (including law enforcement by citizens). However, though a majority of victims do wish to be compensated by their offenders,[19] Shapland's study showed that while those receiving compensation were significantly more positive about the courts than those who were not, neither their attitude towards the police nor their preparedness to report offences was in any way affected. She concluded that her study gave 'no support' to the idea that compensating the victim would increase general co-operation with the criminal justice system.[20] In terms of penal theory, as the White Paper, *Crime, Justice and Protecting the Public* illustrates, increased opportunities for compensation by offenders can be seen as a primary means of restoring the social equity that was disturbed by the offence;[1] while at a societal level, offender compensation is thought to re-establish the kind of cohesion associated with a Durkheimian organic model in which restitutive law plays a major role.[2] Whether the present emphasis on compensation and restitution will regenerate ideas of a society characterised by individual responsibility for harm to others is a moot point, but what is beyond question is the political mileage associated with such emphasis.

Like state-funded compensation, it seems churlish to question the goodness and simplicity of proposals for compensation by the offender. In part the argument relies upon a characterisation of legal history in which, before his rights became subordinated to the state's interest in crime, the victim could proceed at will

and Planning Unit paper 42), J Pointing ed *Alternatives to Custody* (1987, Basil Blackwell), C Williams 'Reparation and mediation in the criminal justice system' (1986) 136 New LJ 1106-1108, and S Walklate 'Reparation: a Merseyside view' (1986) 36 BJ Crim 267-279. Restitution may also reduce punitive feelings against offenders, W Harrell 'Aggression against a remorseful offender: the effects of self-blame and concern for the victim' 107 J Social Psychology 267-275, and B Galaway 'The use of restitution' (1977) 23 Crime and Delinquency 57-67.

19 M Hough and P Mayhew *Taking Account of Crime* (1985, Home Office Research Study 85) pp 44-45, and Shapland et al (1985) pp 121-123.

20 Shapland, p 139.

1 Home Office (1990, Cm 965). See generally A Ashworth *Sentencing and Penal Policy* (1983, Weidenfeld and Nicolson) passim.

2 A Bottoms 'Neglected features of contemporary penal systems' in eds D Garland and P Young *The Power to Punish* (1983, Heinemann) pp 198-199. See also R Boldt 'Restitution, criminal law and the ideology of individuality' (1987) 77 J Criminal Law and Criminology 962-1022, and N Christie 'Conflicts as property' (1977) 27 BJ Crim 1-15.

against his assailant,[3] but whether there was ever, as the romantically inclined have supposed, a 'golden age' of the victim, is open to question.[4] Nevertheless, the notion that offender compensation is a pure working out of an offence against the individual remains persuasive. In 1974, for example, the Canada Law Reform Commission published a working paper which commences a discussion of restitution with a sentiment so beguiling that it makes one wonder why it is not a universal feature of our penal system:

> 'Doesn't it seem to be a rejection of common sense that a convicted offender is rarely made to pay for the damage he has done? Isn't it surprising that the victim generally gets nothing for his loss? Restitution — making the offender pay or work to restore the damage . . . [with compensation by the state where this is not possible] would seem to be the natural thing for sentencing policy and practice.'[5]

There are however, two main difficulties. The first stems from the very proliferation of benefits claimed for compensation by offenders. The issue here is what priority is to be attached to these various objectives when it comes to such matters as the allocation of scarce resources and the determination of their operational parameters. Reviewing the programmes developed in the United States, Scutt observed

> 'originally endorsed as a means of bringing the victim back into the criminal justice system and giving due and proper consideration to his or her needs, an analysis of the schemes operating in the United States recently concluded that the major force behind most of them was that of rehabilitating the offender. The victim was not seen as a prime beneficiary.'[6]

3 J Greenberg 'The victim in historical perspective' (1984) 40 J Social Issues 77-101, A Harland 'Monetary remedies for the victims of crime: assessing the role of the criminal courts' (1982) 30 U Calif Los Angeles LR 52-128 and 'One hundred years of restitution' (1983) 8 Victimology 190-203, S Schafer *Compensation and Restitution to Victims of Crime* (1970, Patterson Smith) pp 9-11, M Wolfgang 'Victim compensation in crimes of personal violence' (1965) 50 Minn LR 223-241.

4 R Epstein 'Crime and tort: old wine in new bottles' in R Barnett and J Hagel eds *Assessing the Criminal: Restitution, Retribution and the Legal Process* (1977, Ballinger Books) 231-257.

5 Canada Law Reform Commission *Restitution and Compensation* (1974, Working paper 5) 5. P Stenning and S Ciano 'Restitution and Compensation and Fines' (1975) Ottawa LR 316-329.

6 J Scutt 'Victims, offenders and restitution: real alternatives or panacea?' (1982) 56 Aust LJ 156-167, 162.

While giving priority to the offender will disappoint the victim and dissatisfy some of those otherwise in favour of restitution, it does at least resolve another matter connected with this proliferation of objectives, namely, how to formulate a research instrument that would be sensitive enough to discriminate between them in the attempt to discover whether any or all of them were being realised in practice.

The second main difficulty lies in the organisational and operational realities of ensuring routine compensation by offenders, which Klein identified in a powerful critique some years ago,[7] many of which have been identified in earlier chapters. To put the matter shortly, these principally involve: the competing demands of other penal objectives in any given case, the impecuniosity of the offender and the need to ensure equity for those dependent on him, the unavailability of discovery which is routine in civil litigation, the unsuitability of criminal courts should the offender wish to challenge the extent of his liability or the victim's assessment of non-pecuniary loss, the implications for plea-bargaining, the reluctance of the criminal courts to become involved in further debt collection, the paradox of offenders being threatened with imprisonment for default in the payment of what is in essence a settlement of their civil liability, the pressure to trade liberty or leniency for compensation, the problem of sentencing the very poor and the very rich, and the determination of victims' needs. Nor is this all, for there will be other difficulties in the choice of operational parameters where there is conflict about the programme's objectives. Depending on whether a compensation/restitution programme scheme is principally designed to benefit the offender or the victim, pressure will be brought to bear on the other to co-operate to make the programme effective, but what if the victim makes unreasonable or even dishonest demands. or refuses to help? At what point does it become unethical to request compliance with the programme's objectives?[8]

Admittedly not all of these difficulties will affect all proposals for offender compensation equally. Where compensation is available only on conviction, the question of victim co-operation assumes little significance. On the other hand, this is clearly of importance in mediation programmes of which restitution by the offender forms a part. Likewise the unsuitability to a

---

7 J Klein 'Revitalising restitution: flogging a dead horse that may have been killed in a just cause' (1978) 20 Crim LQ 383-408.

8 Scutt (1982) p 164.

reparation scheme of the offender or of the offence committed will be of little significance if the offender has sufficient means to pay the ideal assessment of the victim's injury by way of a compensation order. However, if it is expected that offenders are to reimburse their victims in whole or in part in any case in which it is possible, by whatever judicial or extra-judicial device, then there will inevitably remain some victims who will go uncompensated. This is so simply because there has never been full enforcement of the criminal justice system, and it would take a significant re-orientation of criminal justice priorities, including a substantial increase in funding, to ensure that all offenders, where known, were made amenable to some variety of victim reimbursement.

Klein argued that any proposals to make restitution a central goal of the criminal justice system would create philosophical, legal and operational problems of an acute nature, and that such proposals were fundamentally dishonest since they would never be able to deliver what they promised; in short, 'the assumption that correctional restitution will probably assist a significant proportion of victims of crime is probably unwarranted.'[9] His misgivings are germane to the 1990 White Paper's conception of offender compensation as an integral part of punishment in the community,[10] in particular as the realisation of the more modest goals of s 35 of the Powers of Criminal Courts Act 1973 has proved problematic.

(1) The use of compensation orders

While the criminal courts have, since 1972, enjoyed a wide power to order convicted persons to compensate their victims, all the research conducted to date shows that it has been relatively infrequently used in personal injury cases.[11] As Newburn's important 1988 study confirms,[12] things have changed very little despite the introduction in 1982 of the statutory preference for compensation over a fine where the offender's means cannot meet both, and the exhortations from successive Home Secretaries and

---

9 (1978) p 401.
10 Home Office (1990) ch 4.
11 P Softley *Compensation for Injury* (1976, Home Office Research Unit Bulletin No 3) and *Compensation Orders in Magistrates' Courts* (1978, Home Office Research Study 43), J Vennard 'Magistrates' assessments of compensation for injury' [1979] Crim LR 510-523, and Shapland et al (1985) pp 136–137.
12 Op cit.

others, that magistrates should order compensation wherever possible.[13] With the introduction in the Criminal Justice Act 1988 of the duty to give reasons where a court does not make an order, there is a further opportunity to conduct research into both the manner in which the courts discharge this duty and the increase or otherwise in the making of compensation orders in consequence of it.

Newburn's study involved three components, a national survey of 271 magistrates' courts all of which were sent the same form asking questions about their assessment of the suitability for compensation of a specified number of cases,[14] a focused sample taken from four magistrates' courts with the specific objective of studying the enforcement of compensation orders, and interviews with magistrates, enforcement staff, justices' clerks and victims. Despite the variations in the workload and case composition of the respondent courts, the survey was felt to be representative of magistrates' courts generally. The survey yielded 1,313 returns in which there was an identifiable victim and where compensation was theoretically possible, and in 903 cases an order was made. Personal injuries, Newburn found

'were reported in 134 of the cases . . . and in 70 cases (52%) compensation was awarded. Although this is a high proportion compared to the figures contained in *Criminal Statistics*, nevertheless it still illustrates the relatively poor chance of receiving compensation for injury as compared with compensation for material loss'.[15]

In these cases the success rate for 866 victims reporting such loss was 75%.

The *Criminal Statistics England and Wales 1988* show that, in round numbers, 108,000 compensation orders were made in 1988 in conjunction with another sentence, and a further 4,500 were made as the sole sentence. The vast majority of orders — 99,100 — were made following conviction by magistrates (other than for summary motoring offences).[16] This represented 13%

---

13 See especially 55 HC Official Report (5th series) cols 1445-1446 (3 May 1973), Times, 4 May 1976, 971 HC Official Report (5th series) cols 387-388 (26 July 1979), Guardian, 24 March 1982, 428 HL Official Report (5th series) cols 1386-1388 (31 March 1982), and the launch of the *Victim's Charter* Times, 23 February 1990.

14 (1988) p 5. Aspects of the enforcement study were considered in chapter 10, supra, pp 268–269.

15 (1988) p 22. Shapland et al (1985) p 137 also noted a success rate higher than was the case nationally.

16 Home Office (1989, Cm 498) paras 7.38-7.39, and table 7.24.

of all offenders sentenced. The proportionate use of compensation orders is slightly higher in magistrates' courts than in the Crown Court, where orders were made against 9,200 offenders (9% of all offenders sentenced), though the proportion of orders made for indictable offences tried summarily was 21% of offenders sentenced. These proportions have remained very much the same for a number of years.

Turning to personal injury, 12,600 offenders were ordered to pay compensation on summary conviction of an indictable offence of violence against the person, and at the Crown Court there were 3,000 such offenders. Sexual offences hardly registered at all: 100 following summary conviction and less than 50 in the Crown Court. These totals represent 34% and 19% respectively of all offenders sentenced for these offences. By comparison, theft and burglary accounted for nearly 50% of the total number of all orders made in relation to indictable offences in 1988, though the proportionate use of compensation for indictable offences was highest for persons sentenced for criminal damage (67% at magistrates' courts and 23% at the Crown Court). Although one must be very careful about average figures, the average amount ordered to be paid by magistrates in the case of violence against the person was £87, and in the case of sexual offences, £131. In the Crown Court, these amounts were £233 and £221 respectively. By comparison, the highest average figure in the magistrates' court for any one offence was £213 (criminal damage) and the average for all offences was £118; in the Crown Court these averages were £3,664 (fraud) and £1,140 respectively. These amounts are patently very low by comparison with the kind of awards routinely made by the Board, though of course for the Scheme there is in any event the lower limit. Nevertheless, even if the average figure in magistrates' courts (£87) was an amount payable only in respect of general damages, it is an amount commensurate with virtually the lowest figures on the Home Office's tariff, payable in respect of a black eye (£100) or a minor cut (£75-200). As it is unlikely that all 12,600 victims sustained only such minor injury, the primary reason for these low figures, and thus a primary obstacle to full restitution by the offender, is almost certainly that in most cases the court considered that this was all the offender could afford, irrespective of the tariff value of the injury.[17]

So far as summary offences are concerned, the vast majority

17 Home Office *Criminal Statistics England and Wales: Supplementary Tables 1988 vol 4* tables S4.9(A)-S4.11(B).

of compensation orders, in both absolute and relative terms, are for criminal damage, followed by railway (fare dodging) and social security offences. When viewed as a proportion of all convictions, Newburn noted that in 1985 compensation was awarded in 10,478 cases, or 5%, of non-indictable assaults;[18] the proportion has hardly varied. Neither has the use of compensation orders as the sole sentence increased very greatly since that power was introduced in 1982. In 1988, about 4,500 such orders were made, being 4.2% of the total ordered but less than 0.5% of the total of all offenders sentenced.[19]

It should be clear from earlier chapters, that the continuing low level of compensation orders for personal injury has not been a consequence only of poor communication between police and victims, of the absence of institutional responsibility for presenting the victim's interest in compensation, of the insufficiency of the offender's means or of the difficulty of assessing non-pecuniary loss; it is also a question of attitude of mind. In much the same way as justices' clerks and the police have disputed any responsibility for raising the matter of compensation at the trial, magistrates themselves are clearly quite ambivalent about compensation.

'It also became clear in the course of the interviews that magistrates regard compensation as a relatively minor matter. Whilst they were unanimous in their support of the idea of compensation, they repeatedly stressed that in practice compensation was one of their final considerations in court. Magistrates continued to think of compensation as an ancillary matter. This came out clearly when magistrates were questioned about their attitudes to compensation and punishment. The research showed that magistrates are generally unwilling to use compensation as a sole penalty, preferring to combine it with a fine, probation or, in some cases, absolute or conditional discharge. The rationale for this is that compensation, they feel, is not a sufficient punishment, returning one only to the status quo ante.'[20]

This feeling may indeed stem from some of the very substantial penal ambiguities that attend compensation orders as sentences

---

18 (1988) p 4.
19 Home Office (1989) para 7.39.
20 Newburn (1988) p 48. Very similar views were expressed by sheriffs concerning the equivalent Scottish legislation, G Maher and C Docherty *Compensation Orders in the Scottish Criminal Courts* (1988, Scottish Office) pp 31-32.

in their own right, but even if such feeling exists only at an impressionistic level, it has real impact. These feelings are evidently independent of any of the institutional and operational problems that attend the making and enforcement of compensation orders, and thus will persist notwithstanding their amelioration. That is another reason why the notion of a victim compensation fund existing quite separately from any sentencing issues is attractive to many.

C. A VICTIM COMPENSATION FUND

There can be little doubt but that there has existed for some years a compensation gap, comprising those 'victims of violence who cannot apply to the CICB, but whose assailant is not caught, or is quite properly adjudged by the court to lack the means to comply with a compensation order, or indeed fails to make payment either in full or even at all when an order is made against him.'[1] This gap will widen as the lower limit for the Scheme is raised in order to give priority to those victims sustaining serious injury, and if there is at the same time no increase in the rate of orders made by the criminal courts. But even if there were an increase consequent on the various statutory and other changes discussed above, there would still remain a number of victims whose injuries are below the Scheme's limit and whose assailants are never convicted, have insufficient means or who fail to comply with the order. The Home Affairs Committee's recommendation in 1985 was that 'a person suffering physical injuries as a result of the crime, who is deprived of any other redress for the reasons we have outlined, should be granted the right to apply to the registrar of the Small Claims Court to have his claim assessed with a view to repayment out of central funds of the sum so awarded.'[2] The Committee made no attempt even to outline the administrative and other procedures that such application would entail, and it is unsurprising that the government found it unacceptable, offering

1 House of Commons, Home Affairs Committee *Compensation and Support for Victims of Crime* (1984-85, HC 43) para 53.
2 Id.

'no substantial advantage over the removal of the CICB lower limit' and being open to the same objections, 'particularly as regards cost.'[3]

An alternative that has attracted some attention is the idea of a victim compensation fund.[4] There are in fact a variety of proposals which depend on the existence of such a fund, some modest, some ambitious, but they all raise questions about their funding, administration, scope and cost. Two modest proposals proceed from the assumption that an offender has been convicted of an offence causing personal injury. One of these proposes that, following the present procedures for the determination of a compensation order, the victim is paid the full amount at once from a central fund, the enforcing court then seeking reimbursement from the offender according to the terms of the order. This proposal, which reflects the procedures for the recovery of costs, was mentioned by at least a quarter of the magistrates interviewed by Newburn as an alternative to the present haphazard delivery of compensation,[5] and was viewed favourably by the Hodgson Committee which thought its modest reach and cost more realistic a suggestion than some others.[6] Though the White Paper published in 1990 placed considerable emphasis on offender compensation, it made no recommendation on this idea.[7] Amounting to no more than a subsidy underwriting the risk that the offender may default, this proposal does nothing to assist victims whose convicted offenders are not ordered to make compensation or can only make compensation for an amount less than the ideal assessment of the victim's injury.

A variation on this proposal recommended by the Home Affairs Committee in 1990 as part of its review of the administration of the CICB, was that courts could make a 'mixed order' upon conviction, in which some of the ideal assessment of the victim's injury would be paid for by the offender under a compensation

---

3 Home Office *Compensation and Support for Victims of Crime* (1985, Cmnd 9457) para 18.
4 Wasik (1978) and (1984) Shapland et al (1985) ch 10, House of Commons (1984-85) paras 35-36, and A Samuels 'A strategy for compensation for the victims of crime' (1984) 44 Law Soc Gaz 3434-3435.
5 (1988) p 47.
6 Hodgson (1984).
7 Home Office (1990) para 1.10.

order, the balance coming from the Board.[8] One obvious problem here is that this arrangement could only operate where the injury could be valued at more than the Scheme's lower limit, and both the offender and the Board would no doubt wish to make representations as to how the award is to be divided between them. In any event, it is highly unlikely that the Board would welcome other institutions committing its funds to the compensation of victims whom it has not approved under the terms of the Scheme.

The second proposal which assumes the conviction of an offender contemplates the criminal court making an order for the ideal assessment of the victim's injury wholly independently of the question of the offender's means, which order is then payable in full and at once from a central fund. The court may then proceed to determine whether the offender should make a contribution by way of 'compensation' to that fund, at which point it takes into account the factors currently applicable to orders under s 35 of the Powers of Criminal Courts Act 1973. The advantages of this proposal are that in determining what contribution the offender should make, the court will, as is currently the case, be able to take into account, for example, the competing claims of the offender's dependants, the likelihood of his complying with the order with moneys legitimately acquired, and any prior sentencing considerations apt in his case, none of which factors will in any way diminish the victim's full recovery of compensation. In minor cases it will frequently be possible to require of the offender a payment equal to the ideal assessment of the victim's injury, but where an attack has more serious consequences, this may not be possible. Nevertheless, there is no objection to requiring some payment from the offender, even if it is but token.

This proposal raises two main difficulties, one practical, the other theoretical. The practical question relates to the funding of the inevitable shortfall between what can be recouped from offenders, and the amounts paid out to victims. In the first place, we would have to make some reasonable estimate of what that shortfall would total. In 1988, compensation orders were made by magistrates in 34% of cases of assault and violence against the person. These were cases in which the offender had some means, and there were no prior sentencing claims. As a starting point it might be assumed that the fund would thus have to meet three times the amount ordered in 1988, but this could as well increase by 10%-20% depending on the success with which orders are enforced. However, since we do not know whether the cases in which compensation was ordered were representative in terms of the extent of the injuries which victims sustained, it may be quite wrong to take as the starting point this simple proportionate increase. Nevertheless, some estimate will have to be made prior to any allocation of funds from other sources. Apart from the taxpayer, the Hodgson Committee considered the cumulated proceeds of fines, the proceeds of forfeiture and of confiscation, together with contributions by the offender, as possible sources from which the deficit could be met.[9] Then, as now, a difficulty lies in quantifying this sum, and thus in determining whether there would have to be some additional subvention from the taxpayer, and for how much. That in turn would raise questions about which department's budget would have to bear such expenditure, which would inevitably pose problems of resource allocation for that department.

The theoretical objection to these arrangements is 'that the interposition of a such a fund would break the link which a

9 Hodgson (1984) pp 63-64. In the United States, 'Son of Sam' statutes appropriate to the victims or their dependants the royalties payable to an offender for the media depiction of his offences against them, but they generate considerable theoretical and practical difficulties; see R Inz, 'Compensating the victim from the proceeds of the criminal's story' (1978) 14 Columbia J Law and Social Problems 93-122, and M Goldberg '"Publication rights" agreements in sensational criminal cases' (1983) 68 Cornell LR 686-705. In 1965 a private member's Bill was sponsored in an attempt to appropriate the proceeds of offenders' reminiscences, but this was prompted by the desire to see that crime should not pay, rather than to compensate their victims, of whom there was no mention in the debates, Criminal Reminiscences (Sale of) Bill 1965 264 HL Official Report (5th series) cols 281-282 (16 March 1965). Of further interest is the hostile reception that greeted the publication in national newspapers of the former Chief Constable of West Yorkshire's account of his involvement in the detection of Peter Sutcliffe, the 'Yorkshire Ripper'. Critics argued that it was unjust that he should receive any payment for these memoirs while Sutcliffe's victims themselves were unable to obtain damages for the injuries he had caused them, Times, 29 June 1983, and 434 HL Official Report (5th series) cols 125-127 (27 July 1982). Similarly, there has been criticism firstly of the profits made by the makers of a film portraying the role of Buster Edwards, one of the gang who robbed a mail train in 1963 of £2.5m and which left a train guard seriously injured and without redress (Sunday Times, 7 August 1988), and secondly of the payments reportedly made to the Kray twins, currently serving life imprisonment for murder, as part of the making of a film of their lives (Times, 8 May 1990). The latter has apparently prompted a Home Office review with the intention of introducing legislation.

compensation order at present creates between offenders and their victims: payment to a fund would seem no more to be reparation than payment of a fine.'[10] To this a number of points could be made, centred firstly on the question, to whom would the payment seem no more than that of a fine, and secondly on the question, would it matter? If we are concerned about offenders' perceptions, we would need to know how they currently view the payment of monetary penalties and of compensation. If we were then concerned to ascertain whether the link between the offender and the victim supposedly generated by a compensation order had any penal significance, we would have to devise a research project whereby the offender's perception could be translated into measurable effects in terms of the objectives of reparation. Every element of such an undertaking would be problematic, not least determining what the objectives of the link between offenders and victims are, and what priority should attach to them. From the offender's perspective, there may indeed be little to choose between the names of the payment he has to make. From the victims' perspective, the matter may appear somewhat simpler. There is no doubt that victims are pleased to be compensated by their offenders, but given the choice: full compensation every time from a fund to which their offender may have to contribute, or only the chance of an order fully or partially meeting the ideal assessment of their injuries (and which may not be fulfilled), would the victim choose to be compensated from the fund or only from the offender? The matter is at large, but as an issue of social policy we might take the view that whatever the victim's preference, as between restitutive purity and full compensation, the latter is to be preferred.

Finally, there is the very much more ambitious proposal that such a fund should be available whether the offender is convicted or not; in effect a criminal injuries compensation scheme but with a lower limit and whose funds are not wholly derived from general revenue. This would of course meet the objection to the two proposals just discussed, that they would be available only where there has been a conviction, but it is equally open to many other objections, including, as the Hodgson Committee observed, those of finance and administration.[11] For the Board, the Chairman considered that these constituted insuperable problems, and if a newly created body were given the task of determining such claims, that would merely reproduce in another form all the

10 Hodgson (1984) p 64.
11 Id. See also Wasik (1978) pp 608-611.

complex issues that have attended the non-statutory Scheme. Superficially attractive, such a proposal faces formidable objections, yet these leave unanswered the arguably legitimate claims of victims whose injuries do not meet the Scheme's lower limit, or whose offenders are apprehended but only cautioned or who, though convicted, are not amenable to a compensation order.

But these kinds of proposals in turn beg the basic question, why should victims of crimes of violence be singled out from others who also run the risk of uncompensated injury.[12] Though many have echoed the doubts Atiyah voiced 20 years ago concerning the wisdom of establishing the Scheme,[13] it is clearly well entrenched as the appropriate vehicle for delivering compensation to victims of personal crime,[14] and given the effort that has gone into its revision, together with the unwillingness, inertia and obstacles that have to date attended any suggestion that there may be another way of compensating accident victims,[15] looks set for a further 25 years. However, two factors may prompt a reconsideration.

The first concerns the implications of the 1990 White Paper. If compensation is to become a prominent feature of the community penalty, more thought will have to be given to its relationship to other non-custodial sentences, and to the matter of providing compensation where victims are not eligible under the Scheme and whose offenders cannot be ordered to make any or some compensation. The various suggestions that have been made for a victim compensation fund which go beyond the simple notion of a subsidy, and which rely on proceeds confiscated from offenders and supplemented from general revenue, while settling a number of the systemic and operational shortcomings of

---

12 Ralph Gibson LJ, *Reid v Rush & Tompkins Group plc* [1989] 3 All ER 228 at 235-236.

13 P Atiyah *Accidents, Compensation and the Law* (1970, 1st edn, Weidenfeld and Nicolson) p 324.

14 The Board is widely regarded by the administrators of other criminal injury compensation schemes to be a model of its kind, with virtually unrivalled experience in the field. It is a founder member of the International Association of Crime Victim Compensation Boards which meets biennially; CICB (1986) para 49. The Board was also influential in the formulation of the *European Convention on the Compensation of Victims of Violent Crimes*, 428 HL Official Report (5th series) cols 1386-1387 (31 March 1982).

15 The conclusion reached by Harris et al (1986) p 327 was that the deficiencies in the damages system as revealed by their survey were 'too deep-rooted to be removed by any modification of the system.'

compensation orders, nevertheless have their own problems, not least of funding and administration. In short, the penal system is not apt to deliver compensation routinely and fully to victims of personal crimes; the question then is one of priority. There may well be benefits from offender compensation (which, if victims were in any event appropriately compensated from an independent source, would mostly benefit the offender, if at all, rather than the victim), but since not all offenders would be well placed to compensate, there would necessarily be a proliferation of funds and of sources for compensation, without any clear allocation of policy objectives as between these various arrangements. To the extent that objectives are unclear, it will be correspondingly difficult to determine efficacy.

If compensating victims is to take priority, the question then is whether that would not be better, and less divisively, achieved through a comprehensive accident compensation programme. When considering such a proposal, it is as well to acknowledge that the Scheme has, since 1964, amounted to a state-funded programme for the compensation of the victims of intentional torts to the person. However, its greater significance lies in the values that it represents, both about the kinds of victims who deserve to be compensated, and about the proper approach to the delivery of compensation for illness and injury. The Scheme reinforces popular norms delineating the deviant from the law-abiding; it revalues certain kinds of suffering by treating discretely and uniquely the injuries sustained by the 'innocent' victim of crime. Because it is only to the deserving victim that the Scheme is addressed, eligibility criteria in particular concerning the applicant's conduct or biography play a significant role, more so than is to be found in tort law or in industrial injuries. The just deserts model implicit in this conception thus requires attention to be paid to the causes, rather than to the consequences, of the injury, a distinction which lies at the centre of the compensation debate. The Scheme is a paradigm of a cause-based approach to compensation and as such is antithetical to the kinds of proposals made by Atiyah and others.[16] To dismantle it as part of a broader accident compensation strategy which also embraces those victims currently beyond its eligibility criteria, in particular the lower limit, would thus require not merely the acceptance of a consequence-based approach to the compensation of victims of personal crime, but also the substantial

---

16 J Stapleton *Disease and the Compensation Debate* (1986, Oxford UP).

abandonment of the symbolic values associated with the Scheme.

The second factor can be more shortly stated. It is already the case, as has been documented earlier in this chapter, that the Scheme has reached and indeed exceeded saturation point in terms of its administration, not only because of any procedural inefficiencies in the Board. The Scheme is, to a degree, a victim of its own success. But how will it cope with the demands that will inevitably be made upon it as the number of applicants increases both absolutely and as a proportion of notifiable offences against the person? The government's policy of encouraging victims to seek compensation is clear, yet there must be a limit to the number of changes that could be made to the terms and the structure of the Scheme that are compatible with its remaining a credible institution.

Appendices

**Criminal Injuries Compensation Board
Blythswood House, 200 West Regent Street,
Glasgow, G2 4SW
Telephone 041-221 0945**

CRIMINAL INJURIES COMPENSATION SCHEME

1990 SCHEME

A Scheme for compensating vicitims of crimes of violence was announced in both Houses of Parliament on 24 June 1964 and in its original form came into force on 1 August 1964. The Scheme has since been modified in a number of respects. The 1990 revision below applies to all applications for compensation received by the Board on or after 1 February 1990 subject to the exceptions set out in paragraph 28. The 1990 Scheme also applies to applications received by the Board before 1 February 1990 to the extent set out in paragraph 29.

Requests for application forms and all enquiries should be directed to the above address.

THE SCHEME

Administration

1. The Compensation Scheme will be administered by the Criminal Injuries Compensation Board, which will be assisted by appropriate staff. Appointments to the Board will be made by the Secretary of State, after consultation with the Lord Chancellor and, where appropriate, the Lord Advocate. A person may only be appointed to be a member of the Board if he is a barrister practising in England and Wales, an advocate practising in Scotland, a solicitor practising in England and Wales or Scotland or a person who holds or has held judicial office in England and Wales or Scotland. The Chairman and other members of the Board will be appointed to serve for up to five years in the first instance, and their apointments will be renewable for such periods as the Secretary of State considers appropriate. The Chairman and other members will not serve on the Board beyond the age of 72, or other ceasing to be qualified for appointment, whichever is the earlier except that, where the Secretary of State considers it to be in the interests of the Scheme to extend a particular appointment beyond the age of 72 or after retirement from legal practice, he may do so. The Secretary of State may, if he thinks fit terminate a member's appointment on the grounds of incapacity or misbehaviour.

2. The Board will be provided with money through a Grant-in-Aid out of which payments for compensation awarded in accordance with the principles set out below will be made. Their net expenditure will fall on the Votes of the Home Office and the Scottish Home and Health Department.

3. The Board, or such members of the Board's staff as the Board may designate, will be entirely responsible for deciding what compensation should be paid in individual cases and their decisions will not be subject to appeal or to Ministerial review. The general working of the Scheme will, however, be kept under review by the Government, and the Board will submit annually to the Home Secretary and the Secretary of State for Scotland a full report on the operation of the Scheme, together with their accounts. The report and accounts will be open to debate in Parliament.

INF 1 (1/90).

Scope of the Scheme

4. The Board will entertain applications for ex gratia payments of compensation in any case where the applicant or, in the case of an application by a spouse or dependant (see paragraphs 15 and 16 below), the deceased, sustained in Great Britain, or on a British vessel, aircraft or hovercraft or on, under or above an installation in a designated area within the meaning of section 1 subsection (7) of the Continental Shelf Act 1964 or any waters within 500 metres of such an installation, or in a lighthouse off the coast of the United Kingdom, personal injury directly attributable —

    (a) to a crime of violence (including arson or poisoning);
      or

    (b) to the apprehension or attempted apprehension of an offender or a suspected offender or to the prevention or attempted prevention of an offence or to the giving of help to any constable who is engaged in any such activity; or

    (c) to an offence of trespass on a railway.

Applications for compensation will be entertained only if made within three years of the incident giving rise to the injury, except that the Board may in exceptional cases waive this requirement. A decision by the Chairman not to waive the time limit will be final. In considering for the purposes of this paragraph whether any act is a criminal act a person's conduct will be treated as constituting an offence notwithstanding that he may not be convicted of the offence by reason of age, insanity or diplomatic immunity.

5. Compensation will not be payable unless the Board are satisfied that the injury was one for which the total amount of compensation payable after deduction of social security benefits, but before any other deductions under the Scheme, would not be less than the minimum amount of compensation. This shall be £750. The application of the minimum level shall not, however, affect the payment of funeral expenses under paragraph 15 below or, where the victim has died otherwise than in consequence of an injury for which compensation would have been payable to him under the terms of the Scheme, any sum payable to a dependant or relative of his under paragraph 16.

6. The Board may withhold or reduce compensation if they consider that—

(a) the applicant has not taken, without delay, all reasonable steps to inform the police, or any other authority considered by the Board to be appropriate for the purpose, of the circumstances of the injury and to co-operate with the police or other authority in bringing the offender to justice; or

(b) the applicant has failed to give all reasonable assistance to the Board or other authority in connection with the application; or

(c) having regard to the conduct of the applicant before, during or after the events giving rise to the claim or to his character as shown by his criminal convictions or unlawful conduct—and, in applications under paragraphs 15 and 16 below, to the conduct or character as shown by the criminal convictions or unlawful conduct, of the deceased and of the applicant—it is inappropriate that a full award, or any award at all, be granted.

Further, compensation will not be payable—

(d) in the case of an application under paragraph 4*(b)* above where the injury was sustained accidentally, unless the Board are satisfied that the applicant was at the time taking an exceptional risk which was justified in all the circumstances.

7. Compensation will not be payable unless the Board are satisfied that there is no possibility that a person responsible for causing the injury will benefit from an award.

8. Where the victim and any person responsible for the injuries which are the subject of the application (whether that person actually inflicted them or not) were living in the same household at the time of the injuries as members of the same family, compensation will be paid only where—

(a) the person responsible has been prosecuted in connection with the offence, except where the Board consider that there are practical, technical or other good reasons why a prosecution has not been brought; and

(b) in the case of violence between adults in the family, the Board are satisfied that the person responsible and the applicant stopped living in the same household before the application was made and seem unlikely to live together again; and

(c) in the case of an application under this paragraph by or on behalf of a minor, ie a person under 18 years of age, the Board are satisfied that it would not be against the minor's interest to make a full or reduced award.

For the purposes of this paragraph, a man and a woman living together as husband and wife shall be treated as members of the same family.

9. If in the opinion of the Board it is in the interests of the applicant (whether or not a minor or a person under an incapacity) so to do, the Board may pay the amount of any award to any trustee or trustees to hold on such trusts for the benefit of all or any of the following persons, namely the applicant and any spouse, widow or widower, relatives and dependants of the applicant and with such provisions for their respective maintenance, education and benefit and with such powers and provisions for the investment and management of the fund and for the remuneration of the trustee or trustees as the Board shall think fit. Subject to this the Board will

have a general discretion in any case in which they have awarded compensation to make special arrangements for its administration. In this paragraph "relatives" means all persons claiming descent from the applicant's grandparents and "dependants" means all persons who in the opinion of the Board are dependent on him wholly or partially for the provision of the ordinary necessities of life.

10. The Board will consider applications for compensation arising out of acts of rape and other sexual offences both in respect of pain, suffering and shock and in respect of loss of earnings due to consequent pregnancy, and, where the victim is ineligible for a maternity grant under the National Insurance Scheme, in respect of the expenses of childbirth. Compensation will not be payable for the maintenance of any child born as a result of a sexual offence, except that where a woman is awarded compensation for rape the Board shall award the additional sum of £5,000 in respect of each child born alive having been conceived as a result of the rape which the applicant intends to keep.

11. Applications for compensation for personal injury attributable to traffic offences will be excluded from the Scheme, except where such injury is due to a deliberate attempt to run the victim down.

Basis of compensation

12. Subject to the other provisions of this Scheme, compensation will be assessed on the basis of common law damages and will normally take the form of a lump sum payment, although the Board may make alternative arrangements in accordance with paragraph 9 above. More than one payment may be made where an applicant's eligibility for compensation has been established but a final award cannot be calculated in the first instance—for example where only a provisional medical assessment can be given. In a case in which an interim award has been made, the Board may decide to make a reduced award, increase any reduction already made or refuse to make any further payment at any stage before receiving notification of acceptance of a final award.

13. Although the Board's decisions in a case will normally be final, they will have discretion to reconsider a case after a final award of compensation has been accepted where there has been such a serious change in the applicant's medical condition that injustice would occur if the original assessment of compensation were allowed to stand, or where the victim has since died as a result of his injuries. A case will not be re-opened more than three years after the date of the final award unless the Board are satisfied, on the basis of evidence presented with the application for re-opening the case, that the renewed application can be considered without a need for extensive enquiries. A decision by the Chairman that a case may not be re-opened will be final.

14. Compensation will be limited as follows—

(a) the rate of net loss of earnings or earning capacity to be taken into account shall not exceed one and a half times the gross average industrial earnings at the date of assessment (as published in the Department of Employment Gazette and adjusted as considered appropriate by the Board);

(b) there shall be no element comparable to exemplary or punitive damages.

Where an applicant has lost earnings or earning capacity as a result of the injury, he may be required by the Board to produce evidence thereof in such manner and form as the Board may specify.

15. Where the victim has died in consequence of the injury, no compensation other than funeral expenses will be payable for the benefit of his estate, but the Board will be able to entertain applications from any person who is a dependant of the victim within the meaning of section 1(3) of the Fatal Accidents Act 1976 or who is a relative of the victim within the meaning of Schedule 1 to the Damages (Scotland) Act 1976. Compensation will be payable in accordance with the other provisions of this Scheme to any such dependant or relative. Funeral expenses to an amount considered reasonable by the Board will be paid in appropriate cases, even where the person bearing the cost of the funeral is otherwise ineligible to claim under this Scheme. Applications may be made under this paragraph where the victim has died from his injuries even if an award has been made to the victim in his lifetime. Such cases will be subject to conditions set out in paragraph 13 for the re-opening of cases and compensation payable to the applicant will be reduced by the amount paid to the victim.

16. Where the victim has died otherwise than in consequence of the injury, the Board may make an award to such dependant or relative as is mentioned in paragraph 15 in respect of loss of wages, expenses and liabilities incurred by the victim before death as a result of the injury whether or not the application for compensation in respect of the injury has been made before the death.

17. Compensation will not be payable for the loss of or damage to clothing or any property whatsoever arising from the injury unless the Board are satisfied that the property was relied upon by the victim as a physical aid.

18. The cost of private medical treatment will be payable by the Board only if the Board consider that, in all the circumstances, both the private treatment and the cost of it are reasonable.

19. Compensation will be reduced by the full value of any present or future entitlement to—
(a) United Kingdom social security benefits;
(b) any criminal injury compensation awards made under or pursuant to statutory arrangements in force at the relevant time in Northern Ireland;
(c) social security benefits, compensation awards or similar payments whatsoever from the funds of other countries; or
(d) payments under insurance arrangements except as excluded below which may accrue, as a result of the injury or death, to the benefit of the person to whom the award is made.

In assessing this entitlement, account will be taken of any income tax liability likely to reduce the value of such benefits and, in the case of an application under paragraph 15, the value of such benefits will not be reduced to take account of prospects of remarriage. If, in the opinion of the Board, an applicant may be eligible for any such benefits the Board may refuse to make an award until the applicant has taken such steps as the Board consider reasonable to claim them. Subject to paragraph 18 above, the Board will disregard monies paid or payable to the victim or his dependants as a result of or in consequence of insurance personally effected, paid for and maintained by the personal income of the victim or, in the case of a person under the age of 18, by his parent.

20. Where the victim is alive compensation will be reduced to take account of any pension accruing as a result of the injury. Where the victim has died in consequence of the injury, and any pension is payable for the benefit of the person to whom the award is made as a result of the death of the victim, the compensation will similarly be reduced to take account of the value of that pension. Where such pensions are taxable, one-half of their value will be deducted;

where they are not taxable, eg where a lump sum payment not subject to income tax is made, they will be deducted in full. For the purposes of this paragraph, "pension" means any payment payable as a result of the injury or death, in pursuance of pension or other rights whatsoever connected with the victim's employment, and includes any gratuity of that kind and similar benefits payable under insurance policies paid for by employers. Pension rights accruing solely as a result of payments by the victim or a dependant will be disregarded.

21. When a civil court has given judgement providing for payment of a claim for damages or a claim for damages has been settled on terms providing for payment of money, or when payment of compensation has been ordered by a criminal court, in respect of personal injuries, compensation by the Board in respect of the same injuries will be reduced by the amount of any payment received under such an order or settlement. When a civil court has assessed damages, as opposed to giving judgement for damages agreed by the parties, but the person entitled to such damages has not yet received the full sum awarded, he will not be precluded from applying to the Board, but the Board's assessment of compensation will not exceed the sum assessed by the court. Furthermore, a person who is compensated by the Board will be required to undertake to repay them from any damages, settlement or compensation he may subsequently obtain in respect of his injuries. In arriving at their assessment of compensation the Board will not be bound by any finding of contributory negligence by any court; but will be entirely bound by the terms of the Scheme.

Procedure for determining applications

22. Every application will be made to the Board in writing as soon as possible after the event on a form obtainable from the Board's offices. The initial decision on an application will be taken by a single member of the Board, or by any member of the Board's staff to whom the Board has given authority to determine applications on the Board's behalf. Where an award is made the applicant will be given a breakdown of the assessment of compensation, except where the Board consider this inappropriate, and where an award is refused or reduced, reasons for the decision will be given. If the applicant is not satisfied with the decision he may apply for an oral hearing which, if granted, will be held before at least two members of the Board excluding any member who made the original decision. The application for a hearing must be made within three months of notification of the initial decision; however the Board may waive this time limit where an extension is requested with good reason within the three month period, or where it is otherwise in the interests of justice to do so. A decision by the Chairman not to waive the time limit will be final. It will also be open to a member of the Board, or a designated member of the Board's staff, where he considers that he cannot make a just and proper decision himself to refer the application for a hearing before at least two members of the Board. One of whom may be the member who, in such a case, decided to refer the application to a hearing. An applicant will have no title to an award offered until the Board have received notification in writing that he accepts it.

23. Applications for hearings must be made in writing on a form supplied by the Board and should be supported by reasons together with any additional evidence which may assist the Board to decide whether a hearing should be granted. If the reasons in support of the application suggest that the initial decision was based on information obtained by or submitted to the Board which was incomplete or erroneous, the application may be remitted for reconsideration by the member of the Board who made the initial decision or, where this is not practicable or where the initial decision was made by a member of the Board's staff, by any member of the Board. In such cases it will still be open for the applicant to apply in writing for a hearing if he remains dissatisfied after his case has been reconsidered and the three-month limitation period in paragraph 22 will start from the date of notification of the reconsidered decision.

24. An applicant will be entitled to an oral hearing only if—

    (a) no award was made on the ground that any award would be less than the sum specified in paragraph 5 of the Scheme and it appears that applying the principles set out in paragraph 26 below, the Board might make an award; or

    (b) an award was made and it appears that, applying the principles set out in paragraph 26 below, the Board might make a larger award; or

    (c) no award or a reduced award was made and there is a dispute as to the material facts or conclusions upon which the initial or reconsidered decision was based or it appears that the decision may have been wrong in law or principle.

An application for a hearing which appears likely to fail the foregoing criteria may be reviewed by not less than two members of the Board other than any member who made the initial or reconsidered decision. If it is considered on review that if any facts or conclusions which are disputed were resolved in the applicant's favour it would have made no difference to the initial or reconsidered decision, or that for any other reason an oral hearing would serve no useful purpose, the application for a hearing will be refused. A decision to refuse an application for a hearing will be final.

25. It will be for the applicant to make out his case at the hearing, and where appropriate this will extend to satisfying the Board that compensation should not be withheld or reduced under the terms of paragraph 6 or paragraph 8. The applicant and a member of the Board's staff will be able to call, examine and cross-examine witnesses. The Board will be entitled to take into account any relevant hearsay, opinion or written evidence, whether or not the author gives oral evidence at the hearing. The Board will reach their decision solely in the light of evidence brought out at the hearing, and all the information and evidence made available to the Board members at the hearing will be made available to the applicant at, if not before, the hearing. The Board may adjourn a hearing for any reason, and where the only issue remaining is the assessment of compensation may remit the application to a Single Member of the Board for determination in the absence of the applicant but subject to the applicant's right to apply under paragraph 22 above for a further hearing if he is not satisfied with the final assessment of compensation. While it will be open to the applicant to bring a friend or legal adviser to assist him in putting his case, the Board will not pay the cost of legal representation. They will, however, have discretion to pay the expenses of the applicant and witnesses at a hearing. If an applicant fails to attend a hearing and has offered no reasonable excuse for his non attendance the Board at the hearing may dismiss his application. A person whose application has been dismissed by the Board for failure to attend a hearing may apply in writing to the Chairman of the Board for his application to be reinstated. A decision by the Chairman that an application should not be reinstated will be final.

26. At the hearing the amount of compensation assessed by a Single Member of the Board or a designated member of the Board's staff will not be altered except upon the same principles as the Court of Appeal in England or the Court of Session in Scotland would alter an assessment of damages made by a trial judge.

27. Procedure at hearings will be as informal as is consistent with the proper determination of applications, and hearings will in general be in private. The Board will have discretion to permit observers, such as representatives of the press, radio and television, to attend hearings provided that written undertakings are given that the anonymity of the applicant and other parties will not in any way be infringed by subsequent reporting. The Board will have power to publish information about its decisions in individual cases; this power will be limited only by the need to preserve the anonymity of applicants and other parties.

Implementation

28. The provisions of this Scheme will take effect from 1 February 1990. All applications for compensation received by the Board on or after 1 February 1990 will be dealt with under the terms of this Scheme except that in relation to applications in respect of injuries incurred before that date the following provisions of the 1990 Scheme shall not apply—

    (a) Paragraph 4(c);

    (b) Paragraph 8, but only in respect of injuries incurred before 1 October 1979 where paragraph 7 of the 1969 Scheme will continue to apply—

    (c) Paragraph 10 but only insofar as it requires the Board to award an additional sum of £5,000 in the circumstances therein prescribed;

    (d) Paragraphs 15 and 16 but only insofar as they enable the Board to entertain applications from a person who is a dependant within the meaning of section 1(3)(b) of the Fatal Accidents Act 1976 or who is a relative within the meaning of paragraph 1(aa) of Schedule 1 to the Damages (Scotland) Act 1976 other than such a person who is applying only for funeral expenses.

29. Applications for compensation received by the Board before 1 February 1990 will continue to be dealt with in accordance with paragraph 25 of the Scheme which came into operation on 1 October 1979 ("the 1979 Scheme") or the Scheme which came into operation on 21 May 1969 ("the 1969 Scheme") except that the following paragraphs of this Scheme will apply in addition to or in substitution for provisions of these Schemes as specified below—

    (a) Paragraph 3 of this Scheme will apply in substitution for paragraph 4 of the 1969 Scheme and paragraph 3 of the 1979 Scheme;

    (b) Paragraph 6(c) of this Scheme will apply in substitution for paragraph 17 of the 1969 Scheme and paragraph 6(c) of the 1979 Scheme;

    (c) Paragraph 14 of this Scheme will apply additionally to applications otherwise falling to be considered under the 1969 or 1979 Schemes but only insofar as it allows the Board to require an applicant to produce evidence of loss of earnings or earning capacity;

    (d) Paragraphs 22, 23 and 25 of this Scheme will apply in substitution for paragraphs 21 and 22 of the 1969 Scheme and paragraphs 22 and 23 of the 1979 Scheme;

    (e) Paragraph 26 of this Scheme will apply additionally to applications otherwise falling to be considered under the 1969 or 1979 Schemes;

    (f) Paragraph 27 of this Scheme will apply in substitution for paragraph 23 of the 1969 Scheme and paragraph 24 of the 1979 Scheme.

30. Applications to re-open cases received before 1 February 1990 will continue to be dealt with under the terms of paragraph 25 of the 1979 Scheme. Applications to re-open cases received on or after 1 February 1990 will be considered and determined under the terms of this Scheme.

**Criminal Injuries Compensation Board
Blythswood House, 200 West Regent Street,
Glasgow, G2 4SW
Telephone 041-221 0945**

CRIMINAL INJURIES COMPENSATION SCHEME

Application Form—Injury

FOR OFFICIAL USE ONLY

Reference Number

PLEASE READ THE NOTES ON THIS PAGE CAREFULLY BEFORE YOU START TO FILL IN THE FORM

1 Use this form to apply for compensation if you have been injured as a direct result of a crime of violence.

2 If the person who was injured has died, do not use this form. Please write to the Board and ask for a **fatal application form.** If they died otherwise than from the injury, ask for a **fatal (paragraph 16) application form.**

3 If you are applying on behalf of someone
   who is under 18
   or who cannot fill the form in
   or who is unable for any reason to
       manage their own affairs
you must be sure to complete section 2 and the authorisation at section 11. The person who was injured should sign the form as well, if possible.

4 If you are under 18 and you complete the form yourself, you must ask your parent or guardian or another person who has parental responsibility to complete section 2 on the form and to sign the authorisation at section 11.

5 Check by reading the **Criminal Injuries Compensation Scheme** that you appear to be eligible for compensation. If you did not receive a copy of the Scheme with this form then contact the above address and ask for one to be sent to you.

6 If the incident in which you received your injuries happened more than three years ago, the Board will be unable to consider your application unless there are exceptional circumstances. Paragraph 4 of the Scheme refers. You should state the reasons for delay in making the application at Section 4 of this form or in a separate letter.

7 Read all sections on this form and give all the information asked for. Some of the questions can be answered with a tick in the box which applies. Where necessary please write **don't know** or **doesn't apply** rather than leave a blank unless asked to do so. If you need more space for your answers, use a separate sheet of paper or send a letter and attach it securely to this form.

8 When you are asked to give a date, write it in the box provided using numbers only. For example, if the date was February 17th 1989 you should write

date month year

9 You will receive an acknowledgement within a few weeks telling you that your application has been registered and informing you of your personal reference number. **You must use this number whenever you contact the Board.** If you change your address, write to the Board immediately informing us of your old and new addresses.

Use black ballpoint pen or ink because we may need to photocopy this form.

Remember to sign and date this form at the end.

Write in BLOCK CAPITALS and tick the boxes that apply.

Experience has shown that these are all points which can cause delay to your application.

1 Details of the injured person

FOR OFFICIAL USE ONLY

Mr ☐   Mrs ☐   Miss ☐   Ms ☐   Other ☐ (Please State) ▢

Family Name ▢

First Name(s) ▢

Date of Birth: ▢ ▢ ▢
date month year

National Insurance Number ▢

Sex ☐

Marital Status: Single ☐   Married ☐   Divorced ☐   Separated ☐   Widow ☐   Widower ☐

Address: ▢

Postcode ▢

Day time Telephone Number ▢

Occupation and Grade or Rank at time of incident ▢

Employee Number ▢

2 Details of person making an application on behalf of someone else

This section must be completed by an adult if the injured person is under the age of 18 or the injured person is incapable of handling their own affairs.

If you are the injured person and are 18 years or over please leave this section blank and go to section 3.

If you are not the injured person but are applying on their behalf, please enter your details below.

Mr ☐   Mrs ☐   Miss ☐   Ms ☐   Other ☐ (Please State) ▢

Family Name ▢

First Name(s) ▢

Date of Birth: ▢ ▢ ▢
date month year

Relationship to the injured person or status ▢

Relationship Code ☐

Address: ▢

Postcode ▢

Day time Telephone Number ▢

3 Details of representatives

It is not essential to have a Solicitor, Victim Support Scheme or Trade Union, etc to act for you in connection with this application, but if you do choose to be represented please enter the details below. We will then correspond with your representatives direct. If you change your representatives, notify the Board in writing immediately.

Name of Representatives ▢

Address ▢

Representative Code ☐

Representative's Reference Number to be quoted ▢

4 Details of incident

When did the incident in which you were injured happen?

| | | | | | am ☐ pm ☐ |
date month year time

As clearly as you can, please describe the incident in which you were injured. If the incident happened more than three years ago, you should also explain why you have not applied to the Board before now.

Were there any witnesses?

Please give the names and addresses of any people who saw the incident or who could give any information about it.

Where did the incident happen? (Give FULL address)

What is the name of the person who injured you? Please give this if you know it. If you do not know it, the Board may still be able to deal with your application.

Were you and the person who injured you living together as members of the same family at the time of the incident?

Yes ☐   No ☐

Was the incident reported to the Police?

Yes ☐   No ☐

If the incident was not reported to the police, please explain why.

If the incident was reported to the police, please give the information requested below

(a) the name of the person who reported it

(b) the date on which it was reported

| | | |
date month year

(c) the name of the Police Station at which it was reported

(d) the name and number of the Police Officer involved

(e) the crime reference number

(f) was a written statement made?

Yes ☐   No ☐

FOR OFFICIAL USE ONLY

Date

Time

Police Code

Enq. Type

6 Absence from work, school or college and any loss of earnings

How long were you away from work, school or college as a result of your injuries?

[ ] [ ] [ ] to [ ] [ ] [ ]   OR   [ ]
date month year   date month year   not absent

Have you lost any earnings as a result of the incident?

Yes [ ]   No [ ]

If you are employed, please state your take home pay at the date of your injury. This should include overtime, bonuses etc but after deducting tax and National Insurance contributions.

£ [ ]   weekly [ ]   monthly [ ]

If your employment situation changes after completion of this form, please inform the Board.

What payments have you received from your employers for the time you were off work because of your injuries?

[ ]

If you continued to lose earnings when you went back to work because of your injuries, please give details.

[ ]

Please note that there is a limit to the amount of compensation for loss of earnings the Scheme can provide.

Please give the name and address of your employers, school or college at the time of the incident.

If you had just started or were due to start a new job when you were injured, please give the names and addresses of both the new and previous employers.

[ ]

Telephone number [ ]

If you are self-employed, or your earnings are in the form of fees or a share of profits, please state the total loss sustained by yourself.

£ [ ]

In addition, if you are self-employed please provide a separate detailed account with this form. You should be prepared, if required, to produce documents to support your claim, such as certified accounts and notices of assessments to income tax.

7 Receipt of state benefits

Have you received any Social Security Benefits including Unemployment Benefit as a result of the incident?

Yes [ ]   No [ ]

Please list the benefits you have received since the incident.

[ ]

Please give the full address of the relevant benefit office(s).

[ ]

Please note that benefits received as a result of the incident are deducted in full from any loss of earnings. If you are entitled to claim benefits but do not do so, the Board may still reduce compensation by the full value of these benefits. The Board may refuse to make an award until you have taken reasonable steps to claim benefits for which you are eligible.

8 Out of pocket expenses

Please give details including amounts, of any out of pocket expenses such as dental costs, fares to hospital for treatment and repair or replacement of physical aids. Normally the Board will only refund such expenses if receipts are provided. Please note the Board cannot compensate for lost or damaged clothing.

Repairs to or replacement of damaged dentures, spectacles, etc. Claim only if this expense has not already been met in full by the National Health Service or the Department of Social Security (DSS).

[ ]

Any other expenses eg extra fares to hospital, prescriptions, etc.

[ ]

FOR OFFICIAL USE ONLY

Informant Code

Enq. Type

Enq. Type

Details of incident (continued)

Did the incident result in criminal proceedings?

Yes ☐   No ☐

If yes, please give
(a) the name of the court

(b) the result and date

If the incident was reported to an authority other than the police, please give

(a) the date on which it was reported

☐☐☐
date month year

(b) the name and address of the authority

Informant Code

Enq. Type

---

5 Details of injuries and medical treatment

What injuries did you receive?

Have you fully recovered from your physical injuries and any psychological consequences?

Yes ☐   No ☐

If not please describe your symptoms.

Are you still receiving treatment?

Yes ☐   No ☐

Have the injuries left any permanent scarring or deformity?

Yes ☐   No ☐

If yes, then you may later be asked to send photographs, in which case the Board will contribute towards the cost.

PLEASE DO NOT SEND ANY PHOTOGRAPHS UNLESS ASKED

If you received hospital treatment for your injuries, please give the name and address of the hospital, and, if possible, your hospital reference number.

Hospital Address

Hospital Code

Hospital reference No:

Date as in-patient: ☐☐☐ to ☐☐☐

Date as out-patient: ☐☐☐ to ☐☐☐

Second hospital attended if applicable

Hospital Address

Hospital Code

Hospital reference No:

Date as in-patient: ☐☐☐ to ☐☐☐

Date as out-patient: ☐☐☐ to ☐☐☐

Please give the FULL name and address of your own G.P.

Have you consulted him/her as a result of your injuries?

Yes ☐   No ☐

If you received or are still receiving treatment from any other hospital or doctor or dentist please give names and addresses.

Informant Code

Enq. Type

9 **Payments and compensation from other sources**

If you have received compensation for your injuries from any other sources, please give details.

Include compensation orders made by criminal courts, damages received through civil claims, or similar payments from any other sources. The Board will deduct any amount received in this way from any award they may make.

Please give details of any pension or gratuity from your employers, or payments from an insurance company or similar body, which you have received or are likely to receive as a result of your injuries. Please state the amounts received and the companies involved.

Who paid the premiums for any insurance policy?

10 **Previous applications by the person who was injured**

Have you made a previous application to the Board for compensation?

Yes ☐   No ☐

If yes, please give

the date of the incident

the date of the application

the Board's reference number

11 Signature and authorisation

PLEASE READ THIS SECTION CAREFULLY BEFORE YOU SIGN THE FORM.

I certify that all the statements I have made in this application form are true to the best of my knowledge, and that this is my only application to the Board in connection with this incident.

I undertake to tell the Board of any changes that might affect their decision on whether I am entitled to compensation and, if I am, to what amount.

I agree to give the Board all reasonable assistance, particularly in obtaining medical reports, if they are needed.

I authorise the following to assist the Board in considering my application:

The Police, to give any relevant information, including copies of any statements I made to them and a list of any convictions which may be recorded against me.

The Hospitals I attended, and the doctors, dentists and others who treated me, to give reports on my injuries and treatment.

My employers, to give information about my earnings, pension rights and other relevant matters.

Any Government Departments, local authorities or other public agencies in Great Britain or elsewhere from which I received Social Security Benefits or any other payments, to give any relevant information.

Any Government-sponsored training or rehabilitation unit that I have attended, to give any relevant information.

I authorise the Board to ask any court responsible for enforcing a compensation order in my favour to hold any outstanding money received as a result of the order until the Board informs it that I have accepted or rejected their decision of final assessment.

I understand that the Board may inform the authorities and persons mentioned above that I have made this application, and tell them their decision.

IF YOU ARE MAKING AN APPLICATION ON BEHALF OF SOMEONE ELSE, SEE NOTE 3 ON THE FRONT OF THIS FORM AND THEN COMPLETE THE FOLLOWING DETAILS

Is the person who was injured under 18 years of age?

Yes ☐   No ☐

If yes, please send a photocopy of their full birth certificate.

If you do not have parental rights for this child, please give the name and address of the person who does

Name

Address

Postcode

If the person who was injured is over 18, do they normally manage their own affairs?

Yes ☐   No ☐

Signature of person making the application

date

Signature of person who was injured

date

Printed in the United Kingdom for HMSO
Dd8224406 4.90 C600 5360 12521

A GUIDE TO THE CRIMINAL INJURIES COMPENSATION SCHEME

INTRODUCTION

The aim of this guide is to summarise some of the more important aspects and conditions of the Criminal Injuries Compensation Scheme, and to provide applicants with enough information about its interpretation by the Board to help them apply with the minimum of trouble and research. It must be emphasised, however, that the guide is an aid and not a substitute for the Scheme itself and cannot cover every situation; each case is determined by the Board on its own merits and solely in accordance with the relevant provisions of the Scheme. Some applications are, of course, less straightforward than others. Thus, while the guide should enable most applications to be made without assistance, there will be some cases in which applicants may have to think carefully whether to obtain the services of a solicitor or other adviser first. The Board do not, however, pay for the cost of legal advice or representation.

Throughout the guide references are made to **paragraphs** of the Scheme. If you did not receive a copy of the Scheme with this guide you can send for one, and any further forms or information you may require, to:

Criminal Injuries Compensation Board
Blythswood House
200 West Regent Street
GLASGOW
G2 4SW   Telephone No: 041-221 0945

This guide is issued on the authority of the Board and replaces the last explanatory document of this kind dated April 1987 and referred to as "The Statement".

February 1990

WHO CAN APPLY

1. Under **paragraph 4** of the Scheme you can apply for compensation if you sustained personal injury directly attributable –

   (a) to a crime of violence (including arson or poisoning)

   (b) to an incident when you were trying to stop someone from committing a crime or when you were trying to apprehend a suspect after a crime or when you were trying to help the police apprehend someone

   (c) to an offence of trespass on a railway (this applies only to incidents after 31 January 1990, and now allows the Board to consider applications from people who suffer mental injury after witnessing suicides on railway tracks).

2. **"Crime of Violence"**. There is no legal definition of the term "crime of violence". Most crimes of violence of course involve force to the person, e.g. assaults and woundings. Where it is not obvious the Board will look to the nature of the crime rather than its consequences.

3. **"Personal Injury"**. This can include mental injury directly attributable to a crime of violence or threat of violence. Shock directly attributable to the loss of possessions is not within the Scheme.

4. **"Directly attributable"**. Personal injury is "directly attributable" if the incident from which the injury arose would be considered by a reasonable person who knew all the facts to be a substantial cause of the injury, but not necessarily the only cause.

5. **Fatalities**. You can also apply for compensation if you are a dependant or relative of someone who died from criminal injuries (**paragraph 15**) or who was injured but died from some other cause (**paragraph 16**). If you are not a relative or dependant but you paid for or towards the funeral of someone who died from criminal injuries, you can claim reasonable funeral expenses.

WHAT INJURIES QUALIFY

Scope of the Scheme.

6. The injury must have been sustained in Great Britain or one of the other places set out in **paragraph 4** of the Scheme. Injuries sustained elsewhere, say on holiday abroad, are not covered. In this case there

could be a remedy under a similar scheme in force in the country concerned.

Immunity of offender.

7. You can apply for compensation even if the injuries were caused by someone who could not be held responsible under the criminal law, because they were too young, or insane (**paragraph 4**). For example, a child below the age of 10 years (8 years in Scotland) is considered legally incapable of committing a crime. If, as a matter of fact, the child's conduct would have amounted to a crime of violence if committed by an adult the victim is entitled to apply for compensation from the Board.

The lower limit for compensation.

8. Under **paragraph 5** of the Scheme no compensation can be paid unless the Board are satisfied that the amount payable after deduction of social security benefits (but before any other deductions under the Scheme) would not be less than the minimum award of £750.

9. Compensation is assessed on the basis of "common law" damages (**paragraph 12**). This means that, subject to the other provisions of the Scheme, the Board will award what a civil court would award in "damages" for the same injury. However, the effect of the lower limit in the Scheme prevents the Board from making an award if the damages a court could award would be less than £750. Moreover, even if the total sum payable is equal to or more than £750, an application might still have to be disallowed on account of the victim's entitlement to Social Security benefits. Under **paragraph 19** of the Scheme all such benefits received as a result of the injury have to be deducted in full. So if the balance of compensation payable after deduction of such benefits is less than £750 then no compensation can be paid at all.

10. The lower limit will usually apply when the injuries sustained are of a minor nature, e.g. cuts, bruises or sprains where there has been no more than minor medical treatment and where there is no remaining visible scarring, or which have not necessitated more than 3 to 4 weeks absence from work. Whilst the Board take into account shock and emotional disturbance, and will give more weight to this if the victim is elderly, compensation would not normally be awarded for temporary shock, distress or emotional upset alone if no more than the inevitable reaction to an unpleasant experience. You will find further information about the level of awards for particular injuries in the enclosed leaflet.

Accidental injury.

11. As a general rule accidental injury is not covered by the Scheme. The Board can only compensate for accidental injury if you were engaged in one of the law enforcement activities set out in **paragraph 4(b)** of the Scheme, and the injury was sustained in circumstances in which you could be said to have been taking an "exceptional risk which was

justified in all the circumstances" (see **paragraph 6(d)**).

12. Whether the Board can accept you were taking an exceptional risk will depend on the facts. People who fall over when running towards an incident or going to apprehend an offender are unlikely to satisfy the test. Likewise a person injured climbing or jumping over such things as walls or fences will not usually be taking an exceptional risk, unless the action is essential and the person does not know or cannot see what is on the other side. But an act which would not be regarded as constituting an exceptional risk in daylight, may well be so at night.

Road traffic offences.

13. The general rule is that compensation is not payable under the Scheme for injuries caused as the result of traffic offences on the public highway (**paragraph 11**). In such cases the victim's remedy is through the driver's insurance company or, if the driver was uninsured or unidentified, through the Motor Insurer's Bureau (MIB). The address of the Motor Insurer's Bureau is:

> New Garden House
> 78 Hatton Garden
> LONDON EC1N 8JQ

14. There is one situation in which the MIB cannot help. That is where the victim was deliberately run down by a driver who cannot be traced and whose identity is unknown. In this case the victim should apply to the Board for compensation under **paragraph 11** of this Scheme.

Injury caused by animals.

15. Sometimes applications are received which involve attacks by animals, usually dogs. Such cases are not covered by the Scheme unless what has happened amounts to an assault as, for example, where a dog's owner deliberately sets the dog upon some person.

Violence within the family.

16. Under **paragraph 8** of the Scheme, if you and the person who injured you were living together in the same household at the time of the incident compensation cannot be paid unless:

> (a) the person who injured you has been prosecuted (unless there are good reasons why this could not happen) and

> (b) you and the person who injured you have stopped living together for good.

● A man and a woman living together as husband and wife, even if they are not married, are treated as members of the same family.

● If it was a child who was injured condition (b) above does not apply but the Board must be satisfied that it would not be against the child's interest to make an award. Ask for the separate leaflet "Child Abuse and the Criminal Injuries Compensation Scheme".

• **Paragraph 8** of the Scheme does not apply to injuries inflicted by a member of the family before 1 October 1979 for which the Board cannot award compensation in any circumstances. (Paragraph 7 of the 1969 Scheme).

CONDITIONS WHICH APPLY IN ALL CASES

17. Even if there is no doubt that you have sustained "personal injury directly attributable to a crime of violence" for which compensation could be awarded under the Scheme you will also have to show the Board that an award should not be refused or reduced for one of the reasons set out in **paragraph 6** of the Scheme. You should read this paragraph with particular care. The following notes are to help you anticipate the Board's likely approach.

Informing the police (Paragraph 6(a)).

18. It is not necessary that the offender should have been convicted before an award can be made. Some offenders are never found. However, the Board attach great importance to the duty of every victim of violent crime to inform the police of all the circumstances without delay, and to co-operate with their enquiries and any subsequent prosecution.

19. The condition that the incident should have been reported is particularly important since it is the Board's main safeguard against fraud. A victim who has not reported the circumstances of the injury to the police and can offer no reasonable explanation for not doing so should assume that any application for compensation would be rejected by the Board altogether. Failure to inform the police is unlikely to be excused on the grounds that the victim feared reprisals or did not recognise his assailant or saw no point in reporting it. Reporting such incidents may help the police to prevent further offences against other people.

20. It is for the **victim** to report the incident personally unless he was prevented from doing so because of the nature of his injuries. In this case it is then his duty to contact the police and co-operate with their enquiries as soon as he is able to do so. It is not sufficient to assume that the incident will have been reported by someone else because, even if it has, that person may not have known the full circumstances. Reports by, or the evidence of friends, relatives or workmates will not be sufficient if there was no good reason for the victim not informing the police as well.

21. The victim must report all the relevant circumstances. If he deliberately leaves out any important information or otherwise misleads the police, an application for compensation would usually be rejected.

22. The incident should have been reported to the police by the victim at the **earliest possible opportunity**. Failure to inform the police promptly can prejudice further enquiries. Thus, a victim who fails to report initially and only does so later for the

purposes of claiming compensation from the Board is likely to find his application rejected. In general, the ignorance of rights, duties or the provisions of this Scheme are unlikely to be regarded by the Board as acceptable excuses, particularly in the case of the serious crimes which most citizens would recognise as matters which should have been reported to the police.

23. Exceptional cases. Every case is treated on its merits and the Board will take a more sympathetic view where the delay or complete failure to report the incident to the police is clearly attributable to youth, old age, or some other physical or mental incapacity which rendered it difficult or impossible for the victim to appreciate what to do. The requirement might also be waived if the applicant was unaware that his injury was due to a crime of violence, or only discovered there was a connection long after the event by which time little or no purpose would have been served in reporting it to the police.

24. Informing someone else. It is the police to whom crimes of violence must be reported, and reports made to employers, trade union officials, social workers or others will not generally be regarded by the Board as sufficient. Exceptions may be made, however, in the case of injuries sustained, for example, in mental hospitals and prisons where a prompt report to the appropriate person in authority may be sufficient because this will represent a willingness that the matter should be formally investigated. The "appropriate authority" in the case of a child will often be the child's parents whose own failure to inform the police will not constitute a bar on the child's claim if it would have been unreasonable to expect the child to take the matter any further himself.

Helping the police to prosecute (Paragraph 6(a)).

25. Even if the incident has been promptly reported to the police the Board have discretion to refuse or reduce compensation if the victim subsequently fails to co-operate with the police in bringing the offender to justice.

26. Essentially the Board make a distinction between two situations:

a. An applicant refuses to co-operate with the police, for example, refuses to make a statement, attend an identification parade, name the assailant, attend court or such like conduct. The Board make no award.

b. The applicant was willing to co-operate but in the particular circumstances it was decided by the police or the prosecuting authority that no further action should be taken or prosecution brought. An award will usually be made:

27. As with non-reporting, fear of reprisals, etc., will usually be no excuse. If the victim having at first refused to co-operate with the police subsequently changes his mind and assists them in all respects then the Board may consider making a reduced award.

348 *Appendices*

Conduct and character of the victim (Paragraph 6 (c)).

28. You must be able to convince the Board that you were not in any way responsible for the incident in which you were injured. Otherwise the Board may decide to make no award or a reduced award. The Board can also refuse compensation or reduce it on account of previous criminal convictions. In fatal cases the Board will take account of the conduct and any convictions of the deceased as well.

Conduct "before, during or after the event".

29. "Conduct" means something which can fairly be described as bad conduct or misconduct. It includes provocative behaviour. There is no limit upon the sort of conduct that the Board can take into consideration, but no reduction will be made on account of "contributory negligence" unless it can be said to constitute misconduct.

30. Fighting. Compensation will not usually be awarded in the following circumstances –

a. if the victim, without reasonable cause, struck the first blow, regardless of the degree of retaliation or the consequences

b. where the conduct of the victim was calculated or intended to provoke violence

c. if the injury or death occurred in a fight in which the victim had voluntarily agreed to take part. This is so even if the consequences of such an agreement go far beyond what the victim expects. A victim who invites someone "outside" for what he intends should be a fist fight will not usually be compensated even if he ends up with the most serious injury. The fact that the offender goes further and uses a weapon will only make a difference . in exceptional circumstances

d. if the crime of violence formed part of a pattern of violence in which the victim or the applicant had been a voluntary participant, e.g. if there was a history of assaults involving the victim and the assailant where the victim had previously taken the role of the assailant

e. where the victim or the applicant had attempted to revenge himself against the assailant.

31. Provocative words or behaviour. Conduct of this kind may result either in a reduced award or in the rejection of the application altogether. In each case the Board will consider whether the violence done was in or out of proportion to the victim's provocation.

32. Alcohol or drug related incidents. The Board receive many applications in which drink, and sometimes drugs have been a substantial cause of the victim's misfortune. Many of these incidents occur in places and situations which the victim might have avoided had he been sober or not willing to run some kind of risk. In such circumstances the Board may make an award but only after looking very carefully at the circumstances to ensure that the applicant's conduct "before, during or after the events giving rise to the claim" was not such that it would be inappropriate to make a payment from public funds.

33. Gangs and terrorists. A member of a violent gang will rarely be awarded compensation even if the circumstances in which he sustained his injury were unconnected with membership of the gang. Anyone convicted of terrorist activities would be refused compensation by the Board whatever the circumstances of the incident giving rise to the claim.

34. Immoral conduct. This is not in itself a reason for refusing or reducing an award but in some cases immoral conduct may amount to provocative conduct justifying refusal or reduction for other reasons.

35. Unlawful conduct. An applicant injured in the course of committing a serious crime will usually receive no award.

36. Conduct of children playing dangerous games. These cases present two problems. First the applicant must show that a crime of violence was committed. The mere fact that a game was dangerous will not of itself be sufficient. Secondly, even if a crime of violence is established, the Board will not make an award where there is nothing to choose between the conduct of the child who inflicted the injury and the victim. To do so would merely be compensating the loser. In one case, for example, 11 and 12 year old boys were firing stones from catapults at each other. One boy received a serious eye injury. That was an assault, thus a crime of violence, but the application was rejected. In cases where the children are of different ages or take unequal parts in the game, a full or reduced award may be made depending on the degree of their participation and their understanding of the risks involved.

"Character as shown by criminal convictions".

37. This part of **paragraph 6(c)** of the Scheme gives the Board discretion to refuse or reduce compensation because of the applicant's (or the deceased's) past record of criminal offences, whenever committed. The Board can take account of convictions which are entirely unconnected with the incident in which the applicant was injured. Any attempt the applicant has made to reform himself will also be taken into consideration.

38. The Board may completely reject an application if the applicant has –

a. one conviction for a serious crime of violence, e.g. murder, manslaughter, rape, wounding or inflicting grievous bodily harm

b. one conviction for some other very serious crime, e.g. drug smuggling in quantity

c. more than one recent conviction for less serious crimes of violence, e.g. assault, burglary, theft or criminal damage; or

d. numerous convictions for dishonesty of a serious nature.

39. Each case is judged on its merits and in some circumstances even a conviction for a serious crime of violence will not be regarded as a complete bar. For example the Board would be likely to approach sympathetically an application from a person with a bad record of convictions who had been injured while assisting the police to uphold the law or genuinely giving help to someone who was under attack.

Where offender may benefit.

40. Under **paragraph 7** of the Scheme no compensation can be paid in any case unless the Board are satisfied there is no possibility that any person responsible for causing the injury may benefit from an award as could happen if, for example, the victim and the offender were still living under the same roof.

HOW AND WHEN TO APPLY

41. If you have been injured as the direct result of a crime of violence and decide to apply for compensation you should complete an **Injury** application form and send it to the Board as soon as possible after the incident (**paragraph 22**). Application forms can be obtained by contacting the Board's office at the address shown at the start of this guide. If the person who was injured had died, ask for a **fatal** application form. If death occurred otherwise than as a result of the injury ask for a **fatal (paragraph 16)** application form.

42. Time limits. Do not delay making your application. Applications must in any event be made within three years of the date of the incident giving rise to the injury. The Board cannot consider applications made outside this period unless the circumstances are exceptional (**paragraph 4**).

43. The three year limitation period is the same as in the civil courts and exists because late claims can be difficult to investigate. The Scheme has received considerable publicity over the years and the fact that an applicant was unaware of its existence or its provisions is unlikely to be regarded as an acceptable reason for not making an application within three years.

44. The Board will, however, give sympathetic consideration to late applications from or on behalf of victims whose ability to help themselves is or was impaired, and to those who were under the age of 18 at the time of the incident. In addition the Board will give careful consideration to late claims by persons whose injuries were not immediately attributable to the incident provided the application is made as soon as possible after discovering the cause.

45. Applications on behalf of children. An application on behalf of a person under the age of 18 must be made by an adult with parental rights over the child. The reason for this is that a child cannot legally decide for itself whether to accept the Board's determinations and if the application is not made and conducted by the right person on the child's behalf

there may be unnecessary delay before compensation can be paid. A copy of the child's birth certificate must be enclosed with the application form.

46. Usually, the person to make the application will be one of the child's natural parents. Sometimes this may be impossible, e.g. if the child has been subjected to abuse within the family. If the child is in care the Board will expect the application to be made by the authority to whom care has been granted. Usually, in such cases, the application will be signed by the Director of Social Services or other responsible officer on the authority's behalf. In other cases the Board will expect the application to be made and signed by the person having parental rights over the child for the time being. Where there is no one legally entitled to act for the child help should be sought from the Official Solicitor for England and Wales; for a Scottish child, the Board will require the appointment of a tutor or curator. The Board does not make these arrangements itself; wherever possible all the necessary formalities should be completed on the child's behalf before an application is made.

47. Wards of Court must first obtain leave from the Court to apply to the Board.

48. Mental incapacity. Applications in respect of adults who are legally incapable of managing their own affairs, whether they have been rendered so as the result of a criminal injury or otherwise, must be made by a person properly authorised to act on the victim's behalf. In England and Wales it may be necessary to secure the appointment of a Receiver by applying to the Court of Protection before the application is made. The Court will require medical evidence that the person is "incapable by reason of mental disorder as defined in the Mental Health Act 1983 of managing and administering his/her property and affairs". In Scotland it will be necessary for those acting on behalf of the victim to seek the appointment of a curator. In these cases the victim's family or friends should always consider the desirability of taking medical and legal advice before making any application for compensation.

HOW THE BOARD DEALS WITH APPLICATIONS

49. Every application will be acknowledged by the Board as soon as practicable after receipt. The applicant will be given a **personal reference** number which must always be quoted in subsequent communications with the Board.

50. The Board have a duty to check the information you give. You will have to sign a section of the application form giving the Board permission to write to the police, hospital, doctor, employers or anyone else to confirm what you have said about your injuries and loss of earnings. You may be asked by the Board to provide details of any financial loss yourself (**paragraph 14**) and you have a general duty to give all reasonable assistance to the Board in connection with your application (**paragraph 6(b)**). All enquiries made by the Board are dealt with in confidence.

51. The necessary enquiries always involve a delay of some kind in every case and you should not look for an early decision on your application. The Board always have many thousands of applications under consideration and the people with whom the checks have to be made are usually very busy too. It will help therefore not to write to or telephone the Board just to ask about progress, because this in itself causes delay. Once you have received an acknowledgement you can be sure that the enquiries on your case have been started and you will be contacted as soon as possible.

52. Generally the Board concentrate first on an applicant's eligibility under the Scheme because there is no point in calling for detailed medical evidence if compensation is likely to be refused, e.g. because the incident was not reported to the police. Sometimes it may be necessary to defer any decision until the outcome of any criminal proceedings against the offender is known, but the Board will only do this if they consider that the proceedings are likely to have a bearing on the victim's application for compensation.

53. Interim awards. Wherever possible the Board will try to resolve an application by a once only lump sum payment of compensation (**a final award**). But to do this the Board need to have a clear medical prognosis, and in some cases this can take a long time to obtain. In such cases, providing the applicant is in all respects eligible for compensation, the Board may make one or more interim awards on account. But the Board will usually only take this course if there is evidence of need or hardship or −

    (a) when the final award is likely to be substantial, and

    (b) there has already been − or it appears that there will inevitably be − a substantial delay before a final award can be made.

Photographs and Inspections.

54. When the Board have completed their enquiries and are satisfied that you seem to be eligible for compensation you may be sent a form asking whether you have fully recovered from your injuries. If there is any serious scarring you may be asked at this stage to provide photographs of a specified type (for which a standard fee will be offered) to help the Board assess the proper amount of compensation. Please do not send photographs unless asked; any sent without request will of course be considered but the cost will not be reimbursed unless they enable the Board to assess the extent of the injury **once it has fully healed.** Photographs taken shortly after the incident which caused the injury will not usually help.

55. If it is impossible to assess the extent of your injuries on the basis of photographs you may be asked to attend one of the Board's regional hearings centres so that a member of the Board can inspect your injuries before assessing compensation. An applicant is not called for an inspection unless the Board have already decided that he is entitled to an award, or a reduced award. However, before making a final determination, the Board can take account of any

fresh information (e.g. about further criminal convictions) between the date of calling for the inspection and the date of the Board's determination which would affect the applicant's eligibility under the Scheme.

HOW COMPENSATION IS ASSESSED

56. Compensation is assessed on the same basis as "common law damages" (**paragraph 12**). This means that if the incident which caused the injury occurred in England or Wales compensation will be assessed in accordance with the rules of law in England and Wales; if the incident occurred in Scotland, compensation will be assessed under Scottish law. But there are some respects in which the Scheme differs from the law as applied in the Courts. For example under **paragraph 19** the Board are required to deduct the **full** value of any benefits received by the victim as a result of the injuries sustained and under **paragraph 14** there is a limit on the amount of lost earnings or earnings capacity the Board can take into account. The following notes give an outline of the way the Board calculate the final sum payable.

Injury cases.

57. Damages are assessed under two broad headings:

- **General Damages.** This is compensation for the injury itself, for the pain and suffering, and for any loss of facility. If the Board are satisfied that there will be a continuing financial loss or reduction in future earning capacity, compensation will be included for this as well.

- **Special Damages.** This is compensation for financial loss already sustained as a result of the injury calculated to the date of the award. Depending on the circumstances it could include:

    • earnings lost through time off work, calculated usually from figures supplied by the applicant's employers, or from accounts.

    • out-of-pocket expenses such as dental costs, fares to hospital for treatment and repair to or replacement of certain personal items. Normally the Board will only refund such expenses if receipts are provided.

NOTE: The 1990 Scheme does not allow the Board to compensate for the loss of or damage to **clothing** or other property unless the property was relied upon by the victim as a physical aid (**paragraph 17**).

58. Private medical treatment. The Board will not compensate for the cost of private treatment unless satisfied that it was reasonable to obtain treatment privately. Where the Board are so satisfied compensation will not exceed a reasonable amount (**paragraph 18**).

Fatal cases.

59. Where the victim dies as a result of a criminal injury the Board will assess compensation for the dependants or relatives of the victim in accordance with the Fatal Accidents Act 1976, for incidents occurring in England or Wales and in accordance with the Damages (Scotland) Act 1976 for incidents occurring in Scotland.

60. Compensation in either case is based primarily on the **financial dependency** of the dependant or relative of the victim. In Scottish law this element is referred to as "Loss of Support". The Board can make no award unless satisfied by evidence in support of the application that the applicant depended upon the victim financially. A financial dependency cannot be founded on social security benefits.

61. In addition, the Board may award compensation under the following headings:

● **Bereavement.**

England and Wales. Under the Fatal Accidents legislation the bereavement award is a fixed sum of £3,500 which is payable for the benefit:

  a. of the wife or husband of the deceased; and

  b. where the deceased was a minor who was never married:–

    i. of his parents if he was legitimate; and

    ii. of his mother, if he was illegitimate.

    In the case of the death of a minor under (b) (i) above the sum of £3,500 is divided equally between the deceased's parents.

Scotland. An award of compensation for "Loss of Society" may be made to any member of the deceased's **immediate family** within the meaning of section 10(2) of the Damages (Scotland) Act 1976. In this case the Board will require evidence to show the kind of relationship enjoyed between the relative and the deceased.

● **Funeral expenses.** The person who paid for the funeral expenses will be awarded a reasonable sum in compensation, even if that person is otherwise ineligible to claim under the Scheme (**paragraph 15**). The cost of a tombstone may be met if it is reasonable but no award can be made for a memorial, for newspaper intimations, wreaths, flowers or other expenditure.

● In fatal cases the conduct and previous convictions of both the victim and the applicant must be taken into account **paragraph 6(c)**.

● No compensation other than funeral expenses is payable for the benefit of the victim's **estate**.

● The lower limit for compensation (**paragraph 5**) does not affect the payment of funeral expenses or claims under **paragraph 16** which can be met even if the sum payable is less than £750.

NOTIFICATION OF THE BOARD'S DETERMINATION

62. If the Board make you an award of compensation you will be given a breakdown of the assessment, if this is appropriate. You will also be informed of the amounts which have been deducted in respect of compensation you may have received from other sources, e.g. from the offender through a compensation order made by a criminal court (**paragraph 20**). If your application has been disallowed you will be given reasons for the decision.

HEARINGS

63. If you are not satisfied with the Board's final decision on your application you will be able to apply for a hearing which, if granted, will be held before at least two members of the Board excluding any member who made the original decision. You will have three months from the date of notification of the Board's decision to ask for a hearing. A note about hearings will be sent to you with the Board's decision (**paragraphs 23, 24 and 25**).

64. An applicant does not become entitled to be paid an award made by the Board until they have received notification in writing that he accepts it (**paragraph 22**). If you are made an award with which you are dissatisfied and are granted an oral hearing no part of the award will become payable, if at all, until your case has been considered at the hearing.

65. The Board do not permit the televising or recording of the proceedings at any hearing. Permission for observers to attend hearings will be granted only by prior arrangement.

SECTIONS 35-38, POWERS OF CRIMINAL COURTS ACT 1973

Compensation orders

35 Compensation orders against convicted persons

[(1) Subject to the provisions of this Part of this Act and to section 40 of the Magistrates' Courts Act 1980 (which imposes a monetary limit on the powers of a magistrates' court under this section), a court by or before which a person is convicted of an offence, instead of or in addition to dealing with him in any other way, may, on application or otherwise, make an order (in this Act referred to as 'a compensation order') requiring him to pay compensation for any personal injury, loss or damage resulting from that offence or any other offence which is taken into consideration by the court in determining sentence [or to make payments for funeral expenses or bereavement in respect of a death resulting from any such offence, other than a death due to an accident arising out of the presence of a motor vehicle on a road; and a court shall give reasons, on passing sentence, if it does not make such an order in a case where this section empowers it to do so].]

[(1A) Compensation under subsection (1) above shall be of such amount as the court considers appropriate, having regard to any evidence and to any representations that are made by or on behalf of the accused or the prosecutor.]

(2) In the case of an offence under the Theft Act 1968, where the property in question is recovered, any damage to the property occurring while it was out of the owner's possession shall be treated for the purposes of subsection (1) above as having resulted from the offence, however and by whomsoever the damage was caused.

[(3) A compensation order may only be made in respect of injury, loss or damage (other than loss suffered by a person's dependants in consequence of his death) which was due to an accident arising out of the presence of a motor vehicle on a road, if—

    (a) it is in respect of damage which is treated by subsection (2) above as resulting from an offence under the Theft Act 1968; or (*b*) it is in respect of injury, loss or damage as respects which—

(i) the offender is uninsured in relation to the use of the vehicle; and

(ii) compensation is not payable under any arrangements to which the Secretary of State is a party;

and, where a compensation order is made in respect of injury, loss or damage due to such an accident, the amount to be paid may include an amount representing the whole or part of any loss of or reduction in preferential rates of insurance attributable to the accident.

(3A) A vehicle the use of which is exempted from insurance by section 144 of the Road Traffic Act 1972 is not uninsured for the purposes of subsection (3) above.

(3B) A compensation order in respect of funeral expenses may be made for the benefit of anyone who incurred the expenses.

(3C) A compensation order in respect of bereavement may only be made for the benefit of a person for whose benefit a claim for damages for bereavement could be made under section 1A of the Fatal Accidents Act 1976.

(3D) The amount of compensation in respect of bereavement shall not exceed the amount for the time being specified in section 1A(3) of the Fatal Accidents Act 1976.]

(4) In determining whether to make a compensation order against any person, and in determining the amount to be paid by any person under such an order, the court shall have regard to his means so far as they appear or are known to the court.

[(4) In determining whether to make a compensation order against any person, and in determining the amount to be paid by any person under such an order, it shall be the duty of the court—

(*a*) to have regard to his means so far as they appear or are known to the court; and

(*b*) in a case where it is proposed to make against him both a compensation order and a confiscation order under Part VI of the Criminal Justice Act 1988, also to have regard to its duty under section 72(7) of that Act (duty where the court considers that the offender's means are insufficient to satisfy both orders in full to order the payment out of sums recovered under the confiscation order of sums due under the compensation order).]

[(4A) Where the court considers—

(a) that it would be appropriate both to impose a fine and to make a compensation order; but

(b) that the offender has insufficient means to pay both an appropriate fine and appropriate compensation, the court shall give preference to compensation (though it may impose a fine as well).]

(5) . . .

NOTE

Sub-s (4): prospectively substituted by the Criminal Justice Act 1988, s 170(1), Sch 15, paras 38, 40, as from a day to be appointed.

---

36 [Enforcement and appeals]

[(1) A person in whose favour a compensation order is made shall not be entitled to receive the amount due to him until (disregarding any power of a court to grant leave to appeal out of time) there is no further possibility of an appeal on which the order could be varied or set aside.

(2) Rules under section 144 of the Magistrates' Courts Act 1980 may make provision regarding the way in which the magistrates' court for the time being having functions (by virtue of section 41(1) of the Administration of Justice Act 1970) in relation to the enforcement of a compensation order is to deal with money paid in satisfaction of the order where the entitlement of the person in whose favour it was made is suspended.

(3) The Court of Appeal may by order annul or vary any compensation order made by the court of trial, although the conviction is not quashed; and the order, if annulled, shall not take effect and, if varied, shall take effect as varied.

(4) Where the House of Lords restores a conviction, it may make any compensation order which the court of trial could have made.

(5) Where a compensation order has been made against any

person in respect of an offence taken into consideration in determining his sentence—

    (*a*) the order shall cease to have effect if he successfully appeals against his conviction of the offence or, if more than one, all the offences, of which he was convicted in the proceedings in which the order was made;

    (*b*) he may appeal against the order as if it were part of the sentence imposed in respect of the offence or, if more than one, any of the offences, of which he was so convicted.]

37 Review of compensation orders

[At any time before the person against whom a compensation order has been made has paid into court the whole of the compensation which the order requires him to pay, but at a time when (disregarding any power of a court to grant leave to appeal out of time) there is no further possibility of an appeal on which the order could be varied or set aside, the magistrates' court for the time being having functions in relation to the enforcement of the order may, on the application of the person against whom it was made, discharge the order, or reduce the amount which remains to be paid, if it appears to the court—

    (*a*) that the injury, loss or damage in respect of which the order was made has been held in civil proceedings to be less than it was taken to be for the purposes of the order; or

    (*b*) in the case of an order in respect of the loss of any property, that the property has been recovered by the person in whose favour the order was made; or

    (*c*) that the means of the person against whom the order was made are insufficient to satisfy in full both the order and a confiscation order under Part VI of the Criminal Justice Act 1988 made against him in the same proceedings; or

    (*d*) that the person against whom the order was made has suffered a substantial reduction in his means which was unexpected at the time when the compensation order was made, and that his means seem unlikely to increase for a considerable period;

but where the order was made by the Crown Court, a magistrates' court shall not exercise any power conferred by this section in a case where it is satisfied as mentioned in paragraph (c) or (d) above unless it has first obtained the consent of the Crown Court.]

38 Effect of compensation order on subsequent award of damages in civil proceedings

[(1) This section shall have effect where a compensation order has been made in favour of any person in respect of any injury, loss or damage and a claim by him in civil proceedings for damages in respect of the injury, loss or damage subsequently falls to be determined.

(2) The damages in civil proceedings shall be assessed without regard to the order; but the plaintiff may only recover an amount equal to the aggregate of the following—

(a) any amount by which they exceed the compensation; and

(b) a sum equal to any portion of the compensation which he fails to recover,

and may not enforce the judgment, so far as it relates to a sum such as is mentioned in paragraph (b) above, without the leave of the court.]

Index